THE ITALIAN NAVY AND
FASCIST EXPANSIONISM

1935–1940

CASS SERIES: NAVAL POLICY AND HISTORY
ISSN 1366-9478

Series Editor: Holger Herwig

The series will publish, first and foremost, fresh quality manuscripts by research scholars in the general area of naval policy and history, without national or chronological limitations. Furthermore, it will from time to time issue collections of important articles as well as reprints of classic works.

THE ITALIAN NAVY AND FASCIST EXPANSIONISM 1935–1940

ROBERT MALLETT

University of Leeds

FRANK CASS
LONDON • PORTLAND, OR

First published in 1998 in Great Britain by
FRANK CASS PUBLISHERS
Newbury House, 900 Eastern Avenue
London IG2 7HH

and in the United States of America by
FRANK CASS PUBLISHERS
c/o ISBS, 5804 N.E. Hassalo Street
Portland, Oregon 97213-3644

Website http://www.frankcass.com

British Library Cataloguing in Publication Data:

Mallett, Robert
The Italian navy and fascist expansionism, 1935–40. – (Cass
series. Naval policy and history ; no. 7)
1. Italy. Marina militare – History – 20th century 2. Fascism
Italy 3. World War, 1939–1945 – Naval operations, Italian
4. Italy – History, Naval 5. Italy – Politics and government
– 1922–1945
I. Title
359'.00945'09043

ISBN 0-7146-4878-7 (cloth)
ISBN 0-7146-4432-3 (paper)
ISSN 1366-9478

Library of Congress Cataloging-in-Publication Data:

Mallett, Robert, 1961–
The Italian Navy and fascist expansionism, 1935–40 / Robert
Mallett.
    p.   cm. – (Cass series–naval policy and history, ISSN
1366-9478 ; 7)
Includes bibliographical references and index.
ISBN 0-7146-4878-7 (cloth). – ISBN 0-7146-4432-3 (pbk)
1. Italy–History, Naval–20th century. 2. Italy. Marina–
History–20th century. 3. Sea-power–Italy–History–20th century.
4. Fascism–Italy. 5. Italo-Ethiopian War, 1935–1936–Naval
operations. 6. World War, 1939–1945–Naval operations, Italian.
7. World War, 1939–1945–Campaigns–Mediterranean Sea. I. Title.
II. Series.
DG571.M255   1998
359'.00945'09043–dc21   98-22477
                                                              CIP

Typeset by Vitaset, Paddock Wood, Kent
Printed in Great Britain by
Bookcraft (Bath) Ltd, Midsomer Norton, Somerset

Contents

List of Illustrations

Foreword

From the moment of its demise – and that of its *Duce*, Benito Mussolini – Fascist Italy's history has been the subject of controversy. Fierce debates still rage over the essential questions of Italian foreign policy, especially in the period after 1933, and over the manner in which it entered the Second World War: over whether Mussolini had a predetermined imperial programme that hinged on dominating the Mediterranean, which he had nursed at least since 1922 if not before, or whether he merely improvised policy according to the turns of events, and whether his forays on the European political scene after 1934 were merely the expression of a *politica del bluff* or were based on calculation – or miscalculation. Force clearly played a part in all this, and so the history of the policies pursued by the three armed forces under Fascism, and of the relationship among them and the designs of Mussolini, must lie close to the heart of any such enquiries. And yet detailed, archivally based and scholarly studies of these issues written by Italians are few and far between, and in English they have hitherto been virtually unknown. Now, at least as far as naval history is concerned, that lacuna exists no longer.

Fascist Italy was never a totalitarian state, but Mussolini's political control over his generals and admirals was broadly secure. In Admiral Domenico Cavagnari, his chief of naval staff, he had a reliable functionary whose career outlasted that of his fellow heads of service: Cavagnari took up his post as professional head of the navy in May 1934 and remained at his desk until November 1940, when he was unseated as a result of the disaster at Taranto. As this book makes clear, Cavagnari bore a personal responsibility for a number of crucial decisions that shaped the Italian naval inventory and thus greatly influenced its fighting capabilities in 1940. A 'battleship admiral' with something of a fixation on Jutland, he may well have played the decisive role in blocking the construction of aircraft carriers, thereby exposing the fleet to the full consequences of the limitations of the Italian Air Force. Nor did he have any time for the *mezzi insidiosi* – human torpedoes and *MAS* torpedo-boats – that might have enabled Italy to compensate for its over-all naval inferiority in the Mediterranean. His apparent ability to hold to a political view that directly conflicted with the basic postulates of the strategic planning for which he was responsible, as was the case in the spring of 1935, suggests that Cavagnari's limitations went beyond matters to do with battleships and bases.

Like many of his fellow officers, Cavagnari embodied the mixture of caution and ambition which seems to have been one of the defining characteristics of the armed forces' high command under Fascism. The reasons for caution were well founded: Italy's was always the weaker navy when confronting Great Britain – with or without France – and its geo-strategical position in the Mediterranean (mirrored by its position in the Red Sea) meant that it was confined to a sea whose exits it did not control. The consequences, laid out for the first time here in detail, were that the Italian Navy, aware of its many limitations, sought to avoid a direct confrontation with the Royal Navy at the height of the Abyssinian crisis in 1935, and again in 1939–40. As a consequence of his detailed exploration of the strategic situation during these years, Robert Mallett is able to demonstrate that the Italian Navy would almost certainly have been worsted had it fought in the summer of 1935, or at the time of the Czech crisis in the summer of 1938.

Mussolini's embrace of National Socialist Germany, presented here as the defining feature of his foreign policy from 1936 onwards – if not before – helped pose the strategic task for which the navy had to make provision but offered no tangible benefits. As a means of escaping from the coils of economic weakness and permitting Mussolini to challenge Anglo-French hegemony, it failed to provide any direct compensations, because the Germans were unwilling to enter into a substantive relationship with their Italian allies before war began. In this respect, as in others, the navy found itself facing heavy demands as a result of Mussolini's chosen course without the means to shoulder them. The result of all these factors was that, when war came into sight and the navy issued its operational directives in May 1940, a paralysis of will was reflected in a defensive posture that sought only to protect and defend Italy's position in the Central Mediterranean – the unavoidable outcome of five years in which Mussolini led and Cavagnari sought to follow as best he could.

Robert Mallett's path-breaking study of these issues will be as welcome to political and diplomatic historians as it will to specialists in naval and military affairs. His diligent research – only made possible as a result of the confidence reposed in him by the Italian naval authorities – has opened up a dimension of Italian history that has hitherto been almost entirely neglected. Our knowledge of the inner world which lay behind the facade of Fascism is the richer for it.

John Gooch

Series Editor's Preface

Fascist Italy is enjoying a revisionist renaissance. With the notable exception of MacGregor Knox's 1982 work, *Mussolini Unleashed, 1939–1941*, scholars both in Italy and in the Anglo-Saxon community would have us believe that Benito Mussolini was a benign ruler, bent more on bluster than on expansion. From Renzo De Felice to Gaetano Salvemini, and from Denis Mack Smith to James Sadkovich, we are now being assured that Fascist Italy sought closer ties to Britain and France than to Germany, that it pursued no policy of imperial expansion, and that the Italian navy actually 'won' the war in the Mediterranean. In some bizarre manner, this line of argument seems to be a 'logical' counterpoint to the continuing revisionist claims that Adolf Hitler in 1941 launched a 'pre-emptive' strike against the Soviet Union in order to save Europe from 'Asian barbarism'.

Robert Mallett will have none of this. Rather, on the basis of solid research in the hitherto-classified records of the Italian naval staff at the Ufficio Storico della Marina Militare in Rome, he traces Mussolini's close ties to Adolf Hitler, the *Duce*'s full-blown imperial programme, and the Italian navy's concrete and direct strategic planning against Great Britain in general and the Royal Navy in particular. Specifically, Mallett shows that on the eve of Hitler's 'seizure of power' in January 1933, Mussolini had already laid down new programmes of naval expansion designed to 'drive the British from the eastern Mediterranean'. The formation of the Rome–Berlin 'Axis' (as well as its extension to Tokyo) further stimulated Italian naval planning for war in the Mediterranean and Red Seas. By 1935, on specific orders from Mussolini, the Italian navy redirected its strategic planning away from war with France and/or Yugoslavia and towards a confrontation at sea with Britain. By the following year, it had become a central tenet of Italian planning that this war was to be conducted alongside the German navy. That the Italian navy was woefully unprepared for war in 1939 was the result of financial, material and command weaknesses – not of a lack of desire to confront Britain in the self-proclaimed *mare nostrum*.

In the face of tired and unconvincing revisionist apologias, Mallett's work and conclusions are fresh and powerful: that Mussolini did in fact have a clear and predetermined programme for war against the Western powers alongside Nazi Germany; that the purpose of this war was to drive Britain and France from the Mediterranean; and that their place would be taken by a reconstituted imperial Rome in the form of a new Mediterranean and Red Sea empire. As the author shows convincingly, Mussolini's geopolitical ideas had been set by the time that he led the 'march' on Rome in 1922. It is Mallett's great contribution to have returned scholarship to that simple fact. That he has done so on the basis of a masterful mining of the Italian naval records is an added bonus.

Holger H. Herwig
Series Editor

Acknowledgements

Academic research on the diplomacy and strategic policy of Mussolini's Italy has to date suffered from the general paucity of reliable archival material. I therefore remain privileged that during my research periods in Rome over the period 1993–96, I was permitted to examine among the most important documentary evidence yet to emerge on the Fascist era.

Principally, I am most indebted to the Ufficio Storico della Marina Militare, who granted me special access to the hitherto-classified papers of the Italian naval staff. Detailed scrutiny of these documents allowed me to piece together the major developments in Italian naval policy and planning on the eve of the Second World War. The results will, I trust, demonstrate the true nature of Mussolini's relationship with Hitlerian Germany, as well as the full extent of the *Duce*'s over-ambitious imperial objectives. None of this would have been possible without the support and kindness of signorina Margherita Carducci of the Italian office of defence and naval attaché, London, who paved the way for the entire research project. In turn, I am equally indebted to Admiral Renato Sicurezza and Admiral Mario Buracchia of the Ufficio Storico for their warmth, generosity and continued enthusiasm. Nor can I omit the staff of the archive itself, in particular dottoressa Ester Pennella, whose patience, understanding and good humour made many long hours of painstaking work pass so pleasurably. I also thank them for the photographic evidence contained in this book.

Rome's other archives also proved supportive. The Archivio Storico Diplomatico at the Italian foreign ministry proved to be a treasure store of invaluable diplomatic accounts of the later interwar years. I am grateful to professoressa Silvana Quadri for her help in gaining access to the archive and to dottoressa Stefania Ruggeri for patiently aiding my research. Again, I would also like to thank members of staff both at the archive and in the foreign ministry library for their warmth and expert assistance.

I might briefly mention three of Rome's other archives, where, despite the comparative brevity of my visits, support and assistance proved equally forthcoming. The Ufficio Storico dello Stato Maggiore dell'Esercito kindly provided me with key documents that filled important gaps. I am especially grateful for having seen key memoranda written at the time of the Mediterranean crisis (1935–36), and for the overall Italian strategic blueprint – *PR12* – issued in March 1940. The staff of the Italian state archive – the Archivio Centrale dello Stato – readily and enthusiastically discussed my research ideas with me, and helped me to locate naval ministry papers as well as microfilmed fragments of Mussolini's personal papers. Finally, I wish to thank the Archivio del Museo Centrale del Risorgimento for their kind permission to use the private papers of Alfredo Dall'Olio, head of Mussolini's commissariat for war production.

Although in the main this book is based on Italian materials, a substantial amount of research was also undertaken in the United Kingdom. I would like to express my gratitude to the staff of the Public Record Office, London, for their helpfulness and their kindness. I am also indebted to David Brown and Gus Macalloon of the Naval Historical Branch, London, for furnishing me with Eberhard Weichold's unpublished report on 'Axis' naval policy, David Brown's stimulating paper on Malta, as well as with important primary and secondary sources. I would equally like to express my gratitude to the following institutions and individuals: the Brotherton Library, University of Leeds; the Bodleian Library, Oxford; the London School of Economics Library; the University of Bristol Library; and Philip Powell of the Imperial War Museum.

During four years' research activity many people offered important printed materials, advice, assistance with translation and much appreciated support. In wishing to keep this Preface brief, may I thank each of the following for their particular contribution to this book: Admiral Gino Birindelli, Rear-Admiral Luigi Donini, professore Mariano Gabriele, Dr Eric Grove, Professor Holger Herwig, Andrew Humphrys, Dr Elisabeth Joyce, Professor Ian Kershaw, Dr Christian Leitz, Professor MacGregor Knox, Professor Brian Sullivan, Dr Geoff Waddington, Dr John Whittam and the academic staff of the School of History at the University of the West of England, Bristol. I would like to extend my warmest thanks to Professor John Gooch, who supervised the original PhD dissertation with tireless patience and effortless expertise, and has since become a highly valued friend. I offer my thanks to my parents and parents-in-law for their enthusiasm and very welcome encouragement. Finally, I express the deepest gratitude of all to my wife Jo, whose friendship and understanding helped me overcome many difficulties, and to whom this book is dedicated.

The research for this book was funded through the generosity of the Italian ministry of foreign affairs, the Royal Historical Society and the University of Leeds. To each of these institutions I offer my sincere gratitude. All translations from Italian to English (and thus all errors) are my own.

Abbreviations

ACS	Archivio Centrale dello Stato
APCD	*Atti Parlamentari – Camera dei Deputati*
ASMAE	Archivio Storico del Ministero degli Affari Esteri
BDFA	*British Documents on Foreign Affairs*
Cogefag	*Commissariato generale per le fabbricazioni di guerra*
DBFP	*Documents on British Foreign Policy*
DDI	*I documenti diplomatici italiani*
DGFP	*Documents on German Foreign Policy*
JAIA	Joint Allied Intelligence Agency
MAS	*Motoscafo Anti Sommergibile*
MCRR	Archivio del Museo Centrale del Risorgimento
OOBM	*Opera Omnia di Benito Mussolini*
PRO	Public Record Office
SIM	*Servizio Informazioni Militari*
SIS	*Servizio Informazioni Segreti*
SM	*Savoia Marchetti*
USMM	Ufficio Storico della Marina Militare
USSME	Ufficio Storico del Stato Maggiore dell'Esercito

Glossary of Terms

Africa orientale italiana	Italian East Africa
Commissariato generale per le fabbricazioni di guerra	General commissariat for war production
Commissione suprema di difesa	Supreme defence commission
Direzione generale degli affari di Europa e del Mediterraneo	Department of European and Mediterranean affairs (foreign ministry)
Maricosom (August 1935)	Naval submarine command
Maricost	Naval shipbuilding division
Marinarmi	Naval armaments division
Maristat	Naval staff headquarters
Ministero degli Affari Esteri	Foreign ministry
Ministero dell'Aeronautica	Air ministry
Ministero dell'Africa italiana	Ministry for Italian Africa
Ministero della Guerra	War ministry
Ministero della Marina	Naval ministry
Ministero delle Colonie	Colonial ministry
Norme di Diritto Marittimo di Guerra	Regulations for war at sea
Regia Aeronautica	Royal Italian air force
Regia Marina	Royal Italian navy
Regio Esercito	Royal Italian army
Servizio Informazioni Aeronautica	Italian air force intelligence
Servizio Informazioni Militari	Italian military intelligence
Servizio Informazioni Segreti	Italian naval intelligence
Stato Maggiore generale	Italian supreme high command
Stato Maggiore della Marina	Naval staff
Supermarina (May 1940)	Central naval command
Ufficio piani d'operazioni	Naval war plans office

For Jo

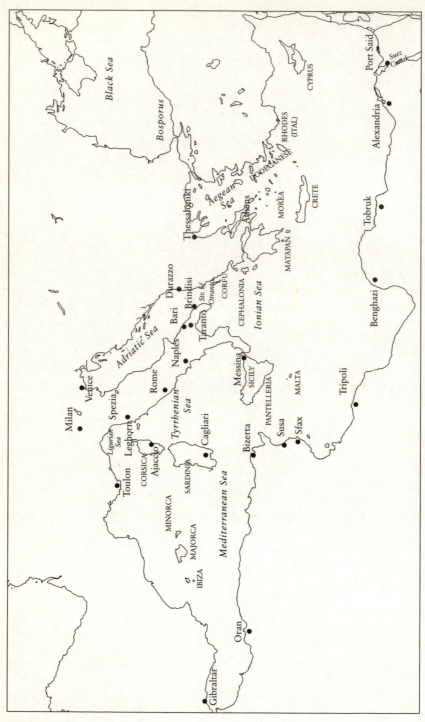

Map of the Key Strategic Points in the Mediterranean

Introduction

Benito Mussolini's belief that Italy should 'banish foreigners from the Mediterranean, beginning with the English', espoused at Fiume in 1919, represented much more than a mere continuum of the expansionist ideas prevalent among Italian nationalists and the post-war liberal governments that pre-dated Fascism.[1] What separated the eventual foreign policy of the Fascist regime from that of its predecessors, was its belief both in revolution at home and in war as a means of fulfilling Italy's imperial destiny. By 1925, the point at which Mussolini proclaimed his dictatorship, the *Duce* iterated that the nation should become 'fascistised' in order to ready it for the eventual confrontation with Italy's principal Mediterranean and Red Sea rivals, Britain and France. Duly, after Italy's ill-fated attempt to capture Corfu in 1923 illustrated the disparity between the British and Italian navies, Mussolini increased Italian military spending (from 2.6 per cent of the overall budget in 1923 to 5.6 per cent by 1931), while at the same time awaiting the alliance with Europe's principal continental power – Germany – which he believed would truly enable Italy to challenge for Mediterranean hegemony.[2]

In the past, Gaetano Salvemini and, more recently, Denis Mack Smith have offered historical assessments of Fascist foreign policy that conclude that no such predetermined imperial programme existed at all. Rather, they argue, Mussolini was simply a blustering opportunist with no clear foreign-policy aims. The interpretation offered by Mussolini's Italian biographer, Renzo De Felice, argues over various volumes that from the mid-1920s onwards the dictator sought agreement with France, and later Britain, and not alliance with Germany in order that his expansionist goals, which mirrored the traditional territorial aspirations of liberal Italy and the House of Savoy, might be secured. In pursuing a foreign policy based on the admittedly unscrupulous notion that Italy would make either one side or the other pay for Italian help, Mussolini simply mirrored the 'policy of the decisive weight' pursued by liberal administrations.[3]

Much of the available evidence does not support either view. On the

1

contrary, it suggests that Mussolini did indeed have a predetermined programme for war against the Western powers alongside Germany, a war whose ultimate objective was to wrest control of the Mediterranean from Anglo-French hands. If anything, this goal formed the basis of Mussolini's thinking even before he assumed control of Italy; at the moment that he led the march on Rome in 1922, in fact.

Examination of the geopolitical ideas prevalent within the Italian naval high command in the period immediately prior to Fascism's rise to power provide an insight into the origins of Mussolini's view – much trumpeted throughout the 1920s and 1930s – that Italy remained 'imprisoned' within the Mediterranean, and should strive to secure free access to the world's oceans. Prior to the Washington Naval Conference of 1922, the then-minister for the navy, Eugenio Bergamasco, stressed that in any war with Italy's principal Mediterranean competitor, France, the Italian strategic position would swiftly become untenable. Italy, he noted in a memorandum to Alfredo Acton, who later became the navy's chief-of-staff under Mussolini, remained reliant on sea-borne imports and in a future war would thus become a victim of any blockade imposed at Gibraltar and Suez. What Italy needed was a fleet composed of both submarines and light surface ships as well as capital ships that the navy could then pit against the enemy at a tactically favourable moment.[4]

Other naval theorists, while on the whole agreeing with this broad geopolitical prognosis, have argued that in any Mediterranean sea war one of the few options open to Italy would be that of taking control of the Sicilian Channel in an attempt to disrupt the Gibraltar–Port Said shipping route – an action which would inevitably provoke a conflict not only with the French, but the British as well. Such a struggle against the overwhelming might of the world's premier maritime nation would, from the Italian point of view, be an unthinkable prospect. Consequently, many within the navy argued that 'Italy's maritime problem could only be solved through political means'.[5]

However, the rise to power of a compatible National Socialist administration in Germany, long anticipated by Mussolini, offered the *Duce* the opportunity slowly to forge an anti-Western alliance with Adolf Hitler, which he duly did from 1935 onwards. In the meantime, the effects of the Nazi rise to power in January 1933 on Italian naval policy were all too visible; Mussolini authorised new programmes of Italian naval building designed not simply to compete with France but also to 'drive the British from the eastern Mediterranean'.[6]

The 1934 programme of naval building focused principally on expanding and modernising Italy's battleship nucleus. The *Littorio*-type battleships laid down, and the remodernisation programmes begun in October 1934, represented confirmation that those in command of the navy believed in the continuing supremacy of the capital ship. In short, this type of vessel represented for the naval leadership the means whereby Italy would become not simply independent of its traditional relationship with Britain, but a great sea power in its own right. Such thinking neatly meshed with Mussolini's belief that the Italian nation should shatter the chains that 'imprisoned it in its own sea', thereby securing a Mediterranean and Red Sea empire of its own.[7]

The question remained, however, of whether a battleship-heavy fleet would be the best way of striving for great power status. Expert opinion within the Italian navy remained divided. After the First World War there emerged in Italy three principal naval schools of thought, each of which challenged for control. The first, the so-called '*innovatori*' ('innovators'), argued that during the recent conflict the large surface fleets operated by the main naval powers had proved worthless in vital operations such as attacking enemy traffic and preventing offensives against native coastal areas. Furthermore, seeking a decisive naval engagement against a foe unwilling to commit its battle fleet had proved more or less impossible. Far preferable was a navy made up of light vessels and submarines supported by air units, which could then launch attacks against the enemy. A second group, the 'evolutionists', also claimed that Italy's past emphasis on the importance of the battleship had been greatly exaggerated. Yet, they by no means believed that this type of vessel had become obsolete. On the contrary, 'evolutionary' thinkers such as the renowned naval strategist Romeo Bernotti felt that new, well-protected and heavily armed capital ships should form the nucleus of a balanced fleet composed of submarines, cruisers, light surface units and aircraft carriers. Italy should also develop a naval air arm based on land.

A third and fundamentally conservative grouping, made up of senior members of the naval staff and including Admiral Thaon di Revel, hero of the Great War and Mussolini's first minister for the navy, did not believe that the days of the capital ship were over. Rather, the so-called 'die-hard' faction remained both tied to the primacy of this class of vessel and, even more significantly, in control of the navy. Certainly, they failed fully to appreciate the lessons that might have been learned from the First World War in terms of aeronaval co-operation and guerrilla tactics. Nor did the position change after Mussolini assumed the naval portfolio, indeed for all the key Italian ministries, in 1925. In August of that year he acceded to the views of his conservatively minded admirals' committee, which argued that Italy did not need aircraft carriers. Thus, a pattern was set whereby the naval high command continued more or less uninterrupted to prepare for a 'Mediterranean Jutland' which the Italian fleet would fight in the waters of the central Mediterranean. In other words, the naval leadership prepared for a decisive encounter involving the deployment of capital ships supported by land-based air units at the most propitious moment in the war.[8]

Yet, even if the supremacy of the battleship remained central to the policy of the navy throughout the interwar period, one of the main problems confronting Mussolini's ambitious programme was financial. Although the Italian representatives at the Washington Conference skilfully negotiated Italian battleship parity with France, Italy's naval budget did not, as we have seen, permit construction of any new vessels of this type until the mid-1930s, partly as a consequence of the global economic downturn of 1929. Despite the belief of those in command of the navy that the battleship constituted 'no mere symbol, but real power', the Italian fleet had only four operational ships of this type, all of which dated from before the Great War. Until 1934, therefore, Italian naval estimates permitted a substantial quantitative increase in fleet strength in terms of cruisers, light surface units and submarines, but the naval ministry announced no battleship building or remodernisation programmes. Fatally, as events in 1935 and during the Second World War were to illustrate, neither had the navy satisfactorily addressed the question of air support for the fleet, at least partly owing to lack of money.[9]

By 1935, the breach with the West that Mussolini had anticipated since at least 1919 having come over the dictator's determination to conquer Ethiopia, the stage was finally set for the creation of an Italo-German alliance, the vehicle whereby Italy would challenge the 'avarice' of the leading European democracies, Britain and France. In the years that were to follow, ideas of Italian naval might and imperial expansion in the Mediterranean and Red Sea developed further as the Rome–Berlin relationship became stronger, and the Italian navy, under the stewardship of its pro-Fascist chief-of-staff, Admiral Domenico Cavagnari, expanded accordingly.[10] In the first instance, this book examines the nature of Mussolini's relations with Hitler's Germany during the period 1935–40 in order to demonstrate the effects the dictator's pro-German policy were to have on naval policy and planning. Second, it examines the evolution of both Italian naval policy and planning for the anti-British and anti-French Mediterranean war which Mussolini envisaged, and ultimately assesses their overall effectiveness.

NOTES

1 S. Morewood, 'Anglo-Italian Rivalry in the Mediterranean and Middle East, 1935–1940', in R. Boyce and E. M. Robertson (eds), *Paths to War: New Essays on the Origins of the Second World War* (Macmillan, London, 1989), p.177; R. J. Bosworth, *Italy: The Least of the Great Powers* (Cambridge University Press, Cambridge, 1979), pp. viii–ix; A. Cassels, 'Was there a Fascist Foreign Policy? Tradition and Novelty', *International History Review*, 5, 2 (1985), pp. 255–7; M. Knox, 'Il fascismo e la politica estera italiana', in R. J. Bosworth and S. Romano

(eds), *La politica estera italiana, 1860–1985* (Il Mulino, Bologna, 1991), pp. 288–91.

2 On these points see Knox, 'Il fascismo e la politica estera italiana', pp. 293–305; on the Corfu incident and the naval confrontation with Britain see J. Barros, *The Corfu Incident of 1923* (Princeton University Press, Princeton, NJ, 1965).

3 G. Salvemini, *Mussolini Diplomatico* (Laterza, Bari, 1952); D. Mack Smith, *Mussolini* (Paladin, London, 1983), pp. 112–13 and p. 197. R. De Felice, *Mussolini il Duce, II: Lo stato totalitario, 1936–1940* (Giulio Eianudi, Turin, 1981), pp. 359–79.

4 The memorandum by Bergamasco is cited in G. Bernardi, *Il disarmo navale fra le due guerre mondiali, 1919–1939* (Ufficio Storico della Marina Militare [hereafter USMM], Rome, 1975), pp. 45–8; on the navy's role in influencing foreign policy see also M. Pizzigallo, 'La Regia Marina e il petrolio: un lungimirante progetto del 1919', *Rivista Marittima*, 109, 10 (1976), p. 62.

5 M. Gabriele, *Operazione C3: Malta* (USMM, Rome, 1965), p. 7.

6 Ibid, pp. 9–10. On Mussolini's need of a German alliance to fulfil his Mediterranean ambitions see J. Petersen's seminal *Hitler e Mussolini: la difficile alleanza* (Laterza, Bari, 1975), pp. 434–44.

7 W. Polastro, 'La Marina Militare italiana nel primo doppoguerra, 1918–1925', *Il Risorgimento*, 3 (1977), pp. 154–5. By 1926 the dictator's notion of his country's imperial destiny, and the navy's concept of Italy as a powerful maritime nation, had become welded into a much-quoted and powerfully succinct geopolitical axiom underlined by him for his service chiefs in the autumn of that year: 'A nation which does not have free access to the sea cannot be considered a free nation; a nation which does not have free access to the oceans cannot be considered a Great Power; Italy must become a Great Power', cited in B. R. Sullivan, 'A Fleet in Being: The Rise and Fall of Italian Sea Power, 1861–1943', *International History Review*, 10, 1 (1988), p. 115.

8 Polastro, 'La Marina Militare italiana', pp. 129–33 and, on the pre-eminence of the conservative naval faction, pp. 153–5; L. Ceva, *Le forze armate* (Unione Tipografico Editrice Torinese [UTET], Turin, 1981), pp. 200–1. The author is grateful to Professor Brian Sullivan for letting him have a copy of his pre-publication paper on renowned Italian naval thinker and strategist admiral Romeo Bernotti, which discusses the question of the Italian naval and air support. Henceforward, B. R. Sullivan, 'Introduction', in R. Bernotti, *Fundamentals of Naval Tactics and Fundamentals of Naval Strategy* (Naval Institute Press, Annapolis, MD, 1998), p. 23. See also Bernardi, *Il disarmo navale*, pp. 272–3; G. Rochat, *Italo Balbo: aviatore e ministro dell'Aeronautica, 1926–1933* (Italo Bovolenta Editore, Ferrara, 1979), p. 91; A. Santoni, 'La mancata risposta della Regia Marina alle teorie del Douhet', in *La figura e l'opera di Giulio Douhet* (Società di Storia Patria, Caserta, 1988), pp. 258–9.

9 On the Italian success at Washington *vis-à-vis* capital ship parity with the French see Bernardi, *Il disarmo navale*, pp. 70–3; J. Blatt, 'The Parity that Meant Superiority: French Naval Policy towards Italy at the Washington Naval Conference, 1921–22, and Interwar French Foreign Policy', *French Historical Studies*, 12, 2 (1981); B. R. Sullivan, 'Italian Naval Power and the Washington Disarmament Conference of 1921–1922', *Diplomacy and Statecraft*, 4, 3 (1993). On the Italian inability to commission new ships see Ufficio Storico della Marina Militare (hereafter USMM), *La Marina italiana durante la seconda guerra mondiale. XXI: L'organizzazione della Marina durante il conflitto, tomo I – efficienza all'apertura delle ostilità*, (Rome, 1972), p. 20. A. Fraccaroli, *Italian Warships of World War II* (Ian Allan, Shepperton, 1968).

10 Knox, 'Il fascismo e la politica estera italiana', p. 304. After the Second World War Cavagnari categorically denied that the navy had ever considered or planned for an anti-British war in the Mediterranean and Red Sea. See, D. Cavagnari, 'La Marina nella vigilia e nel primo periodo della guerra', *Nuova Antologia*, 357 (1947), p. 374. This fundamental political and strategic premise also underpins the more recent work of James Sadkovich. Sadkovich confidently argues that 'during the years prior to 1936, the RMI [the *Regia Marina italiana*] had precluded war with England, assuming that it would have to face only France ... Even after 1936, there was no reason to believe that war with Britain was imminent, nor even probable.' This view is totally erroneous. Sadkovich ignores the substantial evidence to the contrary, including the published accounts of the Cavagnari–Raeder conversations of June 1939, in which the two men discussed the forthcoming 'Axis' war against Britain and France, and which Sadkovich himself cites. J. J. Sadkovich, *The Italian Navy in World War II* (Greenwood Press, Westport, CT, 1994), p. 5, pp. 11–12 and p. 17.

1

Crisis in the Mediterranean

The established view that Fascism's recourse to war over the question of Italian claims in East Africa followed – and resulted from – socio-economic decline at home has been challenged from two principal directions.[1] On the one hand, historians have interpreted Mussolini's decision as forming part of a longer-term ambition to conquer Ethiopia – and for that matter an Italian Mediterranean and Red Sea empire dating from at least 1919 – which by 1925 he had identified as a clear objective.[2] On the other, it has been suggested that Italy's position within the European balance of power explains the logic of the dictator's motives. In short, Mussolini calculated that he could conquer Abyssinia, the limit of his colonial aspirations, with only minimal opposition from Britain and France, and before a rearmed Germany threatened Austria. Afterwards, Italy might then return to its traditionally pro-British and anti-German foreign policy.[3]

A third school of thought argues that attributing single causal factors to Mussolini's reasoning does not adequately explain his rationale. Politico-economic realities played their part, but so too did pressure from certain sections of Italy's ruling class, who believed in overseas expansion. Only when the international configuration favoured it – and when the extent of Italy's economic crisis suggested that territorial aggrandisement might relieve pressure at home – did he take the decision to attack.[4]

As has been exhaustively documented, Mussolini's decision to annex Haile Selassie's East African empire brought Italy to the verge of war with Britain. The strategic dimensions of the resulting Anglo-Italian crisis over 1935–36 were such that any possible confrontation between the two powers would primarily involve the Italian navy. Thus, study of the naval high command's planning to meet this potential conflict offers an additional perspective on the evolution and nature of Mussolini's policy between January and September 1935, the eve of the Italian assault on the Ethiopian empire. In other words, analysis of the navy's role both before and during the Mediterranean crisis permits an assessment of the correlation between the dictator's foreign policy and Italian strategic

7

planning, while at the same time allowing an examination of the naval dimension of the crisis in the Mediterranean.

Interpretations of the strategic balance in the Mediterranean during 1935–36 have resulted in sharply divided opinion. British global over-extension, and London's consequent reluctance to countenance hostilities with Italy, for fear of incurring losses in an albeit victorious war, have formed the basis for a number of important studies. Recently, although agreeing with this broad view, Steven Morewood has maintained that Britain's regional commanders were far from pessimistic about their prospects given the genuine weaknesses of the Italian armed forces, which if engaged would not have offered any serious challenge to British military capability.[5]

Others argue that Britain was in fact in no position to win a bilateral Mediterranean conflict in 1935, and faced the real possibility of defeat at the hands of Italian armed forces, particularly as the Royal Navy remained vulnerable to submarine and air attack. This thesis has recently evolved into a notion of Italy's being able to exploit British debility to coerce London into moderating its political opposition to the conquest of Abyssinia.[6]

This chapter tests Renzo De Felice's thesis that Mussolini planned limited colonial expansion following agreement with Paris and London, and ordered Italian operational planning merely as a precaution against British aggression during the summer of 1935. It also questions the argument that Italian military planning simply constituted an attempt to bolster a diplomatic policy that aimed to 'coerce' Britain into a political agreement. Finally, the nature and capabilities of Italian naval and air power will also be addressed. Analysis of Italian policy here turns on two issues: the extent of Mussolini's awareness of the naval implications of an aggressive, expansionist Mediterranean policy; and the likely effectiveness of the operational planning that emerged. This chapter will argue that Mussolini had planned to conquer Ethiopia militarily as a whole – even if doing so met with London's opposition and resulted in an Italo-British war, which the Italian naval high command appeared reluctant to contemplate. It will subsequently support the argument that in the crisis with Britain that resulted, the Italian naval and air threat was far less serious than had been considered at the time.

The Background to the Mediterranean Crisis

The root causes of the Italo-Abyssinia war pre-dated the Fascist regime of Benito Mussolini by some 25 years. Italian attempts at colonial expansion in East Africa had led to a war with Abyssinia in 1895, after the initial landings in the Red Sea in early 1885. The outcome of this conflict saw the Ethiopian armies, under the command of Emperor Menelik, resoundingly defeat the Italians at the battle of Adowa in 1896. Thereafter the territory remained the only African nation free of European colonisers, while the Italians nurtured a simmering desire for revenge for what they regarded as a national humiliation.[7]

The belief that Italy should 'avenge' Adowa in order to restore national pride eventually developed into a stock-in-trade of the Fascist government, for whom inherited notions of colonial expansion and imperialism were central tenets. As early as 1919, Mussolini evoked a new Italian Mediterranean hegemony by announcing at Fiume that 'the first thing to be done is to banish foreigners from the Mediterranean beginning with the English'. By the time he assumed power in 1922, the idea that Italy remained 'imprisoned' within its own sea, whose doors were Gibraltar and Suez, was an established component of the *Duce*'s geopolitical thinking.[8]

The Ethiopian empire offered one avenue for the realisation of Mussolini's expansionist goals. A successful Italian conquest would at one and the same time serve to 'coalesce' the Italian population into a 'cohesive' national unit, while simultaneously illustrating that 'proletarian' Italy now demanded its place in the world alongside the 'rich nations'. Similarly, it would also mark the first step in Italy's 'march to the oceans'. From 1925 onwards, the idea of establishing an imperial foothold in East Africa took root. By 1932, Emilio De Bono, the minister for colonies, had already begun concrete planning for possible offensive operations against Abyssinia. At the end of December 1934, Mussolini issued his famous directive ordering the 'destruction of the Abyssinian armed forces and the total conquest of Ethiopia'. Over the year that followed, and despite claims that he was prepared to negotiate with Paris and London over Italian claims in East Africa, Mussolini pursued a policy that never lost sight of these specific aims.[9]

The general political and strategic situation in Europe, as well as the balance of forces within Italy itself, influenced Mussolini's decision as to the timing of his planned colonial war. After issuing instructions in February 1934 for the planning of a war of conquest against Abyssinia in 1935, the dictator secured at least the initial support of the colonial ministry, the navy and air force, as well as important elements within the ministry of foreign affairs, by promising to avenge the defeat at Adowa. Then, with French fears of a newly resurgent German Reich plainly in evidence – fears fuelled throughout 1933 by Adolf Hitler's rearmament demands and Germany's departure from both the League of Nations and the Disarmament Conference – Mussolini obtained from Pierre Laval, the French foreign minister, a clear 'free hand' in East Africa in return for the promise of Italian support in maintaining Austrian independence.[10]

Although the government in Rome did not feel altogether immune from the threat of German revisionism, and especially so after the attempted Nazi coup in Austria in July 1934, which effectively poisoned Italo-German relations until well into 1935, Mussolini was very much alive to the possibilities Nazi revanchism offered him. Even before assuming power in 1922, he believed that the 'avarice of the Western powers' would inevitably push Italy into an eventual alliance with Germany. In subsequent years, Mussolini regularly stressed that Italy's moment of destiny, at which point it would become a world power, would come only when a new powerful and politically sympathetic German state arose from the ashes of the Weimar Republic. By late 1934 that moment was fast approaching.[11]

Yet, on the eve of his Ethiopian campaign, it better suited the dictator's purposes to exploit Franco-British fears of Hitler's Reich than openly seek alliance with Berlin. In the first instance, such a policy would forestall any unchecked growth in German continental hegemony, which could create much internal alarm within Italy and hence jeopardise the Ethiopian venture. Second, it would secure French and British approval of his colonial plans in return for supposed Italian support against Germany. Put simply, Italy could not risk a war in Africa without French backing, which might in turn help convince the British, who, even if against Italian expansionism on the continent of Africa, remained unlikely to act alone.[12]

That Mussolini's eventual agreements with Laval directly helped shape events in the Mediterranean and East Africa later in 1935 seems beyond doubt. The accords, concluded between 4 and 8 January of that year, covered a range of issues of interest to both countries, including Italian rights in Tunisia and new territorial arrangements in Libya and in Eritrea, one of Italy's two existing East African territories.

But the pivotal decisions reached between the two men were those concerning joint consultation in the event of a German threat to Austrian independence, and the connected question of an Italian programme of colonial expansion in Ethiopia. Scholars have argued that Laval, eager to secure Italian support against Germany, offered Mussolini freedom of action in Ethiopia, which the French foreign minister later claimed had never extended as far as direct military intervention. [Mussolini, on the other hand, deliberately or otherwise, chose to assume that France really would support Italy, and expressed anger at the French decision to join in the imposition of League sanctions later that year.] More recently, historians have argued that in any case Mussolini regarded the Italo-French agreement as merely temporary. Having already privately stated his intention of establishing closer relations with Berlin once the accords with Laval had served their purpose, he informed De Bono that Ethiopia was but the first stage in a greater imperial design. There is much to be said for this argument. Outward Italian enthusiasm for the joint military agreements that followed the political ones lasted only until the successful occupation of Abyssinia in May 1936. At that point there were already 'some early signs of an Italo-German *rapprochement*'.[13]

So much for the political and diplomatic background to the Italo-Ethiopian war. But what of the naval policy being formulated by Rome at this critical juncture? In the period that immediately followed the rise to power of German National Socialism, the ideas of a new era of Italian naval power and imperial might were to move a step closer towards realisation. Over the years 1933–34 the primary importance of the battleship within the thinking of the naval staff was confirmed. In October 1933 the naval ministry announced that it planned radically to re-modernise two of its four ageing battleships – the *Conte di Cavour* and the *Giulio Cesare* – originally laid down in 1910. The following month Admiral Gino Ducci, the naval chief-of-staff, issued the first of a series of memoranda for Mussolini on the question of future naval building. The current estimates, he began, amounted to some 855 million lire, of which 300 million should be allocated to additional remodernisation pro-grammes for Italy's two other battleships, the *Andrea Doria* and the *Caio Duilio*. The remainder of the budget should go towards construction of a new class of battleship. The rationale behind the naval staff's thinking was clear:

> The factors which justify our demands for new naval construction amounting to 555 million lire are based on the (extensive) shortages in certain types of ships currently being faced by our navy, and in particular shortages which become all too apparent when the Italian fleet is compared with that fleet – the French – which it is assumed will be our most likely future adversary.

Apart from a total absence of modern capital ships, Ducci added, the navy also lacked vessels 'considered vital in the defence of national com-munications in time of war'. Both questions should be addressed without delay. By March 1934, after sustained pressure from the new under-secretary of state for the navy, the avowedly pro-Fascist Admiral Domenico Cavagnari, and in view of the fact that the French had laid down the *Dunkerque* class in 1932, the navy had its way and Mussolini allowed work on two new 35,000 ton ships – the *Littorio* and the *Vittorio Veneto* – to begin immediately. Building started in October of that year, while work also began on a new programme to expand the submarine arm.[14]

However, the policy direction being taken by the naval high command during 1934 did not, of course, mirror the foreign policy being pursued by Mussolini, who, by early 1935, had concluded a political and military agreement with the French. Nevertheless, Domenico Cavagnari, by now chief-of-staff as well as under-secretary at the naval ministry, expressed himself in full agreement with the dictator's policy, and on 15 January

11

1935 laid out his reasons in a rather vague memorandum for Mussolini. Therein, outlining the naval high command's broad assent to the policy being pursued by the *Duce*, he argued that 'as regards our expansion in Abyssinia, we may conclude as follows: now or never'. None the less, he added, the completion of Italy's imperial programme in East Africa depended on securing the agreement not only of the French but also of the British. London effectively controlled the Suez Canal, which lay *en route* to Ethiopia. Although it remained unlikely that Britain would ever close this waterway to Italian traffic, London's interests in this part of the world were substantial, and any direct confrontation with a British government that felt those interests to be at risk should be avoided at all costs. Rome should secure a political agreement with London before operations began. He concluded that any further agreements with interested states should categorically stress that Italy guaranteed only their economic interests in Abyssinia after a successful conquest. The political destiny of any territory won through war would not be negotiable and it would remain in Italian hands – a view clearly in line with Mussolini's directive on the total conquest of Abyssinia issued on 30 December 1934.[15]

Other key figures within the Italian military establishment were far from convinced that a war of conquest in Africa appeared such a good idea. General Federico Baistrocchi, under-secretary at the war ministry, expressed initial reserve at the planned operation. Marshal Pietro Badoglio, head of the Italian supreme high command (the *Stato Maggiore generale*), exhibited outright disapproval of it. After visiting Eritrea, he argued that the overall level of Italian unpreparedness was staggering. Worse, Badoglio added, a colonial war of the kind Mussolini had in mind might weaken Italy's European defences at a time of great international uncertainty. For him, Germany posed the biggest threat to Italy and, as he told a gathering of the Italian service chiefs in September 1934, an alliance with France represented the best means of countering this menace. Mussolini's war in Africa was simply an extravagance that the nation could ill afford. As he noted in a letter to De Bono written earlier that year, it had to be asked whether the idea would ever be worth the material and financial costs it would incur: '*E proprio il caso, qui, di dire se il gioco varrà la candela.*' But, Mussolini appeared clearly intent on his war in Ethiopia, a war which for him constituted the first stage in Italy's imperial mission. In any case, Badoglio's disapproval counted for little. Since 1927 the marshal had exercised only nominal power as head of the Italian high command; Mussolini assumed responsibility for the armed forces and dealt with the service chiefs individually. As the events of 1935 unfolded, it became increasingly clear that the dictator alone made major strategic decisions.[16]

During 1934, Mussolini had focused on the idea of aggression against Ethiopia, issuing his infamous directive to that effect on 30 December.

Concomitantly, the dictator spoke publicly, at Taranto in September 1934, of Italy's need to become a sea power and dominate the Mediterranean before finally authorising the capital ship building requested by the naval staff the following month. Yet, this very capital ship programme would be nowhere near complete before the Ethiopian venture got underway in 1935. Not surprisingly, Cavagnari, although backing the Abyssinian venture, called for a political settlement with London over Italian claims in East Africa in order to avoid the possibility of a naval confrontation. This suggested that Mussolini's Ethiopian plan would either be a gamble or needed to take place under the cover of a diplomatic agreement, as in fact suggested by the navy's chief-of-staff. This serves only to highlight the inconsistencies in Mussolini's politico-military policy as a whole. On the one hand, he demanded an Italian fleet able to dominate the Mediterranean; but, on the other, he ordered the attack on Abyssinia at a time when the navy would be in a weak position, particularly with regard to capital ships, and able to mount only a very limited challenge to the British should they oppose Fascist expansionism on mainland Africa. London did oppose Italian designs on Ethiopia, and Italian naval policy thus appeared ill designed to support Mussolini's diplomacy.[17]

Cavagnari's warning that Italy should at all costs avoid confrontation with Britain over Mussolini's plans to annex Abyssinia proved to be prophetic. At first, however, the signals from London were not altogether negative, largely because the Fascist administration had not yet made totally clear its intentions on the African continent. On 8 January, Leonardo Vitetti, the chargé d'affaires at the Italian embassy in London, informed Fulvio Suvich, the under-secretary of state for foreign affairs, that the British colonial office had no objection to Italian territorial gains at the expense of Abyssinia. Indeed, Sir Robert Vansittart, permanent under-secretary at the foreign office, hoped that a successful settlement of Italian claims to the Ogaden region might even place relations between Addis Ababa and Rome on a sounder footing. If there were reservations, Vitetti added, they were simply based on British concerns that the grazing rights of tribesmen from neighbouring British Somaliland (whose undemarcated frontier with Ethiopia had helped create the Wal Wal incident of 5–6 December 1934) should be protected; once these rights were assured, he concluded, Britain would offer little resistance.[18]

The fact was, however, that Mussolini had little interest merely in securing part of the vast Ethiopian empire. On the contrary, he had already clearly signalled his intention of conquering the entire territory. During the afternoon of 25 January 1935, the Italian dictator, in his capacity as minister for foreign affairs, sent a telegram to Paris asking Laval whether London could now be informed as to the nature of the recent Italo-French agreement on the future of Ethiopia. That day, he also secretly informed Count Dino Grandi, Italy's foreign minister until 1932 and now ambassador to London, that he did not expect any objections from Laval in informing the British government of the 'secret agreement' reached between Italy and France. In so doing, he conveyed to Grandi his intention radically to 'resolve the Ethiopian question' either by imposing direct Italian dominion by force, or 'by whatever means might become dictated by future events'. The British, Mussolini stressed, were on no account to be informed of this and Grandi should take every care to keep the information strictly secret. Rather, the ambassador should only inform London's political establishment that none of Britain's interests in the region was in any way under threat, in order that no immediate opposition to Italy's intended policy might arise. Most probably, military operations would get underway the following October. In the meantime, the *Duce* needed to complete his preparations with minimal interference from outside powers. On 26 January, Mussolini received word from Paris that Laval had no objection to London being informed of the Italo-French agreement on Abyssinia.[19]

Mussolini's plan to mislead London over his intended aggression against Ethiopia rapidly encountered difficulties. British suspicion about what lay behind the dictator's proclaimed intention to secure a 'peaceful' solution to Italian claims against Abyssinia became apparent the moment that Vitetti presented those claims to London on 29 January. Grandi proved equally unsuccessful at the beginning of February. Informing Mussolini of his meeting with Vansittart and British foreign secretary Sir John Simon, he noted a clear British reserve towards any idea of altering the political *status quo* in East Africa to Italy's advantage – even if undertaken as a result of tripartite negotiations involving the French. Neither Simon nor Vansittart appeared convinced that the Laval–Mussolini accords would not create political complications on a vast scale, in particular with the League of Nations, of which Britain was an important member.[20]

In reply to Grandi's insistence that Italy had no plans to go to war over Abyssinia, but merely wished to protect its regional interests against aggression by securing London's support in preventing arms from reaching Abyssinia, Simon replied that Britain could not possibly discriminate between Rome and Addis Ababa in such a way. Nor would he give any assurances that London would not offer political support to the Ethiopian government. Moreover, Vansittart evidently left Grandi with the distinct impression that he suspected much greater Italian designs were afoot than Rome had so far admitted, which might in turn threaten Britain's own imperial possessions. Vansittart's suspicions were clearly not unwarranted. Rome's military build-up in East Africa in February and March served to illustrate the disparity between the pacifist statements being made by Grandi in London, and the political and strategic realities of the actual situation only too clearly.[21]

Mussolini's attempt to misinform the British government as to his true intentions in East Africa suggests that he expected London to object to his planned conquest of the Ethiopian empire. Yet, Cavagnari had already stressed that winning British assent prior to initiating the campaign in Abyssinia was a vital prerequisite to its success. His reasons for advancing such advice were clearly based on his conception of British naval might, which Italy simply could not match. This factor became increasingly central to Italian naval staff thinking as the crisis in Italo-Ethiopian relations quickly developed into an Anglo-Italian crisis during the spring and summer of that year.

Sea power played a major role in British domination of Mediterranean and Middle Eastern affairs. Not only did London control key points within the inland sea such as Gibraltar, Malta and Suez, but it also exerted massive political influence in the region as a consequence of Britain's overall strategic capability, which Mussolini readily acknowledged and resented. In the face of such realities, the dictator's initial political strategy contained a degree of duplicity: evidently, he had attempted to win London's consent to the 'peaceful' establishment of a new political and economic *status quo* in Abyssinia, in order then to use the pretext of Abyssinian 'aggression' to launch military operations aimed at conquering the entire territory.

Throughout the months of February and March, the naval staff in Rome became increasingly aware that British suspicions towards Mussolini's policy in East Africa might create complications. On 3 March the naval attaché in London, Ferrante Capponi, warned the naval ministry that the British Admiralty were eager to keep the Mediterranean Fleet at full strength in the event of possible international tension ahead. He went on:

> the British naval authorities ... seem determined that the Mediterranean should not be weakened in these uncertain times. An officer of the Naval Intelligence Division, who informed me of this British decision, was also at pains to emphasise that the presence of the two aforementioned ships [the battleship *Royal Sovereign* and the destroyer *Despatch*] in the eastern Mediterranean, had nothing whatsoever to do with the Abyssinian question, but was simply connected to British interests in the region, such as those at Cyprus, Palestine, Egypt, etc.[22]

Not surprisingly, the coincidental arrival at the foreign ministry of an official British note expressing concern at Italy's military measures in East Africa generated anxiety in Rome. Cavagnari, influenced by Capponi's report on Britain's reinforcement of the Red Sea, advised Mussolini that London now viewed any Italian presence on the Horn of Africa as a threat to its own regional presence. From East Africa, 'the new Italy' could menace British possessions such as Kenya, Uganda and Tanganyika, as well as threaten imperial communications, particularly those with India. For this reason, the British government had shown itself to be opposed to Italian expansion in Abyssinia, and was therefore likely to invoke the mechanism of the League of Nations – that 'formidable obstacle' to nations, like Italy, in need of living space – to block it. The 'arbitrary' nature of the League covenant had already been exposed, Cavagnari added. Although the British were preventing Italy from finding its 'breathing space', they had stood aside while Japan recently operated in direct violation of the League. They were unlikely to stand aside again. Italy would find itself in conflict with a British government that rejected Rome's wish to reach a direct agreement over Ethiopia, and that intended to place the matter before Geneva.

In the event of Article 16's being applied, the Italian navy could do little to prevent British closure of the Suez Canal, which would seriously undermine Italy's war effort in East Africa. Gibraltar and the main British naval base at Alexandria were beyond its operational range. The Italian armed forces could attack Malta, but then the island did not constitute 'Britain's Achilles heel in the Mediterranean'. But, Cavagnari added, there was a solution to Italy's strategic dilemma vis-à-vis British sea power. The mere threat of confrontation with Italy would create complications for Britain, in that it would wreck the Anglo–French–Italian bloc on which both Paris and London relied to counter future German attempts at achieving continental hegemony. Were Italy to abandon its ties with Britain and France, the former risked seeing Germany installed at the French Channel ports. Rather than find Germany at Calais, Britain would much prefer to see Italy in Abyssinia. British public opinion remained unlikely to support any war with Rome and would demand that London kept its 'hands off' Italy.

European events were unfolding very quickly, and before long the British and French would have need of Italian support. While continuing military preparations in East Africa, Mussolini should seek to discredit Abyssinia as a barbaric state that still permitted slavery and had to secure its removal from the League of Nations. After he had achieved this, Italy might demand a mandate or protectorate over the territory, gradually imposing direct dominion. Britain, the admiral reminded Mussolini, would prefer to find Italy installed in Ethiopia rather than states that it regarded as unreliable. Once Italy secured control over this territory, it would be straightforward enough to create air bases there that threatened British communications in the Red Sea.[23]

The change in Cavagnari's thinking is remarkable. Now no longer believing that Mussolini should attempt to secure outright British approval of his intended occupation of Ethiopia, as set out two months earlier, the chief-of-staff suggested that the dictator might, on the contrary, exploit British fears of German revisionism. In so doing, he might prevent the Italo-Abyssinian question coming before the Geneva Assembly. The admiral also suggested that Mussolini threaten to withdraw his support for Britain and France in order to make them more appreciative of the value of Italian 'friendship'. In other words, Cavagnari recommended coercion as a tactic. His statements regarding the threat Italy constituted to British imperial possessions and Red Sea communications, once successfully in possession of the entire horn of Africa, amounted to an endorsement of Mussolini's wider imperial ambitions. In that respect, they would not have displeased the dictator. What remains equally striking is that the admiral, as in his earlier memorandum, paid limited attention to the naval balance in the Mediterranean, or indeed to naval issues. Cavagnari's avowal that any implementation of League legislation that resulted in a closure of Suez threatened to undermine Mussolini's plan, and that the fleet could do little to prevent such an eventuality, suggests that he sought to avoid confrontation with the Royal Navy.

Cavagnari's views amount to a clear appeal that Mussolini exercise caution. The naval high command appeared increasingly alarmed at the prospect of war against Britain over Ethiopia, a likelihood they had dismissed too lightly in January. Cavagnari became more apprehensive at this prospect as Mussolini's bellicosity towards Britain grew increasingly pronounced in the months that lay ahead. One can therefore interpret the memorandum as an attempt on the part of the navy's leadership to restrain the dictator from any action that might generate hostility with Britain. Cavagnari's note marked a clear departure from that of 15 January, in that he now clearly recognised Britain's growing *sang froid* for what it actually was – opposition to Fascist expansionism. The navy was in no position to challenge a British government opposed to Mussolini's territorial ambitions – particularly if London chose to close the Suez Canal to any Italian expeditionary force. Cavagnari's underlying message was clear: Mussolini should seek a political compromise and not immediately pursue a policy intent on the all-out military conquest of the Ethiopian empire.[24]

Restraint, however, was not on Mussolini's mind. On 8 March he informed De Bono, now the high commissioner for East Africa, that he planned to make unlimited resources available for Italy's imminent war against the Abyssinians. As he had already informed Grandi in late January, he foresaw operations beginning that autumn – in September or October. Showing clear resolve to proceed despite clear evidence of British objections, and notwithstanding the serious misgivings emanating from the naval high command, Mussolini then replied to De Bono's original request for three divisions for use in East Africa by informing him that he would make ten available. This, he concluded, guaranteed that Italy would achieve its overall aims and ensured that there could be no repetition of the humiliating Italian defeat at Adowa.[25]

Four days later, Badoglio again expressed to Mussolini his own reservations as to the wisdom of initiating the campaign against Ethiopia.

In his opinion, Italian Somaliland, Italy's other principal East African territory, was not adequately prepared logistically for use as a main base of operations. Eritrea, on the other hand, remained desperately short of water, a factor that had hampered General Baratieri's campaign in 1896. Before the *Duce* authorised sending any additional divisions, this serious deficiency needed to be examined and resolved. Finally, Badoglio stressed that air power would be crucial to the success of the campaign (Mussolini had ordered the deployment of 300 aircraft to the region). This meant that agreement with Britain and Egypt was essential: only by securing such agreement could Egyptian air space be crossed, and Egyptian and Sudanese air bases be used by Italian air units for supply purposes.[26]

Badoglio, like Cavagnari, evidently saw the dangers for Italy in a rift with Britain, especially at a time when German revanchism appeared evident – on 9 March Hitler announced his decision to disregard part of the Versailles Treaty and re-establish the German air force. But, equally, the marshal appeared envious of De Bono's key role in the planning of the Ethiopian war, a fact that explains his earlier attempts to stall preparations in an endeavour to win control of them. In any case, by 21 March Badoglio signalled his final assent to the operation's proceeding that autumn, as Mussolini demanded, the volume of *matériel* the dictator had committed having underlined his determination to carry it out. Nevertheless, Badoglio had not been alone in questioning the wisdom of the venture. Both he and Cavagnari had grown increasingly anxious about the attitude of the London government and emphasised to Mussolini the need for an accommodation with Britain.[27]

If, as Cavagnari argued, Italy played a crucial role in British and French policy towards Germany and this role offered Rome clear advantages as regards its East African policy, then the price for potential Italian support was raised still further in mid-March. The week after the announcement of the reconstitution of the *Luftwaffe*, Hitler declared that Germany now also intended to reintroduce peacetime conscription and create an army of 36 divisions, a measure which again directly contravened the Versailles settlement.

The *Führer*'s decision, which coincided with growing tension between Italy and Britain over Abyssinia and was clearly designed to create divisions among the Locarno powers, in turn offered Mussolini considerable political leverage. If he could exploit Paris' and London's need of Italy in the defence of Austria, the latter might prove more flexible over the question of Italian expansion in East Africa. That London seemed evidently troubled by German rearmament had been well emphasised by the official communiqué condemning the German action issued on 18 March, and by Simon's visit to Berlin later that month. Moreover, Pompeo Aloisi, *chef de cabinet* at the foreign ministry, outlined for Mussolini his belief that Britain had become terrified of unbridled German expansionism careering out of control, and, even more seriously, of a possible alliance between Europe's two main revisionist powers, Nazi Germany and Fascist Italy. In the light of this situation, Mussolini, faced with British antipathy towards his own expansionist policies, merely needed the opportunity to make the price of Italian 'co-operation' plain.[28]

Hitler's burgeoning revisionism also held much more long-term promise for Mussolini, however, for it finally offered him the opportunity to create his great Fascist Mediterranean empire. In a conversation with the Hungarian prime minister Gombos that spring, he stressed that Rome's alliance with Paris would only ever be a marriage of convenience; Germany held the key to Italy's imperial future. Conquering Ethiopia was, for Mussolini, simply the first step in a larger programme aimed at building an Italian empire stretching from the Mediterranean to the Indian Ocean. After Abyssinia, the dictator intended to set his sights on Egypt and the Sudan, as he told a senior Italian diplomat that March, and in the months and years that followed Mussolini showed that this did not amount to mere bluff. If Fascist Italy could only remove the one obstacle to closer co-operation with Germany – the Austrian question – that had so embittered bilateral relations during 1934, then the way lay open for a powerful new Italo-German coalition that could transform dreams into reality. In the early months of 1935, the conditions for a tentative *rapprochement* between Rome and Berlin were clearly favourable. But, all the same, Mussolini would need to tread carefully, for the memories of July 1934 were still fresh in Italy.[29]

The fact that Mussolini was prepared to commit ten divisions to the imminent war with Ethiopia explains the dictator's decision to call for a conference of the Locarno powers at Stresa in northern Italy that April. He needed to be sure that Italy could rely on an Anglo-French show of support in the event of complications in Austria once the units were deployed in Africa. This implied that the dictator had to reach an accommodation with London – especially so in view of Britain's reported hostility to his plans. The anti-German stance assumed by Italy at the Stresa meeting was thus 'bogus', a 'tactical' manoeuvre designed merely to demonstrate apparent solidarity with Paris and London, when alliance with Germany and conquest well beyond the borders of Abyssinia were secretly on Mussolini's mind.[30]

However, the time for an Italo-German alliance was not yet ripe, not least because a widespread fear of Germany prevailed within Italy. Rome's attitude towards Berlin, argued a firmly anti-German Pompeo Aloisi in a memorandum for Mussolini, needed to be outwardly firm, otherwise future negotiations would not be possible. Italy should keep an open door to Berlin in the event that relations improved. This improvement could then prove 'useful' if not 'necessary' to Italy at a later date. For Mussolini, an outward show of support for Paris and London therefore remained desirable. The dictator already faced anxiety as regards the German threat to Austria from senior Italian figures such as Badoglio as well as from other elements within the foreign ministry. He could not take the risk of Hitler staging a coup that involved Austria after the Italo-Abyssinian conflict had begun. This might clearly call his judgement into question and undermine his position internally. Germany had to be kept in check, at least for the time being.[31]

As regards Germany, the evidence suggests that Mussolini's policy had some effect. It can have been no coincidence that upon learning of the Stresa conference, German foreign minister Konstantin von Neurath acted to reassure the *Duce* that for the moment the Austrian question would remain 'excluded from discussion between Italy and ourselves'. In addition, Neurath gave Mussolini the categorical assurance that 'we have no aggressive intentions against anyone and least of all against Italy', a view repeated to Suvich by the Reich's ambassador to Rome, Ulrich von Hassell. Once the conference got underway in mid-April, Hitler's rotund henchman, Field Marshal Hermann Goering, gave further reassurances to Giuseppe Renzetti, Mussolini's unofficial envoy to Berlin, who then informed Rome that the German government seemed prepared to give a categorical guarantee of Austrian independence should Mussolini require it.[32]

Mussolini now turned his attention to Britain's attitude over the Italo-Abyssinian question. Prior to Stresa, he had received a further indication that London remained firmly against an Italian empire in East Africa. Gino Buti, head of the foreign ministry's political affairs department, as Cavagnari had done before him, warned the Italian leader that the British government continued to remain hostile to any Italian empire that potentially posed a threat to British imperial communications. At Stresa, he concluded, Britain should be warned that Italy fully intended to guarantee the security of her existing East African territories against Ethiopian aggression, and that any British effort to involve the League in this affair weakened the solidarity of those states opposed to German expansionism.[33]

Once at the conference, the dictator preferred not to raise the issue directly within the main forum. Discussion of Italy's intentions in Abyssinia therefore took place behind the scenes, among British and Italian diplomats. The published accounts of these conversations, between Geoffrey Thompson of the Egyptian department and Guarnaschelli, his opposite number, clearly reveal that the British once again left the Italians in no doubt as to the extent of their opposition to any military conquest of Ethiopia. In their encounter on 12 April, Thompson, in reply to Guarnaschelli's assertion that the Italo-Abyssinian issue would 'not be settled by Conciliation Commissions' (by which he meant that Italy would never accept League arbitration), replied that 'Italy could expect no co-operation from the United Kingdom in any attack on Ethiopia'. Any such act of aggression, he continued, 'might well react adversely upon Anglo-Italian relations'. Then, in a clear attempt to exploit presumed British fears of German expansionism, the Italian representatives assumed a more coercive attitude. During a second meeting later that day, Thompson and Guarnaschelli were joined by Vitetti from the London embassy, who proceeded to argue that, thanks to Britain and France, Italy had been 'denied any of the colonial fruits of victory over Germany' in 1919. Now, he added, 'Germany was once more becoming a threat, and her demand for equal rights was understood to include the rights to overseas possessions', a clear hint that Britain would need help – Italian help – in restraining Germany. Once more, Thompson replied that Britain would not countenance Italian aggression in East Africa. From this, the Italians could only conclude that Britain continued to be opposed to Mussolini's planned war of conquest against Ethiopia.[34]

After receiving some assurance from Berlin that discussion of the delicate Austrian question was temporarily off the agenda, Mussolini travelled to Stresa with the clear intention of sounding out the British, albeit indirectly via officials from the foreign ministry. Guarnaschelli's and Vitetti's attempts to exploit Britain's fear of Germany in an effort to reach an accommodation over Ethiopia, were evidently the product of ideas first expressed by Cavagnari and Aloisi. The former had argued that Rome should demonstrate to the British the advantages an Italian protectorate in Ethiopia offered them in preventing the African expansion of 'another country' – a veiled reference to the threat posed by German colonial claims. The usefulness of citing the German threat to British interests had in turn been elaborated for Mussolini by Aloisi just a few weeks before Stresa. The tactic simply met with further continued resistance from British foreign office officials. Therefore, the argument that, because he had succeeded in adding the expression 'Europe' to the word 'peace' in the final Stresa communiqué, Mussolini believed that Britain 'would not oppose him over Ethiopia' cannot be sustained in the light of the available evidence. Quite clearly, the dictator met with continued British resistance to his plans from at least early February onwards, and during Stresa and its immediate aftermath, British officials appeared no more compliant. On 15 April Simon attempted to raise the Ethiopian issue at Geneva. Shortly afterwards, Mussolini instructed Grandi to inform London that Italy would never accept its proposal for League arbitration in Italy's dispute with Abyssinia.[35]

The Anglo-Italian Crisis, April–September 1935

The effect that continued British opposition had on the Italian dictator's thinking, as well as his lingering suspicion of Hitler's true intentions regarding Austria, was reflected in the order that he gave directly to

Cavagnari, sometime during the Stresa conference, to prepare for possible hostilities against both countries. On 14 April the admiral instructed the naval staff that the changing political situation required the navy's war plans office to prepare new operational plans, under hypotheses that had until recently seemed unlikely. Two scenarios for war faced the Italian navy and its new French ally. The first was conflict with Germany, which had already formed the basis of a recent exercise undertaken in the Mediterranean by the first naval squadron, but which now needed examining anew. The second was that the Italian and French fleets might face a war against Britain.[36]

Cavagnari's order flatly contradicted his own thoughts on war against the British as set out for Mussolini in early March. At that point, he had warned against confronting Britain and its navy, whose bases at Gibraltar and Alexandria lay beyond the navy's operational range and capability. The one position that Italy might attack with some success, he had argued at the time, was Malta, although such an operation in itself would not unduly affect Britain's overall position in the Mediterranean. Most astonishing of all was the idea that France might back such a war against Britain, particularly as Cavagnari explicitly emphasised that France would never oppose British policy for reasons of strategic expediency. Mussolini clearly intended to confront Britain, militarily if necessary, over its hostility towards his imperial plans in East Africa. As events were to prove, Italy's fleet lacked the capability to realise this scenario and the naval high command remained reluctant even to contemplate it.[37]

The possibility of a war against Germany formed the basis of the Italo-French alliance concluded in early January. Hence, it is hardly surprising that, as Cavagnari noted, naval plans for such a contingency already existed. Yet, before Stresa, Mussolini received assurances from the foreign ministry in Berlin, as well as from his emissary Renzetti, that senior Nazis foresaw no forcible solution to Germany's Austrian question. Clearly, the dictator did not take such German assurances for granted. A second memorandum from Cavagnari on 24 April ordered the war plans office to make ready fresh proposals for a possible undeclared war against the German navy should Berlin make any attempt to occupy Austria. Operations were to take place within the framework of the Italo-French alliance, he added. Yugoslavia seemed likely, at least initially, to remain neutral, although the chances were that Belgrade might eventually support Berlin. Cavagnari therefore ordered the navy's planners to concentrate on planning for four strategic operations: attacking and destroying all German merchant and naval traffic in the Mediterranean, Red Sea and Indian Ocean; co-operating with France in undertaking a submarine offensive against German ships operating in the Atlantic; preventing the German navy from mounting attacks on metropolitan France or Italy, or their respective colonial possessions; and keeping Yugoslav forces under close surveillance, while at the same time preventing Germany from making use of Yugoslav or Turkish bases. In the absence of any agreement between the Italian and French naval staffs, Cavagnari did not mention how he expected future operations to be co-ordinated or even who was to command the units in question.

Having said this, Cavagnari remained very reluctant to countenance any notion of an Italo-British naval conflict. In his first directive to the naval staff of 14 April he 'assumed' that such a war might be possible only in co-operation with France – by his own admission, an unlikely political and strategic possibility. His extreme reservation at Mussolini's current line of policy is even more evident in his second order issued ten days later. This focused primarily on the idea of an Italo-French confrontation with Germany and devoted very little attention to the idea of war against Britain. Only at the very end did Cavagnari reluctantly discuss such an eventuality:

> Nevertheless, I would like us to undertake this study and thereby take into consideration the preparations that will become necessary should the alarming idea of such a conflict become a reality.
> We will need to develop plans for operations by combined air and undersea forces in the event that British naval forces are ordered to abandon Malta and make for Gibraltar.[38]

It is not surprising that Cavagnari should order the navy's planners to direct their planning for potential operations solely against enemy forces abandoning Malta. The Italian fleet at this point had barely begun its programme of new building and possessed only two capital ships, the *Doria* and the *Duilio*, both of which dated from 1912. To make matters even worse, the navy had no night-fighting capability. Nor did it have much by way of an independent air arm, despite requests from the naval ministry in January 1935 that the question of air support for fleet operations be addressed more seriously. This explains Cavagnari's rationale in regarding Gibraltar and Alexandria as beyond range: a markedly inferior Italian navy bereft of air support and unable to operate by night would, in the event of a Mediterranean war breaking out, find itself confronted with a British enemy in possession of greater numbers of modern capital ships supported by aircraft carriers and able to conduct nocturnal operations. The one strategic advantage enjoyed by Italy – its much-lauded submarine arm – lacked anything approaching the appropriate level of preparation for war against the British in the spring of 1935. Similarly, the navy had to date not yet fully considered the importance of anti-submarine or mine warfare.[39]

It is with these points in mind that one must assess the first plan of operations for war against Britain produced by the war planners on

16 May. Outlining the political dimension of the conflict, the naval staff, probably out of desperation, expected France to enter the war on Italy's side. Britain, in the meantime, could count on bases in Egypt, Palestine and the Middle East, a clear indication that the navy's planners regarded protecting the Suez Canal as London's main focus of attention, and its closure as Italy's greatest fear, as already expressed by Cavagnari. The plans office identified two principal strategic theatres: (1) Malta and the central Mediterranean in general; (2) the Red Sea. The navy's main task should be the destruction of all enemy forces in the central Mediterranean, which it would carry out in two phases. In the first instance, the war plans office recommended launching an aeronaval offensive against Malta designed to destroy all British bases on the island and force its abandonment. In the meantime, the planners suggested that a minefield be laid in the Sicilian Channel (Straits of Sicily).

Phase two involved the Italian fleet attacking British forces abandoning Malta and heading either for Gibraltar or Alexandria. Under both hypotheses, the navy and the air force would mount further combined attacks whose clear objective had to be the destruction of all enemy naval forces at sea. The main Italian battle squadrons based in Sicily would, along with the submarine arm and units from the air force, seek out and attack the enemy at the most opportune moment. If the British were successfully to redeploy to Gibraltar, no offensive operations were possible. Were the British to move their forces to Alexandria, on the other hand, then the air force should attack them there and eventually be supported in this action by the navy. There always remained the risk of Britain's reinforcing its Mediterranean Fleet from home waters and even of London closing the Suez Canal. Notably, in accordance with views expressed by Cavagnari to Mussolini in early March, the plans office could offer nothing to counter the latter eventuality. As regards the Red Sea theatre, air units were to attack the bases at Aden and on the island of Perim, while submarine forces destroyed British naval units based in the region.[40]

Behind the plan clearly lurked the shadow of Domenico Cavagnari. Once again, there is no reference as to how the alliance with France might function in operational terms, despite the fact that the entire plan appeared to hinge on just such a contingency. Any idea of joint operations with the French remained an undeveloped assumption. The navy continued to believe that a surface fleet offensive was possible only against Malta or within the central Mediterranean – the only strategic theatre considered as within the range of the navy – a conception that changed little in the years to follow. How the naval staff expected to counter the closure of the Suez Canal, and how this would affect the lines of communication with East Africa, was simply not addressed. The only option the planners regarded as feasible in this theatre – an attack by air and sea forces against

Aden and Perim – could not in itself resolve the problem of keeping open the Red Sea lines of communication with East Africa.

Taken as a whole, the plan simply served to emphasise the navy's perceptions of its own limitations, while in turn revealing Cavagnari's evident reluctance to countenance the idea of any Italo-British confrontation. France, he had already argued in March, would never enter an anti-British coalition. This meant that far from being able to dominate the Mediterranean, the navy, if forced to operate unilaterally, had open to it only the possibility of attacking the British fleet in the central region of the sea. Beyond that, the Italian navy's options were severely restricted, as its leadership were reluctant to attack enemy positions at Gibraltar and Alexandria. Neither did the navy's high command believe that it could oppose the closure of Suez – especially if it faced the possibility of Britain's reinforcing its Mediterranean position still further. Despite weaknesses in its conventional arms, the naval staff did not examine other realistic options such as guerrilla warfare; a surprising fact, given the successful Italian use of such tactics during the First World War. Cavagnari did give this possibility more serious consideration a month later, although not until October did the naval staff authorise guerrilla-warfare preparations to begin in earnest.[41]

Apart from the navy's operational weaknesses, there also remained the question of interservice co-operation and co-ordination, particularly as its plan called for close air support in the proposed attacks on Malta and the British fleet. Given Badoglio's initial resistance to the Ethiopian venture as a whole, it seemed unlikely that he would ever support the idea of a war against Britain. This explains the fact that the headquarters of the supreme high command continued to be unaware that Mussolini envisaged war against Britain some three months after the dictator issued his original directive in April. Within the pyramidic political structure of Fascist Italy, the various chiefs-of-staff dealt directly with Mussolini over the question of conflict with Britain. On receiving their orders from him, they simply proceeded to prepare their respective plans in isolation from one another. Effectively, this left Italy with no central co-ordinating military authority other than the dictator.[42]

On 23 May Cavagnari informed air staff headquarters in Rome that under the aegis of *Plan B* – the code-name for the entire anti-British operation – the air force should offer the maximum support to the naval offensive against Malta currently under consideration. Outlining the principal objectives of the plan, Cavagnari did not, however, give any indication that he desired closer collaboration between the two planning offices. On the contrary, he simply requested that air cover be provided for the navy's planned offensive against the British Mediterranean Fleet and its bases, as ordered by Mussolini a month earlier.[43]

Two weeks later, during a meeting between the respective deputy chiefs-of-staff for the two services, Pietro Pinna of the air force informed his counterpart Guido Vanutelli that, although he could make aircraft available for the offensive against Malta and any British fleet operating in proximity to Sicily, air force planning, too, seemed likely to remain limited in scope. The air staff regarded Gibraltar as beyond the range of Italy's bomber squadrons, and prospects for an air offensive in the eastern Mediterranean were no more promising:

> As far as operations in the eastern Mediterranean are concerned, General Pinna informs me that an air strip is currently being built on Rhodes and that a similar facility could be made available at Tobruk, although given the distances involved it is highly unlikely that either Alexandria or the Suez Canal can be subjected to sustained and effective aerial bombardment from these positions.
>
> Such operations may only become foreseeable when bombers of greater range currently in production enter into service.

Once again, no mention was made during the meeting of any need to engage in joint planning, and neither was there any indication as to whether the two staffs planned exercises aimed at co-ordinating their respective operations. By late June, with the international temperature rising dramatically, General Giuseppe Valle, chief-of-staff at the air ministry, merely announced that the *Regia Aeronautica*'s planning had focused on attacking 'similar' objectives to those identified by the navy. In concluding, he limited himself to advising Cavagnari that, although Alexandria could, in fact, be attacked from the air, Italian air units could not strike effectively against Suez, adding that air support for fleet operations would be 'as effective as was possible with the means currently available'.[44]

The absence of interservice co-operation, in particular between the staffs of the navy and air force, is striking. The need to conduct combined air and sea operations against a British enemy armed with superior means and vast experience of sea warfare suggested that carefully co-ordinated planning was an absolute necessity. In reality none existed, with alarming consequences for Italy as the threat of war with Britain grew over the summer. Moreover, the air force planners evidently agreed that Italian prospects were limited largely to strikes against Malta and British naval forces in the central Mediterranean. Like their naval counterparts, they offered no means of countering the possible closure of Suez to Italian traffic; nor did they foresee any possibility of placing Gibraltar under attack. This suggested that Italy, highly dependent on imported raw materials, would be unable militarily to challenge any imposition of a blockade at the outset of the conflict. Finally, despite concluding an air pact with France in May, the air force high command also gave no indication that they foresaw combined operations with the French air force taking place against Britain.[45]

While the air and navy staffs pessimistically assessed the prospect of the possible conflict with Britain ordered by Mussolini, Rome concentrated its political efforts on attempting to reduce the level of British disapproval for its policy of expansion in East Africa. In early May, Grandi again attempted to win Vansittart's and Simon's assent to a bilateral agreement between Britain and Italy similar to that concluded with Laval in January. Yet again, and on the dictator's express instructions, he avoided any mention of the fact that Mussolini intended to conquer the whole of Ethiopia by force. Once more, he failed. Italy could expect no support from Britain if it found itself at war with the Ethiopian empire; British public opinion would be markedly hostile to any such an eventuality. The London government, he informed Mussolini later that month, simply refused to countenance any agreement on the lines of the Italo-French accords.[46]

Becoming increasingly intransigent, Mussolini continued to emphasise his determination to settle the Italo-Abyssinian question 'radically'. On 14 May he delivered a speech to the Italian senate in which he argued that Italy could not avoid being temporarily weakened in Europe as a result of its commitment to Africa. It was precisely in order to guarantee Italian security on the European mainland that 'we intend to have our backs covered in Africa', he argued. Four days later he ordered De Bono to have all Italian forces in East Africa ready for war by no later than October. Acknowledging that the British government opposed his plans, Mussolini stressed that he planned to declare war on Britain if it attempted to block Italian policy.[47]

In the meantime Aloisi, in a clear attempt to forestall any possible application of the covenant before the Italian campaign began that autumn, worked assiduously at Geneva to ensure that the Italo-Abyssinian dispute did not come before the League. At the same time, he continued, as he had done prior to Stresa, to advise Mussolini that London and Paris remained eager to maintain Italian friendship in view of the growing threat posed by Germany, and did not wish to see the front established at the conference collapse so quickly. In short, he argued, if Mussolini threatened both to abandon Stresa and to take Italy out of the League, then Britain and France might become more favourably disposed to Italian colonial aspirations.[48]

The dictator lost no time in applying this advice. On 21 May Mussolini gave an audience to Sir Eric Drummond, the British ambassador to Rome, during which he argued that Italy's position with regard to Ethiopia barely differed from that of the French in Morocco or the British in Egypt. Although the government in London seemed attached to the principle of collective security, it had not hesitated to protect its own interests in Egypt when it felt them to be under threat. Therefore, Italy would also defend her rights in East Africa, even if it meant going to war against the whole Ethiopian empire in order to do so. If Britain and France continued to oppose Italy's colonial policy, then he intended quite simply to leave the League of Nations.[49]

While Italian relations with London soured further, Mussolini sought to improve those with Berlin. On 18 May, during the course of a speech to the Fascist chamber of deputies, he openly condemned 'those who would wish to nail us to the Brenner', while continuing to deny Italy its rights to colonial spoils – an open attack on the policy being pursued by Paris and London. So, too, did Mussolini emphasise publicly that there was now but one impediment to improving Italo-German relations – the question of guaranteeing Austrian independence – a statement that met with much enthusiastic applause. Losing no time, Hitler finally made an open declaration of Germany's intent to refrain from interfering in Austria's internal affairs. In a speech delivered to the Reichstag three days later the *Führer* affirmed that 'Germany neither intends nor wishes to interfere in the internal affairs of Austria, to annex Austria, or to conclude an "Anschluss"'.[50]

This was precisely the sort of guarantee of continued Austrian independence that Mussolini had been seeking since October 1934. During his meeting with Hassell at the end of May, the dictator could not have appeared more effusive in his gratitude. Stressing that he fully appreciated the significance of Hitler's declaration, Mussolini continued that 'he did indeed value the *Führer*'s statement as constituting a decided step forward along the road to [a] German–Italian understanding'. Both men agreed that a mutual 'hands off' formula would now apply to Austria. In turn, Mussolini also openly acknowledged Hassell's emphasis on Germany's 'neutrality and reserve in the Abyssinian question'.[51]

The reasons for Mussolini's gratitude were clear. At the time of Stresa, he had again attempted to secure a German guarantee of Austrian territorial integrity, in order to assure himself that an *Anschluss* would not take place once Italy was committed in Africa. Any such event could destabilise the Mussolini regime internally, for he had already faced considerable opposition from an Italian establishment deeply concerned at the grave risks he planned to take. However, despite certain reassurances having been given to Rome by senior German officials such as Neurath and Goering, Mussolini did not appear completely to believe them. This led him to order Cavagnari to prepare for a possible war should Berlin attempt a sudden annexation of Austria. Now, with the public assertion by Hitler that the Reich posed no threat to the continued existence of Austria, and with Goering having made additional promises that Germany would not supply the Abyssinians with aircraft, the threat of such a war subsided, and bilateral relations improved markedly. So much so, in fact, that, following a complaint from Hitler in mid-June that he disliked and mistrusted the Italian ambassador to Berlin, Vittorio Cerruti, Mussolini recalled him immediately and replaced him with Bernardo Attolico from the Moscow embassy. In the light of this *rapprochement*, the *Duce* could now concentrate his efforts on countering mounting British opposition to his planned campaign against Ethiopia, secure in the knowledge that Berlin would not launch a sudden coup north of the Brenner Pass.[52]

If the cautious political *détente* being reached with Berlin reduced Mussolini's fears of an Austro-German union at a time of Italian vulnerability, it did little to assuage the concerns of Cavagnari and the naval staff, who throughout that summer viewed a possible war against Britain with mounting anxiety. With the conclusion of the Anglo-German Naval Agreement in mid-June – which fixed future German capital ship building at 35 per cent of that of Britain – there arose a further complication. A few days before London and Berlin signed the agreement, Cavagnari stressed in a memorandum for Mussolini that the Anglo-German deal might well initiate a new French building programme:

> Given the nature of our relations with France, it seems that we cannot fail to take that country's point of view into serious consideration.
> Therefore, given past precedents we should expect that the concession that Germany can now build to within 35% of the overall tonnage of the British fleet will offer the French navy the pretext to demand an increase in its own naval tonnage.

Mussolini evidently agreed with this view, for he had already expressed his concern that the naval agreement might affect the balance of power between the 'medium-sized' maritime nations, and had called for a general agreement on naval armaments.[53]

For the moment, however, the most serious and immediate problem facing Cavagnari did not concern the navy's long-term building policy with regard to the French. On the contrary, the Italian naval leadership feared losses in an Italo-British confrontation, as ordered by Mussolini in April, which could well leave the fleet's operational level seriously reduced for many years. This meant that the naval high command should avoid such a war at all costs.

On 19 June, the day after London and Berlin had signed the naval accord, Cavagnari, in a report for Mussolini, again voiced his reluctance to confront the Royal Navy. In mid-May the naval staff had already begun to address the question of substantially strengthening Italy's qualitative and quantitative naval capability. The progress of the various studies undertaken will be addressed more fully in the following chapter. Here, one might stress that its high command viewed current Italian prospects in a war with Britain with evident pessimism. Beginning by informing

Mussolini that he had prepared the navy for the conflict foreseen by the dictator as best he could, Cavagnari went on to stress that Italy would nevertheless find itself confronted by a greatly superior enemy and without any semblance of air support for its fleet:

> It remains obvious that, if war against Britain were to break out, the task of the navy would be an extremely onerous one, and could only be carried out if it were to perform with an extraordinary boldness which, if present from the very outset of hostilities, might bring about initial successes that would all the same be difficult to consolidate, being reliant on the effectiveness of the air force and the contribution of the naval air arm such as it is. Thereafter, the navy could only attempt to resist enemy pressure that would gradually grow heavier by the day.

Clearly, having studied the war plans office's plan to attack Malta produced in May, and noting the evident limitations contained within it, Cavagnari preferred not to mention it to Mussolini. Rather, the chief-of-staff argued that not launching a naval offensive but protecting lines of communication with Africa remained the navy's principal concern – a strategic view he continued to hold in the years that followed. In addition, he stressed that guerrilla warfare remained the only realistic means that the navy had of striking offensively at the British fleet, both within the Mediterranean and outside. The problem was that Italy did not as yet possess the means to carry out such a strategy, and such means should be built without further delay. Specifically, the high command requested: eight new submarines of the medium-sized *Sirena* class, and two more with minelaying capability; 12 fast motor torpedo-boats (*MAS – Motoscafo Anti Sommergibile*); two *Oriani*-class destroyers; two *Orsa* destroyer escorts; and two *Climene*-type torpedo boats. Work was to commence on these vessels as quickly as possible, in order that they might be ready for use in a war against the British. The only problem, of course, was that the units in question would not be ready before the Italian invasion of Ethiopia, scheduled to begin that October.[54]

Who could doubt that Cavagnari's report sought to demonstrate to Mussolini the slender chances for success the Italian navy had should war break out with Britain? Yet again, the chief-of-staff tried to impress upon the dictator the limitations facing the fleet in such a war. Even though the navy's planners considered an attack on Malta as one of the few options available, Cavagnari, who had already argued that such an operation would not alter unduly the strategic balance in Italy's favour, did not mention the plan to the *Duce*. Clearly, he feared that Mussolini might order him to proceed with an offensive that neither he nor the naval staff believed likely to succeed, and which would in any case incur potentially heavy naval losses. After Giuseppe Valle and Pietro Pinna of the air staff had shown themselves openly pessimistic about Italian prospects against the British in the Mediterranean, Cavagnari quickly informed Mussolini that Italy's fleet would face any future war with little or no air support. The only offensive strategy which he did suggest to the dictator – launching a guerrilla war with currently non-existent weapons – constituted an obvious attempt to deter Mussolini from considering hostilities against Britain. Any offensive using '*mezzi insidiosi*' required considerable preparation and, vitally, additional naval building, which would take many months to complete. Once informed of this fact, Cavagnari evidently hoped that Mussolini would reconsider his plan to attack the British fleet and resolve the Italo-Abyssinian dispute politically, as he had originally suggested in March. By early July, he also began to argue that the navy could do very little to protect lines of communication with Libya and East Africa from British attack.[55]

Over the rest of that summer, relations between London and Rome were to worsen considerably, making the threat of war appear more likely. On 14 June Aloisi yet again warned Mussolini that Britain remained intransigent towards Italian claims in East Africa, and that the British government merely intended to use the League of Nations as a means of protecting its own imperial interests. This, Aloisi argued, suggested that Italy should remain within the League framework and itself use the threat of departure from that framework as a means of coercion. Some ten days later, Mussolini, in his encounter with the British minister for League of Nations' Affairs, Anthony Eden, employed precisely this tactic. Rejecting Eden's proposal that Abyssinia might cede the province of Ogaden to Italy in return for an outlet to the sea at Zeila in British Somaliland, he insisted that Britain should leave Italy to settle the matter itself. Under a system of Italian control similar to that of Britain in Egypt, Ethiopia would become transformed to the mutual advantage of all concerned, and no longer pose any threat to regional security. In achieving this, he, Mussolini, would be resolutely determined, and Britain should not place Italy in the position where it might have to leave the League of Nations in protest over the matter. By 5 July, Grandi in London warned Vansittart that Britain had already seriously damaged its relations with Rome and, should it now seek French support in opposing Italy, further risked wrecking the Locarno agreements and splitting Europe into two opposing blocs.[56]

[Mussolini appeared most eager to preserve Italian friendship with France that summer in order to ensure that Paris would not, as Cavagnari had predicted, support Britain's stance over Abyssinia.] This meant upholding the idea that Rome would back a French war against Germany should the latter attempt to annex Austria or attack metropolitan France. In return for this pledge of Italian military support, Laval would, at least in Mussolini's mind, then continue to offer Italy *carte blanche* in East Africa and, more important, not back Britain's opposition to the Italian plan. In early July, an Italian pledge of military support for France led to the conclusion of the Gamelin–Badoglio agreements, which foresaw combined military operations to counter possible German aggression against France or Austria.[57]

This further move towards an Italo-French military alliance could not but influence the navy's views of Italy's strategic position in the Mediterranean. Initially, the naval staff, ordered by Mussolini to conclude an agreement of their own with the French navy, believed that in view of the air pact signed in May, and the Gamelin–Badoglio military agreements concluded in early July, France might now back a naval war against Britain. Under the aegis of the Franco-Italian accords, war against Germany remained the hypothesis that governed naval planning. But, in view of the current political crisis with Britain, war against the Royal Navy remained a clear possibility, and any Italo-French alliance should also cover this contingency.

Guardedly more optimistic about the Italian fleet's prospects in such a conflict than he had been in May, Cavagnari now argued that only with French support might it be possible to assert greater dominance over the western Mediterranean and thereby achieve control of the sea route from Gibraltar to Malta. If the Royal Navy deployed units to the eastern basin of the sea the British could easily capture the Dodecanese, and, even more seriously, sever all Italian lines of communication with Suez and the Red Sea. Italy could do very little to counter this eventuality except request French protection for Italian merchant shipping *en route* via Gibraltar to Italy. Concomitantly, Italian air and underwater units based at Augusta in southern Italy, and a similar force operating from a swiftly occupied Cephalonia in western Greece, might prevent the enemy from penetrating the central Mediterranean from the eastern basin. In any case, it had become vitally important that Paris and Rome now conclude a naval agreement in order to clarify how the alliance would operate in time of war; an obvious sign that Cavagnari viewed any alliance with France as conjecture.[58]

Certainly, the chief-of-staff's logic appeared over-optimistic and was based on a rather crude *quid pro quo*. If, he calculated, Italy guaranteed to support France in any war against Germany, then this might persuade the French to counter any potential threat faced by the Italians, including one from Britain. As Guido Vanutelli, the deputy chief-of-staff, summed up in a memorandum to Cavagnari of 2 July, Italy 'would be giving much in return for nothing' if it backed France against Germany without gaining some measure of security in the Mediterranean.[59]

But, as Cavagnari had himself expressly indicated that March, it appeared unlikely that Paris would assume any position diametrically opposed to that of the British. Similarly, the first versions of *Plan B* in May had not discussed such a possibility in any depth. Cavagnari's report for Mussolini in mid-June did not mention it at all. Therefore, any idea of an alliance with France based on the hypothesis that it operated against both Germany and Britain remained wildly unrealistic. Even in the event that it did become a reality, the naval staff still did not believe that much could be done to win control of the eastern Mediterranean from the British, who in any war were expected to close the Suez Canal and the Dardanelles and to sever all Italian communications with East Africa. This action could only serve to undermine the Italian military campaign about to get underway on the African continent.

By early August, and in the face of increasing British opposition to any Italian designs against the Ethiopian empire, King Victor Emanuel warned Mussolini that he should not count on French support for Italy in any war against Britain. If anything, this suggests that it had been the dictator who had ordered the navy to consider the possibilities offered by French backing, should war break out with Britain over the Italian dispute with Addis Ababa. Given that this slender likelihood had failed to materialise, Italy faced the prospect of war against Britain alone. On 9 August the dictator thus ordered Badoglio to consider which options were open to Italy should it find itself facing such a war.[60]

Four days later, Badoglio convened a meeting of the supreme high command, attended by each of the chiefs-of-staff and their respective deputies, and ordered them to report, for Mussolini's benefit, how Italy might best conduct the threatened war with Britain. Their conclusions were almost universally gloomy. The navy, which of all the Italian armed forces would be the most heavily committed in such a conflict, found itself at a massive disadvantage if confronted with British sea power. Although Cavagnari and his freshly appointed deputy, Admiral Wladimiro Pini, emphasised that the Italian fleet would certainly be on a full war footing by 30 August, they lost no time in stressing that the odds remained heavily weighted against them. At that time, the navy had only two operational capital ships – the unmodernised *Duilio* and *Doria* – which, although able to boast of a reasonable level of armament, had no protection whatsoever against submarine attack. Italy's much-vaunted submarine fleet in practice also offered very little by way of offensive capability. No more than 20 submarines could be kept at sea at any one time, and many of the operational theatres were some distance from their metropolitan bases, which effectively reduced their range greatly. Similarly, the success of any undersea offensive depended on the operations in question being supported by air actions, and Italy's naval air arm could not be considered a serious threat. Nor, as Giuseppe Valle outlined, did it appear likely that the air force's ageing aircraft offered much by way of additional support. The situation remained unlikely to improve markedly until June 1936, he added.

The navy could do little to defend the Dodecanese Islands, could mount little by way of offensive operations in the Red Sea, and would find its base at Tobruk heavily exposed to enemy attack. In effect, the naval high command could not guarantee that communications with East Africa would remain intact in time of war. Against this picture of Italian inferiority, Cavagnari outlined the extent of British naval power. The Royal Navy operated a fleet composed of 15 battleships armed with 38cm or 40cm main guns, of which Italy possessed not even one. It had some 60 heavy cruisers against Italy's 13, and around 100 destroyers as opposed to Italy's 50. Moreover, the Royal Navy had an aircraft-carrier capability, and each vessel carried around 40 aircraft able to conduct reconnaissance and bombing operations. Italy had no such vessels. Only in submarines did Italy match the British fleet – both operated some 50 to 60 units.

This massive naval superiority was matched by British control of the Mediterranean exits. Quite simply, Britain could blockade Italy within this sea and engage its fleet inside without major difficulty. Although the Italian navy might consider taking Malta, Italy would not be able to hold the island permanently. The British, Cavagnari added, would be able to mount offensive operations against the Italian mainland with great ease. His final statement represented a succinct résumé of his reasons for opposing war against Britain as expressed to Mussolini since early March:

> Italy's total lack of battleship capability and the limited operational value of its air force render the possibility of war against Britain an extremely onerous undertaking.
>
> If we already had our new capital ship nucleus, we might then be able to reach somewhat different conclusions, even if only from the point of view that Britain might not then wish to take the risk of engaging us in any war.
>
> The two old battleships *Duilio* and *Doria* cannot be deployed to any theatre of strategic operations. They will therefore be assigned to the defence of Augusta, Naples or La Maddalena.[61]

The record of this critical meeting is highly revealing. In the first place, Badoglio's involvement in the planning for a possible confrontation with the British signalled a fleeting augmentation of his personal role as head of the supreme high command. Second, the document still further demonstrates Cavagnari's persistent reluctance to contemplate a war against the Royal Navy. In turn, if the account of the meeting is examined alongside the earlier arguments of both the air and navy staffs, then clearly neither believed that they could seriously counter British armed hostility to Italian aggression on the African continent, being unable to challenge that power for control of the Mediterranean and Red Sea. For the navy, whose quantitative inferiority remained obvious and whose submarine and air arms were unprepared for war, the only serious possibility for carrying an offensive to the British lay with guerrilla warfare. However, neither the means nor the appropriately trained men were ready before the attack on Ethiopia got underway in early October. By 10 September, provisional experiments with the equipment in question were still in progress, and only the following year were satisfactory results obtained, by which time Italy had taken Ethiopia and avoided war with Britain.[62]

As Cavagnari pointed out to Badoglio, the Italian armed forces could only hope that, following a very public avowal of Italy's supposed intention to fight, Britain, not wishing to risk losses affecting its overall imperial defence capability, might hesitate to initiate hostilities, thus permitting the war in Africa to proceed unopposed. In other words, Rome should now pursue a policy based on bluff in order to secure the planned conquest of the entire Ethiopian empire. This suggested that Mussolini and Italian diplomacy had to find the solution to the Mediterranean crisis. The military solution asked for by the dictator was simply not possible.[63]

After the high command had met, Mussolini, increasingly determined not to be thwarted, ordered an intensification of preparations for war against Ethiopia. At the same time he warned Paris that the French government should at all costs seek to prevent any armed clash between Italy and Great Britain. Italy, he stressed, would not be able to find forces to deploy on three fronts: Ethiopia, the Italo-Austrian frontier and the Mediterranean.[64]

Then, on 20 August, the naval staff suddenly learned that London seemed likely to reinforce the Mediterranean Fleet with units from home waters, just as they had predicted in their original plan of operations that May. A fresh study by the war plans office noted that a British formation composed of units from both naval stations was highly unlikely to deploy to Malta, given the risk of an Italian attack, but would assume positions at either end of the Mediterranean – beyond the range of the Italian surface fleet. The Home Fleet seemed certain to remain at Gibraltar, while the rest of the new formation deployed to bases in the eastern basin. From these positions, the Royal Navy were expected to undertake the following operations: from the western basin, to mount a bombardment of the Ligurian coastline in north-west Italy with heavy cruisers and battleships; to attack shipping leaving Ligurian ports with submarines and cruisers; to attack the same ports from the air; and to attack other, southerly, naval facilities at La Maddalena, Cagliari, Trapani, Palermo and Naples using the same combination of means. From the eastern basin the British would use a similar array of naval power in order to penetrate the Aegean Sea with the objectives of disrupting communications with the Black Sea and capturing the Dodecanese Islands. Both formations would ultimately combine in order to attack any convoys attempting to reach Africa via the Sicilian Channel. The Italian navy's ability to counter this remained limited. In the western Mediterranean, a force of torpedo-boats supported by cruisers might be kept at the ready to attack at dawn any British force heading towards Liguria. On the island of Sardinia light naval units should be prepared to operate either north of the Tunisian coast or between that island and Sicily. Finally, cruisers and destroyers should also be ready to undertake night operations against the British in the lower Ionian Sea.[65]

The success of the plan depended on the Italian fleet's ability to prevent the British from launching their attacks against the western metropolitan coastline, the Dodecanese or Italian communications. As such, the new version of *Plan B* therefore appeared markedly more defensive in nature than that originally ordered by Mussolini in mid-April. It is true that part I of the new plan discussed the possibility of attacking Malta and subsequently any British fleet abandoning the island. But, as noted above, Cavagnari had practically dismissed the idea during the meeting of the supreme high command the week before. In any case, the naval staff clearly believed that the Royal Navy did not plan to deploy in strength to the island. Besides the obvious quantitative disparity between the British and Italian navies, it should simply be repeated that the Italian fleet remained without air cover at sea, had no night fighting capability and no anti-submarine tactics or means at its disposal. The likely success or failure of the new *Plan B* must be considered with these facts in mind.

The conclusions reached by the naval high command in the days before the outbreak of the Italo-Ethiopian war only served to confirm that the Italian fleet could not hope to withstand the rigours of a war against the Royal Navy. On 19 September, after the war plans office issued directives for *Plan B* to the naval divisions concerned, the naval leadership concluded that, although Italy enjoyed an optimum strategic position in the Mediterranean, it lacked the means to exploit such an advantage. The British navy could, they argued, simply counter any operation of the *Marina* by deploying more powerful and more numerous naval units. Evidently, it would never be possible for Italy to secure control of the Mediterranean in the face of such odds.[66]

Mussolini had been fully aware that the Italian armed forces could do little to challenge the British in any Mediterranean and Red Sea war. Yet, the *Duce* also knew that London sought to avoid an Anglo-Italian clash. During a meeting with Drummond on 23 September, Mussolini received a personal assurance that neither the foreign secretary Samuel Hoare nor the British cabinet wanted to 'humiliate Italy', close the Suez Canal or to impose 'military sanctions' against Italy. Believing himself now free from the threat of British intervention, Mussolini promised Drummond that Italy posed no threat to Britain's imperial interests. Shortly afterwards, the dictator finally ordered the Italian expeditionary force to attack Ethiopia on 3 October.[67]

We might conclude this chapter by reiterating some key political and strategic points. Mussolini's designs on Ethiopia, which dated from at least 1925, were not an end in themselves but formed part of a much greater imperial design that encompassed the entire Mediterranean and Red Sea, and constituted a first step in 'demolishing' the British Empire. Far from seeking agreement with London, as recommended by Badoglio and an increasingly nervous Cavagnari, Mussolini at first sought to mislead the Ramsay MacDonald coalition government and then, in the face of continued British political resistance to his plans to wage war in Africa, ordered his armed forces to prepare to attack Britain's position in the Mediterranean in mid-April 1935.[68]

In addition, his earlier alliance with Laval had not been concluded from a genuine fear of any on-going German threat. On the contrary, it amounted to a temporary expedient aimed at forestalling a premature German action against Austria, an action that threatened both the *Duce*'s East African enterprise and his domestic political position. The French 'alliance' was to be discarded once Italo-German relations were strengthened after the strains imposed upon them by the traumas of July 1934. An alignment with Berlin and not the Western powers held the key to Mussolini's future dreams of empire.

In turn, Britain's continued, albeit expected, opposition to his plans to assault the Ethiopian empire by force of arms, evident since early February 1935, angered Mussolini. So much so that he ordered Cavagnari to prepare to wage war against the Royal Navy and its bases at a time when Italian naval rearmament was far from complete, air cover for the fleet was almost totally lacking, and the submarine arm was largely unready for war – only 20 vessels could put to sea at any one time, while many of the anticipated operational theatres were too distant from its metropolitan bases. Despite repeated attempts by Cavagnari to warn him that the navy could achieve little in any possible Italo-British conflict, and that the French – until recently considered a future foe by the *Marina*'s planners – would not offer support despite the military agreements reached over 1935, only in mid-September, after Britain had reinforced its Mediterranean position, did Mussolini finally reach a political understanding with London. Had he actually ordered the armed forces to war with Britain there can be little doubt that they would have faced defeat at the hands of greatly superior forces.

Ultimately, Britain paid a heavy price for failing to confront Mussolini's aggression with force. In the period that followed, the *Duce*, eventually buoyed by his successful military campaign in Africa and his stubborn resistance to British pressure to reach a compromise settlement, showed all too clearly that he intended to mount a challenge to the hegemony of both Britain and France in the Mediterranean alongside Italy's new German ally.

NOTES

1 G. W. Baer, *The Coming of the Italian–Ethiopian War* (Harvard University Press, Cambridge, MA, 1967), p. 35; F. Catalano, *L'economia italiana di guerra: la politica economico-finanziaria del Fascismo dalla guerra d'Etiopia alla caduta del regime, 1935–1943* (Istituto Nazionale per la Storia, Milan, 1969), p. 7; G. Rochat, *Militari e politici nella preparazione della campagna d'Etiopia: studio e documenti, 1932–1936* (Franco Angeli, Milan, 1971), p. 105; On the supposed stalling of Fascism's ideological dynamic see Cassels, 'Was There a Fascist Foreign Policy?', p. 259.

2 J. Petersen, 'La politica estera Fascista come problema storiografico', *Storia Contemporanea*, 3, 4 (1972), especially pp. 700–5; Mack Smith, *Mussolini*, p. 202; Knox, 'Il Fascismo e la politica estera', p. 301 and on Mussolini's overall imperial and geopolitical thinking, pp. 296–322.

3 R. De Felice, *Mussolini il Duce. I. Gli anni del consenso, 1929–1936* (Giulio Einaudi, Turin, 1974), pp. 597–616.

4 R. Mori, *Mussolini e la conquista dell'Etiopia* (Felice le Monnier, Florence, 1978), p. 4.

5 N. H. Gibbs, *Grand Strategy. Volume I, Rearmament Policy in History of the Second World War, United Kingdom Military Series*, ed. J. R. M. Butler (Her Majesty's Stationery Office, London, 1976), pp. 189–98; A. Marder, 'The Royal Navy and the Ethiopian Crisis of 1935–36', *American Historical Review*, 75, 5 (1969), pp. 1341–5; S. Roskill, *Naval Policy Between the Wars. Volume II: The Period of Reluctant Rearmament, 1930–1939* (Collins, London, 1976), p. 263; for a newer analysis see S. Morewood, 'The Chiefs-of-Staff, the "Men on the Spot", and the Italo-Abyssinian Emergency, 1935–36', in D. Richardson and G. Stone (eds), *Decisions and Diplomacy – Essays in Twentieth Century International History* (LSE/Routledge, London, 1995), pp. 93 and 102.

6 R. Quartararo, 'Imperial Defence in the Mediterranean on the Eve of the Ethiopian Crisis (July–October 1935)', *Historical Journal*, 20, 1 (1977), pp. 200–3 and 220. The idea that Italy had achieved 'naval hegemony' in the Mediterranean by mid-1935 is also expressed in R. N. Salerno, 'Multilateral Strategy and Diplomacy: The Anglo-German Naval Agreement and the Mediterranean Crisis of 1935–1936', *Journal of Strategic Studies*, 17, 2 (1994). On the idea that Italian plans would have 'guaranteed' success in the event of war with Britain see F. Minniti, '"Il nemico vero": gli obiettivi dei piani di operazione contro la Gran Bretagna nel contesto etiopico (maggio 1935–maggio 1936)', *Storia Contemporanea*, 26, 4 (1995), pp. 576–7 and 593.

7 J. Gooch, *Esercito, stato e società in Italia, 1870–1915* (Franco Angeli, Milan, 1994), Ch. 5.

8 On the Fascist belief that Adowa should be avenged see A. J. P. Taylor, *The Origins of the Second World War* (Penguin, London, 1987), pp. 118–19; Knox, 'Il fascismo e la politica estera italiana', p. 321. For the idea that imperialism was 'implicit in fascism', see C. J. Lowe and F. Marzari, *Italian Foreign Policy, 1870–1940* (Routledge, London, 1975), p. 240.

9 Lowe and Marzari, *Italian Foreign Policy*, pp. 240–1; Mori, *Mussolini e la conquista dell'Etiopia*, p. 1. For an assessment of how a forward policy in East Africa had also taken hold within the Italian foreign ministry, see M. Michaelis, 'Italy's strategy in the Mediterranean, 1935–39', in M. J. Cohen and M. Kolinsky (eds), *Britain and the Middle East in the 1930s* (Macmillan, London, 1992), p. 45. *I documenti diplomatici italiani* (*DDI*), settima serie, 1922–35, vol. XVI (Istituto Poligrafico dello Stato, Rome, 1990), 358, memorandum by Mussolini, 30/12/1934. In August of 1934 Mussolini had informed the heads of the armed forces that the situation

in Europe at that moment was 'so uncertain that the Italian armed forces should be kept on a state of alert in case they were called upon to respond to sudden crises such as the one that had occurred at the end of July', a clear reference to the attempted Nazi coup in Austria. But, he continued, 'as far as Abyssinia is concerned, our general line of conduct must be such as to give the impression that we are remaining faithful to our treaty of friendship with that country. All idle gossip, either in Italy or the Italian colonies, with regard to our aggressive intentions in Abyssinia should be silenced by whatever means. These voices could prove extremely costly to us at a later date.' Ufficio Storico della Marina Militare, Rome, Direzioni Generali, (USMM, DG), 8-G, Mussolini to under-secretaries of state for war, navy and air force, 10/8/1934. (*Note*: Italy, along with France and Britain, was a signatory of the tripartite agreement on Abyssinia concluded in 1906. In 1928 the Fascist administration had concluded a bilateral treaty of friendship with the Ethiopian empire.)

10 Petersen, *Hitler e Mussolini*, pp. 336–44; Laval claimed that France 'did not intend to impede Italian penetration in Abyssinia', see *DDI*, 7, XVI, 399, meeting between Mussolini and Laval, 6/1/1935.

11 Petersen, *Hitler e Mussolini*, p. 11; B. R. Sullivan, 'The Italian Armed Forces, 1918–40', in M. J. Cohen and M. Kolinsky (eds), *Military Effectiveness. Volume II: The Interwar Period* (Allen & Unwin, Boston, MA, 1988), p. 175; Knox, 'Il Fascismo e la politica estera italiana', pp. 304–6.

12 G. Weinberg, *The Foreign Policy of Hitler's Germany. Volume I: Diplomatic Revolution in Europe, 1933–36* (University of Chicago Press, Chicago, IL, 1970), pp. 196–7; On the effects that German policy in Austria was already having in Italy at this time see *Documents on German Foreign Policy* (hereafter *DGFP*), series C, (vols III–VI) (Her Majesty's Stationery Office, London, 1957–83), vol. III, 118, 'Political Report', Hassell to foreign ministry, 25/7/1934. The possibility of an Italo-German war over the question of Austria was discussed by the supreme high command in September 1934. See L. Ceva, 'Appunti per una storia dello Stato Maggiore generale fino alla vigilia della "non-belligeranza", giugno 1925 – luglio 1939', *Storia Contemporanea*, 10, 2 (1979), pp. 222–7.

13 Baer, *The Coming of the Italian–Ethiopian War*, p. 78; G. Buccianti, *Verso gli accordi Mussolini-Laval: il riavvicinamento italo-francese fra il 1931 e il 1934* (Giuffrè Editore, Milan, 1984), pp. 248–9; N. Rostow, *Anglo-French Relations, 1934–36* (Macmillan, London, 1984), p. 77; Weinberg, *Diplomatic Revolution in Europe*, pp. 196–7; on the 'temporary' nature of the Franco-Italian alliance see R. J. Young, 'Soldiers and Diplomats: The French Embassy and Franco-Italian Relations, 1935–6', *Journal of Strategic Studies*, 7, 1 (1984), pp. 75–80; 'French Military Intelligence and the Franco-Italian Alliance, 1933–1939', *The Historical Journal*, 28, 1 (1985), pp. 148–9 and 161–2.

14 USMM, DG, 0-C, 'Programma di costruzioni navali', Ducci to naval ministry, 29/11/1933. For subsequent memoranda on the subject of new battleship programmes for the navy, see Bernardi, *Il disarmo navale*, p. 596; USMM, DG, 0-C1, 'Quesiti per il relatore bilancio esercizio 1935–1936: programma navale italiano per il 1934–35 e 1935–36', unsigned memorandum, 5/2/1934. On the evolution of the *Littorio* ships see W. H. Garzke and R. O. Dullin, *Battleships: Axis and Neutral Battleships in World War II* (Naval Institute Press, Annapolis, MD, 1985), pp. 371–81. On the submarine arm see USMM, *L'organizzazione della Marina durante il conflitto, tomo 1*, p. 79. The vessels in question were subsequently laid down from August 1935 onwards see Fraccaroli, *Italian Warships of World War II*, pp. 135–9.

15 De Felice, *Gli anni del consenso*, pp. 638–40.

16 On the views of Baistrocchi and Badoglio see ibid., pp. 633–6; Badoglio to De Bono, 12/5/1934, in Rochat, *Militari e politici*, pp. 324–7. On Badoglio's role in the high command after 1927, see P. Pieri and G. Rochat, *Badoglio* (UTET, Turin, 1974), p. 563. The royal decree law of 6 February 1927 effectively stripped Badoglio of all responsibility for the Italian armed forces leaving them under the control of Mussolini, although the former remained publicly Italy's most senior military figure. Thereafter, Badoglio retained a purely consultative role, in theory keeping the dictator informed of military developments and being informed himself of these developments by the various under-secretaries of state. Ceva, 'Appunti per una storia dello Stato Maggiore generale', pp. 213–14, 220, 229 and 250; idem, *La condotta italiana della guerra. Cavallero el il Comando Supremo, 1941–1942* (Feltrinelli Editore, Milan, 1975), pp. 23–7.

17 In September 1934, one month before building of the new *Littorio* class began, Mussolini made a speech at Taranto, Italy's principal naval base, emphasising the importance of sea power in fulfilling the nation's imperial destiny. 'We will become a great nation when we are able to dominate the sea. Rome could not have conquered its empire without first having crushed the naval might of Carthage. In order that the Mediterranean, which is not an ocean and which has two entrances guarded by others, will not remain a jail that stifles our life force, we must become powerful on that sea.' *Opera Omnia di Benito Mussolini* (OOBM) (various volumes) (La Fenice, Florence and Rome, 1951–80), vol. XXVI, pp. 322–4.

18 *DDI*, 7, XVI, 415, Vitetti to Suvich, 8/1/1935. For an account of the incident at Wal Wal see Baer, *The Coming of the Italian–Ethiopian War*, Ch. 3.

19 *DDI*, 7, XVI, 490, Mussolini to Grandi/Pignatti, 25/1/1935, 492, Mussolini to Grandi, 25/1/1935 and 494, Pignatti to Mussolini, 26/1/1935; Petersen, *Hitler e Mussolini*, p. 343.

20 Mori, *Mussolini e la conquista dell'Etiopia*, p. 12.

21 *DDI*, 7, XVI, 523, Grandi to Mussolini, 1/2/1935. In mid-February, Vitetti informed both John Simon and Geoffrey Thompson of the Foreign Office that Italy's strategic preparations in East Africa were merely precautionary and designed to protect Rome's interests there should they come under attack. See *DDI*, 7, XVI, 585, Vitetti to Mussolini, 13/2/1935 (two separate dispatches). See also 638, Grandi to Mussolini, 22/2/1935 and 670, Grandi to Mussolini, 27/2/1935.

22 Archivio Storico del Ministero degli Affari Esteri (ASMAE), Rome, Ambasciata di Londra, busta: 891, fascicolo: 2, Capponi to naval staff, 3/3/1935.

23 *DDI*, 7, XVI, 677 (appendix), British embassy to Italian foreign ministry, 28/2/1935 and 694, Cavagnari to Mussolini, 4/3/1935.

24 Both Renzo De Felice and Lucio Ceva argue that naval staff reservations with regard to the planned operation against Ethiopia did not surface until later that year, at the point at which Britain reinforced the Mediterranean station with units from the Home Fleet. As Cavagnari's letter of 4 March clearly shows, the navy's high command expressed considerable anxiety about Britain's attitude towards Mussolini's plan much earlier. De Felice, *Gli anni del consenso*, pp. 637–8; Ceva, 'Appunti per una storia dello Stato Maggiore generale', p. 229.

25 *DDI*, 7, XVI, 707, Mussolini to De Bono, 8/3/1935; Rochat, *Militari e politici*, pp. 406–8. For the view that Mussolini was intent on a total conquest of Abyssinia and not any form of negotiated settlement see Mori, *Mussolini e la conquista dell'Etiopia*, pp. 72–6; M. Knox, 'The Fascist Regime, its Foreign Policy and its Wars: An "Anti-Fascist Orthodoxy?"', *Contemporary European History*, 4, 3 (1995), p. 362.

26 Badoglio's memorandum for Mussolini is cited in Rochat, *Militari e politici*, pp. 408–11.

27 Ibid., pp. 121–2; E. M. Robertson, *Mussolini as Empire Builder: Europe and Africa, 1932–36* (Macmillan, London, 1977), pp. 96–100.

28 A copy of the communiqué was presented to Fulvio Suvich by Eric Drummond on the date of its despatch to Berlin. *DDI*, 7, XVI, 756, meeting between Suvich and Drummond, 18/3/1935 and 797, Aloisi to Mussolini, 23/3/1935.

29 M. Knox, 'L'ultima guerra dell'Italia Fascista', in B. Micheletti and P. Poggio (eds), *L'Italia in guerra, 1940–43* (Annali della Fondazione 'Luigi Marchetti', Brescia, 1990–91), p. 19. On the possibilities of an *'intesa'* between Rome and Berlin see *DGFP*, C, IV, 164, 'Political Report. Subject: Italian Foreign Policy', Hassell to foreign ministry, 21/6/1935. Weinberg argues that strained relations between Italy and the British and French over Abyssinia, and German 'neutrality' and aloofness towards the issue, at this point created the appropriate conditions for a *rapprochement*. Furthermore, although the Nazi administration would not affirm Austrian independence, it was prepared to agree to a 'temporary accommodation' not based on achieving total control of the country. Weinberg, *Diplomatic Revolution in Europe*, pp. 232–3. For the idea that Mussolini's overtures to Hitler during the spring of 1935 were merely the product of his anxiety as regards Italy's current European position at a time of growing commitment to the Abyssinian venture, see M. Funke, 'Le relazioni italo-tedesche al momento del conflitto etiopico e delle sanzioni della Società delle Nazioni', *Storia Contemporanea*, 2, 3 (1975), pp. 480–1. For the view that Mussolini regarded an Austro-German *Anschluss* as the principal means of winning German support against the western powers from as early as 1927, see Knox, 'Il Fascismo e la politica estera italiana', p. 306. On improved Italo-German relations in the spring of 1935 see R. H. Whealey, 'Mussolini's Ideological Diplomacy: An Unpublished Document', *Journal of Modern History*, 39, 4 (1967), p. 432.

   On Hitler's ideas of forging with Italy the 'nucleus of a new Europe' and in winning Italian consent to an *Anschluss* as a means of securing this see M. Messerschmidt, 'Foreign Policy and Preparation for War', in W. Deist *et al.* (eds), *Germany and the Second World War: Volume I: The Build-Up of German Aggression* (Clarendon Press, Oxford, 1990), p. 548. Hitler's notion that the Abyssinian affair offered an ideal opportunity to strengthen relations between Rome and Berlin is also discussed by K. Hildebrand, *The Foreign Policy of the Third Reich* (Batsford, London, 1973), p. 41. For the argument that Britain's weak handling of the Abyssinian issue redefined Hitler's view of the former, and gradually consolidated his enthusiasm for a 'combination of the Fascist powers' that might easily be 'transformed into a world-wide anti-British alliance' see G. Waddington, '*Hassgegner*: German Views of Great Britain in the Later 1930s', *History*, 81, 261 (1996), pp. 27–30.

30 For the view held by senior diplomats at the foreign ministry that Austria constituted Italy's own *'zona demilitarizzata'* see *DDI*, 7, XVI, 852, Buti to Suvich, 2/4/1935. The idea for such a conference was first raised by an unsigned foreign ministry memorandum which set out the Italian line to be taken at the Anglo–French–Italian conversations held in Paris to discuss the problem of German rearmament on 23 March 1935. See *DDI*, 7, XVI, 785, 'Tesi da sostenere a Parigi', 22/3/1935. On the origins of this idea see 798, Drummond to Mussolini, 23/3/1935, and on Mussolini's stance at Stresa see Knox, 'The Fascist Regime, its Foreign Policy and its Wars', p. 362.

31 Ceva, 'Appunti per una storia dello Stato Maggiore generale', p. 228; Robertson, *Mussolini as Empire Builder*, pp. 98–100; *DDI*, 7, XVI, 851, Aloisi to Mussolini, 2/4/1935; on Aloisi, see Mori, *Mussolini e la conquista dell'Etiopia*, p. 247. If Mussolini did regard Stresa as a means of preventing further German acts of

revanchism at a crucial moment for Italy's expansionist programme, then the evidence suggests that his strategy met with some success. On 29 March Ulrich von Hassell, the German ambassador in Rome, warned Berlin that the Italian foreign ministry saw a military clash with Germany as 'inevitable' and that Stresa would lead to 'a close coalition against Germany'. However, he also added that 'even Mussolini, who, in view of the action he may be expected to take against Ethiopia during the next 12 months, would naturally prefer to avoid warlike developments in Europe', but 'sees no other way out unless Germany changes course at the eleventh hour'. *DGFP*, C, III, 563, Hassell to foreign ministry, 29/3/1935. Similarly, on 1 April, Hassell again warned of the need to prevent Italy from 'swinging more or less unconditionally over to the Franco-British side the next time the question of disarmament came up', and that to achieve this Mussolini should be given assurances that Germany did not intend a forceful solution of the Austrian problem. *DGFP*, C, IV, 5, Hassell to Neurath, 1/4/1935.

32 *DGFP*, C, IV, 6, Neurath to Hassell, 4/4/1935. See also *DDI*, 7, XVI, 874, meeting between Suvich and Hassell, 6/4/1935. In October 1934 Mussolini emphasised to Hassell: '1) that Austria was a German country, 2) that she must be independent.' He went on, 'Much would be gained ... if the Führer were to make a clear public statement on a suitable occasion to the effect that Germany recognised Austria's independence and would not interfere in her internal affairs.' *DGFP*, C, III, 266, Hassell to foreign ministry, 23/10/1934. On 2 May 1935, Cerutti, acting under Mussolini's instructions, asked for such a guarantee once more and was informed by Neurath that Hitler could not for the moment make such a promise in public. However, he was able to give the ambassador a formal assurance on behalf of the *Führer* that an *Anschluss* was not on the agenda. *DDI*, ottava serie, (vols I–IV and XII–XIII) (Istituto Poligrafico dello Stato, Rome, 1952–92), vol. I, 125, Cerruti to Mussolini, 2/5/1935. For Renzetti's report see *DDI*, 7, XVI, 908, report by Renzetti for the ministry for popular culture, 11/4/1935 and 915, Cerruti to Mussolini, 13/4/1935.

33 *DDI*, 7, XVI, 846, Buti to Mussolini, 1/4/1935.

34 Renato Mori maintains that Mussolini rejected any idea of discussing the Abyssinian question at Stresa for fear that he might meet British disapproval of his plan. Rather, he intended to present London with a *fait accompli* over the issue – as the Japanese had done over Manchuria in 1931–32. Mori, *Mussolini e la conquista dell'Etiopia*, p. 21. For the view that British silence over Ethiopia at Stresa led Mussolini to believe that 'an implicit agreement similar to that reached with Laval in January had also been struck with the British', see Lowe and Marzari, *Italian Foreign Policy, 1870–1940*, p. 264; Baer, *The Coming of the Italian–Ethiopian War*, p. 122; D. Grandi, *Il mio paese: ricordi autobiografici* (Il Mulino, Bologna, 1985), p. 391. For the argument that the French played the major part in keeping the Italo-Ethiopian dispute off the main agenda at Stresa see De Felice, *Gli anni del consenso*, pp. 661–2. Accounts of the back room talks at Stresa can be found in *Documents on British Foreign Policy* (hereafter *DBFP*), series 2 (vols XIII–XVIII), vol. XIV (Her Majesty's Stationery Office, London, 1949–57), 230 and 232, conversations between Thompson, Guarnaschelli and Vitetti at Stresa, 12/4/1935; *DDI*, 8, I, 70, Buti to Suvich, 23/4/1935 and 71, 'Conversazioni di Stresa per la questione etiopica (11, 12 e 13 aprile 1935)', Vitetti to Buti, 23/4/1935.

35 *DDI*, 7, XVI, 694, Cavagnari to Mussolini, 4/3/1935; the colonial question in Hitler's foreign policy is discussed by Hildebrand, *The Foreign Policy of the Third Reich*, pp. 39–40; A. Hillgruber, 'England's Place in Hitler's Plans for World Dominion', *Journal of Contemporary History*, 9, 1 (1974), p. 13. On Stresa, see, for example, Taylor, *Origins of the Second World War*, p. 119; Robertson, *Mussolini*

as Empire Builder, p. 131. On Mussolini's reaction to Simon's move, see *DDI*, 8, I, 60, Mussolini to Grandi, 20/4/1935.

36 Given that Mussolini dealt directly with the various heads of the armed forces it is likely that the order was transmitted personally. His directive is referred to in a letter from Cavagnari to the war ministry in late May. See USMM, DG 0-L, 'Operazione "B"', Cavagnari to army staff, 23/5/1935; USMM, DG 1-D, 'Piani di guerra', Cavagnari to naval staff, 14/4/1935.

37 *DDI*, 7, XVI, 694, Cavagnari to Mussolini, 4/3/1935.

38 On the agreements concluded between the two air forces and armies see Young, 'Soldiers and Diplomats', pp. 77–8; USMM, DG, 1-D, 'Piani di guerra', Cavagnari to naval staff, 24/4/1935. It should be noted that Cavagnari foresaw the British as remaining strictly neutral in any war against Germany.

39 In January 1935 the naval ministry expressed its concern that Italy remained without an effective air arm. All 115 aircraft operated by the navy entirely for reconnaissance purposes were in need of replacement. The Italian fleet, it argued, needed air support in order to undertake offensive aeronaval operations. Over the previous year, several aeronaval exercises had been undertaken but the results had proved decidedly modest. See *Atti Parlamentari – Camera dei deputati*, (*APCD*), legislatura XXIX, sessione 1934–35, documenti 439–51A, 'Stato di previsione della spesa del ministero della Marina', 29/1/1935. On the submarine arm see USMM, *La Marina italiana nella seconda guerra mondiale. XIII: I sommergibili in Mediterraneo* (USMM, Rome, 1967), p. 9. The naval ministry did not establish a submarine command until August 1935. Furthermore, the official history of the Mediterranean underwater arm adds that the Italian submarine was slow in submersion and was regarded as a 'static' weapon and not as a 'mobile' and 'manoeuvrable' one, adding that the overall performance was disappointing (p. 17). On the failure to develop an anti-submarine and mine-warfare capability see USMM, *La Marina italiana nella seconda guerra mondiale. XXII: La lotta antisommergibile* (USMM, Rome, 1978), pp. 1–3 and USMM, *La Marina italiana nella seconda guerra mondiale. XVIII: La guerra di mine* (USMM, Rome, 1966), pp. 75–6.

40 USMM, DG, 1-D, 'Documento di guerra L.G.10 – Piano B', naval war plans office, 16/5/1935.

41 USMM, *La Marina italiana nella seconda guerra mondiale. XIV: I mezzi d'assalto* (USMM, Rome, 1964), p. 7.

42 Minniti, '"Il nemico vero"', pp. 580–1; M. Knox, 'The Italian Armed Forces, 1940–3', in A. R. Millett and W. Murray (eds), *Military Effectiveness. Volume III: The Second World War* (Allen & Unwin, Boston, MA, 1988).

43 USMM, DG, 2-A, 'Operazione B', Cavagnari to air staff, 23/5/1935. Cavagnari's memorandum also contained a specific request that the air force contribute to the building of air bases designed to house new units of the naval air arm at the key coastal positions of Tobruk and Massawa. The existing base on Leros in the Dodecanese should, he added, be upgraded to house aircraft of greater operational range. On the same day, 23 May, Cavagnari also requested that the war ministry, responsible for providing the artillery used in defending Italy's naval bases, place its port defences on partial alert. While the navy remained responsible for organising harbour defence as a whole, the army partly provided the means in terms of anti-aircraft weapons for example. In turn, this then implies that the two services ought to have co-ordinated their respective efforts closely. Yet again, the evidence suggests that co-operation remained limited to the respective services simply making the other aware of their latest contingencies. See USMM, DG, 0-L, 'Operazione B', Cavagnari to war ministry, 23/5/1935.

44 USMM, DG, 2-A, Vanutelli to Cavagnari, 6/6/1935. The new air units referred to by Pinna as 'currently in production' were the *Savoia Marchetti (SM)* 81 bomber which proved of little real operational value and was quickly superseded by the *SM* 79. For an accurate analysis of the *Aeronautica*'s likely effectiveness at undertaking bombing operations see Morewood, 'The Chiefs of Staff. the "Men on the Spot" and the Italo-Abyssinian Emergency', p. 93. The idea that Italy lacked an effective bomber arm at the height of the Mediterranean Crisis, and that this compelled the naval high command to consider developing '*mezzi insidiosi e d'assalto*', which might be used in attacks on British warships in harbour, is discussed in USMM, *I mezzi d'assalto*, p. 6. Valle's letter to Cavagnari can be found in USMM, DG, 2-A, 'Operazione B', Valle to Cavagnari, 27/6/1935. Valle maintained that the air force would concentrate maximum efforts on attacking Malta and British naval units operating in the Sicilian Channel and the Red Sea. Gibraltar, he confirmed, could not be attacked by Italian bombers, although air operations might now be launched against Alexandria from the base currently being built at Tobruk. The Suez Canal, although within range of the bomber squadron based on Leros, remained a difficult target for the *Aeronautica* to strike, and the results were unlikely to prove significant.

45 The Italo-French air pact signed on 13 May, covered only the eventuality of a war against Germany. See DDI, 8, I, 196, 'Accordo di collaborazione aerea tra Italia e Francia', 13/5/1935; Young, 'Soldiers and Diplomats', p. 78. On the question of Italian dependence on imported staple raw materials see M. Knox, 'Conquest, Foreign and Domestic, in Fascist Italy and Nazi Germany', *Journal of Modern History*, 56, 1 (1984), pp. 46–7.

46 *DDI*, 8, I, 134, Grandi to Mussolini, 3/5/1935 and for Simon's assertion that London would not conclude any bilateral deal with Rome over Abyssinia see 210, Grandi to Mussolini, 15/5/1935.

47 Cited in Mori, *Mussolini e la conquista dell'Etiopia*, p. 27; *DDI*, 8, I, 247, Mussolini to De Bono, 18/5/1935.

48 Mori, *Mussolini e la conquista dell'Etiopia*, pp. 27–9. Mori argues that the British government continually delayed bringing the Italo-Abyssinian dispute before the Geneva assembly for fear of alienating Italy at a time of a growing German menace in continental Europe. This view is also expressed in R. A. C. Parker, *Chamberlain and Appeasement: British Policy and the Coming of the Second World War* (Macmillan, London, 1993), p. 49; A. L. Goldman, 'Sir Robert Vansittart's Search for Italian Co-operation Against Hitler, 1933–36', *Journal of Contemporary History*, 9, 3 (1974), pp. 114–15; *DDI*, 8, I, 235, 'Questione etiopica', Aloisi to Mussolini, 16/5/1935.

49 *DDI*, 8, I, 253, meeting between Mussolini and Drummond, 21/5/1935.

50 OOBM, XXVII, pp. 78–9. This section of the *Führer*'s speech is cited in Baer, *The Coming of the Italian–Ethiopian War*, pp. 160–1. The Hitler speech came at a time when, after the German introduction of military service, the Stresa conference, etc., the *Führer* evidently felt it 'crucial to ease the situation through nominally conciliatory gestures. Hence, the Hitler "peace speech" of 21 May 1935, and its specific guarantees to Austria, echoing what had been said in diplomatic circles over the previous weeks and aimed, through placating Mussolini, at driving a wedge through the Stresa signatories.' Letter to the author from Professor Ian Kershaw, University of Sheffield, 1/10/1997.

51 *DGFP*, C, III, 266, Hassell to foreign ministry, 23/10/1934; *DGFP*, C, IV, 121, Hassell to foreign ministry, 31/5/1935.

52 *DDI*, 8, I, 419, Renzetti to Ciano, 21/6/1935; 521, fn 2. On Goering's prohibition of aircraft sales to Ethiopia and Mussolini's belief that this heralded a new Italo-

German *rapprochement* see *DGFP*, C, IV, 109, Hassell to foreign ministry, 26/5/1935.

53 ASMAE, Affari Politici: Italia, busta: 27, fascicolo: 2, 'Conversazioni navali anglo-tedesche', Cavagnari to Mussolini, 15/6/1935; *DDI*, 8, I, 376, Mussolini to various Italian embassies, 14/6/1935. On 21 June Fulvio Suvich informed Hassell that 'in itself Italy had only a secondary interest in this Pact, since the spheres of action of the German and Italian fleets lay far apart'. But, he added, 'France was watching the birth of German sea power with anxiety' which meant that Italy could not help but be 'primarily interested ... in the possible repercussions of the German–British Agreement on other powers. In particular, any French decision to strengthen their own fleet as a result of the German–British Agreement ... would be of far-reaching and unwelcome significance to Italy. Therefore Italy had substantially not taken up any attitude towards the German–British Agreement, but had reserved her full position in case of such repercussions.' *DGFP*, C, IV, 162, Hassell to foreign ministry, 21/6/1935. A memorandum by the Italian foreign ministry for Mussolini of 22 June argued that the new agreement signalled Berlin's renunciation of a naval armaments race with Britain, but that, none the less, were Germany to build up to the allowed 35 per cent limit on capital ships, other naval powers would be compelled to begin new programmes themselves. Most affected of all by the Anglo-German alignment were the French. ASMAE, Aff. Pol: Italia, b: 27 f: 2, 'Pro-memoria per Sua Eccellenza il Capo del Governo', unsigned, 22/6/1935.

54 USMM, Cartelle Numerate (CN), busta: 2765, fascicolo: 5, 'Notizie per le nuove costruzioni', Cavagnari to the President of the construction planning division, 12/5/1935; USMM, DG, 8-G, Cavagnari to Mussolini, 19/6/1935. The submarines of the *Sirena* class were laid down as the *Perla* class in August and September 1935. Twelve fast MAS of the *Baglietto*, *Picchiotti* and *CRDA* types were launched between April 1936 and February 1937. Four *Oriani*-class destroyers and four *Orsa* destroyer escorts were launched between October 1935 and April 1936. For details see Fraccaroli, *Italian Warships of World War II*.

55 USMM, DG, 0-N, 'Operazione B', Cavagnari to colonial ministry, 3/7/1935.

56 *DDI*, 8, I, 377, 'La questione etiopica e la Società delle Nazioni', Aloisi to Mussolini, 14/6/1935, 430, 431, 433, meetings between Mussolini and Eden, 24–25/6/1935; 485, Grandi to Mussolini, 5/7/1935. On 9 July Grandi, after having also discussed the burgeoning crisis with Samuel Hoare, who assumed responsibility for the foreign office on 7 June, warned Mussolini that there remained every chance that Britain might well persuade France to support it over the Italo-Abyssinian question. See 511, Grandi to Mussolini, 9/7/1935. Earl of Avon, *The Eden Memoirs. Volume I: Facing the Dictators* (Cassell, London, 1962), pp. 221–30.

57 *DDI*, 8, I, 480, 'Riassunto dell'accordo Gamelin–Badoglio', Suvich to Mussolini 3/7/1935. On 10 July Mussolini then instructed Cerruti, the ambassador-designate to Paris, to stress 'at every available opportunity' the idea that the military agreements concluded were of the maximum importance to Italy, while at the same time making clear the dictator's reasons for his policy against Abyssinia. Just as he had ordered Grandi, so too did Mussolini instruct Cerruti to make no mention of the fact that Italy intended a total military conquest of the Ethiopian empire. *DDI*, 8, I, 521, Mussolini to Cerruti, 10/7/1935. For the view that the Gamelin–Badoglio talks resulted in a 'genuine military alliance' see Young, 'Soldiers and Diplomats', p. 78. For evidence of the store set by Gamelin on the alliance see M. S. Alexander, *The Republic in Danger: General Maurice Gamelin and the Politics of French Defence, 1933–1940* (Cambridge University Press, Cambridge, 1992), pp. 52–3.

58 USMM, DG, 1-D, '"Piano C" – Pro-memoria sulle operazioni navali', memorandum by the office of the naval chief-of-staff, 1/7/1935.

59 USMM, DG, 1-D, 'Pro-memoria sugli eventuali accordi navali del "Piano C"', Vanutelli to Cavagnari, 2/7/1935. Although the deputy chief-of-staff made no direct reference to joint Franco-Italian operations against the British, he argued that any military alliance between two states should examine every possible contingency for war. In terms of the Mediterranean, Rome and Paris should ensure that the alliance offered the means of guaranteeing free passage through the entrances to that sea at Gibraltar, the Dardanelles, Suez, and the Straits of Bab el Mandeb in the southern Red Sea.

60 For evidence of increasing British hostility towards Mussolini's policy in East Africa in late July and early August, see *DDI*, 8, I, 640, Aloisi to Mussolini, 1/8/1935 fn 1, 654, Aloisi to Mussolini, 2/8/1935, 657, Grandi to Mussolini, 3/8/1935 and 684, Suvich to Mussolini, 7/8/1935; Victor Emanuel's letter to Mussolini is cited in Rochat, *Militari e politici*, p. 225, note 27.

61 USMM, DG, 8-G, 'Ufficio di Stato Maggiore generale, processo verbale della riunione del 13 agosto 1935'; Rochat, *Militari e politici*, pp. 226–9. As regards Malta it should be noted that the British Admiralty did not believe Italy could hold the island, even assuming that it successfully captured it in the first place. As Britain's First Sea Lord, Ernle Chatfield, emphasised to William Fisher, commander-in-chief of the Mediterranean Fleet, on 25 August, 'Malta is a minor matter in the long run ... if Italy is mad enough to challenge us, it is at the ends of the Mediterranean [that] she will be defeated and, knowing that her communications with Abyssinia are cut, you yourself will have a freer hand in the Central Mediterranean and Malta, even if it is demolished, will come back again.' Chatfield to Fisher, 25/8/1935, cited in Marder, 'The Royal Navy and the Ethiopian Crisis', p. 1331.

62 Rochat, *Militari e politici*, p. 231 and pp. 227–9; for Badoglio's subsequent reporting of this see Badoglio to Mussolini, 9/8/1935. On the naval staff's development of the 'guerrilla warfare' arm at the time of the Anglo-Italian emergency see USMM, *I mezzi d'assalto*, p. 7.

63 In the light of new evidence Quartararo's view that 'British positions in the Mediterranean, in Egypt and the Middle East were seriously challenged by Italy's military, air and naval forces' is ill founded. Quartararo, 'Imperial Defence in the Mediterranean', p. 220. Minniti, in support of the arguments of De Felice, maintains that the Italian plans in question were defensive in nature and designed to coerce Britain into reaching the political agreement which Mussolini supposedly sought; an agreement that would see Italian influence in the Mediterranean and Africa grow with British and French consent. As the evidence clearly illustrates, this had not been the case. The Italian armed forces had in fact been ordered to prepare for war with Britain should the latter attempt to oppose by force Mussolini's planned war of conquest in East Africa. The attack on Malta, considered by the navy in May/July and briefly mentioned during the high command meeting of August, hardly constituted a defensive strategy, and must therefore be seen as an attempt to cripple the British fleet. See De Felice, *Gli anni del consenso*, pp. 679–91; Minniti, '"Il nemico vero"', pp. 576 and 593.

64 *DDI*, 8, I, 788, Mussolini to De Bono, 21/8/1935 and 815, Mussolini to Cerruti, 25/8/1935; Rochat, *Militari e politici*, p. 230.

65 Precisely when the naval staff became aware of the British decision to reinforce the Mediterranean station remains unclear. Reinforcement of the Red Sea had been under consideration by the Admiralty plans division since 22 July, while the strengthening of the Mediterranean Fleet had been the subject of discussions by

the chiefs-of-staff since 6 August. See Morewood, 'The Chiefs of Staff, the "Men on the Spot" and the Italo-Abyssinian Emergency', p. 87.

On 13 August Capponi, the Italian naval attaché, informed the naval ministry that he remained unaware of likely British fleet movements, at the same time warning that Britain now viewed the strategic situation in the Mediterranean as potentially grave. He added that the traditional friendship with Italy would in no way prevent London from considering this problem seriously. ASMAE, Amb. Londra, b: 891 f: 2, 'Questione italo-etiopica: Atteggiamento inglese nei riguardi A.O. – Dislocazioni di navi', Capponi to naval ministry, 13/8/1935. Three days later Grandi informed the foreign ministry that to the best of his knowledge Britain planned no 'special measures' with regard to the Italo-Abyssinian dispute. ASMAE, Amb. Londra, b:881 f:4, Grandi to foreign ministry, 16/8/1935. The new naval plan can be found in USMM, DG, 0-E, 'Piano B – dislocazione iniziale ed impiego del naviglio di superfice', naval war plans office, 20/8/1935. The orders based on this hypothesis were eventually despatched to the first and second naval squadrons on 13 September, four days before the Home Fleet arrived in the Mediterranean. See Minniti, '"Il nemico vero"', p. 581.

66 USMM, DG, 1-E, 'Riunione Stato Maggiore', 19/9/1935. The next day a naval staff report – 'Esame della situazione' – placed great emphasis on the fact that the naval high command had predicted that British resistance to Mussolini's Ethiopian venture would lead London to intervene militarily in the matter. The Royal Navy, the report continued, had been placed on a genuine war footing and could be expected to blockade the Mediterranean, annihilate the Italian naval and merchant fleets, destroy the Littorio class currently under construction, block the Suez Canal and ultimately prevent any further Italian expansion overseas. The Italian navy had until recently pursued a policy based on war with France and Yugoslavia, a contingency for which Italy's naval inferiority could be countered by the fact that land based air units and land forces would play a decisive role. In any conflict with Britain the navy could offer little by way of resistance. USMM, DG, 8-G, 'Esame della situazione', unsigned report, 20/9/1935.

67 DDI, 8, II, 166, meeting between Mussolini and Drummond, 23/9/1935.

68 Knox, 'Il Fascismo e la politica estera italiana', p. 296.

2

Plans for Expansion

The crisis in the Mediterranean during the spring and summer of 1935 illustrated graphically the disparity between Mussolini's imperialist aspirations and Italy's strategic weakness. Yet the Italian fleet's marked inferiority when faced with the might of the Royal Navy, and London's obvious opposition to Fascist expansionism, by no means tempered Mussolini's thirst for territorial aggrandisement. On the contrary, confrontation with Britain, and, subsequently, France, only served to make him more resolute, in particular because London had given ground in the face of a possible Italo-British war.[1]

Between October 1935 and the Italian declaration of war in June 1940, the dictator's determination to achieve Italian hegemony in the Mediterranean began to take on a new impetus. In the first instance, the rearmament drive begun in 1933 assumed still greater importance. Over the period 1935–39 Italian military expenditure as a whole reached 89.5 per cent of Britain's, and outstripped the French rearmament budget by 22.8 per cent. Despite raw-materials shortages that effectively delayed work on the *Littorio* programme, Italy's naval estimates increased between the fiscal years 1934–35 and 1935–36, largely to accommodate the new construction requested by Cavagnari in June 1935. Further budget increases in the subsequent period from 1936–38 followed in response to building programmes announced by France and Britain, Rome's principal Mediterranean competitors.[2]

But, even if rearmed, Italy alone could never hope to challenge the combined might of the Anglo-French *entente*. What Italy needed was a powerful ally that could support Mussolini's drive towards Mediterranean supremacy and the quest for new raw materials sources through political, economic and military support. Hitler's newly revived German Reich would prove to be this ally.[3]

By the spring of 1935 a clear *détente* had already taken place between Rome and Berlin after the tensions over Austria in 1934. As relations with the Western powers worsened throughout the remainder of 1935 and into

48

1936, Mussolini strove to strengthen this *rapprochement*, which, ever since his rise to power, he had seen as the motor that would drive his imperialist programme. On 6 January 1936 he signalled to Berlin's envoy, Hassell, that should Austria 'become a German satellite, he would have no objection'. Later that spring, he confirmed that Rome would not oppose a German remilitarisation of the Rhineland – the Locarno agreements notwithstanding. The outbreak of the Spanish Civil War in July, and the subsequent intervention of Italy and Germany on the side of Franco's nationalist rebels, further strengthened relations. In November Mussolini made his famous declaration that an 'Axis' had been formed between Rome and Berlin.[4]

To speak of the 'Axis' as a military and political alliance of some import is greatly to overestimate the realities of its mechanics. As many scholars have noted, its value often seemed intrinsically political, even propagandistic; little or no attempt was made to achieve even a marginal level of strategic collaboration until some two years after its inception. Even then, the level and extent of German–Italian co-operation remained limited, as discussed later. Yet, as this chapter will illustrate, there can be little doubt that improved relations between Rome and Berlin had a profound effect on Mussolini's Mediterranean imperialist aims, and the course of naval policy and planning as a whole. In other words, the 'shaping of the Axis' at the political level gradually led Cavagnari and the naval high command to consider the possibility of an Italo-German naval alliance that might operate against Britain and France. Therefore, the qualitative arguments on the future evolution of the navy, as discussed by its plans office over 1935–36, must be examined with this fact in mind. Indeed, so, too, must the financial, material and political impediments that shaped the eventual course of naval policy. Finally, this chapter addresses the problem of Italy's shortage of bases, and the evolution of naval operational planning during the course of, and after, the Italo-Ethiopian war.[5]

Evolution of Naval Policy in the Shadow of the Rome–Berlin Rapprochement, *October 1935–December 1936*

Mussolini's principal concern throughout the first nine months of 1935 had been to ensure that Italy successfully conquered the entire Ethiopian empire, and not merely gained control of specific Abyssinian provinces. Once the Italians had launched the invasion from Eritrea on 3 October this overall objective assumed even greater importance, for the dictator's very prestige rested on the establishment of an Italian empire in East Africa, and a military defeat resonant of Adowa in 1896 simply could not be contemplated.[6]

In order to achieve this goal, the *Duce* needed to be sure that London would not resort to stronger political or even military measures aimed at halting the Italian annexation in its tracks, particularly as Italy had not the means to oppose such measures. Subsequently, he continued ordering Grandi and other key Italian diplomats to inform the British government that the military operations being undertaken by Italy in no way threatened its regional interests.[7]

By 5 October Mussolini had received some measure of assurance from Aloisi that Laval would not permit economic sanctions to develop into military ones, although the French would fully back any implementation of the former. At the same time, Laval warned that the French government, even if disposed to show favour towards Italy, now totally supported London.[8]

But Mussolini remained suspicious of Britain's true intentions. His continued anxiety that London might launch a preventive war, despite its assurances to the contrary, consequently became reflected in the thinking of a decidedly nervous naval staff. The week before the Italian offensive, the naval high command, clearly worried that the Royal Navy might attempt to attack and destroy the first naval squadron, which included the navy's two ageing battleships *Doria* and *Duilio*, concluded that it should be redeployed from Gaeta to Naples. The week after the offensive began, Cavagnari, worried that an attack on the Italian fleet could be imminent, warned Italy's naval divisional commanders that there remained every likelihood that economic sanctions would develop into military ones. Should this be the case, he added, Britain might provoke a war by deliberately staging an 'incident'. All Italian naval units were to ensure that no confrontation of any kind should take place with British naval forces.[9]

Understandably, Cavagnari and the high command were principally concerned with the question of losses. This issue had dominated naval staff policy throughout the course of early 1935, when the admiral had repeatedly warned Mussolini that the navy could not face war against Britain – a war which it had not envisaged to date and which would inevitably reduce severely its operational capability against the *Marina*'s traditional rival, France. But, the arrival of the British Home Fleet in the Mediterranean in mid-September, and the real threat of conflict with Britain, radically changed Cavagnari's thinking, leading to the reorientation of Italian naval policy as a whole. The British were now the enemy, he wrote in a memorandum for Mussolini in late October, and one diametrically opposed to any Italian expansionism:

> Recent events have served to open everyone's eyes, in fact they have opened them wide. Britain has shown itself to be opposed to all our aspirations in principle; a strengthening of Italy's position in the

Mediterranean through colonial expansion, will invariably meet with
the direct opposition of Great Britain because this country regards it as
running counter to its own imperial interests.

Seizing the moment, the chief-of-staff argued that had Italy's new
battleships been available, British 'arrogance' would not have been so
pronounced. This clearly suggested, he continued, that the Italian fleet
should expand still further to meet the inevitable challenges Italy would
face in its future confrontations with Britain.[10]

Cavagnari's earlier opposition to an Italo-British naval confrontation
had disappeared. The navy's thinking now followed the tenor of
Mussolini's foreign policy that had challenged London over Abyssinia,
and placed a future Italo-British conflict firmly on the agenda. In part,
the shift reflected the *Duce*'s fear that London planned to wage war against
Italy over the Abyssinian question. But, the new developments in the naval
staff's central policy now also concurred with Mussolini's avowed belief
that Britain planned to check future Fascist expansionism by securing total
French political, naval and military support. On 26 October, two days
after Cavagnari had penned his memorandum, Mussolini warned ambassador Cerruti, now installed in Paris, that he had seen:

> a document whose contents were extremely serious, for they illustrate
> all too clearly what the real aims of British policy are: war against Italy,
> with the active support of France, and with the full complicity of Geneva.
>
> The document I am sending you is to all intents and purposes the
> offer of a full military alliance against Italy, that goes beyond the
> imposition of sanctions. Clearly the pretext of an attack on the British
> fleet by Italy is merely being used as a cover. What the British really
> have in mind is moving from economic sanctions to military ones in
> order to force Italy to back down in the face of the combined fleets,
> armies and air forces of Britain and France.[11]

Not surprisingly, Italy's naval leadership soon came to regard the
hypothesis of war against Britain and France as the basis for all naval
planning, and by early 1936 the navy's planners were considering future
naval programmes with this very contingency in mind.

As Rome's relations with London and Paris deteriorated over the
remainder of 1935, and in particular following the League's decision to
impose economic sanctions, Mussolini strove further to strengthen Italy's
links with Hitler's Reich. While Paris and London, although seeming to
do very little in reality, spoke publicly of the need for determined action
against what now turned out to be clear Italian aggression on the African
continent, Mussolini agreed that a meeting should take place between
Mario Roatta, head of Italian military intelligence (the *Servizio Informazioni Militari*), and Wilhelm Canaris, his German counterpart.[12]

At the same time, the Fascist government acted to strengthen political and economic ties between Rome and Berlin. In late September, Hans Frank, Germany's minister for justice, informed Mussolini's emissary, Count Vernarecci di Fossombrone, that Italy and Germany should resolve the Austrian question, the only remaining stumbling block to closer relations, and reach a wide-ranging political agreement. During the same meeting, Frank also suggested that the Reich might meet Italian demands for raw materials in the event of League sanctions being imposed. One month later, Bernardo Attolico reported, after a conversation with Hjalmar Schacht, the president of the *Reichsbank*, that Germany indeed appeared eager to improve trading links with Italy, and in particular now offered to supply coal.[13]

By 11 November, Fossombrone, having reported to Mussolini and returned to Germany, informed Rome that Berlin had approved the forming of a special Italo-German committee in order to organise supplies for Italy during the period in which limited sanctions were in operation. A few days later, on 16 November, Mussolini unequivocally announced to Hassell in Rome that 'Stresa was over and done with', and that France had now moved ever closer to Britain. 'Italy and Germany', he concluded, 'were nations little favoured by fortune; when one or the other raised their head, there stood Britain the possessor, ready to deal them a heavy blow.' In December the *Duce* refused to enter negotiations proposed by London aimed at settling the Italo-Abyssinian dispute, on the grounds that Italy could not do so when facing the embargo on oil supplies currently under consideration by the League. His motives were clear: while Paris and London deliberated, he would press on with a total conquest of Abyssinia. By 28 December, Mussolini had further reduced Rome's links with the Locarno powers by denouncing his January agreement with Laval.[14]

Mussolini's moves to strengthen Rome's ties with Berlin did not go wholly unopposed. By the end of 1935, the more Anglophile factions of the Italian establishment, represented largely by career diplomats at the *Palazzo Chigi* and headed by Fulvio Suvich, openly argued in favour of re-establishing Italy's old rapport with London. They also warned of the dangers Italy faced should Germany become installed in Austria. But Mussolini, who had now ensured that Cavagnari, as did all the chiefs-of-staff dependent on the dictator's patronage, demonstrated outward support for his anti-British line, and had also secured the loyalty of Badoglio after placing him in charge of operations in East Africa at the point when those conducted by De Bono had stalled in mid-November, was clearly in no mood for dissent. Early in the new year, as League sanctions began to place increasing strain on the Italian economy, he informed Berlin, via Hassell (and without informing the Italian foreign ministry), that he no longer objected to greater German influence in

Austrian affairs. At the same time Mussolini repeated his mid-November assertion that for him Stresa was dead. A few months later, he dismissed under-secretary Suvich and promoted his youthful and, more important, pro-German son-in-law Galeazzo Ciano to the post of minister for foreign affairs. By that point, Rome and Berlin were already on the path to a much closer political understanding.[15]

Further evidence of strained relations between Italy and the Western powers emerged during early 1936. On 10 January the Italian naval ministry received a report from Capponi in London, which noted that British political circles openly boasted of a naval and military alliance having been formed between Britain and France. Four days later, the naval attaché warned naval staff headquarters that for the British Admiralty the Mediterranean had now become a focus for concern that would not simply end with the conclusion of the present tension. London, he argued, had recently concluded strategic agreements not only with the French, but also with other Mediterranean powers such as Greece and Turkey. Furthermore, Britain had greatly strengthened its position in the Mediterranean recently and British rearmament, now proceeding at breakneck speed, had at least partly been motivated by the crisis in relations between Rome and London.[16]

For Mussolini, this tension with Paris and London proved to be the justification for a further refusal of co-operation. On 9 December 1935 senior representatives of the Italian navy had arrived in London for the conference on naval limitation, called by Britain the previous summer. Almost immediately, Mussolini signalled his intention not to participate. On 3 January, three days before he informed Hassell of a relaxation in Italian policy over Austria, the *Duce* ordered Admiral Raineri Biscia, the head of the Italian delegation, to enter into no discussions that aimed to re-examine the question of battleship parity with France established at Washington in 1921–22. The British, he then informed a gathering of the naval high command in mid-February, should be told that Italy had entered the London conversations in good faith, anticipating a marked improvement in mutual political relations. This had not taken place. Now Italy faced not only economic sanctions but the prospect of a League embargo on oil. He could countenance no agreement signed under such conditions. For the moment, Italy would therefore not be a signatory of the treaty.[17]

Mussolini saw the threat of Italian abstention from the London naval agreement, which, according to Grandi, Britain feared owing to the Japanese withdrawal from the conference in mid-January, as the means of forestalling a possible League ban on petroleum imports. But, even more ominously, he clearly had no intention of sanctioning fresh agreements aimed at limiting naval building, at a time when the navy's planners were already beginning to consider long-term strategic policies based on the idea of a Mediterranean war against France and Britain – a conflict

Mussolini had since at least 1919 regarded as unavoidable if Italy were to conquer a substantial empire of its own.

By December 1935, the navy's planners had produced the first plans for a substantial quantitative increase in Italian naval capability. Subsequently, Cavagnari, like all chiefs-of-staff eager to see his service expand under his stewardship, presented the dictator with proposals for naval expansion that included further capital-ship remodernisation and construction, and which also requested an aircraft carrier. However, Mussolini deferred them momentarily, until Geneva's position on raw materials sanctions became clearer.[18]

Nevertheless, the navy's planners continued to study the building requirements the Italian fleet would likely need to consider in the event of a future naval confrontation with either the British or the French fleets. Very early in 1936, the war plans office prepared a lengthy report based on the hypothesis that such a conflict might well find Italy's fleet facing a British enemy able to operate at both ends of the Mediterranean. The Italian navy could best counter this by building a large escape fleet – a *'flotta d'evasione'* – able to break out of the Mediterranean, win control of its exits, and operate outside that sea alongside friendly naval powers such as Germany.

This vast building programme would include nine or ten capital ships, four aircraft carriers, 36 cruisers, and between 46 and 75 new submarines. The chief obstacle to its completion would invariably be Italy's limited industrial base. The building in question needed to take place alongside work already being undertaken by shipyards. Industry therefore needed to expand accordingly in order to build an additional 445,000 tons of shipping between 1936 and 1942. Otherwise, construction of the 'escape fleet' would take at least 24 years to complete under current conditions. The only realistic alternative to building such an extensive new fleet, the planners argued, would be a more modest building programme based on continuing the naval ministry's current policy of simply replacing old vessels with new ones. This proposed programme – the *'programma minimo'* – comprised two new *Littorio*-class battleships, three heavy cruisers, eight destroyer escorts, 22 destroyers and torpedo-boats, and four submarines, all to be built between the current fiscal year and the one for 1941–42. Under this hypothesis, no aircraft-carrier construction would be necessary, presumably because land-based air units would provide support for the fleet at sea. In any event, the naval staff urged discretion: the new Italian fleet should not increase in size in a manner that might cause international concern.[19]

This, then, appeared to be the stark choice facing Mussolini. An Italian fleet able to dominate the Mediterranean, secure control of its key exits at Gibraltar and Suez, and subsequently to break out of that sea and wage a naval war alongside the German navy against the might of Britain, and quite possibly France, would either require a vast increase in Italian industrial capacity, which remained beyond the nation's means, or otherwise would take at least 24 years to reach completion. Such a programme, even if realisable, also needed to take account of Italy's marked shortage of bases outside the Mediterranean, as well as the likely response of the other main naval powers. In short, the British and French could well increase their building in response, thus necessitating further Italian programmes.

In tone, the memorandum appeared strongly permeated by the thinking of Cavagnari, who had the previous year outlined the gravity of Italy's naval and geopolitical situation *vis-à-vis* Britain, and who now demonstrated the price Mussolini needed to pay in order to achieve his dreams of wresting control of the Mediterranean from Britain. The alternative could only be a naval policy that simply replaced decommissioned ships, and which continued to plan for a fleet operating only within that sea. However, the lengthy plans office report clearly hinted that a future alliance with Germany had become a considered possibility within naval staff thinking – a direct consequence of Mussolini's markedly improved relations with Berlin. Gradually, as the dictator's attempts at strengthening ties with Berlin grew apace over 1936 and 1937, so did this increasingly become a fundamental tenet of the navy's policy – although neither Germany nor Italy made greater moves towards staff conversations until early 1939. Subsequently, by September 1937, the naval staff had begun to focus its construction policy on the concept of Italy and Germany's building a combined fleet half the size of Britain's. The move towards such a policy effectively removed the need for an Italian ocean-going navy. As will be seen later, the *Regia Marina*'s high command expected Germany to engage the British fleet in the Atlantic while the Italian fleet concentrated its efforts exclusively in the Mediterranean and Red Sea.[20]

Justification for the new direction of Italian naval policy was not long in coming. By mid-February 1936, the naval leadership believed that the French naval staff had now begun to plan for a conflict against an Italo-German combination, in which France would fight alongside a Royal Navy that would in theory already have dispatched its Home Fleet to the Far East. In order to be able to undertake a war of this kind, the French marine ministry had reportedly requested an increase in overall fleet capability to equal that of the combined German and Italian navies – precisely as Cavagnari had feared the year before, following the conclusion of the Anglo-German treaty. Under a plan developed by the French naval strategist Vice-Admiral Raoul Castex, operations had apparently been envisaged against Sardinia and Italy's western coastline, as well as against the Italian and German battle fleets. Meanwhile, Castex also recommended that land offensives should be launched in the Balkans and North Africa.[21]

The acquisition by the Italian naval staff of such information, was further compounded by news from London that the British and French navies had recently participated in joint conversations. Shortly before the report on recent trends in French strategic planning arrived in Rome, Capponi reported from London that:

> the recent conversations between the British and French naval delegations could only have been centred on the current situation in the Mediterranean, and in particular in the support France could offer the British in any war against us.

Britain, Capponi concluded, would only reduce its operational strength in the region at the moment when the French were able to increase theirs accordingly. Hostility with Britain, it seemed, was becoming an increasing possibility.[22]

Throughout that spring, Mussolini shifted ever closer to an alignment with Hitler's Reich. For him, the inevitable breach with the Western democracies had finally taken place; Britain had shown itself intrinsically opposed to Italian expansionism. In the *Duce*'s mind, this could mean only one thing: an Italian alliance with Germany. As he stressed to Hassell in late January 1936:

> We cannot openly show France and England our position toward Germany. Not yet! One must move slowly and cautiously. But between Germany and Italy there is a common fate. That is becoming stronger and stronger. That cannot be denied. Germany and Italy are congruent cases. One day we shall meet whether we want to or not. But we want to! Because we must. [Mussolini pounded his fist on the table.][23]

In mid-February, amid news from East Africa that Badoglio's latest offensive had proved successful, Mussolini signalled his assent to Berlin's occupation of the demilitarised Rhineland in response to the recently concluded Franco-Soviet Pact. In a meeting with Hassell on 22 February, the *Duce* yet again repeated his assertion that 'Stresa was finally dead', and left the German ambassador with the clear impression that 'Mussolini would not take part in action by Britain and France against Germany occasioned by an alleged breach by Germany of the Locarno Treaty'. Concluding that Italy would now 'stand aside', Hitler occupied the region on 7 March.[24]

At the end of that month, Rome and Berlin concluded an agreement, based on the Canaris–Roatta conversations of September 1935, for collaboration between the German and Italian secret police. Then, in the first days of April, Mussolini took a still more significant step towards establishing a closer political understanding with Germany. At the time of his Rome meetings with Hans Frank, the *Duce* ordered Bernardo

Attolico to inform Berlin that Italy would not take part in staff talks with Britain and France, and neither would it enter any discussions with the Locarno powers whose scope appeared anti-German. That spring, both governments also authorised a number of German–Italian exchange visits aimed at improving bilateral relations, culminating with that of Edda Ciano, Mussolini's daughter, in June.[25]

Meanwhile, relations with London did not improve. As the Italian war in Africa drew towards its successful conclusion – the Rhineland crisis having done much to reduce the likelihood of a League imposition of oil sanctions on Italy – a report from Grandi in London claimed that Britain not only viewed Fascist Italy with marked hostility, but also regarded the creation of an Italian empire in East Africa as a threat to its imperial interests, as predicted by Cavagnari the year before. By mid-April, the naval ministry was faced with additional reports from Capponi in London, which claimed that official British circles now openly spoke of the menace posed by Mussolini's Italy to Britain's interests in the region, and of the need to revise totally the nation's strategic position in the Mediterranean.[26]

Clearly eager to protect Italy's own strategic and political regional interests, the naval staff urged that immediate attention be given to the question of occupying Albania and protecting the Adriatic from attack by enemy naval and air units based in Greece. By so doing, they stressed, Italy could safeguard its communications with East Africa and the Dodecanese Islands in the event of a future Mediterranean war.[27]

With the end of the Italo-Abyssinian conflict in early May, the imminent threat of hostilities against Britain subsided. The subsequent announcement that London now planned to demobilise its forces in the Mediterranean came as a great relief for Cavagnari and the high command, who since early 1935 had consistently regarded confrontation with Britain with trepidation. Indeed, from the moment that the British announced their decision, Capponi in London persistently sought to secure precise dates for the departure of the units from the Home Fleet still in Mediterranean waters. His anxieties were relieved when the Admiralty informed him that the fleet would leave for Britain on 17 July. In the meantime, Mussolini had already publicly announced that Italy had conquered the entire Ethiopian empire, just as he originally planned.[28]

For the Italian naval staff, the period immediately after the conclusion of Italy's war with Abyssinia became increasingly dominated by British rearmament, and by what they regarded as substantial efforts on the part of London once more to assert British pre-eminence within the confines of the Mediterranean. Throughout June and July 1936, a stream of reports reached *SIM* and its naval counterpart the *Servizio Informazioni Segreti* (*SIS*), many of which originated from the London embassy, which argued that the British government now planned to reinforce Malta and return the Mediterranean Fleet to its base there. The British had also allegedly begun considering the possibility of creating a new naval base on Cyprus. In mid-July the newly installed Galeazzo Ciano warned that, according to information he had recently received, Britain now planned further to consolidate its place in Mediterranean affairs by holding naval talks with Turkey. The naval staff promptly concluded that from its bases in Malta, Turkey, Greece and Egypt, as well as from its potential new position on Cyprus, Britain could easily dominate the Mediterranean and place all Italian naval bases, themselves inadequately defended, under attack. Considerable sums of scarce money, and a minimum period of at least five years were required, before the position with regard to Britain could even marginally improve.[29]

It was precisely this geopolitical reality – British and French domination of Italy's *mare nostrum* – that Mussolini had always detested and appeared so determined to overturn. Therefore, it could hardly be surprising that Paris' and London's attempts at normalising relations with Mussolini over that summer failed as the *Duce*, his resentment mounting, moved Rome steadily closer towards an alliance with Berlin that could challenge the hegemony of the Western powers conclusively. Adding further fuel to the dictator's bitterness over the British stranglehold in the Mediterranean was his personal animosity towards Anthony Eden, now British foreign secretary, whose firm sanctionist line he had particularly despised. Moreover, the election of Léon Blum's leftist Popular Front coalition in France now made friendship with Germany appear more attractive than ever. Only through this friendship could Italy finally break the bars of its Mediterranean prison, which Britain appeared eager to strengthen.[30]

With the war in Africa over and with the problem of sanctions consequently lifted, Mussolini could now consider how best to develop the Italian fleet, his principal military weapon for seeking to win control of the Mediterranean. During the course of a strongly anti-British speech delivered to the Fascist chamber of deputies earlier that year, Cavagnari announced the new Italian naval estimates for the period 1936–37. While trumpeting the great value of the Italian fleet as a 'potent instrument of Mussolinian policy', Cavagnari did not declare exactly what the programme entailed: 'The political moment does not allow of it, and it would not be wise today to formulate precise naval programmes.' His reasons for doing so were clear. Mussolini, uncertain as to how the League embargo on raw materials might affect Italy, preferred still to delay his decision on the new Italian building, requested by the chief-of-staff in December 1935 until the situation became clearer. Raw-materials shortages had already forced a general slowdown in Italian armaments production as a whole; a slowdown that effectively forced the building work on the new *Littorio*-class battleships to be put back by some 12 months. In such a climate, Rome simply could not contemplate new construction programmes for the navy.[31]

Indeed, one of the few projects undertaken by the naval ministry during the early part of 1936, the design and building of six small motor boats (*barchini*) each loaded with 300 kg of explosive and destined for use against enemy vessels, did not entail substantial use of raw materials. Nor did its sister project, the production of man-guided torpedoes. Thus, the naval leadership approved the project in January 1936, at a time when the risk of war with Britain remained acute and when raw materials were particularly scarce. With the end of the Mediterranean crisis that summer any immediate threat of war against Britain disappeared. Accordingly, Cavagnari ordered the suspension of all guerrilla warfare experiments, preferring to devote time and materials to the future evolution of the Italian battle fleet. He only authorised further development of these '*mezzi insidiosi*' afresh in late 1938, when German claims against Czechoslovakia once again threatened to the bring the Italian navy into a European war against Britain and France. Cavagnari's intermittent interest in this form of warfare suggests that the naval staff rather unwisely took such tactics into serious consideration only at times when the risk of conflict seemed real, and subsequently the threat to the main battle fleet greater. In so doing, they effectively overlooked a potentially valuable and certainly highly economical form of warfare that might have been used to great effect in the summer of 1940.[32]

In the early months of summer, Cavagnari returned once more to the question of future naval building. In a memorandum of 25 June, the chief-of-staff argued that the proposed programme he had submitted for Mussolini's consideration in late December constituted the maximum effort the nation could offer in preparing a new battle fleet. Mussolini evidently agreed, although only partly. Rejecting the naval staff's proposal for a massive escape fleet, as outlined in January, the dictator ordered that a much smaller programme be initiated. By July, he had allocated a further 1,108,000,000 lire for a substantial number of small naval units and submarines. However, Cavagnari's request for further capital-ship construction had also been turned down by Mussolini, leaving the plans office to conclude that in the face of substantial increases in the British naval estimates, 'the strength of our fleet relative to that of the British will not be improved to our advantage', on the basis of current Italian building policy. Although the Italian fleet would eventually possess adequate numbers of light surface vessels, submarines and cruisers, it still lacked a sufficient number of capital ships, and remained without aircraft carriers. They urged, therefore, that although war against the British Empire could be regarded as many years away, the government should seriously consider ordering one or possibly two new battleships as well as an aircraft carrier at the beginning of the next fiscal year.[33]

Mussolini's rejection of Cavagnari's demands for greater naval construction in the summer of 1936 raises the question of the naval ministry's position as regards the allocation of funds. After all, given the primacy of its role in any eventual conflict within the Mediterranean, one might suppose that spending on naval building should have been given priority. On the surface, however, the navy's share of the Italian military budget suggests that it fared rather poorly against the other armed forces. The overall figures for the later interwar period (1938–40) show that on average the army enjoyed a 51 per cent share of total expenditure, the air force 28 per cent and the navy a mere 21 per cent (see Table 1).

Table 1
Comparative budgets for the Italian armed forces 1934–40

financial year	army	air force	navy	total budget estimate
1934–35	2,639	810	1,310	4,759
1935–36	7,093	2,241	2,850	12,184
1936–37	9,050	3,628	3,423	16,101
1937–38	5,794	3,923	2,970	12,687
1938–39	6,685	4,296	3,429	14,410
1939–40	14,868	6,944	5,206	27,018

Note: Figures in millions of lire.
Source: F. Minniti, 'Il problema degli armamenti nella preparazione militare italiana dal 1935 al 1943', *Storia Contemporanea*, 9, 1 (1978).

Against these figures must be offset the fact that both the army and the air force, in the words of Brian Sullivan, 'were forced to divert a large share of their resources to the wars in East Africa and Spain in 1935–40', whereas the navy, being less committed in these theatres, could preserve its resources and enter the war in June 1940 better prepared. None the less, it remained clear that, while the naval high command understandably did not win Mussolini's financial backing for their ambitious 'escape fleet' programme, they also failed to secure funds to begin the rather more modest programme of capital-ship construction recommended by Cavagnari in December 1935. Effectively, the huge financial cost of conquering Abyssinia and the national shortage of raw materials prevented any major programme of naval building beginning at a time when existing naval programmes had already suffered serious setbacks. In turn, such facts amply suggest that in purely economic terms Italy, whose economy had experienced a serious trade deficit over 1935, could not possibly sustain Mussolini's grandiose expansionist policies.[34]

The summer months of 1936 saw not only the naval high command's plans for capital ship building temporarily shelved but also, fatally as it eventually transpired, any idea of developing an aircraft carrier rejected. In August 1925 the navy's admirals' committee had opposed the building of such vessels on the grounds that the main theatres of operations foreseen for the fleet – the Tyrrhenian and Adriatic seas and the stretches of sea between Malta and Tunisia and Sardinia and the Balearics – could be covered by land-based air units. This implied, as one observer noted, that the navy held firm to its 'Jutland' mentality and continued to advocate the primacy of the capital ship. Nevertheless, by September 1935, with Italo-British tension at its height, Cavagnari had ordered the naval staff to consider the matter again, and in December asked Mussolini to authorise building to begin.[35]

The consequent emergence of the plans office proposal for an 'escape fleet' the following January contained an important statement on the value of aircraft carriers to the navy. The naval planners stressed that for any fleet operations being staged in theatres over 2,000 nautical miles from the nearest air base, only carrier-borne units could provide air support. Therefore, they recommended that at least three, and possibly even four, 20,000-ton vessels be designed and built as part of the proposed pro- gramme for an ocean-going fleet, should it be accepted. Air operations within the Mediterranean alone could be undertaken by land-based units, and therefore aircraft-carrier construction did not form part of the alternative policy forwarded by the naval staff, the *programma minimo*.[36]

By 15 August, with the immediate prospects of war against the Royal Navy having evaporated, and without any likelihood of the ambitious 'escape fleet' programme being financed by the Fascist administration, Cavagnari torpedoed the entire embryonic project; the navy's construc- tion board still apparently had not fully decided whether aircraft carriers would prove useful in a Mediterranean conflict.[37]

Influence from naval armaments firms with a vested interest in capital- ship building, and who were closely connected with the upper echelons of the navy, may have played a part in his decision. On 3 August Cavagnari had forwarded to Mussolini a letter by Massimo Rocca of Ansaldo Steel, which, along with O. T. O. Terni, were Italy's principal shipbuilders. The note stressed that Italy should make every effort to continue exploiting Britain's temporary global naval weakness, one that London was gradually rectifying, by increasing its own naval building accordingly. Dismissing the value of an aircraft carrier to a country like Italy, which 'enjoys a central position in the Mediterranean', Rocca argued that fleet air support could easily be supplied by land-based units and by a seaplane carrier – which the fleet already possessed in the *Miraglia* – and that the navy should place greater emphasis on increasing battleship capability. Therefore, he urged that the remodernisation and new building programmes be acceler- ated, and suggested that the naval ministry be allowed to commission a further four *Littorio*-class vessels, all to be completed by 1943.[38]

It did indeed transpire that the naval leadership rejected the idea of carrier-borne air support and opted for further battleship building, although not quite on the scale proposed by Rocca. On 15 August Cavagnari ruled out all plans for aircraft-carrier development; across the report of the naval construction board of 8 August he had written in red pencil the word 'No!!!'. By early the following year, it finally became clear that the next major naval building programme would see funds allocated to further remodernisation work on the remaining two older battleships, the *Doria* and the *Duilio,* and to the laying down of two more *Littorio*-class battleships in 1938.[39]

Although, as is discussed later, the navy's planners were to continue pressing for aircraft-carrier construction in the years that followed, the naval ministry commissioned no ships of this type before the outbreak of war in 1940. As noted above, pressure from naval armaments firms may have influenced this decision; but, then, so did Cavagnari's own 'battle-ship' mentality. He remained fixed on the concept of the battleship, a philosophy which he had shared with his conservatively minded predecessors from the early 1920s onwards, and 'doubted aircraft posed a serious threat to modern battleships'. In any case, he failed to learn the lessons of the crisis with Britain the previous year, at which point air cover for the fleet had been practically non-existent. It proved a disastrous error of judgement. As Eberhard Weichold, the German Admiral in Rome during the war, noted in 1951:

> The Italian fleet did not contain a single aircraft carrier, for with France as the prospective enemy, the navy had been built upon the assumption that operations would be confined to the Tyrrhenian Sea. Carriers were regarded as complicated and vulnerable vessels and it had been decided to do without them in the belief that their functions could be covered by shore-based aircraft. During the war, however, the range of shore-based planes proved insufficient for reconnaissance and fleet operations beyond the central Mediterranean, with the result that Italian air reconnaissance of Gibraltar and Alexandria, the main British bases in the Mediterranean, was always inadequate.[40]

In turning down the navy's idea of building a powerful escape fleet, and in delaying work on new battleship programmes during the summer of 1936, Mussolini demonstrated his understanding of the economic and material limitations facing Italian naval policy. This made the attraction of political and military alliances with other, more powerful, revisionist states all the greater, for only by forming part of such an alliance could a materially and financially weak Italy hope to challenge the hegemony of its comparatively much stronger competitors in the Mediterranean, Britain and France.

As Table 2 illustrates, the Italian position with regard to strategic raw materials remained very weak when compared to the chief industrialised nations, despite Mussolini's attempts to improve overall production in the final years before the war. If one adds to these figures the fact that Italy met its annual coal requirement of 12 million tons and its petroleum needs of two million tons largely through costly importation, then the deficiencies of the national industrial economy become all too apparent.[41]

Table 2
Comparative annual output of staple raw materials, 1938/39

	Germany	USA	Britain	France	Italy
Coal	187.9	n/a	236.8	47.6 (1938)	1.0 (1938)
Pig Iron	8.2	n/a	n/a	n/a	1.05
Steel	22.3	28.8	10.7	6.1	2.3

Note: Figures given in millions of tons (n/a – not available).
Sources: G. Schreiber, 'Political and Military Developments in the Mediterranean Area', in W. Deist *et al.* (eds), *Germany and the Second World War, Vol. III* (Clarendon Press, Oxford, 1995); B. R. Sullivan, 'The Italian Armed Forces, 1918–1940', in A. R. Millett and W. Murray (eds), *Military Effectiveness, Vol. II* (Allen & Unwin, Boston, MA, 1988).

Thus, Germany's immediate willingness to recognise the new Italian empire, Britain's starkly contrasting opposition to recognition, and the convergence of Italian and German policy with regard to the Spanish Civil War that erupted in July 1936, provided Mussolini with the framework for moving Italy one step closer towards such an alliance. For Hitler, too, collaboration with Rome, even if a 'second-best' association, offered clear political advantages – it constituted the means of making Britain more agreeable to his planned expansion in central and eastern Europe.[42]

Mussolini's appointment of the pro-German Ciano to the post of foreign minister on 9 June marked a further move towards this closer understanding. Hassell, the German ambassador, concluded that Fulvio Suvich's policy – 'fanatically' aimed at maintaining Austrian independence – had not endeared him to Mussolini, who clearly wished to build on the recent Italo-German *rapprochement* and promptly placed his son-in-law in the post of foreign minister. The change of foreign ministers, the German ambassador informed Berlin, had to be considered as a clear 're-orientation' of Italian policy towards Germany.[43]

With fear of British 'encirclement' in the Mediterranean widespread within the Italian establishment, Mussolini now had the liberty to strengthen his ties to Berlin with less fear of opposition. After he repeatedly affirmed his opinion that Austria should remain an independent state, 'but a *German* Austria which could conduct no policy other than a *German* one', Berlin and Vienna reached a mutual understanding with Rome's outward approval. From that point, mid-July 1936, the formation of the 'Axis' was placed firmly on the agenda.[44]

By January 1937, the effects of this new understanding on the direction of Mussolini's foreign and naval policy were apparent. Mussolini's search for Mediterranean hegemony, the fundamental basis for the Italian alliance with Berlin, led to the possibilities of a German–Japanese–Italian naval coalition being discussed during Goering's meetings with Mussolini. Later that year, the Italian naval staff came to consider the possibilities such an alignment offered as the means of challenging Britain within the Mediterranean and Red Sea.[45]

Prior to Ciano's well-documented visit to Berlin that October, and the subsequent announcement by Mussolini, during a speech in Milan the following month, that an 'Axis' had been formed between Rome and Berlin, the *Duce* illustrated very clearly his determination to challenge Paris and London over Mediterranean affairs. At the beginning of September 1936, Mussolini informed Grandi in London of a disturbing new 'anti-Italian' trend now noticeable in British policy. In particular, he noted that King George V had recently toured the Mediterranean without visiting Italy; that the first lord of the Admiralty, Sir Samuel Hoare, had recently inspected British bases in the Mediterranean and at Malta; that the Italian language had been suppressed on Malta; that Britain had concluded an anti-Italian military agreement with Egypt; and that the British were planning a new naval base in the Adriatic. Such 'provocative' gestures by no means surprised the dictator but, he concluded, Italy should now pursue a similarly negative line of policy in the non-intervention committee meetings, which had been set up in order to prevent outside intervention in Spain. Grandi, 'should not even concede the minimum requests put forward by Great Britain (and France)'.[46]

Mussolini's reasons for instructing the Italian ambassador to adopt this tactic were clearly not governed by a mere desire for spiteful reciprocity. On the contrary, the *Duce* seemed determined to use the excuse that London now threatened to encircle Italy as a means of thwarting Anglo-French attempts at blocking Italo-German aid to the Nationalist armies in Spain. Hence, his instruction to Grandi not to co-operate in the workings of the non-intervention machinery. The reasoning behind Mussolini's attitude was clear: the motivation for Fascist intervention alongside Germany in the Spanish conflagration had been based on his determination to avoid at all costs a Franco-Spanish Popular Front bloc that might undermine Italy's Mediterranean position. It might also be added that successful support for Franco's Nationalists in Spain offered the possibility that the Italian navy might find itself in possession of Balearic bases, from where it might one day threaten Anglo-French communications in that region. Therefore, it suited Mussolini's purposes to wreck any British or French attempts at blocking Italian intervention. In achieving this, Rome's relationship with Berlin would invariably prove invaluable; London and Paris clearly did not wish to risk intervention in Spain becoming a *casus belli* that would envelop the whole of Europe.[47]

Ciano's journey to Berlin in late October certainly led to broad agreement with Hitler over bilateral policy in Spain. Both men agreed that Berlin and Rome should continue to aid Franco and that recognition of his government once established should be immediate. But, more important, the discussions also led to Hitler and the Italian foreign minister offering each other an 'institutional guarantee' for future co-operation, and saw aired their mutual desire to create 'a loose alliance formed for [a] war of expansion'.[48]

The effects of this new alignment were to be immediately felt on Mussolini's strategic policy as a whole. On 31 October, the week after Ciano made his momentous journey to Germany, Mussolini, in a conversation with Giuseppe Bottai, the minister for education, spoke of his belief that Italy's next war – against the British in the Mediterranean – would be brief. Italy, he stressed, could sustain such a war, and he expressed himself very much impressed with the idea voiced by general Alberto Pariani, the under-secretary at the war ministry, of a lightning war, *'una guerra brigantesca'*.[49]

The idea of such a conflict subsequently became the principal theme of two supreme high command meetings chaired by Badoglio that were held at the end of 1936. In the first of these, which took place at the headquarters of the *Stato Maggiore generale* on the morning of 5 November, Badoglio began by outlining that Italy's military effort, which would now focus primarily on the Mediterranean, had become linked to that of Germany after Mussolini's proclamation of the 'Axis' four days earlier. The military agreements concluded with France during 1935 were, he continued, to be considered dead because they were directed against Italy's new German ally.

In addition to confirming Italy's relationship with Berlin to the gathered service chiefs, a relationship which Badoglio increasingly opposed in the months and years ahead, two aspects of the marshal's role within the Italian military apparatus emerge from the record of the meetings. First, his position with regard to the chiefs-of-staff had not altered. Although he retained nominal power as the head of the high command, the first meeting revealed that key discussions, such as those on military spending the previous summer, continued to take place between the individual commanders and Mussolini alone. This meant, for instance, that Badoglio appeared unaware that Mussolini ordered Giuseppe Valle to create an air force comprising 3,000 new aircraft and able to wrest Mediterranean air superiority from the British and French by 1938. As regards the individual chiefs-of-staff, they quickly made use of the meeting to demand further increases in their own budgets in order to accommodate additional spending that would be incurred in Spain, and, in the case of the navy, in strengthening the defences on the island of Pantelleria and improving the naval base at Tobruk.

Second, Badoglio's attitude during this encounter and the subsequent high command meeting of 17 December illustrates his determination to prevent plans being developed for any offensive in the Mediterranean as well as his mistrust of Berlin. On 5 November Badoglio emphasised to the military commanders the need to ensure that metropolitan defences were strong and well organised before they even considered any other contingency. The question of 'guaranteeing Italy's way of life in the Mediterranean', as Mussolini put it, held the possibility for all sorts of 'nasty surprises' if Italy's European defences remained weak – a clear sign that Badoglio disliked the *Duce*'s new shift towards Berlin.

During the second meeting the following month, Badoglio expressed these sentiments even more forcefully. Italy's major overseas possessions were still in the process of development. If Italy were to become involved in any war with countries whose own colonies bordered either Libya or Italian East Africa (Britain and France) within the next few years, these territories would need to be reinforced with forces from the mainland. This would invariably weaken national defences and therefore the chiefs-of-staff should not seriously consider it an option. Pariani and Cavagnari none the less expressed their belief that a sudden offensive aimed at seizing the Suez Canal and linking Libya and Abyssinia through a conquest of the Sudan – both stated objectives of Mussolini – remained possible. If the army and air force launched a lightning war from eastern Libya while the western frontier was stoutly defended, and the navy conducted supporting naval operations from its new base at Tobruk, the limited British forces based in the Sudan would not be able to resist. But Badoglio remained wholeheartedly against any such offensive. Seizing on Valle's statement that the air force remained unsure as to who had overall command of air units based in Ethiopia and the Aegean, he quickly blocked the idea, arguing that before plans of any sort were developed, a clear system of command for all forces operating in all territories needed to be established. With this he terminated the meeting.[50]

Apart from anything else, the evidence provided by these crucial encounters between Badoglio and the respective heads of the armed forces demonstrates that Mussolini had negotiated his understanding with Berlin as a precursor to further Italian armed conquest – or, at least, that Badoglio feared that he had done so. As Pariani noted during the meeting in December, 'our empire is being formed', and his plans for an offensive against Suez and the Sudan offered a means of bringing about the ideas expressed by Mussolini since at least 1919 – that Italy should, and would, dominate the Mediterranean. Of particular interest, however, is the attitude of Cavagnari, who unreservedly backed the idea of any war of conquest undertaken by the army, and who some two years later continued to do so in the belief that Italy would win the conflict with minimal naval involvement. The navy would merely protect supply lines with Libya, and prevent the junction of the Anglo-French fleets based at either end of the Mediterranean through use of light surface craft and submarines. Thus, the admiral's precious battle fleet did not require deployment, and would remain 'in being'. Finally, the meetings confirmed Badoglio's subordinate position. The marshal subsequently failed to achieve control of the unitary Italian military command under discussion at this time and vetoed early in 1937, and demonstrably failed to prevent planning for the operation against Suez and the Sudan from proceeding in the period which followed. His opposition to the German alliance did not appear to be fashionable in Italy's military circles at this time. Mussolini, his prestige high over the victory in Ethiopia, would run the military himself.[51]

Although within the naval high command the formation of an Italo-German connection met with no obvious opposition, there were elements who questioned the need to plan for war against Britain. The subject had been raised by the head of the naval war plans office in a memorandum for Cavagnari of 13 December. Therein he argued for a return to the navy's traditionally anti-French policy on the basis that Britain would most probably remain neutral in any clash involving the 'Axis' powers and a likely alignment composed of France, Russia and Turkey. The British, even if opposed to an Italo-German alignment, were too preoccupied with Japanese expansionism in the Far East to pay close attention to events elsewhere. Indeed, Japanese designs against Australia and northern China compelled not only London to pause before declaring war, but quite possibly Moscow as well. This suggested that Britain – 'conservative by nature' – and Russia might not enter a war France was losing if the threat from Japan proved great enough. Naval plans, therefore, should in future be developed with this eventuality firmly in mind.[52]

In view of British opposition to Mussolini's conquest of Abyssinia the previous year, and in the light of the outwardly hostile views of Hitler, Mussolini and Ciano towards England, their 'mutual enemy', this seems a surprising, even naïve, recommendation, especially as Cavagnari voiced his outward approval for a war of conquest against British African territory just four days later. Certainly, the argument gained no ground. By the spring of 1937, Wladimiro Pini, the navy's deputy chief-of-staff, had replied to the memorandum by arguing that Britain remained far too interested in forestalling Italy's development as a nation to be possibly discounted as an enemy. Moreover, a war solely against the French remained an unlikely eventuality given the nature of the Anglo-French relationship. As such, the navy's principal hypothesis for war – *alfa uno* – had become and would remain focused on the idea of war against Britain in the Mediterranean. All naval planning should in future concentrate solely on this idea. With the emergence of the concept of a global naval alliance composed of the three principal dictator states during 1937, Italian naval planning did just that.[53]

Battleships and Bases

So much for the relationship between, and evolution of, Mussolini's foreign and naval policy during and immediately after the Mediterranean crisis. But how effective was the new Italian fleet likely to be? More important, would it have sufficient numbers of well-placed, and well-defended bases?

Cavagnari believed in the efficacy of the capital ship, a vessel that had been central to Italian conceptions of naval power since before the First World War, and largely remained so in its aftermath. Therefore, the *Littorio*-class ships laid down in 1934 and 1938 represented the centrepiece of the new Italian fleet, and, as discussed later, were to be deployed at the point in any war when a decisive naval operation required the engagement of the most powerful surface units. Having a declared displacement of 35,000 tons, the *Littorios*, in theory, complied with the limitations for this type of ship established at Washington in 1922. In reality, they weighed in at over 42,000 tons, and were capable of a top speed of 31.3 knots. The limitations of the Italian armaments industry meant that the maximum gun size possible was 15 inches, but even so, the weapons were exceptionally powerful, more powerful in fact than many larger-calibre weapons.[54] Indeed, the performance of Italy's heavy naval armaments compared very favourably with that of other major naval powers, including Britain (see Table 3).

Table 3
Comparative battleship gun performance of the main naval powers

gun calibre	nation	penetration @ muzzle
16"/50	USA	32.62"
16"/52	Germany	31.72"
16"/45	USA	29.74"
16"/45	UK	29.03"
15"/50	Italy	32.07"
15"/50	France	30.93"
15"/42	UK	29.28"
15"/47	Germany	29.17"

Note: Figures given in inches.
Source: W. H. Garzke and R. O. Dullin, *Battleships: Axis and Neutral Battleships in World War II* (Naval Institute Press, Annapolis, MD, 1985).

However, these flagships of the Italian navy were highly vulnerable to air attack, partly because their 12 90-mm guns were inefficiently placed in single mounts rather than in pairs (thus increasing the size of the target presented to enemy aircraft), but also because the guns frequently failed, leaving the ship without fully operational batteries. In addition the damage-control equipment was of a poor standard, and in particular the lack of power-driven pumps could lead to progressive flooding.[55]

Although the ships demonstrated an apparent advantage in the exceptional fire power of their main guns, it should be noted that the quality of Italian naval ordnance was often of a lower level than that of other countries, given the limitations of Italian industry and the need for raw-material substitution. Also, when compared with the naval armaments of other navies, in particular the British and German, the Italian guns appear to have had too large a spread. Apart from this, any inferiority in anti-aircraft defences was invariably made worse by the fact that the naval programmes announced by the naval ministry between 1933 and 1937 made no provision for aircraft-carrier construction. In effect, this suggested that should the main battle fleet attempt operations against British-controlled Mediterranean positions, such as Gibraltar or Suez, it would find itself inadequately protected and dependent on air support from land bases. Given the almost total absence of co-operation between the air force and navy staffs during 1935, the prospects for effective air support in future did not look at all promising. Ultimately, the *Littorios* may have been fine ships, but, from Italy's strategic point of view, they could do little to counter British control of the Mediterranean exits. It seems that the naval high command had not learned the lessons of 1935; the rhetoric of the regime bemoaned Italian imprisonment within its own sea, but, throughout the interwar period, naval technology had not been employed realistically to challenge the hegemony of the Royal Navy and its French ally. This only served to reduce the operational range of the main battle squadrons, which were dependent on land-based air support.[56]

Similarly, the battleship-remodernisation programmes initiated by the naval ministry in 1933 raise questions about the overall strategic value the ships consequently represented. Older histories of the Italian navy viewed the rebuilding of the *Cavour* and *Doria* classes as a significant technological achievement; the improved protection, armaments and speed of the vessels being regarded as giving the ships a strategic value directly equivalent to that of the *Littorios*. In practice, however, this was very far from being the case. The navy had undertaken the updating of the four vessels in question, over the period 1933–40, primarily as something of a stop-gap measure, aimed at giving the Italian fleet temporary battleship capability while newer vessels were under construction. Remodernisation remained a cheaper option than designing and building new vessels from scratch. As such, these vessels were to prove 'extremely vulnerable to modern ordnance' and subsequently of very little real value once the European conflict began. The remodernised vessels proved slower than their newer counterparts, which, in turn, created problems in determining the composition of the battle squadrons.[57]

The Italian cruiser squadrons, while numerically impressive on paper, were equally flawed in design. Largely built for speed, the ships only achieved high performance at the expense of armoured protection. Indeed, as one writer has noted of the *Capitani Romani* class, 'It was immediately evident that no protection would be possible in order to maintain both the armament and speed required of the vessels', a defect whose implications in time of war remain obvious. The Fascist regime also made much of Italy's submarine fleet, which by 1939 was the world's largest. Again, the number of such vessels did not reflect their operational value. Most of the underwater arm had been built for daytime operations and was therefore wholly unprepared for the nocturnal demands eventually made upon it. This was further compounded by poor manoeuvrability and communications, and a slow rate of submersion, as well as by the 'static' nature of Italian underwater naval tactics. Even more serious was the fact that Italian submarines were often cursed by internal leakages of poisonous fumes when submerged. On one particular occasion this resulted in the temporary insanity of an entire crew operating in the Red Sea.[58]

These marked deficiencies were partly the product of flaws in the conceptual and design processes – which, for instance, led to the building of fast cruisers that were inadequately protected – as well as a reflection of Italy's low-level economic and industrial base. As already noted, the national economy operated in deficit, and this was to remain a problem for the Fascist government throughout the 1930s. The concomitant shortage of raw materials constituted a major obstacle for Italian armaments industries. Import substitution, the attempted solution, could never be an alternative to the real, but extremely costly, genuine article, and drastic shortages of primary raw materials dogged and ultimately delayed the future progress of Italian naval programmes. Similarly, shortages of fuel were greatly to reduce the fleet's capability to undertake peacetime exercises, and equally placed limitations on its operational possibilities in time of war.

In face of such marked disadvantages, the creation of a fleet as numerically large as that possessed by Italy in 1940 remains something of an achievement, and in turn offered clear advantages. By the late 1930s the navy had offered Mussolini increased political power in the world of international affairs. In short, although the Italian fleet would never realistically be able to win a single-handed war against its British counterpart, Britain's fear of incurring capital-ship losses, thereby reducing its global operational capability, meant that the Admiralty in London would be unwilling to engage with a naval force as numerically large as Italy's, as was the case during 1935–36.

There is evidence that the British overestimated the qualitative strength of the Italian navy at this time, basing their perceptions more on its quantitative expansion than on any improved operational capability. This could have had implications within the political sphere, for the Fascist administration, as has already been shown, was far from slow to note British concern at the growth of Italian military potential in the later interwar period.[59]

Italian naval theorists had noted British predominance in the Mediterranean through its control of key geostrategic positions such as Gibraltar, Malta and Port Said since at least the early 1920s. Yet, it was not until 1934 that the naval leadership devoted serious attention to the navy's position with regard to bases, and began to argue that existing port facilities be strengthened and new ones built. Then, in late March 1935, amid growing British diplomatic opposition to Mussolini's expansionist plans in East Africa, Cavagnari spoke publicly of Italy's clear need to improve the defences of its base facilities in the Mediterranean, which at that point he considered to be well below the level required for a modern navy. After the Abyssinian crisis confirmed the strategic foothold enjoyed by the armed forces of the British Empire within the Mediterranean and its environs, the naval staff addressed the question much more vigorously, and spending on the improvement of harbour facilities rose accordingly.[60]

In June 1936 the war plans office highlighted the vulnerability of Italy's principal metropolitan naval facilities (Augusta, La Spezia, Naples, Cagliari, Trapani, Palermo and Messina) to enemy attack in a report which subsequently recommended that the naval ministry consider building a major new base for its battle fleet at Gaeta, a few miles north of Naples. From there, the Italian naval squadrons could very easily be deployed, should the naval high command require them to undertake operations in the central Mediterranean or either of the two basins. The additional strengthening of naval bases at Leros in the Dodecanese and Tobruk in Libya would, the planners added, offer the Italian navy a means of deploying submarines and light surface vessels in any future war against Britain in the eastern Mediterranean.[61]

A subsequent report by the navy's planners in August 1936 placed further emphasis on the huge operational advantages enjoyed by the Royal Navy and the Royal Air Force, from the point of view of base facilities, during the recent period of tension. In particular, the naval staff pointed out that the British had swiftly reinforced both Gibraltar and Malta – important in controlling the Mediterranean Atlantic entrance and launching operations against the Italian mainland and the Italian fleet respectively – at the onset of the emergency. Alexandria and Haifa in the eastern Mediterranean had meanwhile provided the British fleets with harbour facilities which, like Gibraltar, the Italian armed forces could not have placed under attack. Faced with the possibility of an air offensive against Malta, the British had simply strengthened the island's defences, evacuated their naval forces and moved them to other bases. At the same time, Britain had also been able to turn to the Greek government for additional base facilities, even to the point of constructing a new naval base on Cyprus.

The somewhat gloomy assessment continued by highlighting Britain's ability to increase the garrison of the Suez Canal to 8,500 men by making use of Egyptian troops, as well as its ability to place large numbers of air units at Gibraltar and Malta, along with Suez itself. Finally, the report stressed that at Aden Britain had also undertaken notable operational improvements. Subsequently, if French Mediterranean bases such as those at Bizerte in Tunisia, Oran in Algeria and Toulon in France were added to this formidable array of facilities, then enemy control within that sea could only be regarded as total.[62]

Cavagnari, now pressing Mussolini to consider a substantial increase in Italian naval capability, reacted promptly to the views of the plans office. In mid-August 1936 the naval ministry produced a report for Mussolini commissioned by the chief-of-staff, which argued that the Libyan port of Tobruk, whose vulnerability to enemy attack had been exposed during the tension with Britain during 1935, should become a naval base of some significance. Arguing that the location offered excellent reconnaissance and early-warning facilities, the study also maintained that naval units operating out of Libya could protect metropolitan waters, house units destined for operations against Suez and, in conjunction with Italian bases in the Dodecanese, provide a sound chain of defence that might counter enemy units attempting to pass from the western Mediterranean to the eastern basin. Tobruk should consequently be regarded as a 'frontier outpost' in need of protection against air and land offensives that Britain might mount from Egypt. By November, Mussolini had authorised Cavagnari to initiate the necessary strategic improvements that would transform the harbour into a significant naval port. The following month, the chief-of-staff, in a meeting of the Italian high command, emphasised the great value Tobruk had in supporting any land offensive aimed at taking the Suez Canal and the Sudan.[63]

The navy's efforts to improve its position as regards bases continued in the period up to the outbreak of war in June 1940, as will be discussed later, although they met with varied success. By November 1936, Mussolini's quest to achieve regional air parity with Britain and France led him to allocate funds to the air force to carry out improvements to its bases in Libya, from where Pariani's planned land offensive against Suez would be launched. Although in January 1937 Mussolini approved plans drawn up by Cavagnari aimed at strengthening the defences of the island of Pantelleria – an island crucial to the defence of the central Mediterranean, and hence to the success of the entire plan in that it would be needed in the defence of sea traffic with North Africa – the chief-of-staff later complained that the government had not yet made any extra money available for the project.[64]

In Italian East Africa, meanwhile, the naval ministry made considerable efforts to improve the principal naval facilities in the region at Massawa and Assab in Eritrea and Mogadishu in Somaliland. Even though by 1940 an intensive work programme had seen installed arsenals, stores, anti-aircraft defences and radio stations, only Massawa could be considered adequately defended. Moreover, although the naval staff were frequently to request the building of a new naval base at Chisimaio in Somaliland, in order to launch possible operations against the British in the Indian Ocean, the port was not built before the outbreak of war, as will be discussed more fully.[65]

Cavagnari's efforts to improve the navy's base facilities in readiness for the approaching war with Britain did see an increase in spending for this contingency from 352.8 million lire for the fiscal year 1932–33 (22 per cent of the overall estimate) to 1,147.2 million lire for the period 1939–40 (42 per cent of the estimate). There had also been an additional allocation of 591 million lire in 1938 to develop colonial ports. However, the naval ministry did not approve the major new base at Gaeta requested by the plans office in June 1936, and also turned down a later proposal for a major new base at Milazzo in northern Sicily. Taranto remained the principal base for the battle fleet, and the continued vulnerability of this port in time of war was to be ruthlessly exposed by RAF torpedo bombers in November 1940. Meanwhile, other Italian ports remained equally vulnerable, despite the sums expended on improving them. As the naval staff concluded in November 1939, Italy had spent great sums of money on building a large fleet whose principal naval bases were poorly equipped and highly vulnerable to air attack. In the meantime, port defences in Italian East Africa had only been designed to defend against enemy attack from the sea; no thought had been given to the possibility that they might face a land offensive.[66]

The Evolution of Plan B and Further Developments in Italian Naval Strategy

At the point when Mussolini's policy towards Abyssinia brought the Italian fleet close to conflict with the Royal Navy during the spring and summer of 1935, Cavagnari showed himself to be markedly opposed to any idea of war with Britain. Yet, the navy's net inferiority did not appear to temper Mussolini's willingness to commit the Italian fleet to fight the British once the armed forces launched their attack on Abyssinia in October. Indeed, as London's attitude towards him hardened over that autumn and winter, and particularly after the dictator had shown no evidence of wishing to agree to a negotiated settlement of the Italo-Abyssinian dispute, so did he increasingly consider waging war against the British. The plans prepared by the navy's war plans office during the period of the Italo-Abyssinian War included a possible raid by cruisers on the British bases at Alexandria and Haifa, and a guerrilla operation using block ships aimed at bottling up the Grand Harbour at Malta.[67]

Certainly, London, although aware that Italy's overall strategic position in the Mediterranean remained weak (and especially so as it imported some 76 per cent of all imports by sea via Gibraltar and Suez), believed that Mussolini might order a 'mad dog act' rather than face defeat by League action. In particular, the Admiralty feared the effects of Italian air operations against its fleet in the narrow waters of the Mediterranean, especially as anti-aircraft ammunition remained in short supply, a fact of which Mussolini had been made fully aware, thanks to the effectiveness of Italian military intelligence. Thus, although British regional commanders such as Admiral Sir William Fisher believed that the ships of the Royal Navy could 'blow the Italians out of the water', and the Mediterranean Fleet could easily and quickly win control of the central Mediterranean in order to sever Italy's communications with East Africa, the London government refused to give the order. With the menace of Hitler and Imperial Japan on the horizon, Whitehall would not risk losses that might affect Britain's overall defence capability.[68]

It remains debatable how much damage Italian air and sea operations could have inflicted upon the global capability of the Royal Navy. At the onset of the Italo-Abyssinian War, Cavagnari had ordered the Italian fleet to maintain a strictly defensive footing in the Mediterranean. On 9 October the chief-of-staff warned all Italian naval units, now ready to operate in the positions determined by the naval high command on 20 August, that the Royal Navy might provoke an incident that could lead to an armed conflict, and that each department should, accordingly, exercise extreme caution.[69]

A plans office memorandum issued five days later noted the limitations that affected Italian strategy. Should Britain declare hostilities it would also immediately blockade the Mediterranean. Subsequently, the British would launch operations aimed at capturing Tobruk and the Dodecanese, given that the Royal Navy certainly sought to prevent an Italian attack on the Suez Canal. From a strategic point of view, the planners recommended that the first naval squadron be deployed to Taranto, while the second might be dispersed between Messina and Palermo (Sicily), and Trapani and Cagliari (Sardinia) in the Tyrrhenian Sea. Once established in these positions, both forces should aim to control enemy movements through the Sicilian Channel and launch operations in either basin.

The British, the report then warned, were very likely to establish a naval base at Navarino in Greece, and from there quickly launch offensive operations in the central and eastern Mediterranean. Once they had done so, it concluded, the two Italian naval squadrons would find their possibilities greatly reduced. It remained imperative, however, that neither the positions in the Tyrrhenian nor that at Taranto be abandoned under any circumstances.[70]

Aside from confirming the importance to the Italian navy of controlling the central Mediterranean, a strategic conception that dominated all naval planning in the period that preceded the Second World War, the report also focused on the crucial significance of the eastern Mediterranean basin to the current situation. In particular, the naval high command noted that the British would invariably attempt to counter any Italian threat to the Suez Canal, which had of course already been identified as a principal factor in maintaining communications with East Africa. The report also demonstrated that for the naval leadership the advantage lay with the British, who, as naval strategist Romeo Bernotti had argued two days earlier, would probably keep their overwhelming naval power at the ready, leaving the initiation of any offensive to Italy. In other words, the Royal Navy were unlikely to launch attacks on the Italian mainland, Italian possessions or the Italian fleet unless Italy had first taken the initiative. If it were to do so, however, there was little the Italian fleet could do to oppose it, other than attack the enemy in the Sicilian Channel. Neither, Bernotti had argued, were the British Admiralty likely to commit aircraft carriers or battleships in the initial stages of any conflict, but rather would keep these ready to counter any Italian operation aimed at disrupting the blockade. British naval operations in either basin were therefore likely to be undertaken by light naval forces and submarines.[71]

Certainly, Italy's naval leadership had little intention of initiating hostilities at this moment. As a meeting of the naval staff concluded on 17 October, the only option for an offensive operation lay with the possible attack on Malta that the planners had discussed the previous May. Yet, the naval leadership discounted the likely effectiveness of this action at that point and neither had the possibility of such an offensive been mentioned to Mussolini by Cavagnari. In any case, as the meeting noted, any successful prosecution of the attack remained entirely dependent on the question of guaranteeing air support. Therefore, ultimate responsibility for the planning and execution of any such attack lay with the staff of the *Aeronautica*. Ten days before, a member of the naval staff had informed Cavagnari that the training of air force pilots for operations against enemy ships and bases had not yet even begun.[72]

Yet, Mussolini showed himself resolutely determined to strike at the British should they thwart his East African campaign, notwithstanding the navy's reservations. On 11 September, days before the arrival of the Home Fleet in the Mediterranean, Mussolini secretly ordered a surprise attack on the British Red Sea base at Aden; a possibility which the navy's planners had already considered the previous May, and which, in conjunction with a planned army offensive aimed at taking the Suez Canal, would secure Italian communications through the Red Sea with East Africa. Mussolini this time gave the order not to Cavagnari, who had opposed the idea of any confrontation with the British from the very beginning of the Mediterranean crisis, but to Alessandro Lessona, the minister for colonies, whom he evidently trusted. Strange as his decision may appear on the surface, its logic becomes clearer on closer examination. The military commands in East Africa, including that of the navy, were directly responsible not to the chiefs-of-staff in Rome but to the regional high commissioner, himself answerable primarily to Lessona. Clearly, Mussolini was determined to ensure that the Italian armed forces replied promptly and aggressively should Britain attempt to block Italian operations against Abyssinia.[73]

The naval staff subsequently maintained that the success of any operations planned for the Red Sea also remained contingent on close support from units of the air force. In particular, they emphasised that any attack on Aden could be carried out only from the air, but that air and sea co-operation would be essential in striking other principal targets, such as the island of Perim in the southern Red Sea, and in defending the naval bases at Massawa and Assab.[74]

As early as 1 November, however, the war plans office had already stressed that guaranteeing air support for the planned operations would be problematic. The aircraft deployed to the East African command barely sufficed to provide defensive cover for the naval bases at Assab and Massawa, let alone the launching of an attack against Aden. What would be required was a further commitment of air units to the region that might provide defensive cover as well as offering the possibility of mounting aggressive operations.[75]

On 12 December an evidently anxious Cavagnari duly asked the air and army staffs in Rome whether they were seriously considering the offensives ordered by Mussolini – and, if so, whether air support for the planned naval operations would be forthcoming. Valle replied that Italian air units were available for the proposed attacks on Perim, the anchorage at Khor Novarat, and the island of Camaran. The air offensive against Aden, he added cautiously, might be possible 'eventually'. He intended to hand over responsibility for the operations to the authority *de facto* responsible for them, the high commissioner in Asmara, who would then examine the possibilities in greater detail. Meanwhile, on 23 December, Federico Baistrocchi, under-secretary at the war ministry, also emphasised that planning for East Africa was the responsibility of the high commissioner, but that in any case no detailed plans had been formulated by the army for the attack on Egypt; Cavagnari should not concern himself unduly. That same day Valle confirmed that air force units comprising *Ca.111* and *SM.81* bombers were available to support all planned naval operations in the Red Sea, and would also be able to attack Aden. However, detailed planning for the actions in question had yet to get underway, he added, and would not do so until the Italian high commissioner in East Africa had considered the matter.[76]

Early in 1936 the commander-in-chief of naval forces in East Africa, Admiral Vittorio Tur, warned Cavagnari that the Red Sea situation now mirrored exactly the geostrategic position in the Mediterranean. Britain, in controlling the key points at Suez and Aden, could exercise total control over the entire *Mar Rosso*, thereby effectively severing all Italian communications with East Africa at will. Moreover, any idea of attacking Perim should now be discounted. Britain had considerably strengthened its positions on the island, and an Italian offensive aimed at capturing it could no longer be considered. Similarly, any planned air offensives in the region were not only doomed to failure, but would lead to the total destruction of all Italian colonial air bases.[77]

Not surprisingly, Mussolini's surprise attack against Aden was never launched. The naval high command also dismissed similar sudden operations against Alexandria and Haifa. The naval leadership wisely seemed prepared to commit only light forces to enterprises that might have resulted in a moral success, but little else. Moreover, the naval staff had already established the previous May that attacking any such objectives would not be possible without air cover, and the air staff doubted the effectiveness of any air attack on Alexandria.[78]

In the immediate wake of the Mediterranean crisis, the navy's strategic thinking continued to encompass the idea that Italy should seek to dominate the central region of that sea. In so doing, the metropolitan coastline could be protected, communications with North Africa safeguarded, and the junction at the centre of the sea of enemy fleets operating in either basin prevented. Naval strategists, such as Giuseppe Romagna of the Italian naval academy, argued that the recent Italo-British tension had not been unequivocally resolved, and that future conflict in the Mediterranean remained inevitable. Italy's maritime capability did not make it likely that it would emerge victorious from any fleet encounter with Britain. Therefore, the principal option open to its naval high command lay in strengthening the strategic position in the Sicilian Channel and preventing enemy vessels from obtaining free transit of the Mediterranean, thereby challenging British dominion of that sea. At the same time, the navy should make every effort to halt the movement of British petroleum traffic from Haifa in Palestine. By deploying greater numbers of submarines and aircraft to Sicily and southern Sardinia, by greatly fortifying Pantelleria and the islet of Pelagia, and by establishing a network of hydrophone stations in the region, Italy could dominate this stretch of water and exercise greater control over the entire sea. Britain might then think twice before committing substantial naval forces to the area, leaving Italy to select the moment when any naval encounter might prove most successful.[79]

This view concurred with official naval staff strategic policy. Noting that many of Romagna's recommendations were already under consideration by the war plans office, the navy's planners also argued that an eventual occupation of Albania would further secure Italian dominion in the region. Once Italy had established sound defences on the southern Albanian coastline, it might dissuade the enemy from creating a naval base on Corfu that threatened Italian control of the Adriatic. With the rejection by Mussolini of the 'escape fleet' policy that summer, owing to its vast financial and material costs, any notion of the navy's securing future Italian hegemony of the Mediterranean by winning control of its exits seemed implausible; future naval planning focused rather on winning control of the central regions of the sea. Cavagnari's rejection of aircraft-carrier construction, and even of any idea of converting existing merchant vessels for the task, implied that for the Italian fleet, any war would be a 'Jutland' affair fought close to the navy's main metropolitan bases, with air cover being provided from land-based air units.[80]

The fallacy of this strategy was brutally exposed once Italy found itself at war in 1940. The navy, without adequate air support, suffered a predictable fate. Six of its seven operational battleships were damaged or destroyed as a result of 12 separate attacks, and 10 of these were the result of air actions; as one commentator has recently noted: 'The high speeds of Italian warships offered little protection against strikes by British aircraft.' In the meantime, Italy was to find itself blockaded within the Mediterranean Sea, and at the mercy of enemy fleets, which could 'attack decisively' all lines of communication between the mainland and the colonies.[81]

By the end of 1936, amid the improved relations between Rome and Berlin, the navy's strategic conceptions had become increasingly underpinned by the idea that the army would conduct a land offensive aimed at taking Sudan and the Suez Canal, in which the navy would play only a supporting role. While the navy's planners foresaw possible future offensives against key British positions such as Malta, Alexandria, Aden and Perim, the main thrust of naval strategy concentrated on defending the Sicilian Straits and protecting communications with Libya. Therefore, the combined first and second naval squadrons, composed of the rebuilt *Cavour*-class battleships, heavy cruisers and torpedo-boats would, whether facing a conflict against Britain or France, be deployed to bases in the lower Ionian Sea. From there they might seek a decisive naval confrontation with the enemy in either theatre at the most propitious moment. Meanwhile, two additional groups composed of light cruisers and light surface vessels would be deployed to operate in the western basin and central Mediterranean to act as scouts for the main fleet and to conduct independent actions against the enemy.[82]

Accordingly, further naval staff analysis increasingly centred on improving Italian prospects in such a war. The navy's plans office strongly urged that an occupation of Malta in the early stages of any conflict be considered, as it offered the best means of protecting the Italian fleet and its bases in the Ionian Sea from air attack, although the planners did not give the matter serious attention until late in 1938. Meanwhile, mining of the central Mediterranean as a means of preventing enemy forces from moving from one theatre to another also received increasing attention from 1936 onwards, and so, too, did Italy's need to develop anti-submarine technology.[83]

On a wider level, the naval leadership also addressed the issue of creating a secondary chain of defence in the Mediterranean by reinforcing the Dodecanese Islands of Leros and Rhodes, which, once complete, might, in conjunction with Tobruk, constitute a further means of threatening British communications in that sea. Furthermore, the planners argued, the islands could also be used to protect Italian lines of communication 'in any war of short duration', and could in addition become the starting point for 'surprise operations' in the eastern Mediterranean, given their proximity to both Haifa and Alexandria.[84]

As Jens Petersen has concluded, the Abyssinian crisis marked the moment when Italian foreign policy, driven by Mussolini, finally turned towards the alliance with Berlin, which he had believed since first coming to power would enable him to expel Britain from the Mediterranean, Italy's 'own sea'. After the breach with Britain and France over Ethiopia, the Italian dictator increasingly strengthened his ties with Hitler's Reich. Removing high-level opposition from within the *Palazzo Chigi* by ousting Fulvio Suvich in favour of Galeazzo Ciano, Mussolini declared Austria practically a German satellite, tacitly approved Germany's Rhineland occupation, and promised Hitler that he would enter into no staff conversations with the western European powers. To all intents and purposes, the political protocols that accompanied Ciano's first meeting with Hitler in October 1936 marked the birth of the anti-democratic alliance for war formalised in May 1939. The 'Axis', as Mussolini christened it shortly afterwards, thus became the vehicle for the 'inevitable' clash between the 'decaying' nations of the West and the youthful, energetic totalitarians.[85]

The naval high command and its chief-of-staff, although pessimistic about Italian chances in a war against Britain throughout much of 1935, on the whole agreed with Mussolini that London would oppose all of Fascism's imperial aspirations in principle. Having again expressed caution at the *Duce*'s plans for a surprise attack on Aden, ordered by him in September, the naval staff went on to outline the level of sea power Italy needed to attain in order realistically to mount a naval challenge for control of the Mediterranean and Red Sea exits. The 'escape fleet' concept duly formulated by the navy's planners in January 1936 appeared ambitious to the point of absurdity; Mussolini would not even sanction building two new capital ships, owing to raw-material shortages, let alone a fleet of such enormous dimensions and one so clearly beyond national industrial and economic capability. Therefore, the answer to Italy's maritime problem lay with the German alliance, developed by Mussolini over 1936, and which by 1937 had come to be regarded by Cavagnari and the navy's planners as the means of forcing the enemy to disperse its forces more widely. The answer for Cavagnari lay not with exploiting the potentially highly effective, and certainly cheaper, guerrilla warfare technology at his disposal, nor with creating a genuine aeronaval capability by building aircraft carriers, but rather in the construction of a major battleship-heavy fleet destined for use in a 'Jutland'-style confrontation with the British.

Yet, Cavagnari and the naval high command did not foresee a prominent role for the fleet in the Fascist challenge for Mediterranean hegemony to come. The admiral readily concurred with the Pariani project for a land assault on Egypt and the Sudan, in which the navy simply defended the central Mediterranean and maintained supply lines with the African expeditionary army. Naval policy after Abyssinia, therefore, focused on pressing for new *Littorio*-class ships, improving metropolitan and colonial bases, and concentrating on how best to secure control of the waters in the centre of the sea. This overall strategic concept was to develop during the course of 1937 and 1938, as relations between Rome and Berlin were further strengthened.

NOTES

1 M. Knox, *Mussolini Unleashed: Politics and Strategy in Fascist Italy's Last War, 1939–1941* (Cambridge University Press, Cambridge, 1982), pp. 33–4.
2 Sullivan, 'The Italian Armed Forces', p. 171, also makes the observation that these figures are all the more astonishing if examined alongside the national income figures for the three countries. In 1940 the respective annual incomes stood as follows: Italy: $5.3 billion; France: $12.5 billion; Britain: $21.9 billion. The overall estimate for the naval ministry in 1934–35 totalled 1,304,881,000 lire against 1,609,891,000 for the following fiscal period. The increase of 305,010,000 had been appropriated largely to accommodate new naval construction. See *APCD*, leg. XXIX, sess. 1934–35, doc. 439–51A, 'Stato di previsione della spesa del ministero della Marina', 29/1/1935, and leg. XXIX, sess. 1934–36, doc. 980–1008A, 'Stato di previsione della spesa del ministero della marina', 20/1/1936. In 1935 the French navy, in response to the Italian *Littorio* programme of 1934 and the Anglo-German Naval Agreement of June 1935, obtained government authorisation to build two new 35,000-ton vessels, the funds for which were voted in three tranches in 1938–39. The overall programme (1935–39) included four new capital ships, two aircraft carriers, three cruisers, and some 51 smaller ships. See G. Pedrocini (ed.), *Histoire militaire de la France, Volume 3: De 1871 à 1940* (Presses Universitaires de France. Paris, 1992), pp. 461–2. On the Italian response

to the building of the major naval powers see *APCD*, leg. XXIX, sess. 1934–38, doc. 2115A–227, 'Stato di previsione della spesa: ministero della Marina', 24/2/1938.

3 For Hitler's views see Messerschmidt, 'Foreign Policy and Preparation for War', pp. 547–8; and Waddington, '*Hassgegner*', pp. 24–5.

4 For Mussolini's idea that an alliance with Hitler's Germany would provide the means of winning control of the Mediterranean see G. Weinberg, *The Foreign Policy of Hitler's Germany. Volume II: Starting World War II, 1937–39* (Chicago University Press, Chicago and London, 1980), p. 261. On Austria see *DGFP*, C, IV, 485, Hassell to foreign ministry, 7/1/1936, and 486, Hassell to foreign ministry, 7/1/1936. For the idea that this merely constituted a necessary tactical manoeuvre by Mussolini see De Felice, *Gli anni del consenso*, p. 667. On Mussolini's confirmation that Italy would take no action if Germany broke with Locarno see *DGFP*, C, IV, 574, unsigned memorandum from German embassy in Rome, 20/2/1936, and 579, 'Political Report', Hassell to foreign ministry, 22/2/1936; Weinberg, *Diplomatic Revolution in Europe*, p. 249.

5 Weinberg, *Diplomatic Revolution in Europe*, pp. 331–2; On the continued divergence of views within the 'Axis' see Messerschmidt, 'Foreign Policy and Preparation for War', pp. 632–5. On the Italo-German staff talks of 1939 see L. Ceva, 'Altre notizie sulle conversazioni militari italo-tedesche alla vigilia della seconda guerra mondiale (aprile–giugno 1939)', *Il Risorgimento*, 30, 3 (1978), p. 152; G. Schreiber, 'Political and Military Developments in the Mediterranean Area, 1939–1940', in W. Deist *et al.* (eds), *Germany and the Second World War. Volume III: The Mediterranean, South-East Europe and North Africa, 1939–1941* (Clarendon Press, Oxford, 1995), p. 9. The author is grateful to David Brown of the Naval Historical Branch, London, for kindly letting him see a copy of an unpublished post-war report by Eberhard Weichold (German admiral in Rome, June 1940–March 1943), which makes the point that Hitler authorised limited military conversations to begin only in the spring of 1939. German Historical Series, Vice-Admiral E. Weichold, *Axis Naval Policy and Operations in the Mediterranean, 1939 to May 1943* (Naval Historical Branch, London), p. 1.

6 Mori, *Mussolini e la conquista dell'Etiopia*, pp. 72–6.

7 On this point see *DDI*, 8, II, 218, Mussolini to Grandi, 2/10/1935, 224, Mussolini to Grandi, 2/10/1935, 225 footnote (1), 230 meeting between Suvich and Drummond, 3/10/1935 and 236, Grandi to Mussolini, 4/10/1935.

8 *DDI*, 8, II, 252, Aloisi to Mussolini, 5/10/1935; Mori, *Mussolini e la conquista dell'Etiopia*, p. 79 and pp. 87–8. On Laval's attempts to win British support for France *vis-à-vis* Germany, see Parker, *Chamberlain and Appeasement*, p. 51. For Hassell's view that within Italy the French alliance had not 'worked' at the decisive moment see *DGFP*, C, IV, 323, 'Political Report', Hassell to foreign ministry, 3/10/1935.

9 USMM, DG, 1-E, 'Riunione di Stato Maggiore della Marina', 27/9/1935. Four days after the invasion got under way the naval staff also concluded that movements of the Italian fleet should be kept to a minimum, owing to the severe shortage of fuel. The quantities of fuel in storage, which theoretically were to have kept the navy operational for six months, would in reality suffice for only two and a half months of warfare. See USMM, DG, 1-E, 'Riunione di Stato Maggiore della Marina', 7/10/1935; USMM, DG, 1-A, Cavagnari to all naval departments, 9/10/1935.

10 USMM, CN, b:2684, 'Considerazioni circa la necessità di aumentare la flotta', Cavagnari to Mussolini, 24/10/1935. The expansion of Italian naval power requested by Cavagnari, and eventually presented to Mussolini for consideration

in December 1935, involved a second remodernisation programme aimed at updating the *Duilio* and *Doria*, two more ships of the *Littorio* class and substantial numbers of submarines and light surface vessels. In order to give the new fleet an ocean-going capability, Cavagnari had also ordered the naval staff to develop plans to construct an aircraft carrier. See USMM, CN, b:1727, 'Progetti nuove costruzioni', Cavagnari memorandum, 9/9/1935. The evolution of this policy and the question of air support for the navy are addressed later in this chapter. See Santoni, 'La mancata risposta della Regia Marina alle teorie del Douhet', pp. 260–2; Minniti, '"Il nemico vero"', p. 582. At around the same time as Cavagnari began to consider aircraft-carrier construction and further ship building, the naval ministry also addressed more seriously the need to develop its 'guerrilla warfare' capability. By 10 September, the navy's first submarine group had already begun experimenting with man-guided torpedoes and frogmen armed with mines. From 1 October onwards the experiments in question appear to have proceeded successfully, although by the time they were completed in August 1936, the immediate threat of war with Britain had passed. See USMM, *I mezzi d'assalto*, p. 7.

11 *DDI*, 8, II, 493, Mussolini to Cerruti, 26/10/1935. The unpublished report spoken of by Mussolini can be found in ASMAE, carte Grandi, b: 42, f: 103, unsigned/unheaded appendix to Mussolini's letter. On apparent French support for Britain in the event of Italian aggression see *DDI*, 8, II, 395, Cerruti to Mussolini, 18/10/1935, 428, Suvich to Mussolini, 19/10/1935 and particularly, 547, Grandi to Mussolini, 2/11/1935. For Grandi's view that Britain now aimed to halt Italy's war in East Africa and, by exploiting French fears of an Italo-German agreement over Austria, wreck the Laval–Mussolini agreements and isolate Italy in the Mediterranean see *DDI*, 8, II, 526, Grandi to Mussolini, 31/10/1935.

12 On the question of Anglo-French calls for determined action see Weinberg, *Diplomatic Revolution in Europe*, p. 237. The Roatta–Canaris meeting took place near Verona on 16 and 17 September. Whealey, 'Mussolini's Ideological Diplomacy', pp. 432–3.

13 *DDI*, 8, II, 204, Jacomoni to Mussolini, 29/9/1935 and 537, Attolico to Mussolini, 31/10/1935.

14 *DDI*, 8, II, 608, di Fossombrone to Jacomoni, 11/11/1935. Mussolini ordered Count di Fossombrone to inform Hitler personally that he warmly welcomed any strengthening of bilateral relations, and that he was prepared to settle the Austrian issue, provided the independence of this state could be guaranteed; *DGFP*, C, IV, 414, Hassell to foreign ministry, 16/11/1935. On Mussolini's refusal to negotiate over Abyssinia while under threat of an oil embargo see *DDI*, 8, II, 795, Mussolini to Grandi, 4/12/1935; *DGFP*, C, IV, 457, 'Memorandum by an Official of Department II', Berlin, 12/12/1935. On Mussolini's denunciation of the Italo-French accords see Weinberg, *Diplomatic Revolution in Europe*, p. 238.

15 F. Suvich, *Memorie*, 1932–1936, ed. G. Bianchi (Rizzoli, Milan, 1984), pp. 280–3. On 11 November De Bono refused to undertake the major advance from Makale recommended by Badolglio six days before, and obviously desired by Mussolini, who wished to see the war in East Africa concluded as speedily as possible, given the international tension it had created. Mussolini promptly dismissed De Bono and replaced him with Badoglio. On this point see Badoglio's memorandum to Mussolini cited in Rochat, *Militari e politici*, Badoglio to Mussolini, 5/11/1935, and on De Bono's replacement pp. 235–6. On the effect of sanctions on the Italian economy see Public Record Office (PRO), London, FO 371/20401, 'Italy: Extracts from the Financial and Economic Sections of the Annual Report for 1935', 26/2/1936; and *British Documents on Foreign Affairs. Reports and Papers from the*

Foreign Office and Confidential Print. Part II, Series F: Europe 1919–1939 (BDFA) (vols 11–15), *Volume 12, Southern Europe: Italy, Balkan States and Danubian States, 1935,* ed. D. C. Watt *et al.* (University Publications of America, Washington, DC, 1992), no. 3, Drummond to Eden, 31/1/1936.On the pro-German views of Ciano and on his efforts to forge close links with Berlin see Mori, *Mussolini e la conquista dell'Etiopia*, p. 247; G. B. Guerri, *Galeazzo Ciano: una vita, 1903–1944* (Bompiani, Milan, 1979), pp. 280–1.

16 ASMAE, Amb. Lond, b: 937, f: 2, 'Intesa politico-militare franco-britannica', Capponi to naval ministry, 10/1/1936. On 26 December Grandi had informed Mussolini of the conclusion of naval and military agreements between Paris and London, based on the contingency that the French fleet would support the British if attacked by Italy, in return for Britain's support of France on the Rhine. See *DDI*, 8, II, 918, Grandi to Mussolini, 26/12/1935. On the Anglo-French strategic agreements see also *DDI*, 8, III, 4, Grandi to Mussolini, 2/1/1936. That London's naval, air and military conversations with France 'only confirmed the hopelessness of expecting active military support from the French', is discussed by Marder, 'The Royal Navy and the Ethiopian Crisis, pp. 1348–51. See also R. A. C. Parker, 'Great Britain, France and the Ethiopian Crisis, 1935–1936', *English Historical Review*, 89, 351 (1974), pp. 312 and 327. For French denials that any Anglo-French military agreement existed see *DDI*, 8, II, 926, Cerruti to Mussolini, 28/12/1935; ASMAE, carte Grandi, b: 44, f: 108, sf: 2, ins: 2, 'Intesa navale franco-britannica', foreign ministry to Grandi, 11/11/1935. On the extent of Anglo-French naval co-operation by early 1936 see PRO, ADM 116/3398, 'Meeting Between 1st Sea Lord and French Admiral Robert', 15/1/1936. On British rearmament ASMAE, Amb. Lond, b: 937, f: 2, 'Atteggiamento inglese questione A.O. – apprestamenti bellici e navali', Capponi to naval staff, 14/1/1936; it was not until 25 February 1936 that the British cabinet finally approved a programme of national rearmament.

17 Later, on 3 March, Dino Grandi informed both André Corbin, the French ambassador to London and Robert Craigie, an assistant under-secretary at the foreign office, that while economic sanctions existed Italy would continue to abstain from any new naval agreement. Italy, he stressed, simply wanted freedom of action in determining its own naval programmes. *DDI*, 8, III, 352, Grandi to Mussolini, 3/3/1936. An account of Mussolini's meeting with the naval high command can be found in Bernardi, *Il disarmo navale*, pp. 621–2, 648–9; ASMAE, Aff. Pol. Italia, b: 34, f: 1, memorandum by Cavagnari, undated. During the course of this meeting, Mussolini warned that he fully intended to go to war should the League of Nations go ahead with plans to introduce a further measure aimed at blocking Italian supplies of oil. The dictator ordered Raineri Biscia to return to London and block any implementation of the oil embargo. On this point see also *DDI*, 8, III, 274, Mussolini to Grandi, 22/2/1936. On League preparations to impose an oil sanction see Rostow, *Anglo-French Relations*, pp. 229 and 232; Parker, *Chamberlain and Appeasement*, pp. 55–6.

18 Knox, *Mussolini Unleashed*, p. 20.

19 The plans office memorandum can be found in Archivio Centrale dello Stato (ACS), Rome, Ministero della Marina: Gabinetto, busta:195, 'Studio sul programma navale', naval war plans office, 13/1/1936; see also F. Minniti, 'Il problema degli armamenti nella preparazione militare italiana dal 1935 al 1943', *Storia Contemporanea*, 9, 1 (1978), pp. 42–4.

20 Gabriele, *Operazione C3: Malta*, pp. 13–14. On the navy's gradual orientation towards a construction policy linked directly to that of Germany by September 1937 see Minniti, 'Il problema degli armamenti nella preparazione militare

italiana', p. 44.

21 USMM, DG, 10, 'Note su idee strategiche espresse in Francia', unsigned memorandum, appendix I, 'Suite du rapport n. 119', 22/2/1936.

22 ASMAE, Amb. Lond. b: 937, f: 2, 'Atteggiamento inglese questione A.O.', Capponi to naval ministry, 18/2/1936. Capponi had garnered the information from a conversation with Vice-Admiral Robert, the head of the French naval delegation at the London Conference.

23 Cited in Whealey, 'Mussolini's Ideological Diplomacy', p. 435.

24 On 11 February Hitler decided to reoccupy the demilitarised Rhineland on the Franco-German frontier in direct contravention of Versailles, if he could secure at least Mussolini's acquiescence. On 17 February Hassell sounded out Suvich, who stressed that the likely Italian response to a denunciation of Locarno remained undecided. *DDI*, 8, III, 241, meeting between Suvich and Hassell, Rome, 17/2/1936. Three days later the foreign ministry in Berlin learned that during a conversation with an unnamed confidant, Hassell had been warned that Suvich should on no account be trusted and that in fact Mussolini had already 'precluded any diplomatic or political opposition by Italy if Germany were to denounce the Locarno Pact'. *DGFP*, C, IV, 574, unsigned memorandum, Rome Embassy, 20/2/1936. On 22 February Mussolini informed Hassell that he would not oppose a German occupation of the Rhineland. *DGFP*, C, IV, 579, 'Political Report', Hassell to foreign ministry, 22/2/1936 and *DDI*, 8, III, 275, meeting between Mussolini and Hassell, 22/2/1936. The original Italian record of this meeting quotes Mussolini as having said that he would not object to a German response to the Franco-Soviet treaty, provided that it remained a 'legal' one. See ASMAE, Archivio di Gabinetto, bobina 7, meeting between Mussolini, Suvich and Hassell, 22/2/1936. Weinberg argues that Mussolini in his conversation with Hassell of 22 February, 'still thought it likely that oil sanctions would be instituted – in which case he would leave the League and make Locarno "disappear of its own accord". If the Germans, however, were to act before that time, Italy would not move against them.' Weinberg, *Diplomatic Revolution in Europe*, p. 249.

25 On the Himmler–Bocchini agreement see Robertson, *Mussolini as Empire Builder*, p. 188. For Mussolini's instructions to Attolico see *DDI*, 8 III, 564, Mussolini to Attolico, 2/4/1936; DGFP, C, V, 252, enclosure to memorandum by Neurath, 3/4/1936. On Frank's visit to Rome in early April and on the additional assurances made during this occasion see 255, Hassell to foreign ministry, 4/4/1936.

26 *DDI*, 8, III, 582, Grandi to Mussolini, 4/4/1936; ASMAE, Amb. Lond, b: 937, f: 2, 'Atteggiamento inglese questione A.O.', Capponi to naval ministry, 8/4/1936.

27 USMM, DG, 4-B, 'Questione albanese in caso di conflitto', naval war plans office, 20/4/1936. On Mussolini's early policy towards Albania see E. Di Nolfo, *Mussolini e la politica estera italiana, 1919–1933* (Ledam, Padova, 1960), pp. 173–93; A. Cassels, *Mussolini's Early Diplomacy* (Princeton University Press, Princeton, NJ, 1970), pp. 315–30; H. Stuart Hughes, 'The Early Diplomacy of Italian Fascism: 1922–1932', in G. Craig and F. Gilbert (eds), *The Diplomats, 1919–1939* (Princeton University Press, Princeton, NJ, 1953), p. 223; L. Ceva, '1927: una riunione fra Mussolini e I vertici militari', *Il Politico*, 50, 2 (1985). On the navy's pre-Fascist ambitions in Albania see P. Pastorelli (ed.), *Sidney Sonnino: Carteggio 1914–1916* (Laterza, Bari, 1974), Thaon de Revel to Sonnino, 14/4/1915.

28 On the announcement that Britain would now return the Home Fleet to British waters see ASMAE, Amb. Lond, b: 930, f: 2, foreign ministry to navy, air and colonial ministries, 13/6/1936. On Capponi's endeavours to secure a firm date for the definite withdrawal of British naval forces see ASMAE, Amb. Lond, b: 937,

f: 2, 'Smobilitazione delle forze navali in Mediterraneo', Capponi to naval ministry, 14/7/1935. For Mussolini's announcement on Abyssinia see *OOBM*, 27, pp. 265–6.

29 In the files of the foreign ministry archive in Rome there are a substantial number of reports from Grandi and Vitetti at the London embassy, conveying intelligence on Britain's supposed plans for the future defence of the Mediterranean. See, for example, ASMAE, Amb. Lond, b: 925, f: 1, 'La Gran Bretagna e il Mediterraneo – situazione di Malta', Grandi to foreign ministry, 19/6/1936 and b: 910, f: 2, 'L'Inghilterra e il Mediterraneo – progetto di nuova base a Cipro', Grandi to foreign ministry, 19/6/1936. Ciano's report on Turkey can be found in ASMAE, Amb. Londra, b: 910, f: 2, Ciano to Vitetti, 14/7/1936; ACS, Min. Mar. Gab, b:195, memorandum by Cavagnari, 25/6/1936.

30 On Mussolini's view of Eden's supposed hostility towards Italy see *DDI*, 8, III, 598, Mussolini to Grandi, 6/4/1936 and 652, Mussolini to Grandi, 13/4/1936. For Mussolini's anxiety as regards the emergence of a pro-Soviet administration in Paris see *DGFP*, C, V, 344, Hassell to foreign ministry, 23/5/1936.

31 The full text of Cavagnari's speech to the Italian chamber of deputies can be found in PRO, FO 371/20419, 'Admiral Cavagnari's Speech Before the Chamber of Deputies', 27/3/1936.

32 USMM, *I mezzi d'assalto*, pp. 18–19 and on the lack of interest in guerrilla warfare tactics until September 1938, p. 21.

33 ACS, Min. Mar. Gab. b: 195, memorandum by Cavagnari, 25/6/1936, and unsigned memorandum, 7/1936. The new programme approved by Mussolini permitted construction of 12 *Oriani* class destroyers, 16 *Spica* torpedo boats, 12 *Glauco* (ocean-going) and eight *Perla* (medium-sized) type submarines and 25 *MAS*, all to be complete by July 1938.

34 Sullivan, 'The Italian Armed Forces', pp. 171–2; The budget figures are cited in Minniti, 'Il problema degli armamenti nella preparazione militare italiana', p. 52. For the fiscal year 1935–36 the annual Italian budget deficit, inclusive of spending on the war in East Africa, was estimated by the British foreign office as in excess of 6,500 million lire. See PRO, FO 371/20401, 'Italy: Extracts from the Financial and Economic Sections of the Annual Report for 1935'. See also FO 371/21166, 'Italy. Annual Report, Economic (A) 1936', 30/5/1937; Sullivan, 'The Italian Armed Forces', p. 182; Catalano, *L'economia italiana di guerra*, pp. 25–6.

35 Most major studies of the Italian navy and its role in the Second World War place great emphasis on the lack of adequate air cover for the fleet. See, for example, R. Bernotti, *La guerra sui mari nel conflitto mondiale, 1939–41* (Società Editrice Tirrena, Livorno, 1948), p. 40 and, on the necessity for effective aeronaval co-operation, p. 25; M. Bragadin, *Che ha fatto la Marina, 1940–54?* (Garzanti, Rome, 1950), pp. 13–15; G. Bocca, *Storia d'Italia nella guerra Fascista, 1940–43* (Laterza, Bari, 1969), pp. 128–9; USMM, *L'organizzazone della Marina durante il conflitto, tomo I*, pp. 52–3 and 322–6. On Cavagnari's 'Jutland' mentality see Santoni, 'La mancata risposta della Regia Marina alle teorie del Douhet', pp. 258–60.

36 ACS, Min. Mar. Gab, b: 195, 'Studio sul programma navale'. The plans office report requested 22,000-ton aircraft carriers. For the view that the navy had substantially smaller 14,000-ton vessels in mind see Santoni, 'La mancata risposta della Regia Marina alle teorie del Douhet', p. 260.

37 A memorandum by the naval ministry of 15 August 1936 conveying Cavagnari's categorical rejection of the projected aircraft-carrier construction is cited in Santoni, 'La mancata risposta della Regia Marina alle teorie del Douhet', p. 262.

38 USMM, CN, b:2675, f:9, 'Programmi navali: bilanci', Rocca to Cavagnari, 3/8/1936. On the monopolistic relationship between the main naval-arms companies and the *Marina* after 1925 see L. Ceva and A. Curami, *Industria bellica*

anni trenta (Franco Angeli, Milan, 1992), especially pp. 71–83. On corrupt practices among the arms manufacturers see Bocca, *Storia dell'Italia nella guerra Fascista, 1940–43*, p. 131.

39 On the decision to remodernise the *Doria* and the *Duilio* and build two more *Littorio*-type vessels of 35,000 tons see USMM, CN, b: 2729, f: 4, Cavagnari to Marinarmi/Maricost, 22/2/1937.

40 For the view that Cavagnari remained fixated on the primacy of the battleship see Knox, *Mussolini Unleashed*, p. 21. That his opinion was shared by other members of the naval staff see Santoni, 'La mancata risposta della Regia Marina alle teorie del Douhet', pp. 262–4; Weichold, *Axis Naval Policy and Operations in the Mediterranean*, p. 3.

41 Knox, 'Il fascismo e la politica estera italiana', p. 326; Weinberg, *Diplomatic Revolution in Europe*, pp. 331–2. On the improvement in Italo-Japanese relations, and Mussolini's shift away from supporting the Chinese Nationalists over 1936 and early 1937 see V. Ferretti, 'La politica estera italiana e il Giappone imperiale (gennaio 1934–giugno 1937)', *Storia Contemporanea*, 10, 4/5 (1979), pp. 907–23. The overall level of Italian material weakness and consequently the value to Italy of an alliance with Berlin is discussed in Schreiber, 'Political and Military Developments in the Mediterranean Area', pp. 25–30.

42 Weinberg, *Diplomatic Revolution in Europe*, pp. 332–3. For Hitler's views see Messerschmidt, 'Foreign Policy and Preparation for War', pp. 632–3; Waddington, *Hassgegner*, p. 30.

43 On Ciano's views of a closer understanding between Rome and Berlin see *DGFP*, C, IV, 486, Hassell to foreign ministry, 7/1/1936, and C, V, 381, Hassell to foreign ministry, 18/6/1936. See also Guerri, *Galeazzo Ciano*, pp. 290–1 and the memoirs of the former *chargé d'affaires* at the Berlin Embassy, Massimo Magistrati, which argue that Ciano's attraction to the 'Axis' proved fleeting. M. Magistrati, *L'Italia a Berlino, 1937–1939* (Arnoldo Mondadori, Verona, 1956), p. 17.

44 For Italian attitudes towards Britain see Schreiber, 'Political and Military Developments in the Mediterranean Area', p. 350. A good example of the evidence fuelling Italian fears that Britain now planned to exact revenge on Rome for having humiliated London over the Ethiopian question is to be found in the London embassy papers at the foreign ministry archive in Rome. See ASMAE, Amb. Lond. b: 910, f: 2, 'Politica mediterranea dell'Inghilterra. Colloquio con alto ufficiale britannico', unsigned report for Ciano, 30/7/1936. On Mussolini and Germany see, *DGFP*, C, V, 403, 'Political Report', Hassell to foreign ministry, 25/6/1936 and 457, 'Political Report', Hassell to foreign ministry, 17/7/1936; Schreiber, 'Political and Military Developments in the Mediterranean Area', p. 348; Hildebrand, *The Foreign Policy of the Third Reich*, p. 60. For the view that Berlin remained cautious regarding any strengthening of ties until August, at which point the Canaris–Roatta conversations on mutual assistance to Spain paved the way for high-level discussions, can be found in Weinberg, *Diplomatic Revolution in Europe*, p. 292 and pp. 333–4. The Italian record of the Canaris–Roatta and Canaris–Ciano meetings of 28 August can be found in *DDI*, 8, IV, 685, SIM to foreign ministry, 5/8/1936 and 819, 'Colloqui italo-tedeschi per un'azione comune in Spagna', 28/8/1936.

45 G. Ciano, Ciano's Diplomatic Papers, ed. M. Muggeridge (Odhams Press, London, 1948), 'Conversation Between the Duce and President Goering', 23/1/1937, pp. 80–91.

46 On the Ciano–Hitler meetings, the declaration of the 'Axis' on 1 November and its consequences see Weinberg, *Diplomatic Revolution in Europe*, pp. 335–6; Petersen, *Hitler e Mussolini*, pp. 431–4. The conclusion that Mussolini at this point

had not decided on alliance with Berlin, but on the contrary continued to pursue the 'policy of the decisive weight' – the *politica del peso determinante* – conceived of by Dino Grandi in 1930 as a continuum of liberal Italy's foreign policy, forms the basis of Rosaria Quartararo's study. See R. Quartararo, *Roma tra Londra e Berlino: la politica estera fascista dal 1930 al 1940* (Bonacci, Rome, 1980), pp. 271–2. On Mussolini and Britain see ASMAE, carte Grandi, b: 42, f: 103, sf: 2, Mussolini to Grandi, 5/9/1936; the view that the events mentioned in Mussolini's letter had greatly angered the Fascist government had been noted by Johann von Plessen, the *chargé d'affaires* at the Rome Embassy. See *DGFP*, C, V, 545, 'Anglo-Italian Relations', Plessen to foreign ministry, 17/9/1936.

47 On Grandi's subsequent efforts to delay the procedure whereby alleged breaches of the non-intervention agreement proposed on 1 August by the Blum administration were discussed, see Avon, *Facing the Dictators*, pp. 409–11. On the idea that intervention in the Spanish Civil War offered Mussolini the opportunity to secure gains in the Balearics see F. Bargoni, *L'impegno navale italiano durante la guerra civile spagnola, 1936–1939* (USMM, Rome, 1992), p. 26. Italian and German determination to supply Franco with arms despite the embargo imposed by Paris and London is expressed in the opening statement of the Roatta–Canaris meeting of late August 1936. See *DDI*, 8, IV, 819, 'Colloqui italo-tedeschi per un'azione comune in Spagna', 28/8/1936. For the view that Britain and France were not prepared to risk a wider war over Spain see G. Stone, 'The European Great Powers and the Spanish Civil War, 1936–1939', in R. Boyce and E. M. Robertson (eds), *Paths to War*, p. 217; P. Preston, 'Mussolini's Spanish Adventure: From Limited Risk to War', in P. Preston and A. L. MacKenzie (eds), *The Republic Besieged: Civil War in Spain, 1936–1939* (Edinburgh University Press, Edinburgh, 1996), pp. 37–8.

48 Petersen, *Hitler e Mussolini*, p. 433; Schreiber, 'Political and Military Developments in the Mediterranean Area', p. 351. For the idea that the overtly anti-Bolshevist nature of the 'offensive alliance' proposed by Hitler should merely be regarded as a camouflage for Fascist imperialism in the Mediterranean and Nazi expansionism in the Baltic and eastern Europe, see Messerschmidt, 'Foreign Policy and Preparation for War', p. 633. On the conversations see Ciano, *Diplomatic Papers*, 'Conversation with the Fuehrer', 24/10/1936, pp. 56–61; ASMAE, carte Grandi, b: 42, f: 103, sf: 2, 'Resoconto del primo colloquio Ciano-von Neurath', 21/10/1936 and 'Colloquio del ministro Ciano col Fuhrer', 24/10/1936. On Ciano's enthusiasm for the idea that anti-Bolshevism 'provided an excellent means of casting a cloak' over German rearmament see *DGFP*, C, VI, 14, Hassell to foreign ministry, 6/11/1936.

49 G. Bottai, *Diario 1935–1944*, ed. G. B. Guerri (Rizzoli, Milan, 1994), 31/10/1936.

50 USMM, DG, 0-M, 'Verbale della seduta', supreme high command meetings of 5/11/1936 and 17/12/1936. On Badoglio's position with regard to Mussolini and the Italian armed forces at this point see Knox, *Mussolini Unleashed*, p. 17, and on Pariani's plan and Badoglio's efforts to 'assert control' over it pp. 18–19. On the origins of Pariani's proposed strategy, first developed during the time of the Mediterranean crisis see Minniti, '"Il nemico vero"', p. 584.

51 On the navy's overall strategic thought see Sullivan, 'The Italian Armed Forces', p. 193. At this point Italo-German naval collaboration in Spain appeared already established. On 17 November 1936 a meeting in Rome between members of both navies discussed the co-ordination of submarine operations close to the Spanish coast. The subsequent agreement did not, however, come into full operation. See Bargoni, *L'impegno navale italiano durante la guerra civile spagnola*, pp. 140–1. The view that Erich Raeder, the German navy's commander-in-chief, wished to

create a joint Italo-German naval high command that would face all European developments and not simply those arising out of the Spanish war is discussed in G. Schreiber, *Revisionismus und Weltmachtstreben: Marineführurung und deutsch–italienische Beziehungen, 1919–1944* (Deutsch Verlags-Anstalt, Stuttgart, 1978), p. 101.

52 USMM, DG, 1-A, 'Ipotesi di guerra', naval war plans office to Cavagnari, 13/12/1936.

53 USMM, DG, 1-A, Pini to naval war plans office, 24/3/1937.

54 M. Gabriele and G. Friz, *La politica navale italiana dal 1885 al 1915* (USMM, Rome, 1982), pp. 143–4. On the continuing belief in the primacy of the capital ship after 1918, and in particular on the relationship between naval supporters of this type of vessel and the Fascist regime in the 1920s, see Polastro, 'La Marina Militare italiana', pp. 153–63.

55 Garzke and Dullin, *Axis and Neutral Battleships*, pp. 426–7.

56 The author is grateful to Admiral Gino Birindelli and Rear-Admiral Luigi Donini, both officers in the Italian navy during the 1930s, for pointing out these facts during various interviews in Rome over 1994–95. On these points see also USMM, *L'organizzazione della Marina, tomo I*, pp. 97–8 and pp. 99–106 and more recently Schreiber, 'Political and Military Developments on the Mediterranean Area', p. 89.

57 USMM, *L'organizzazione della Marina, tomo I*, pp. 70–1; Garzke and Dullin, *Axis and Neutral Battleships*, p. 379.

58 E. Ando, 'Capitani Romani – Part I: Design and Construction', in *Warship. Volume II* (Conway Maritime Press, London, 1980), p. 147. Similar failings can be attributed to the heavy cruisers of the *Trento* class and the smaller *Condottieri* class (both the 1st Group (1930) and 2nd Group (1931–32)). As regards Italian destroyers and destroyer escorts, the vessels built after 1922 did attain post-trial speeds of between 30 and 32 knots, but their seaworthiness remained very poor despite various attempts at modification. On these points see USMM, *L'organizzazione della Marina, tomo I*, pp. 71–4 and 81–2. The official history of the Italian submarine arm notes that vessels operating in the Mediterranean were often very noisy even while stationary and immersed, had no protection against enemy anti-submarine technology, were slow, and had a poor level of manoeuvrability. As regards the submersion rate, the Italian time of between 60 and 120 seconds compares poorly with the 30 seconds of the German U-boats. USMM, *I sommergibili in Mediterraneo*, pp. 24–5. The incident in the Red Sea was conveyed to the author during a conversation with Rear-Admiral Luigi Donini, Rome, December 1994.

59 In late 1937 concerned officials at the British foreign office noted that the Italian decision to build new capital ships of 35,000 tons armed with 15" main guns was 'disquieting', and could well place Britain in a 'very awkward position'. PRO, FO 371/21181, minute by Fitzmaurice, 22/9/1937. Although the Admiralty replied that they were not unduly concerned by Italian capital-ship construction, Ernle Chatfield had already informed the Committee of Imperial Defence that summer, 'If now it was decided that Italy was to be considered a probable enemy, it would be a long time before it would be possible to take any defensive measures on that basis.' PRO, CAB 2/6, 'Committee of Imperial Defence: Minutes of the 259th Meeting held on 1 July 1937 – Probability of War with Italy.' For the view that the Italian air force 'completely outclassed' British air power in the Mediterranean see PRO, Air 2/2090, 'The Italian Air Force', Committee of Imperial Defence, Defence Policy (Plan) Sub-Committee, 7/1937. The question of the Mediterranean in Britain's global strategic calculations during 1937–38 is discussed by Lawrence

Pratt. Pratt does not, however, offer analysis on the details of Italian strategic policy or any significant insights into the extent of the Italian armaments programmes that he mentions. See L. Pratt, *East of Malta, West of Suez: Britain's Mediterranean Crisis, 1936–1939* (Cambridge University Press, Cambridge, 1975), pp. 75–105.

60 Gabriele, *Operazione C3: Malta.* pp. 5–7; USMM, *L'organizzazione della Marina, tomo I*, pp. 175–7.

61 ACS, Min. Mar. Gab, b: 195, unsigned memorandum, 25/6/1936.

62 USMM, DG, 0-B10, 'Provvedimenti di competenza dell'ufficio piani di operazioni di Maristat riguardanti il periodo 1 settembre 1934–31 agosto 1936', naval war plans office, 8/1936.

63 USMM, CN, b: 2687, f: 18, 'Apprestamenti settore militare marittimo di Tobruk', naval ministry study commissioned by Cavagnari, 11/8/1936; USMM, CN, b: 2687, f: 12, Cavagnari to Balbo, 11/1936.

64 Discussions on improvements to Italian base facilities took place at various meetings of the supreme high command held between November 1936 and June 1937. See USMM, DG, O-M, 'Verbale della seduta', meetings of 5/11/1936, 22/1/1937, 26/2/1937, 31/3/1937 and 11/6/1937.

65 USMM, *La Marina italiana nella seconda guerra mondiale. X: Le operazioni in Africa orientale* (USMM, Rome, 1961), pp. 3–14.

66 USMM, *L'organizzazione della Marina, tomo I*, p. 176; USMM, DG, 1-A, naval war plans office, 16/11/1939; USMM, *Le operazioni in Africa orientale*, p. 8.

67 On Mussolini's unwillingness to reach any negotiated agreement on the question of Ethiopia, see Mori, *Mussolini e la conquista dell'Etiopia*, pp. 233–41 and 260–1. On these operations see Minniti, '"Il nemico vero"', pp. 585–6.

68 Marder, 'The Royal Navy and the Ethiopian Crisis', pp. 1335–7, 1338, and 1343–5. The idea that Mussolini had been aware of such deficiencies and therefore regarded British reinforcement of the Mediterranean Fleet as a bluff is discussed by De Felice, *Gli anni del consenso*, pp. 679–80. On the divergence of views between Mediterranean naval commanders such as Fisher and Dudley Pound and those of the London government, see Morewood, 'The Chiefs-of-Staff, the "Men on the Spot" and the Italo-Abyssinian Emergency', pp. 92–4. Fisher's views, along with the idea that the Italian naval high command greatly feared an attack on Italy's coastline by a British battle fleet, are discussed in S. Morewood, 'The British Defence of Egypt, 1935–September 1937' (PhD thesis, University of Bristol, 1985), p. 156.

69 USMM, DG, 1-A, Cavagnari to all naval departments, 9/10/1935.

70 USMM, DG, 0-E, 'Dislocazione iniziale delle forze di superficie', naval war plans office, 14/10/1935. On the dispositions to be assumed by the two Italian naval squadrons should Britain declare war see Minniti, '"Il nemico vero"', p. 581.

71 USMM, DG, 1-D, 'Pro-memoria sulle possibilità d'azione britannica nel Mediterraneo', Bernotti to naval war plans office, 12/10/1935. Bernotti's role in influencing naval strategic thought during the period of Italo-British tension is discussed in Sullivan, 'Introduction', in Bernotti, *Fundamentals of Naval Tactics*, pp. 25–6.

72 USMM, DG, 1-D, 'Riunione di Stato Maggiore', 17/10/1935. In a meeting held on 7 October the navy's high command had also concluded that shortages of fuel would greatly reduce the options open to the Italian fleet, whose movements should now be kept to a minimum. See USMM, DG, 1-D, 'Riunione di Stato Maggiore', 7/10/1935. On 29 October Cavagnari duly instructed all naval departments that owing to severe fuel shortages, only the defensive operations recently produced by the plans office could be undertaken. No other ship

movements were to be contemplated unless absolutely essential. See USMM, DG, 0-N, 'Riduzione consumo dei combustibli', 29/10/1935. On lack of air force readiness see USMM, DG, 0-M, Viansino to Cavagnari, 11/10/1935.

73 Ufficio Storico dello Stato Maggiore dell'Esercito (USSME), Rome, N:11, carteggio: 4030, Lessona to the high commissioner, Asmara, 11/9/1935, and on Lessona's political reliability as regards Mussolini and the entire Abyssinian venture see Bottai, *Diario, 1935–1944*, 24/4/1936. Minniti argues that the planned attack on Aden originated not with Mussolini but with Cavagnari and the naval staff. Lessona's memorandum of mid-September leaves no room for doubt that the order had been given by Mussolini himself. See Minniti, '"Il nemico vero"', p. 585. On the Pariani plan to seize the Suez Canal following the launch of land offensives from Eritrea and Libya see pp. 583–4. On the order of command in East Africa see USMM, *Le operazioni in Africa orientale*, p. 13.

74 USMM, DG, 0-L, 'Operazioni offensive in A.O. in caso di applicazione del Piano B', Cavagnari to air and army staffs, 12/12/1935.

75 USMM, DG, 8-C, report by the naval war plans office on the possibilities for aeronaval operations in the Red Sea, 1/11/1935.

76 USMM, DG, 0-L, 'Operazioni offensive in A.O.', Cavagnari to the air and army staffs, 12/12/1935; USSME, H:5, raccolta:RR, carteggio:47, 'Operazioni offensive in A.O. in caso di applicazione del Piano B', Valle to Cavagnari, 12/12/1935. For Baistrocchi's reply see USSME, N:11, c: 4030, Baistrocchi to Cavagnari, 22/12/1935; Minniti, '"Il nemico vero"', pp. 585–6; USSME, N:11, c:4030, 'Operazioni offensive in A.O. in caso di applicazione del Piano "B"', Valle to high commissioner for East Africa/Lessona, 23/12/1935.

77 USMM, DG, 8-A, 'Apprezamento della situazione al 31 gennaio 1936', Tur to Cavagnari, 31/1/1936. The admiral's report only serves to cast further doubt on the eccentric views of Rosaria Quartararo, who in this case has assuredly argued that 'it is a fact that, at the peak of the crisis, Italy could potentially maintain complete control of the Red Sea'. Quartararo, 'Imperial Defence in the Mediterranean', p. 198. On the British plan to bomb Italy's East African aerodromes from positions in Aden and the Sudan and firmly hold both the former and Egypt against 'any form of attack', see Morewood, 'The British Defence of Egypt', pp. 152–4.

78 Minniti, '"Il nemico vero"', p. 586.

79 USMM, DG, 10, 'Considerazioni navali sulla attuale tensione anglo-italiana', Giuseppe Romagna memorandum, Italian naval academy, 4/1936.

80 USMM, DG, 10, 'Considerazioni navali sulla attuale tensione anglo-italiana', naval war plans office to Romagna, 15/4/1936; USMM, DG, 4-B, 'Questione albanese in caso di conflitto', naval war plans office, 20/4/1936. The idea that Cavagnari prepared the navy for a 'Mediterranean Jutland' focused on confrontation between the two enemy battle fleets is discussed in Knox, *Mussolini Unleashed*, p. 21; Santoni, 'La mancata risposta della Regia Marina alle teorie del Douhet', p. 260.

81 Sullivan, 'Introduction', in Bernotti, *Fundamentals of Naval Tactics*, p. 50; USMM, *Le azioni navali nel Mediterraneo, tomo I*, pp. 3–4.

82 On the navy's primary concern with supporting the army attack on Egypt see Sullivan, 'The Italian Armed Forces', p. 193. USMM, DG, 0-E, 'Applicazione documento zero: Costituzione delle squadre', naval war plans office, 27/11/1936; USMM, *Le azioni navali nel Mediterraneo, tomo I*, pp. 12–13.

83 Gabriele, *Operazione C3: Malta*, pp. 13–14. On the greater emphasis placed on the use of mines as part of the central Mediterranean defences see USMM, *La guerra di mine*, p. 76. For the greater interest in anti-submarine warfare from late 1936 onwards see USMM, DG, 5-B, 'Organizzazione della difesa del

traffico', naval war plans office, 17/12/1936; USMM, *La lotta antisommergibile*, pp. 3–4.

84 USMM, DG, 9-A, 'Problema militare marittimo delle isole italiane dell'Egeo', naval war plans office, 1/12/1936.

85 L. Salvatorelli, *Il fascismo nella politica internazionale* (Giulio Einaudi, Rome–Modena, 1956), p. 156.

3

Tension in the Mediterranean

Over the years 1937 and 1938, Mussolini's avowal that war against the British and French remained 'inevitable' led him to seek economic and military alliance with Berlin, the pursuit of which, as discussed in the previous chapter, had underpinned Fascist foreign policy during 1936. In January 1937 he moved still further along this road by hinting to Hermann Goering, as he had done to ambassador Hassell the year before, that Italy would acquiesce in an Austro-German *Anschluss*. In return, the field marshal intimated that Germany would support Italy in any future Mediterranean crisis. Meanwhile, towards London Mussolini demonstrated an outward willingness to reach a *détente* by agreeing to the conclusion of a largely innocuous 'gentlemen's agreement' in early 1937. In reality, the *Duce* merely sought to prevent Berlin from arriving at any agreement of its own with Britain, a tactic he employed again in agreeing to the Easter accords of April 1938, and a tactic which amply demonstrated the level of mistrust permeating the 'Axis' relationship.[1]

Nevertheless, despite such misgivings, Rome clearly needed Berlin's backing if Mussolini's dreams of Italian predominance in the Mediterranean were to be realised. As Hassell reported in February 1937, 'the increasing predominance of Mediterranean interests in Italian policy ... makes German support virtually indispensable given the undeniable divergencies with other Mediterranean Powers'. The price for this support, he added, was already recognised in Italy as being a 'considerable modification' of Italian policy towards a *Gleichschaltung* between Austria and National Socialism. Over the course of that year, Mussolini and Ciano duly spoke of the 'inevitability' of the *Anschluss* that finally occurred in March 1938, while the Italian military began planning in earnest for the confrontation with Britain in the Mediterranean of which Mussolini had so often spoken.[2]

Hitler, now increasingly aware that his long-sought-after understanding with Britain might prove illusory, turned to ideas of aggression as a means of achieving his continental aims during the period covered by this chapter. Now convinced that any German–British *rapprochement* offered limited possibilities, he came to believe that the Rome–Berlin 'Axis' would prove of more use to him in pursuing territorial claims in continental Europe than any agreement with Britain. Indeed, it might act as a 'counter-weight' to the Franco-British policy of co-operation. By the end of 1937, therefore, the *Führer*'s thinking had begun to focus on the concept of a Mediterranean war between Italy and the Western powers sometime during 1938, which would create the perfect diversion for a German coup in central Europe that Britain, faced with problems in the Far East and in Africa, would in any case be in no position to counter. 'The timing for our attacks on the Czechs and Austria', he told a gathering of German military chiefs in November 1937 (the so-called 'Hossbach' conference), 'must be made dependent on the course of the Anglo–French–Italian war', although he opposed any idea of a military alliance with Italy and preferred to maintain Germany's independence of action.[3]

In short, both dictators cautiously appreciated the value a closer German–Italian relationship might have in realising their respective expansionist goals. Mussolini, in the face of internal apprehension, nevertheless chose to align Italy with Germany, in order, as he was to state in February 1939, to 'break the bars' of Italy's Mediterranean prison – Corsica, Tunisia, Cyprus – and 'march to the oceans'.[4]

The great improvement in bilateral relations between Rome and Berlin had clear implications for the direction of Italian naval policy as a whole, and discussion of these forms the basis of the present chapter. The continuing effect of Mussolini's pro-'Axis' policy on the Italian navy's overall planning meant that Italian support for German territorial claims against Czechoslovakia brought the fleet to the brink of war in the autumn of 1938, at a point when the naval armaments programme, already hampered by raw-materials shortages and strained by the burden of additional building, was glaringly incomplete. Cavagnari's role in planning to meet this crisis and the effectiveness of naval operational planning were to be governed by these clear deficiencies.

Planning for War: The Regia Marina's Role in Mussolini's Quest for Mare Nostrum, *January–December 1937*

Goering's avowal – in January 1937 – that the eight Italian battleships boasted of by Mussolini during their meeting would, when placed alongside the eight possessed by the German navy and the 12 of the Japanese fleet, 'constitute a very considerable naval force compared with other countries', greatly impressed the Italian dictator. So much so that, shortly after his encounter with the field marshal, he authorised planning for the remodernisation of the *Doria* class and the building of further

Littorio-class ships, in order that Italy might actually achieve the total in question. By the end of that year, the naval ministry had initiated both programmes, which, when complete, in theory by 1941–42, would help in achieving its objective of dominating the central Mediterranean in a war against Britain and France.[5]

Meanwhile, clearly determined to prevent a Republican victory in Spain's increasingly bitter civil war, a victory that would undermine Italy's political and strategic position in Mediterranean affairs, Mussolini also ordered units of the Italian submarine arm to begin attacking and sinking all 'Red' naval units and merchant vessels destined for Republican ports. By late December 1936, and after Mussolini expressly requested it, senior representatives of both the Italian and the German naval staffs met in Cádiz in southern Spain to discuss future additional support for the Nationalist navy. Bases for operations against Republican shipping and ports were established at Palma on Majorca and Ceuta in Spanish Morocco, and by the first months of 1937, Italian submarines had already begun their campaign against shipping bound for Spanish government ports.[6]

Although Cavagnari and the naval high command came to regard a combination of German and Japanese naval might as the best means of drawing off enemy forces from the Mediterranean, leaving Italy to fight for control of the central Mediterranean and subsequently the Suez Canal, it would clearly be some time before the Italian fleet reached the operational levels boasted of by the dictator. Similarly, Italian intervention in Spain, and the gradual intensification of the submarine offensive over that spring and summer, although signifying Mussolini's determination to ensure a Nationalist victory in the war, again demonstrated to him the limits of Italian power in the face of Anglo-French opposition. In short, Paris and London's imposition of the Nyon agreement later that year served to illustrate for the dictator the geopolitical realities facing Italy and future Italian expansion in the Mediterranean, and served to underline still further the importance of alliance with Germany.

The problems facing the existing capital-ship programme during the course of 1936, owing to shortages of raw materials and fuel deficiencies, were persistent throughout 1937, and indeed for the remainder of the period prior to the outbreak of war in June 1940. Late in 1936, Cavagnari had already warned the naval staff of the dangerously low fuel reserves affecting the operational level of the fleet, stressing that all naval departments should exercise the utmost economy in the use of fuels. The implications of this order were clear: the navy's ability to stage exercises were limited, and in time of war it would also have its operational capability greatly restricted. By 1 January 1940, despite more successful attempts at stockpiling than those of the other armed forces, the navy's storage facilities still only held 1,583,190 tons of fuel – enough for little more than five months of war.[7]

In addition to the problem of fuel, the question of securing and distributing raw materials destined for the navy's building programmes remained equally thorny. After Cavagnari instructed the appropriate naval departments to begin planning additional building in February 1937, it rapidly became clear that existing naval programmes were already in trouble. By April, Mario Falangola of the navy's inspection board warned the chief-of-staff that problems in the production of ships' armour had delayed work on both the *Littorio* and the *Vittorio Veneto*, later advising him that trials were unlikely to get underway until mid-1939, over a year later than originally envisaged.[8]

Table 4

Chief raw-materials requirements of the Italian armaments industries (1940)

Type of material	Overall annual requirement	Total met through importation
Coal	12,061,500	8,900,000
Fuel oils	8,731,420	8,731,420
Iron	1,794,770	1,594,770
Nickel	5,000	5,000
Copper	150,000	149,000
Rubber	22,000	22,000

Note: Figures in tons
Source: Figures derived from F. Minniti, 'Le materie prime nella preparazione bellica dell'Italia, 1935–1943 (parte prima)', *Storia Contemporanea*, 27, 1 (1986), p. 20.

The reasons for such delays are partly explained by Italy's need to import the majority of its raw materials at great cost to its vulnerable national economy. Added to this, Italy's lack of an effective central co-ordinating authority, able to overcome 'administrative confusion' and distribute existing materials equitably and according to need, greatly exacerbated the overall situation. Although the *Commissione suprema di difesa* (the supreme defence commission) did exist, theoretically to manage the national economic and military effort, it lacked the power to do so. Likewise, although Mussolini placed the veteran General Alfredo Dall'Olio in command of a general commissariat for war production (*Cogefag – Commissariato generale per le fabbricazioni di guerra*) during 1935, in an attempt to instill a sense of order into the allocation of materials for the armed forces, this initiative, too, failed. The individual service ministries controlled their own procurement, a factor that could only generate delays and bitter interservice wrangling for industrial resources. Neither did the Fascist administration's failure to introduce greater levels of standardisation do much to improve an already chaotic situation. As regards the naval ministry, although it could dominate the other services in gaining access to the principal Italian arms industries, such levels of material deficiency and bureaucratic chaos could nevertheless only have serious implications: neither of the *Littorio* vessels, originally destined for completion in 1938, entered service until the summer of 1940, after Mussolini had declared war on Britain and France. Furthermore, the second *Littorio* programme authorised by the *Duce* in December 1937 saw only one ship, the *Roma*, completed in mid-1942, by which time Fascist Italy had already lost its war against Britain.[9]

The weakness of the Italian industrial economy, the lack of sufficient quantities of strategic raw materials and the vulnerability to blockade of Italy's position in the Mediterranean, signified for Mussolini that a strengthening of ties with Berlin at the economic level might hold marked advantages in time of war. In early March 1937 Ciano sought to build on the economic relationship developed during the recent Italo-Abyssinian crisis, and ordered Attolico in Berlin to contact Goering and 'discuss the co-ordination of German and Italian action to secure autarky for the case of war'. Since both countries 'were in the same danger', he added, they might establish a joint standing committee to discuss the exchange of raw materials. However, although the two governments did draw up the first of a series of protocols in mid-May, which foresaw Germany supplying coal, iron and other key materials to Italy 'in abnormal times', Germany could only provide significant quantities of coal. Petroleum and rubber supplies needed to be sought elsewhere. Moreover, as late as February 1939, the German–Italian rail network seemed unable to carry even the full annual quota of coal exports – 9 million tons – from Germany to Italy. In effect, there was little Germany could do to help the Italian armaments drive. Worse still, the Italian economy could barely finance a programme of heavy raw-material importation, particularly in view of the fact that by 1939–40 the reserves of the Bank of Italy had dwindled from 20 million lire to 3 million lire, while Mussolini concomitantly had also expended foreign stocks and bonds on costly overseas adventures in Ethiopia, Spain and Albania. Such facts serve further to illustrate, with stark clarity, the disparity between Mussolini's dreams of Italian might and the harsh economic realities facing the Italian exchequer.[10]

Despite these facts, Mussolini's conviction that a war against the western European powers was inevitable grew throughout the course of 1937. By the first months of summer, he had informed Rodolfo Graziani, the Italian viceroy in Somaliland, that in view of this fact the number of Italian troops stationed in Italian East Africa should be increased to 300,000 men by raising an indigenous army, and deploying further contingents there from the metropolitan sphere. In order to make the territory wholly autonomous from the mainland, Mussolini also ordered that an independent defence commission for the colony be established to prepare for the imminent threat of hostilities. The plan to strengthen the

Italian East African territories was no mere precaution, as Mussolini put it, 'against the fact that British rearmament was probably also directed against us'. Rather, it formed part of Italy's overall grand strategy during this period, aimed at establishing a major new naval base in Italian Somaliland, and eventually seizing the Suez Canal and the port of Aden in an attempt to win control of the Red Sea.[11]

In the meantime, over the summer months, the strengthening of the Rome–Berlin alignment grew apace. In May, German foreign minister Konstantin von Neurath visited Rome and invited Mussolini – who during their meeting again declared Austria to be 'a German state' – to the German military manoeuvres that autumn. The *Duce* accepted. However, both Hitler and the German foreign ministry were swift to reject a suggestion, first thought of by Ciano, that the visit might lead to Rome and Berlin concluding a four-power pact with Austria and Hungary, which guaranteed Austrian independence. The refusal, indicative of the fact that Neurath evidently regarded Germany as the 'senior partner in the Axis', in turn revealed much about Italian policy. Clearly aware that the long-awaited *Anschluss* was near, Mussolini and Ciano appeared anxious either to delay it by securing the weight of Austro-Hungarian support on the Italian side of the 'Axis', or, alternatively, to create a bloc of states comprising Yugoslavia, Bulgaria and Romania that might counter too great a German predominance in the Balkans. Naturally, Berlin, eager to execute Germany's intended union with Austria, had little time for such delaying tactics. Therefore, the visit went ahead as planned in late-September, without the conclusion of any such political agreement.[12]

While the preparations for Mussolini's visit to Berlin proceeded, the navy's role in the Spanish Civil War, and specifically its submarine offensive against Republic-bound shipping passing through the Mediterranean, increasingly embittered Rome's relations with London and Paris. Although the initial campaign, which ended in mid-February 1937, had produced somewhat modest results – out of 15 ships attacked only four were hit by torpedoes – a second series of operations involving 48 Italian submarines, as well as Italian aircraft and naval surface units, attacked merchant vessels throughout the Mediterranean from the Aegean to the eastern Spanish coastline. The indiscriminate offensive, which began early in August after Franco had requested and received Mussolini's help in destroying a Soviet military convoy heading from the Black Sea ports to Republican Spain, met with much criticism from within the Italian naval staff. Not only did Cavagnari oppose Italian intervention in Spain *per se*, but appeared equally reluctant to cede the two Italian submarines and two destroyers requested by the Spanish Nationalist navy. His opposition was, however, futile; Mussolini and Ciano made the decisions.[13]

More seriously, Mussolini's actions also brought Italy to the brink of confrontation with Britain and France. Indeed, only Admiralty opposition prevented Anthony Eden from pressing his request for retaliatory action – the sinking of the Nationalist cruiser *Canarias* – any further. As Ernle Chatfield pointed out, for retaliation to be effective it would need to be directed not against the Spanish but the Italians; any such threat of retaliation 'ran counter to Great Britain's official policy of restoring good relations with Mussolini', the stated aim of the Chamberlain administration. At the behest of Yvon Delbos, the French foreign minister, the London government, eager to secure a political solution to the new crisis in the Mediterranean, thus agreed that a conference should be held at Nyon, near Geneva. In the meantime, London took the precaution of strengthening the Mediterranean Fleet by sending four additional destroyers to the area. Evidently impressed by the show of Anglo-French unity, Ciano ordered Cavagnari to suspend the naval campaign against merchant shipping on 4 September, some six days before the first meetings at Nyon took place.[14]

At the Anglo–French–Italian naval staff conversations held in Paris in late September in order to implement the patrol scheme decided upon at the conference, which Italy had not attended 'because of the presence of the Russians', clear divisions were to emerge. According to the Italian record of the meetings, as soon as the three-nation naval discussions began, differences occurred between the Italian delegation and their Anglo-French counterparts. On the very first day of the conference – 27 September – the negotiators representing the Italian naval high command, deputy chief-of-staff Wladimiro Pini and Admiral Raineri-Biscia, a veteran of the London naval conference the year before, evidently relieved that the patrol scheme only referred to 'inhumane' actions, rather surprisingly agreed to an all British–French route through the entire Mediterranean. However, the next day, and following pressure from an enraged Mussolini, who objected to Italy's relegation to secondary status in its 'own sea', the Italians changed their minds and demanded that Italy be assigned a zone in the western Mediterranean, that the Sicilian Channel be divided into three patrol areas, one for each nation, and that Italy's eastern Mediterranean patrol area should cover the Dardanelles and the Suez Canal.

Very swiftly, both the British and the French representatives showed their disapproval of the Italian proposal. Robert Godfroy and César Campinchi of the French ministry of marine strongly opposed any Italian presence in the western Mediterranean – although they were prepared to see the Italian patrol zone extended as far as the Balearic Islands. They equally disliked the idea of subdividing the Sicilian Channel. To do so, they argued, created competing 'compartments' along the Suez–Gibraltar shipping route, and they insisted that the central Mediterranean be controlled exclusively by British and French naval units. Furthermore, they rejected the Italian proposals on the grounds that, if they accepted them, 'they would give Italy an overall patrol area larger than that of the

French navy', a fact which would create considerable public outcry in view of Italian actions that summer. The British, on the other hand, while not wholly against the Italian plan for the Sicilian Channel, were not in favour of ceding control of the Dardanelles to Italy in order to avoid 'antagonising the Soviet Union too much', and joined the French in opposing any substantial presence of the Italian fleet in the western Mediterranean. Neither, as it turned out, did Admiral William James, head of the British delegation, prove willing to permit Italian ships to patrol the waters around the Egyptian coast and the Suez Canal region in particular. 'As regards the eastern Mediterranean', he argued on 29 September, 'he believed it of vital importance that the zone around Suez along with Egyptian coastal waters be patrolled by British units alone.'

Later that same day, however, in a clear attempt to prevent the Italians from demanding greater control of the eastern basin, the British accepted the idea that the Italian navy's ships patrol the waters around Sicily, with the proviso that the Royal Navy cover the area around Suez and the Egyptian coast. This, Pini noted in his report, could only have been a manoeuvre designed to prevent Italy gaining any control of the waters around the Suez Canal. Duly, the Italian delegation, while agreeing to the Anglo-French point of view over Sicily and the western Mediterranean, then pressed for a compromise solution to the eastern Mediterranean question. Admiral Pini stressed that he could not possibly accept a patrol scheme that left Italy 'without access to one of the principal Mediterranean exits', and subsequently proposed that Britain and Italy should jointly patrol the waters off Egypt; the British patrol limit being the island of Karpathos to the east of Crete, while responsibility for the region of sea lying between Crete and the Suez Canal should be assigned to the Italian navy. Pini also demanded that the *Marina* be given responsibility for the waters linking Italian possessions in the Dodecanese and Libya. To his surprise, the British concurred, and the three delegations finally signed an agreement that afternoon which left the Italian navy in control of the shipping routes between the Aegean and North Africa, and with responsibility for patrolling a region of water stretching uninterrupted from the Balearic Islands to Port Said, just as Mussolini had demanded. It is little wonder that Pini, in his official report on the conference, concluded that Italy had won a great moral victory, given that 'the zones assigned to the other naval powers were, on the contrary, separate from one another and not in any way interconnected'.

Nevertheless, the matter did not end there. On the afternoon of 29 September, prior to the final signatures on the agreement and during the course of an official luncheon, members of the French naval staff – apparently after the Russian government had placed pressure on Delbos at Geneva – argued that they could not possibly accept 'Italian control of most of the waters between the Dardenelles and Port Said'. The solution, argued Deleuze, a junior member of the delegation, meant extending Britain's eastern Mediterranean patrol area to the region west of Crete. Not surprisingly, Pini refused to agree. Pointing out that the three delegations had already concluded an agreement, he declared himself opposed to any scheme that severed Italian communications between the Dodecanese and Libya, and that also excluded the Italian fleet from the waters between the Dardenelles and Port Said.

Nor did Pini respond any more favourably to a personal plea from James, who, along with the French Admiral Borrague, shortly afterwards visited the Italians in their hotel and argued that assigning the area between Rhodes and Tobruk to Italy had been an error on his part, and in fact contradicted his own instructions from the Admiralty. His Italian counterpart merely replied that Rome did not accept changes to an agreement demanded by 'other powers which were in any case not present and therefore not authorised to dictate terms'. James and Borrague, aware that they had lost the argument, let the matter quietly drop, leaving Pini to inform Rome that:

> Both admiral Raineri and I were only able to conclude that admiral James had decided to act in support of French wishes. Subsequently we left him in no doubt as to the level of ill-feeling that this had generated among ourselves.[15]

Aside from symbolically emphasising the geostrategic concerns of the principal Mediterranean naval powers, Nyon and the subsequent Paris conference did result in a partial victory for Mussolini, whose angry instructions to Pini and Raineri-Biscia led them to win for Italy a moral success of some note. The Italian navy had taken part in the Paris discussions on the pretext that it would only do so under 'conditions of absolute equality with any other power in the Mediterranean'. Therefore, London, eager to reach a new understanding with Mussolini, felt compelled to ensure Rome's participation at the naval discussions by publicly recognising Italy as a 'great naval power'. Moreover, the eventual outcome saw Rome's submarine offensive that summer go unadmonished as Italian prestige was increased; as Ciano noted, 'from suspicious pirates to the policemen of the Mediterranean, and the Russians whose ships we were sinking excluded'.[16]

Yet, Nyon and Paris had also seen 'collaboration between the British and French fleets of a kind never known before'. Despite something of an increase in Italian prestige, the agreements can only have demonstrated for Mussolini the extent of Anglo-French dominion in the Mediterranean, and Italian impotence in the face of it. In short, the submarine offensive had been halted in its tracks, and Mussolini had not been able to oppose this. Worse still, Mussolini proved unsuccessful in his attempts to secure Germany's participation in the patrol scheme, Hitler clearly not wanting to antagonise the British unduly even if his long-sought-after Anglo-German alliance had failed to materialise. Not surprisingly, Mussolini, although he authorised four Italian submarines to take part in further operations after the Nyon agreement had been concluded, did so in the face of continued opposition from the naval staff, and on the strict proviso that the vessels in question became the ultimate responsibility of Spain's Nationalist navy.[17]

Mussolini soon recovered from his disappointment over Germany's refusal to take part in the Mediterranean patrol scheme; his visit to Berlin between 25–29 September 'strengthened anew the foundations of German–Italian collaboration'. Yet, the value of his journey to Berlin lay not in the conclusion of specific agreements. No political, military or even economic treaty resulted from the meeting of the two dictators, and as Ciano noted, in a sense the voyage added little that was new to the Berlin protocols he had concluded the previous October. Nor did it lie in generating a greater air of trust between the two capitals; prior to the visit, Rome's concern that Neurath's planned visit to London might lead to an Anglo-German agreement had been all too apparent.[18]

Rather, the significance of Mussolini's voyage lay in the experience itself – the impression it created within the *Duce*'s own mind of German power and of the personal qualities of the *Führer*. As historians have concluded, this experience of Nazi Germany had been among the 'most profound' of Mussolini's entire life. His tours of German armaments factories and the impressive military parades the Nazi government staged in his honour created a vision of 'overwhelming strength'. There, for the Italian dictator, was a nation and a man – Hitler – with whom Italy must ally itself. 'Not friendship but mutual veneration was the tie.' Thus, he abandoned any notions of maintaining 'equidistance', Italy's traditional foreign policy under its pre-Fascist Liberal administrations, and 'chose Germany'. As both Ciano and Giuseppe Bottai noted in their diaries, the Rome–Berlin 'Axis' was now the basis of Italian policy. Despite the risks of aligning Italy with 'anti-humanist Germanism', risks which Italy would one day be compelled to confront, the 'Axis' remained a 'formidable reality' of great potential use in furthering Italian aspirations.[19]

The Berlin meetings between the two dictators had, then, not resulted in any specific commitment to co-ordinate their strategic efforts. Nevertheless, in the wake of the visit, the navy's planners did begin to consider the possibilities open to Italy should a German–Italian naval partnership find itself fighting a war against Britain and France. During September 1937, the war plans office outlined future Italian naval policy in a report for Mussolini, in which the planners argued that they might in future be governed by a new political formula: namely, that the total combined fleet strength of the *Regia Marina* and the German navy should eventually reach 50 per cent of that of the combined Anglo-French navies. The navy, the staff report continued, should in any event strive to reach an operational strength equal to 80 per cent of its French counterpart, 40 per cent of the Royal Navy's, and also reach a level 10 per cent larger than that of Germany. If Italian naval building achieved these targets, then the navy's 'relative strength' compared with that of France would improve, as would its position regarding the Royal Navy, taking into account the fact that at most it could deploy only 60 per cent of its fleet in the Mediterranean in time of war. On the other hand, if the theoretical alliance with Germany became a reality, then Britain could only deploy 20 per cent of its fleet to this theatre to operate alongside its French ally, given the Royal Navy's need to commit substantial forces in 'northern naval theatres'. The proportional ratio of naval strength in the Mediterranean would then be 10:6 in the enemy's favour, a balance which the planners regarded as 'acceptable'.

Britain, the report argued, had recently embarked on a massive naval rearmament drive that Mussolini should consider exceptional: British shipyards were building around 116,000 tons of new shipping a year. Ultimately, the overall British fleet strength would comprise 21 capital ships, 11 aircraft carriers, and 15 heavy cruisers. The French, on the other hand, could build up to 56,000 tons of shipping per annum, and the report estimated that the French fleet would, by 1944, be in a position to operate ten capital ships, four aircraft carriers and seven heavy cruisers. In order to counter this most effectively, the plans office stressed that Italy needed two main naval squadrons, each composed of four battleships. To meet this minimum requirement, the naval ministry should consider the construction of two more vessels of the *Littorio* class with 15" guns, improved anti-aircraft defences, better protection and higher speed, and should not hesitate to exceed the 35,000-ton Washington limit. If Mussolini approved this new construction, by 1944 Italy's position *vis-à-vis* the capital ships of the other main European fleets would be as follows:

Italy	Germany	France	Britain
8	10	10	21

However, a further crucial proviso contained within the report centred on the absolute necessity of Italy's possessing at least one aircraft carrier, the building of which Cavagnari had vetoed the previous summer. Despite his categorical rejection of the need for such ships, the planners were convinced that the Italian navy needed air cover from carrier-borne units, whether within the Mediterranean or outside, as the report set out with unmistakable clarity:

If in theory it remains possible to demonstrate the limited use our navy has for an aircraft carrier, such an argument appears flawed when one considers the various exercises undertaken by the fleet over the last ten years. There are regions within the Mediterranean where any intervention by our land-based air forces should be considered as far too onerous an undertaking; there are strategic situations where only carrier-based aircraft would have any chance of success.

Nor would the Italian fleet prove very successful if forced to operate without air cover, as a result of 'possible future alliances', in the 'vast oceanic theatres'. Therefore, the planners urged Mussolini, Italy should construct at least one 15,000-ton vessel of this type able to carry up to 70 aircraft during the period 1938–40, and a second ship during the period from 1941–43.[20]

Ascribing undue political value to the naval staff report on the future requirements of the fleet would clearly be unwise. No binding military agreement between Germany and Italy existed at this time, and exchanges of ideas between the respective naval staffs of the two countries did not take place until June 1939. For its part, the German navy did not at this point envisage war against Britain as a likely possibility, and certainly saw no prospect for any alliance with its Italian counterpart. The German naval staff planned for a two-front war against France and the Soviet Union, in which it hoped that both Italy and Britain would remain neutral. Not until the spring of 1938 did Hitler order Admiral Erich Raeder, commander-in-chief of the *Kriegsmarine*, to consider Britain as a potential adversary.[21]

Furthermore, merely assessing the strength of potential future enemies by, in the words of Gerhard Schreiber, 'counting their battleships', hardly constituted an effective way of planning naval policy. On the contrary, the considerations of future programmes produced by the Italian naval planners should also have examined other factors such as comparative weapons data, levels of training and morale in order to ascertain areas of enemy weakness, and not merely attempted to address numerical strengths in terms of capital ships.[22]

Thus, although the concept of a Rome–Berlin 'Axis', within which Italy might tackle its fundamental clash of interests with the Western powers, made logical sense from Mussolini's point of view, the war plans office report illustrated the disparity between its own planning and the strategic realities facing Italy. The naval staff may well have recognised the value of a German–Italian alliance, and even proposed an Italian building programme linked proportionally to that of the German fleet, but no bilateral agreement to co-ordinate German–Italian naval building existed. Furthermore, although the threats posed by Germany and Japan from 1933 onwards created global strategic difficulties for Paris and London, Italy ultimately failed to gain any significant advantage from this. Britain and France had a large numerical aeronaval preponderance that the

Italians might have countered better had they 'concentrated on the development of naval strength'. Despite being in a good position to concentrate their power against areas such as Egypt, Malta and Tunisia, Italy either failed to develop the forces necessary to exploit this advantage, or began to do so belatedly. Largely, this was due to the domination of Italy's armed forces by the army and its 'Alpine' mentality until the middle of the 1930s; the continued failure of the air and navy staffs to develop a close and effective operational relationship for what would be a primarily aeronaval encounter; and, ultimately, Mussolini's inability or unwillingness to encourage greater interservice collaboration – all themes which will recur later in this study.[23]

Domestic unease at the increasingly pro-German and anti-Western direction of Mussolini's policy did not disappear after the improvement in political relations between Rome and Berlin. On the contrary, public opinion within predominantly Catholic Italy expressed continual hostility towards what it regarded as the paganistic repression prevalent in Nazi Germany, opposition which only grew as Mussolini introduced Draconian measures such as the anti-Jewish laws aimed at overcoming the 'racial immaturity' of the Italian people. Within the political and military establishment, criticism of Mussolini's German policy, fear of its consequences, and outright terror at the idea of a war against the British remained equally widespread. The naval staff, largely opposed to war in 1935, also expressed grave reservations regarding Italian intervention in Spain, and during the Paris naval conference had appeared initially prepared to accept the proposals of their British and French counterparts without complaint, only assuming a more confrontational line following the intervention of a furious Mussolini. Many within Italy's diplomatic corps, too, were opposed to a policy based on war. Yet, for all the *Palazzo Chigi*'s reserve, which exasperated Ciano to the extent that he believed it would take at least 15 years to change the prevalent mentality of the 'sheep' at the foreign ministry, neither Italy's diplomats nor its admirals could shape and determine the direction of policy. Although Mussolini could not entirely control the various élite groups within Italy – economic interests, the church, the monarchy, the military – he could just about dominate them by virtue of the 'uneasy compromise' he and the Fascist Party had reached with them. Thus, the foreign ministry, for instance, had little power, and even Ciano's influence depended upon the patronage of his father-in-law. At most, it would be possible to restrain the dictator, but not change the direction he had chosen for Italy.[24]

That autumn, the further cementing of the German–Italian relationship therefore continued unabated. On 22 October a visit by German foreign minister designate, the former champagne salesman Joachim von Ribbentrop, resulted in Mussolini's decision finally to take Italy out of the League and join the Anti-Comintern Pact alongside Germany and

Japan. The German ambassador to Rome, Hassell, whom Ciano increasingly accused of having insufficient enthusiasm for closer Italo-German relations, and who was in any case not a member of the Nazi Party and lacked direct influence with Hitler, clearly had no place in the new political relationship between Rome and Berlin. Subsequently, after pressure from the Italian foreign minister, who wanted a 'party man' in the job, and for that matter a diplomat who had not enjoyed direct access to Mussolini prior to his rise to power, Hitler removed Hassell and replaced him with the 'unimaginative' yet pro-Axis Hans Georg von Mackensen. Berlin also took great care to keep Rome fully informed of the proposed visit of Viscount Halifax to Germany, seeking to avoid reawakening the Italian suspicions aroused over the planned Neurath voyage to London that summer.[25]

Alberto Pariani's concept of a '*guerra brigantesca*' aimed at taking Suez, which originated in late 1935 and had become the focus for discussion at the supreme high command meeting of December 1936, only to be dismissed as unrealistic by Badoglio, took on increasing importance as relations with Germany improved. Pariani argued, during a conversation with Ciano in February 1938, that while German forces concentrated on winning a conflict against France, Italy might attack the Sudan from its East African possessions and perhaps simultaneously launch the offensive from Libya that would lead to the taking of Egypt. For Pariani, too, the conflict between Italy and the Western powers remained an 'inevitability'. The solution for him was an alliance with Germany that enabled both countries to prepare for a war best undertaken in the spring of 1939, when the armament levels of their enemies would be at their lowest. He enthusiastically approved Ciano's suggestion that Italian forces invade Switzerland in order to support the German attack on France, as well as the foreign minister's idea of staging surprise amphibious landings at Suez and Port Said. Both agreed to approach Mussolini immediately with the proposal of establishing a secret German–Italian war planning committee.[26]

Cavagnari expected the Italian navy's role in the 'march to the oceans' largely to involve defending the central Mediterranean and protecting communications between the mainland and Libya. To this, one might add that naval planning also contemplated staging a possible invasion of Malta as a means of guaranteeing the success of this strategy.

As Mussolini improved Italo-German relations during the course of 1937–38, planning for each of these operations proceeded accordingly. By October 1937, Riccardo Paladini, commander-in-chief of the navy's lower Tyrrhenian division, had produced a lengthy report for the naval staff on how best, in his opinion, the navy might undertake the first part of this strategy and the means necessary for it to prove successful. Defence of the central regions of the Mediterranean, he began, depended on controlling the Straits of Sicily and in attacking enemy forces operating there at night. In the first instance, this entailed the navy's deploying surface, undersea and air units to launch torpedo attacks against any enemy forces attempting to pass from one basin to the other. All naval units assigned to fighting this conflict should be kept in port until the most propitious moment for an encounter. Italy could not easily replace naval vessels – and particularly capital ships – lost in action, and therefore none should be committed until victory seemed likely.

Defence of the Straits of Sicily depended in the first instance on the use of mines, hydrophonic equipment (on shore and aboard submarines and motor boats), aerial reconnaissance, as well as on the timely intervention of surface and submarine forces assigned specifically to this task. Mining should by imperative ensure that the waters between Pantelleria and Sicily were impassable, while submarine units, on the other hand, defended the straits between the former island and Tunisia. The navy might develop Pantelleria into 'a type of large support ship for light and underwater naval units and aircraft', and guns with a range of approximately 30 kilometres should be placed along its coastline in order to bombard enemy ships. As regards air reconnaissance, appropriate base facilities should be established at Augusta and Stagnoni in Sicily, along with Tobruk and Benghazi in Libya. Any naval units assigned to this theatre should include small and medium-sized submarines, light cruisers and torpedo-boats, which would operate between Pantelleria and Africa, the most vulnerable point for the enemy. But, Paladini warned with particular emphasis, were the British and French to commit naval forces that included capital ships to the central Mediterranean theatre, then the region's existing bases at Augusta and Cagliari in Sardinia were likely to prove unable to stage major and possibly decisive naval operations involving the main battle fleet, both being far too small to harbour units of that size. Therefore, he argued in conclusion, a new base should be built at Milazzo near Messina in northern Sicily, able to house vessels up to the 35,000-ton *Littorio* class, protect them from all forms of attack, and at the same time permit their rapid deployment in any of the three main Mediterranean theatres.[27]

Later in this chapter, the naval staff's implementation or otherwise of Paladini's recommendations will be addressed more fully. At this point, it might be noted that the concept of defending the central Mediterranean, and in particular of preventing the British from cutting communications between the metropolitan sphere and North Africa, already constituted a central preoccupation for the navy's planners. At the time of the Ethiopian crisis, the Italian naval high command had believed that the Royal Navy would, if war broke out, carry out air and sea attacks on the Libyan port of Tobruk. Hence, as the war plans office began to consider the possibility of war against Britain in the years preceding the Second World War, planning became dominated by the belief that the navy needed to strengthen the defences between Italy and Libya.[28]

Paladini's emphasis on the co-ordinated use of torpedo-carrying air and sea units remained a controversial question. Air and naval staff co-operation during the course of the Mediterranean crisis had not been very effective. Moreover, neither the navy nor the air force had been able to develop a torpedo bomber, largely, according to the navy's official history, owing to the latter's marked opposition to it. Also, any idea as ambitious as that of building an entirely new naval base in the Straits of Messina able to protect the jewels of the Italian fleet – the *Littorio* battleships – and ensure their timely intervention in any sea war, proved far too costly a concept. Felice Guarneri, the minister for exchange, begged Mussolini at this time to ensure that Italy enjoyed at least ten years of peace before embarking on further costly military adventures.[29]

With national finances in such a parlous condition, the 'Milazzo' plan suggested by Paladini and costing, in his own words, 'several hundred million lire', could not be considered. Therefore, the problem of providing the Italian battle fleet with a well-defended base with ready access to the central Mediterranean theatre was resolved by the naval ministry's decision to expand and upgrade the existing facility at Taranto, which fell under the authority of the Ionian naval division. By 1937, the navy duly approved the '*Mar Grande*' project, which involved the building of a huge 405-metre dry dock, countless stores and workshops and a vast underground tunnel connecting the quayside with the naval arsenal, but work was not fully completed before the outbreak of war.[30]

Similar problems of interservice co-ordination and funding bedevilled naval planning in the other principal Italian theatre of operations, the Red Sea. During the time of the Abyssinian crisis, it will be remembered, Mussolini had ordered that preparations be made for a surprise attack on the British base at Aden, to secure an unimpeded Italian outlet to the Indian Ocean via the Red Sea. In February 1937, the commander of naval forces in Italian East Africa, Guido Bacci di Capaci, produced a detailed study for the naval high command in Rome in which he stressed that, in order truly to fulfil Mussolini's imperial vision, Italy's regional forces should seek to dominate the entire horn of Africa and the southern entrances to the *Mar Rosso* (Red Sea). Aside from recommending that a ground offensive be planned to capture British and French Somaliland, Bacci di Capaci argued that the navy must be able to guarantee 'the free transit of all naval and merchant vessels through the Straits of Bab el Mandeb'. This could be best achieved by taking the French port of Djibouti at the moment war broke out, and launching air operations from existing bases at Assab and other air fields in newly conquered French Somaliland, in order to place Aden and Perim under attack and thereby force their evacuation. Co-operation between the regional military staffs needed to be extremely close in order to plan and execute the operation. It would be highly dangerous, Bacci di Capaci concluded, simply to begin planning 'on the eve of the operation's taking place'. This also required the naval ministry substantially to increase local naval forces.[31]

Not until October, the month after Mussolini's visit to Berlin, did the navy's planners fully begin to consider the options open to Italy in this theatre. At present, noted a naval staff assessment, Italy's two principal bases at Assab and Massawa, of which only the latter was adequately defended, enabled local naval forces to exercise control only over the central and southern regions of the Red Sea. Owing to enemy domination of the Gulf of Aden, the navy could launch no submarine or fleet offensive from these positions against British and French naval units operating in the Indian Ocean. In short, Italy had no control over the southern exit of the Red Sea. A marked absence of naval facilities in Italian Somaliland equally limited the navy's capacity to attack enemy forces in the wider oceanic theatre. Nor were the naval units currently deployed to Italian East Africa sufficient to do much more than wage offensives against Anglo-French communications within the *Mar Rosso*. Therefore, the report concluded, if Italy's strategic effort in the region in any future conflict was to be more than mediocre, then a number of measures needed to be taken. Ocean-going naval vessels should be designed and built for use in this theatre, while the government should also make additional resources available to increase significantly the pace of building work on bases in Italian Somaliland at Mogadishu and Chisimaio. Plans to destroy the port of Aden, 'the real keystone' to control of the Red Sea, should be prepared immediately, while ground operations should also be planned, whose objective would be to capture all enemy bases in British and French Somaliland.[32]

Again, lack of adequate resources hampered planning for the theatre. The port at Chisimaio never achieved the status of a full naval base, the naval ministry eventually fearing that it remained too exposed to attack from British forces in neighbouring Kenya. In the meantime, despite considerable efforts by the navy, finances permitted only the port of Massawa to become an operational base with adequate facilities and defences, while Mussolini authorised the construction of ocean-going naval units specifically for use in the Red Sea and Indian Ocean belatedly, in April 1939. Ultimately, however, work on these did not begin, owing to the outbreak of hostilities that autumn. Strategic planning in this theatre, which the local naval command began seriously only in mid-1939, mirrored that for the Mediterranean, insofar as the naval staff, whose operational base was at Massawa, planned in isolation from the other planning departments, which were located several hundred kilometres away in Addis Ababa and also worked independently of one another.

Under such organisational conditions, it remained unlikely that inter-service collaboration would prove any more fruitful than it had during the international emergency of 1935–36. At the outbreak of war in June 1940, only modest naval forces were based in the region, which, far from being able to wrest control of the Red Sea from the enemy and wage oceanic war against their fleets, could only hope to sustain the shortest of conflicts before capitulating.[33]

Cavagnari believed that, with the building of two additional *Littorio*-class ships, finally approved by Mussolini on 4 December, the Italian navy had the potential to challenge the British and French fleets and assert Italian control over the central Mediterranean. In a letter to Pietro Badoglio in mid-November, the chief-of-staff argued that were the navy able to count on the German and Japanese navies forcing Britain to commit its fleet to naval theatres other than the Mediterranean, then Italy's strategic position within that sea became much more promising. Should such diversions become a reality, the navy might win control of the eastern Mediterranean without German assistance and also achieve hegemony, in conjunction with Japan, in the waters of the Red Sea–Indian Ocean. Having secured Italian maritime domination of these regions, military offensives in Africa, such as the Pariani plan to capture the Suez Canal, could proceed and be completed successfully, thereby markedly improving Italy's economic position and greatly undermining the overall status of the British Empire.[34]

Cavagnari's assertion, in his letter to Badoglio, that the naval staff's strategic planning would, from November 1937 onwards, thus become governed by the criterion, 'Germany allied to Italy against an enemy coalition comprised, at the outbreak of war, of Great Britain, France, the Soviet Union and the smaller Mediterranean powers (excluding Yugo-slavia)', became the central issue for discussion in the supreme high command meeting held on 2 December. During the course of the encounter, which initially dealt with the need to defend Albanian oil exports to Italy via the lower Adriatic in time of war, Pariani's planned assault on Egypt, which he described as 'easy prey' given the small number of enemy troops based there, received a further airing.

While the four Italian and two colonial divisions currently based in Libya protected the territory from French forces in Tunisia, Pariani began, a highly mobile expeditionary force should carry out the attack on Egypt and capture the Suez Canal. In fact, he added, the army had already begun assembling such a force. The navy should ensure that if transporting this army and its supplies were to prove difficult once war had begun, then they should ship it to Libya in peacetime, to which Cavagnari replied that this would indeed be the case and that such a project might ideally be undertaken prior to the outbreak of war. Badoglio, initially cool towards the entire project when Pariani had raised it the previous December, proved so again. 'Before giving a definite reply to this suggestion', he noted, 'I would like accurate studies to be undertaken', and he went on to instruct the naval and air chiefs to assess jointly how the expeditionary force might be supplied. It was important, he noted in conclusion, 'that the various general staffs exercise their intelligence and co-operate closely with one another: a useful exercise even if the ideas which emerge ultimately do not correspond to the realities of war'.

The final item on the agenda that day was how best to organise air and navy co-operation in time of war. Prior to the meeting, Cavagnari, in line with operational contingencies being assessed by the naval staff, which clearly demanded good co-ordination of Italy's air and sea forces, stressed that the Italian fleet required air support in its principal operational theatres, the upper Tyrrhenian, the Adriatic and the Red Sea. At the same time the air force should provide air cover for all of the navy's base facilities. Badoglio, in raising the question, noted that Valle had already assured him that he 'foresaw the intervention of the air force in any naval battle that the navy might one day undertake', adding that once the army had completed its own plans, 'the navy and the air staffs, in a spirit of close collaboration, should examine the question of defending naval bases as well as the contribution the air force might make to naval operations'. Valle concluded that the respective staffs simply needed to reach an agreement on operational procedures, with which Badoglio agreed, before ordering the two chiefs-of-staff to collaborate closely in achieving this goal.[35]

Of primary interest at this meeting is Badoglio's continued opposition to the planning for the land offensive against Egypt, resistance which a year later saw the marshal – on the express orders of Mussolini – forbid any idea of attacking Suez, and give absolute priority to the defence of metropolitan and colonial territories in case of attack, as he had attempted to do in December 1936. Also of note is Badoglio's order to Cavagnari and Valle to collaborate closely in preparing their respective forces for combined operations. The existing evidence gives little indication that this ever took place, and certainly, by the time of Italy's entry into the war, the manner in which air support could be summoned for fleet operations remained chaotic, being governed by bureaucratic procedures that dramatically slowed down the entire process. Moreover, Cavagnari's complaint during the course of the high command meeting that Italy's naval air arm was practically non-existent appears all the more surprising given his own vetoing of aircraft-carrier construction in August 1936. But, in any event, planning for the attack on Suez went ahead in the period that followed, despite Badoglio's clear reservations. The previous April, Mussolini had personally ordered the armed forces to increase their preparations for war against Italy's principal adversary, Britain. The plans produced by Pariani and the army staff during 1938 for an attack on Egypt were designed specifically to realise the *Duce*'s aim of creating a Fascist empire stretching from the Mediterranean to the Indian Ocean.[36]

New Italian Naval Programmes and the Threat of War against Britain and France, January–September 1938

In March 1938, the, for Mussolini inevitable, German–Austrian *Anschluss* finally took place. Hitler's profound gratitude towards the *Duce* after the event, his offer of a military alliance and guarantee of the absolute inviolability of the Brenner frontier during his visit to Rome in May, did much to ensure that the 'close ties of the Axis' had withstood the shock. Thus, although Mussolini pressed London to open talks whose aim should be a *rapprochement* between Britain and Italy that spring, he remained committed to the alliance with Berlin and saw an Anglo-Italian *détente* as no more than a tactical manoeuvre designed to maintain a 'bargaining position' with the West he feared might become diminished after the *Anschluss*. If proof of this commitment were needed, then it came with his public support for German claims against the Sudeten regions of Czechoslovakia, and with his avowal later that year that Italy would fight alongside its German ally.[37]

In the initial months of 1938, naval policy remained governed by the need to strengthen Italy's battle fleet capability through additional long-term building. On 7 January the Italian naval ministry officially announced a major new supplementary building programme for the period 1938–43, planning for which the chief-of-staff had initiated the year before, and which he believed might enable Italy to dominate the central Mediterranean in any war fought alongside Germany and Japan:

> Following meetings held recently at *Palazzo Venezia* between representatives of the ministry of finance, the head of the supreme high command and the under-secretary of state for the navy, the *Duce* has decided that the new programme of naval construction for the *Regia Marina* will amount to two new battleships, twelve destroyers and a notable number of submarines [16].
>
> The two battleships will be named *Roma* and *Impero* and will be laid down at Genoa and Trieste respectively. Construction work on all new vessels will begin immediately.[38]

Almost immediately, the naval plans office warned Cavagnari that, although the second *Littorio* programme met their requirements for improving Italy's 'relative' capital-ship strength in the Mediterranean, as set out in the official report of September 1937, no consideration had

111

been given to their demand for aircraft carriers. Reminding the admiral of their belief that such vessels remained indispensable for the Italian fleet, the planners urged that future naval programmes include at least two ships of this type between 1940 and 1944. Unswayed by their arguments, Cavagnari once again rejected the demands of the navy's planners. In a speech to the Fascist chamber of deputies in mid-March, he affirmed his belief that such ships were of no use to Italy, particularly as they were so vulnerable to modern gunnery and torpedo attack. The latest developments in aircraft technology, and the geographically restricted operational theatres foreseen for the Italian navy, meant that land-based air units provided far more adequate air support than carrier-borne aircraft. Not until July 1941 did Mussolini finally approve the conversion of an old passenger liner – the *Roma* – into an aircraft carrier, after naval staff deliberations had further delayed work approved by the *Duce* the previous January. By the time the project was finally completed, in September 1943, Italy had already signed its armistice with the Western allies and the lack of air cover for the fleet had been brutally exposed.[39]

The naval dimension of the Pariani plan to attack Egypt and the Sudan in early 1939, based on the navy's securing dominion of the central Mediterranean, was a strategy for which the new capital-ship fleet was indispensable. Yet, the existing *Littorio* programme, which had already incurred delays owing to raw-materials shortages throughout 1936 and 1937, suffered still further setbacks during 1938. The naval inspection board now did not expect trials on the vessels in question to begin until well into the following year. In turn, this clearly placed in doubt the ability of Italian naval yards to complete any supplementary programme by 1942, as planned. In short, the navy would certainly not be in any position to dominate the central Mediterranean with a new battleship fleet by the spring of 1939, which in itself gave a hollow ring to any planning by the navy to support the Pariani project.[40]

Indeed, in February 1938, General Alfredo Dall'Olio warned both Mussolini and Cavagnari that they should not initiate any additional naval building unless new supplies of raw materials could be guaranteed. In subordinating the civilian requirements of the Italian nation to its military needs, as Mussolini had already done the year before, the *Duce* should exercise great caution. It would not be wise to deprive the nation as a whole, and therefore upset the 'sensibilities of the masses' inordinately, Dall'Olio concluded. The general suggested that the criteria 'new programmes – new allocation – new availability' should govern armaments policy as a whole.[41]

But, despite Dall'Olio's efforts, the naval staff soon defeated *Cogefag*'s attempts to impose its authority on the building programmes, Mussolini's continued attempts to reassert the authority of the organisation notwithstanding. By May, and following warnings from *Maricost*, the navy's

1. Admiral Domenico Cavagnari, under-secretary of state and chief-of-staff of the Italian navy. Photographed at the Friedrichshaven naval conference, June 1939 (courtesy of the *Ufficio Storico della Marina Militare [USMM]*, Rome).

2. The *Cavour*-class battleship *Conte di Cavour*, originally laid down in 1910 and completely rebuilt between 1933–37. The vessel was sunk by British Swordfish aircraft at Taranto in November 1940 *(USMM).*

3. The *Cavour*-class battleship *Giulio Cesare*, first laid down in 1911 and rebuilt between 1933–37 *(USMM)*.

4. Foreground, the *Conte di Cavour* at her moorings (*USMM*).

5. The 45,000-ton *Littorio*-class battleship *Vittorio Veneto* (*USMM*).

6. The *Littorio*-class battleship *Vittorio Veneto* *(USMM)*.

7. The *Zara*-class heavy cruisers *Pola*, *Zara*, *Gorizia* and *Fiume* at sea, 9 July 1940. Laid down between 1929 and 1931 the ships displaced at between 11,900 and 14,600 tons and carried eight 8" main guns *(USMM)*.

8. The heavy cruisers *Fiume*, *Zara*, *Pola* and *Gorizia* during a training exercise, 1940 *(USMM)*.

9. The heavy cruisers *Fiume* and *Zara* at sea, June 1940 *(USMM)*.

Above: 10. The *Trento*-class heavy cruiser *Trieste* photographed at sea *(USMM)*.

Below: 11. Italian warships at Naples for the Horthy naval review, 26 November 1936 *(USMM)*.

12. Part of Italy's large submarine fleet moored at Naples on the occasion of Admiral Horthy's visit, 26 November 1936 *(USMM)*.

13. Aerial photograph of the Italian fleet at Naples during the 'H' naval review in honour of Hitler, 5 May 1938 *(USMM)*.

14. The naval base at Taranto. Seen here is the first naval squadron moored in the *Mar Piccolo*, November 1938 *(USMM)*.

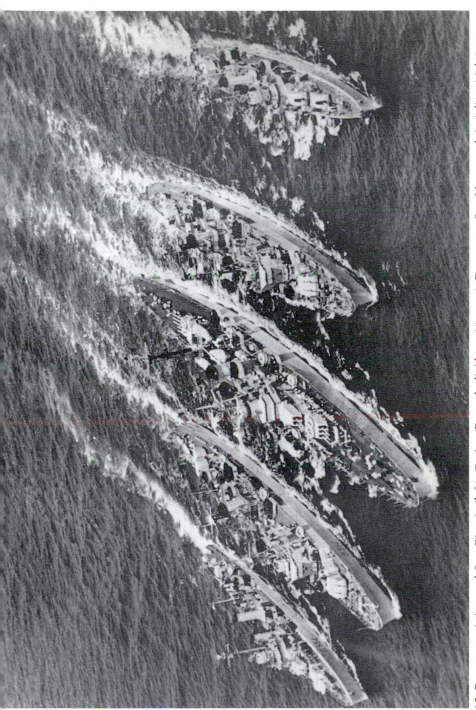

15. Destroyers *Aviere* and *San Giorgio* (left). Cruiser *Duca degli Abruzzi* (centre). Destroyers *San Marco and Artigliere* (right) *(USMM).*

16. *MAS* (special motor torpedo-boat) number 555. The boat was part of the *MAS 555* class armed with one 13mm machine gun, two 17" torpedo tubes and six depth charges. Twenty-one were built between 1940 and 1941, each having a top speed in excess of 41 knots (*USMM*).

shipbuilding division, that shortages of materials were delaying progress on all naval building, Dall'Olio announced that he planned to increase the monthly total of materials destined for new construction work from 7,000 tons to 10,000.[42]

This had evidently not been easy. That July, after he had duly increased the allocations as planned, Dall'Olio informed Mussolini that the navy's programmes had been assigned an extra 31,000 tons of iron in the year to date, bringing the total allocation for the naval ministry to 112,000 tons at a time when *Cogefag* had only received an additional 70,000 tons to replenish its own stocks, which were now seriously depleted. Similarly, the navy demanded increased supplies of copper, nickel and cast-iron, all of which *Cogefag* had conceded, but again without new shipments reaching the commissariat. Despite these endeavours Cavagnari continued to complain that still greater efforts were needed if the Italian building programme were to proceed according to schedule. The additional quantities, he noted, sufficed to keep work going on the *Roma* and *Impero* for the time being, but were not enough to begin building the new ocean-going submarines of the *Cagni* class or the *Capitani Romani* light cruisers, neither of which were laid down until the autumn of 1939. As it transpired, none of the 1938 programme was approaching completion by the time Italy entered the war in June 1940.[43]

By mid-December 1937, Berlin and Rome had concluded an economic agreement guaranteeing mutual support for one another in the event of war against the West. The agreement stipulated that, in 'abnormal times', German and Italian supplies for their respective war efforts be shipped overland, in order to avoid enemy interference with goods in transit at sea. The naval staff, already working under the hypothesis that Italy would conduct its next war alongside Germany and Japan, consequently produced a report, in mid-January 1938, on the manner in which they expected the government to implement this policy once conflict had begun. In time of war, Italy might secure supplies of raw materials from the Scandinavian countries, the nations of central and eastern Europe, Latin America and the United States (bearing in mind the limitations imposed by US neutrality laws). Primarily, Italy should exploit European materials sources as much as possible, while Nationalist Spain might act as a transit point for goods arriving via the Atlantic, given its control over the Straits of Gibraltar, which Madrid could seize from British control. All other routes into the Mediterranean – namely the Suez Canal and the Dardanelles – remained impassable, leaving Italian East Africa dependent on supplies arriving via the Indian Ocean.[44]

The report estimated that the overall annual requirement of the Italian wartime economy was around 20.8 million tons of materials, of which only 12.2 million (58 per cent) could be guaranteed under the above hypothesis. This suggested that the programme of autarky (import substitution), established since the 1920s, should and could reduce the overall import requirement to 17.2 million tons per annum. Stockpiling, therefore, remained the sole means of making up the deficit (3.6 million tons per annum) before the outbreak of war. As regards the Italian possessions in East Africa, these would be isolated from the mainland in wartime and dependent on their own resources. The only way of improving this situation would be through an Italian occupation of Djibouti and, possibly in conjunction with the imperial Japanese navy, naval operations aimed at securing free transit of the Gulf of Aden and the Indian Ocean.[45]

The main problem was that Italo-German political competition in south-eastern Europe had already created friction between Rome and Berlin the year before, a fact which suggested that collaboration in this region, if not in economic affairs in general, might prove anything but fruitful in future. Plainly, Rome had to compete with Germany for key raw materials 'in the closed market of continental Europe', a competition greatly hampered by Italy's economic situation. The campaign for autarky brought few tangible results: by 1939-40, Italy still imported some 80 per cent of its raw materials. The expectation that Spain would support the Italian war effort unequivocally proved optimistic – at the end of the civil war a victorious Franco refused to commit his devastated country to any 'Axis' war effort – while the idea of an alliance with Japan also failed to materialise. Furthermore, once Germany annexed Austria on 12 March, Mussolini's options in Europe were concomitantly reduced, and Italy became 'more dependent on German policy'.[46]

Yet, despite Mussolini's private misgivings at the suddenness of the German action against the Austrian Republic that March, he greeted the long-anticipated *Anschluss* with grudging approval. For him, assent to a German–Austrian union had been the key to Italy's own programme of expansionism. With that event now a reality, the path lay open to pursue the quest for greater Italian hegemony in the Mediterranean. Although he turned down Ribbentrop's offer of a military alliance during the occasion of Hitler's visit to Rome, he privately informed Ciano that eventually he would agree to it, 'because there were a thousand and one reasons why he did not trust the western European democracies'. Concomitantly, so, too, did 'the Italians understand our concern about the fate of the Sudeten Germans', as the German foreign ministry gratefully noted. For the Italian dictator, the Easter Accords concluded with London on 16 April were no more than 'a gesture of little practical significance'. Stresa was now 'dead and buried'. Germany and Italy were 'neighbours', and if the British and French wanted war, Rome and Berlin 'would immediately combine into a bloc and would hold together to the end'.[47]

As relations between Rome and Berlin were further cemented, the naval staff produced two studies – in June and July – which examined

Italian possibilities in any war against Britain and France. As the Paladini report had stressed the previous October, the central Mediterranean assumed vital importance in such a conflict, and indeed the thinking of the navy's planners focused primarily on this theatre. Britain, the first study noted, would deploy its naval forces to the eastern Mediterranean, which meant that maintaining its communications through the Sicilian Channel would be of vital importance in time of war. The Italian navy, in trying to sever British communications between the two Mediterranean theatres, in turn faced having to overcome the problem of Malta, a position which the enemy intended to use to protect its traffic through the Sicilian Channel and to mount offensives against Italy's base at Augusta, the key position in the defence of this theatre. Thus, the need to strengthen Italian defences in this stretch of water became 'indispensable' under this hypothesis for war.[48]

The following month, the naval war plans office produced a general order of naval operations DG 1 (*Direttive Generali*) under its hypothesis *alfa uno* (an Italo-German war against the Western powers), which addressed defence of the central Mediterranean in great detail. The planners identified three principal theatres of war. In the western basin, little success could be expected, and the navy should pursue a defensive strategy only, in order to defend Italy's western coastline and the fleet's principal bases in that region. Meanwhile, in the eastern Mediterranean, the overall objective of Italian strategy was the capture of the Suez Canal, which the navy could undertake only in conjunction with the army. In order to achieve this objective, the enemy should be prevented from winning control of the all-important third operational theatre, the Sicilian Channel. The Italian armed forces could best ensure this by, in the first instance, occupying Albania and the island of Malta, and, in the second, by attacking the enemy within this theatre.

The plans office envisaged two principal operations. The first entailed the navy's creating a system of defence – a '*dispositivo di sbarramento*' – whose aim should be to divide the Mediterranean into two halves, each occupied by the enemy, and subsequently to disrupt communications between them. The defensive system should comprise mobile units (submarines, light surface vessels and aircraft) as well as fixed units (mines, gun emplacements and hydrophone stations), and be established in the regions of water lying between south-west Sardinia, the island of Pantelleria and the Pelagian Islands (Lampedusa, Lampione and Linosa). The navy might also operate similar systems in the region of sea between eastern Sicily and the Albanian coast, as well as in the waters off Libya. Second, *DG 1* recommended that the main battle fleet be kept at the ready to stage decisive naval operations from its bases at Augusta and Tobruk, at the most favourable moment in the war. Furthermore, the *sbarramento* would prove more effective were the navy to stage a guerrilla offensive aimed at 'blockading' other key enemy ports such as Bizerte, Sfax and Sousse in Tunisia. '*Mezzi insidiosi*' – weapons of surprise and rapid exploitation – should be kept at the ready on Pantelleria, and similar operations against other enemy ports and naval units might also be launched from Tobruk and Leros in the Dodecanese. The naval war, the planners concluded, would see the enemy heavily outnumbering the Italo-German coalition. Even so, if this alliance 'took the initiative and initiated an undeclared conflict', then the initial strategic successes might tip the scales in their favour.[49]

At this point, the army staff, too, were planning a 'surprise' operation against French forces in Tunisia, whose objective was to prevent them from attacking Italian lines of communication with North Africa, and units destined for Pariani's Egyptian offensive; an operation Pariani had regarded as best taking place in the spring of 1939. If, however, this date remained the target, then quite clearly none of the Italian armed forces was likely to be ready. The army's plan foresaw combined air and land operations being undertaken, which included the landing of troops by air behind enemy lines, a contingency which by the war ministry's own admission, was still in its infancy. Nor had the air and army staffs discussed the problems of staging such a campaign.[50]

As regards the navy's planning, the absence of any discussion on the issue of air support for the fleet is striking and, along with the naval staff's call for greater army and navy co-operation in carrying out the attacks against Suez and Albania, acted as yet another reminder of the lack of co-ordination between Italy's armed forces. Similarly, although *DG 1* called for fleet operations in the central Mediterranean at the decisive stage of the conflict, the naval ministry did not, of course, foresee the battleship nucleus being complete until 1943. Despite the fact that the Paladini report on defending the central Mediterranean warned of the likelihood of enemy action at night, the naval planners had not addressed this possibility. Nor was there any sign that Italy's alliance with Germany, upon which the entire document's thinking rested, had moved any closer to realisation, Mussolini having rejected closer military ties with Berlin in May. Moreover, the naval plans office also highlighted the importance of staging widespread guerrilla attacks against key enemy naval bases and naval forces, a contingency that had received minimal attention since the end of the Italo-Ethiopian war. Although in 1937 the planners requested that 'good ideas', such as man-guided torpedoes (*maiali*) and other forms of guerrilla warfare, be given more serious consideration, only in late September 1938 did Cavagnari give authorisation for the experiments to resume. The naval leadership appeared not to appreciate the value of this form of warfare until after the outbreak of war; it did not 'fit into *Supermarina*'s Jutland-style operational concept'.[51]

Although Mussolini and Ciano expressed Italy's disinterest in German claims against the Sudeten territories of Czechoslovakia, which Rome regarded as much a 'family affair' as the question of the *Anschluss*, they were nevertheless increasingly eager to discover Berlin's true intentions towards Prague over the summer of 1938.[52] Their reasons for doing so were made quite clear to the Germans. Given the nature of Rome's relations with Germany, any war involving the latter could also include Italy. Therefore, Mussolini regarded it as important that Hitler inform him of his intentions, in order that he 'be able to take in due time the necessary measures on the French frontier'.[53]

Yet, the *Duce* apparently ordered very few military precautions to be taken along the Italian frontier with France. Even by late September, at a moment when 'all states in any way concerned are taking military measures', as Bräuer, the German chargé d'affaires in Paris noted, the 'Franco-Italian frontier remains completely unaffected'. A strange state of affairs, indeed, given Mussolini's firm avowal that 'should France resort to warlike measures against Germany, Mussolini would attack France'.[54]

By late August, Italian enquiries as to how Germany intended to resolve the Czechoslovakian question assumed greater impetus. On 31 August Ernst von Weizsäcker, the state secretary at the foreign ministry, noted that 'the Italian government are now beginning to interest themselves more seriously in the Czechoslovak problem', adding that Attolico, the Italian ambassador, had again spoken of Italy's willingness to strengthen its frontier with France 'in order to exercise a preventative influence', and therefore of its need to know German intentions. On the morning of 2 September, having still received no adequate response from the Germans, Mussolini ordered Ciano to sound out Berlin via Hitler's emissary, Philip of Hesse. Hesse, before leaving Rome to confer with the *Führer*, informed Ciano that he was in possession of 'important facts', but said no more other than that 'no German initiative should be expected before early October'.[55]

That same day, the naval staff – under whose orders it remains unclear – prepared a provisional plan of operations for a 'surprise' war against Britain and France in the Mediterranean, whose ultimate objectives were the capture of the Suez Canal and the occupation of Tunisia. The plan, *DG 1 Op. AG*, aimed to launch a sudden offensive, whose objective was the navy's 'disabling' of enemy positions and forces in order to achieve temporary superiority in the Mediterranean, and secure the two main objectives. Making use only of 'naval units available at the outbreak of hostilities', along with 'guerrilla weapons actually in existence or weapons which might be prepared in just a few days', the plan foresaw a force of torpedo-boats based on Majorca attacking British and French units in Spanish waters at night, while a similar force, or alternatively a solitary submarine, might attack the British battleships *Malaya* in Haifa and *Barham* in Marseilles. The French base at Bizerte should be blockaded by sinking two cargo vessels laden with concrete – the *Enrichetta* and the *Valgiuba* – in the harbour entrance. The navy should undertake a similar operation against Malta using the cargo vessel *Roma*.

DG 1 Op. AG attached special importance to ensuring the success of the attack on the Grand Harbour. If the navy could successfully blockade the British Mediterranean Fleet within its Maltese base, then the main Italian battle squadrons stood a fighting chance against the Home Fleet, which London would inevitably deploy to the Mediterranean, as it had done in 1935. Therefore, once the blockship was in place, the plans office also argued in favour of deploying *MAS* (fast torpedo-boats) to enter the harbour itself, and attack British units within. Although Toulon could not be blockaded, a squadron of Italian torpedo-boats and units of *barchini* – the wooden motor boats loaded with explosives first developed in January 1936 – could attack and sink the French naval forces based there. Submarines were to operate in the waters off Malta and Toulon, while the Sicilian Channel should be blockaded, as already foreseen, with the currently available means. Assuming that the air force had 'received similar orders', it should be instructed not to attack 'centres of population', but the same key naval bases identified as targets by the naval staff. Six days later, after repeated attempts by Mussolini and Ciano to discover whether Hitler planned to attack Czechoslovakia, the war plans office dispatched operational orders in sealed envelopes to *Maricosom*, the submarine command in Rome. On 10 September the navy's high command also secretly issued its directive for an offensive against British and French forces in the Mediterranean to the respective naval departments concerned.[56]

In the meantime, the political climate in Europe assumed crisis proportions. By 10 September, it became clear that both the British and French had mobilised their fleets, and two days later Goering proposed that Mussolini meet Hitler at the Brenner Pass 'no later than 25 September'. On the same day – 12 September – Hitler made a speech at Nuremberg, scene of the annual Nazi rallies, denouncing Czechoslovakia and its president, Edouard Beneš, and 'uttered vague but alarming threats of intervention', a statement that even Mussolini regarded as grave. Nevertheless, the day after, Ciano, in response to an enquiry by Bochko Christic, the Yugoslav minister to Rome, as to what the Italian position was with regard to the Sudeten question, affirmed that Italy intended to support Berlin. 'Although we are not bound to Germany by any military pledges', he stated, 'we had not recently or in the course of this extremely grave development relaxed our ties with Germany in the least, but had publicly given clear proofs of our solidarity with our comrade in the Axis.' By then Cavagnari had already informed all Italian naval commands that the central European crisis could now easily lead to war, and that, 'in accordance with orders he had received', he did not intend to order any major mobilisation of the navy which might be construed by Britain and

France as a precursor to the opening of hostilities. He had, however, ordered preparations to be made for the sudden entry of the Italian navy into a conflict 'in case of emergency'. All naval facilities should therefore remain on full alert.[57]

As it transpired, the world was to wait a further 12 months before war in Europe finally erupted. On 13 September British prime minister Neville Chamberlain informed Hitler that, in view of the current crisis, he proposed to travel to Germany and meet him 'with a view to finding a peaceful solution' to the Sudeten issue. Thus began the first in a series of encounters involving the two men, later joined by Mussolini and French premier Edouard Daladier, which finally resulted in the conclusion of the Munich Agreement. This peacefully dismembered Czechoslovakia and allowed the German-speaking regions to pass under Berlin's control. On learning of Chamberlain's intentions on the evening of 14 September, Mussolini exclaimed, 'There will be no war now', adding that yet again British prestige had taken a serious blow. Even so, Mussolini pledged continued support for Germany in a meeting with Philip of Hesse prior to Munich, informing the *Führer*'s emissary that Italy would enter the war after Britain had declared hostilities. Meanwhile, Pariani told Ciano of his belief that a rapid strike against Suez, making widespread use of poisonous gas, could secure an Italian victory. By 27 September, Mussolini had ordered his chiefs-of-staff to mobilise to ensure Italy's 'armed neutrality' in the event of a war, and instructed Ciano to meet Ribbentrop at Munich and discuss the possibilities for greater Italo-German military co-operation.[58]

Yet, war did not come. Had it done so, and the Italian navy been ordered to war on the basis of directive *DG 1 Op. AG*, then its prospects for success would have been slender indeed. The naval high command viewed an Anglo-French war with alarm: the Italian navy confronted the combined might of the enemy fleets alone, Cavagnari warned Ciano on 26 September. Its only chance for success would come if Japan intervened in the Far East, which in itself brought the threat of an American declaration of war. Moreover, four days earlier an Italian naval intelligence report had already informed the naval staff that two of the main targets for guerrilla operations – Malta and Bizerte – were 'empty'. The British had deployed part of their battle fleet to Gibraltar, while the bulk of it lay at Alexandria, from where *SIS* expected it to attack and occupy the Dodecanese. Only a flotilla of torpedo-boats and three submarines remained at Malta. The French, in the meantime, had assembled their fleet at Toulon, which, the naval planners had noted in September, could not be blockaded. Any idea of blockading and destroying the British Mediterranean Fleet in the port of Valetta, in order to give the Italian battle squadrons a better fighting chance, had therefore evaporated. Italy's two remodernised capital ships, *Cesare* and *Cavour*, faced the entire might of the enemy navies. Nor was

119

there any indication of whether the air staff guaranteed the Italian fleet any measure of air support. Similarly, although Cavagnari issued orders on 27 September for fast convoys to be prepared to carry reinforcements to the Aegean and North Africa, the naval staff had not undertaken to date any serious study on convoying or convoy protection. Only in the aftermath of Munich was the naval war plans office to produce a first study, *DG 10 A2*, which covered support operations for the army's war against Egypt. Likewise, only in the wake of the Czech crisis did the naval staff consider the possibilities of developing further the '*mezzi insidiosi*' called for by their ambitious plan of early September 1938.[59]

Clearly, over 1937 and 1938, Rome's relations with Berlin grew stronger following Mussolini's declaration of the 'Axis' in late 1936. Rome's diplomatic agreements with Britain, in theory aimed at reducing existing tension in the Mediterranean exacerbated by the Italian submarine campaign of mid-1937, proved no more than a façade. Mussolini's real aim was to block any German–British *rapprochement*. Italy, struggling desperately to complete naval-armaments programmes subject to continual delays owing to material and financial deficiencies, needed Berlin's future support if the *Duce*'s Mediterranean and Red Sea ambitions were ever to succeed. London and Berlin were therefore to be kept apart. In turn, British and French joint action in imposing the Nyon and Paris agreements further illustrated to Mussolini the limits of Italian power and his need of an alliance.

Thus, over the summer and autumn months of 1937 the Rome–Berlin alignment sought by Mussolini developed still further, and culminated in his visit to Germany and Hitler's return visit in May of the following year. The effects on Italian naval policy and strategic planning were immediate. In September, as the *Duce* absorbed the military might of Hitler's Reich, the naval high command began to consider the possibilities for an Italo-German and even Japanese naval coalition, which, as Cavagnari argued to Badoglio two months later, might see enough enemy forces drawn off into other theatres, enabling Italy to win control of the eastern Mediterranean and the southern entrances to the Red Sea. In so doing, Italy would secure the free access to the oceans so frequently demanded by Mussolini. In the period which followed, the navy subsequently considered how best to strengthen the central Mediterranean – crucial to the success of the Pariani offensive against Egypt now under serious consideration – secured funds, but not sufficient quantities of materials, for new capital-ship building due for completion in 1943, and developed the first plans for war by June and July of 1938. By then, German revisionism, which first led to the annexation of Austria in March and now threatened war against Czechoslovakia, interrupted Italian long-term naval planning and brought Italy, its dictator trumpeting his support for the *Führer*, almost to the brink of war with the West – a war that would find its incomplete battle squadrons and bases confronting an awesome preponderance of enemy aeronaval power. The political settlement concluded at Munich in September saved the Italian navy from almost certain defeat. In the period that followed, both the navy's leadership and Mussolini were to emphasise, in formalising their alliance with Germany, that Italy could not contemplate a general war for at least three years, at best a highly conservative estimate. In believing Berlin would honour this objective, the dictator proved seriously mistaken.

NOTES

1 For Mussolini's and Ciano's belief that conflict against Britain was inevitable if Italy's 'aspirations' were to be realised and the 'energy' of her population released, see G. Ciano, *Diario: 1937–1943*, ed. R. De Felice (Rizzoli, Milan, 1994), entries for 6/11/1937 and 12/12/1937. On Hitler's reported confirmation that the Mediterranean was an Italian sphere of interest during his May 1938 visit to Rome, see FO 371/22419, 'The Dictators in Rome', Perth to Foreign Office, 16/6/1938. On the Mussolini–Goering encounter, see Weinberg, *Starting World War Two*, pp. 270–4; Ciano, *Diplomatic Papers*, 'Conversation Between the Duce and President Goering', 23/1/1937, pp. 80–91. On the failure of the Anglo-Italian agreement of January 1937, see Weinberg, *Starting World War Two*, p. 275. The view that the 'Axis' merely constituted a 'marriage of convenience' and the Rome–Berlin–Tokyo triangle an 'illusory power-façade' which amounted to no more than a hope that the Western powers would 'refrain from action in a given situation', see Messerschmidt, 'Foreign Policy and Preparation for War', pp. 633–5. For the argument that Italian foreign policy under Ciano remained motivated by a mistrust of Germany and by 'a continuing fear of the German drive to the South-East', see Schreiber, 'Political and Military Developments in the Mediterranean Area', p. 353.
2 *DGFP*, C, VI, 216, 'Political Report', Hassell to foreign ministry, 18/2/1937.
3 On these points, see Waddington, '*Hassgegner*', pp. 32–4. *DGFP*, D, I, 19, 'The Hossbach memorandum', 10/11/1937. The idea that Hitler did not foresee a military alliance with Italy in any war is discussed in Schreiber, *Revisionismus*, p. 115.
4 Sullivan, 'The Italian Armed Forces', p. 180. On internal opposition to the regime's pro-German policy, see Knox, 'Il fascismo e la politica estera italiana', pp. 327–8.
5 See Ciano, *Diplomatic Papers*, 'Conversation between the Duce and President Goering', 23/1/1937, pp. 80-91; USMM, CN, b: 2729, f: 4, Cavagnari to Marinarmi/Maricost, 22/2/1937; Knox, *Mussolini Unleashed*, pp. 20-1. The naval budget allocation for the year 1937–38 amounted to 1,857,891,000 lire. See *APCD*, leg. XXIX, sess. 1934–1937, doc. 1553–79A, 'Previsione della spesa del ministero della Marina', 20/1/1937.
6 Bargoni, *L'impegno navale italiano durante la guerra civile spagnola*, pp. 134–5. As Bargoni notes the orders were given by Mussolini to the naval staff in mid-November 1936 after supplies reaching Spain from Russia had strengthened the Republican armies; on Italo-German naval conversations, see pp. 195-211.
7 USMM, CN, b: 2688, f: 2, Cavagnari to naval staff, 29/10/1936; USMM, DG, 0-N, 'Depositi di nafta esistenti e distribuzione per settore del fabbisogno per 5 mesi di guerra', naval staff, 1/1/1940. The figure of 1.5 million tons contradicts those

offered by Gerhard Schreiber, who claims the figure for the navy to be between 1.7 and 2 million tons. See Schreiber, 'Political and Military Developments in the Mediterranean Area', p. 352.

8 USMM, CN, b: 2688, f: 4, Falangola to Cavagnari, progress reports, 17/4/1937, 28/4/1937 and 4/8/1937.

9 Knox, *Mussolini Unleashed*, pp. 31–3. On the level of friction between the armed services and *Cogefag* over the allocation of materials, see Minniti, 'Le materie prime nella preparazione bellica dell'Italia', p. 9. For examples of Mussolini's attempts to instil order into the anarchic system of raw-materials allocation through creating a descending order of priorities, namely: (1) giving absolute priority to arms production; followed by (2) industries indirectly involved with armaments production; and (3) 'civilian' requirements, see USMM, CN, b: 2724, f: 3, Mussolini to all service ministries, 27/3/1937 and Archivio del Museo Centrale del Risorgimento (MCRR), Rome, carte Dall'Olio, busta: 1122, Mussolini to all service ministries, 31/1/1938. On the *Littorio* class, see Fraccaroli, *Italian Warships of World War II*, p. 19. A fourth vessel of this class – the *Impero* – was never completed, and after the Italian armistice in 1943 became a target ship for the Germans.

10 *DGFP*, C, VI, 247, Hassell to foreign ministry, 5/3/1937. See also Minniti, 'Le materie prime nella preparazione bellica dell'Italia', pp. 25–6. On the Italian–German economic agreement, see *DGFP*, C, VI, 368, 'Secret protocol between the German and Italian governments', 14/5/1937. On the Italian problem with securing its estimated wartime requirement of 8.5 million tons of crude oil per annum, see Schreiber, 'Political and Military Developments in the Mediterranean Area', pp. 25–7. On the question of the limited possibilities offered by the overland rail link between Germany and Italy, see Minniti, 'Le materie prime nella preparazione bellica dell'Italia', p. 28; Weichold, *Axis Naval Policy and Operations in the Mediterranean*, p. 2. For an assessment of Italian state finances, see Knox, *Mussolini Unleashed*, pp. 31–3.

11 Knox, 'Il fascismo e la politica estera italiana', p. 327; USMM, DG, 8-A, Maroni to naval ministry, 3/6/1937.

12 On the German invitation to Mussolini, see *DGFP*, C, VI, 355, memorandum by Neurath, 4/5/1937 and 385, Hassell to foreign ministry, 25/5/1937. On the proposed four-power agreement, see *DGFP*, C, VI, 453, memorandum by Neurath, 7/7/1937, and on the rejection of the idea by Hitler and the German foreign ministry 458, memorandum by Neurath, 12/7/1937 and 461, Neurath to Hassell, 13/7/1937.

13 Details of the first and second submarine offensives ordered by Mussolini, the 'psychological' success of the latter and the risk it brought of war against Britain and France are discussed in detail in Bargoni, *L'impegno navale italiano durante la guerra civile spagnola*, pp. 209 and 280–314. The 'blatant nature' of the attacks and an account of the success of the Italian submarine arm's summer campaign of 1937 can be found in P. Gretton, 'The Nyon Conference: The Naval Aspect', *English Historical Review*, 90, 1 (1975), pp. 104–5. On Cavagnari, see Ciano, *Diario*, 28/8/1937.

14 Gretton, 'The Nyon Conference', pp. 105–7; W. C. Mills, 'The Nyon Conference: Neville Chamberlain, Anthony Eden, and the Appeasement of Italy in 1937', *International History Review*, 15, 1 (1993), pp. 14–15; Ciano, *Diario*, 4/9/1937.

15 On the Paris naval conference of 27–29 September 1937, see Gretton, 'The Nyon Conference', p. 110. The official Italian record of these conversations can be found in USMM, DG, Studi politici, various reports by Wladimiro Pini on the Paris meetings of 27–29/9/1937. For an official account, see Bargoni, *L'impegno navale*

italiano durante la guerra civile spagnola, pp. 324–5. For Mussolini's reaction to Nyon, see Ciano, *Diario*, 14/9/1937, 21/9/1937, 22/9/1937 and 2/10/1937.

16 Ciano, *Diario*, 21/9/1937; Gretton, 'The Nyon Conference', p. 110.

17 On Anglo-French naval co-operation, see Gretton, 'The Nyon Conference', p. 110. For Mussolini's failed attempt to secure Berlin's inclusion in the patrol scheme, see Ciano, *Diario*, 14/9/1937. For the notion that Hitler's view of Britain at this time had become increasingly 'ambivalent' see Messerschmidt, 'Foreign Policy and Preparation for War', p. 637; and Waddington, '*Hassgegner*', pp. 22 and 34. On further Italian naval aid to Spain, see Bargoni, *L'impegno navale italiano durante la guerra civile spagnola*, pp. 330–7.

18 *DGFP*, D, I, 5, Hassell to foreign ministry, 8/10/1937. The view that, although prior to the visit Mussolini 'was by no means willing to endorse all German aspirations', he was, after it, profoundly impressed by Germany and its *Führer* is expressed by Gerhard Weinberg. Weinberg also emphasises that Mussolini had not, contrary to widespread belief in Germany, given Berlin a 'free hand' in Austria, although his policy over the preceding two years made Nazism's presence on the Brenner inevitable. Weinberg, *Starting World War Two*, pp. 279–83. The argument that Mussolini did not accept a formal alliance despite the success of the visit is maintained by Mack Smith, *Mussolini*, p. 250. For the opposite view, that the dictator wished to conclude a working military alliance with Hitler but that this resulted in failure, see Schreiber, *Revisionismus*, p. 109. On the absence of specific agreements, see Weinberg, *Starting World War Two*, pp. 279–80; for Ciano's views, see Ciano, *Diario*, 29/9/1937. On Rome's fear that Neurath's planned visit to London – cancelled in June 1937 as a result of the Leipzig incident – might lead to a formal Anglo-German understanding, see Weinberg, *Starting World War Two*, p. 280; Ciano, *Diplomatic Papers*, 'Conversation with the German Ambassador', 14/6/1937 and 16/6/1937. On the Leipzig affair and the subsequent cancellation of the Neurath trip, see Waddington, '*Hassgegner*', pp. 34–5.

19 For the 'profundity' of Mussolini's experience, see E. Wiskemann, *The Rome-Berlin Axis: A History of the Relations Between Hitler and Mussolini* (Oxford University Press, Oxford, 1949), p. 107. On the impression created on Mussolini, Weinberg, *Starting World War Two*, pp. 281–2. On Mussolini's decision to abandon any notion of '*il peso determinante*', see Lowe and Marzari, *Italian Foreign Policy*, pp. 300–1; Magistrati, *L'Italia a Berlino*, pp. 72–3. For official Italian views of the German alliance, see Ciano, *Diario*, 29/9/1937; Bottai, Diario, 31/10/1937. For German accounts of the Mussolini visit, see *DGFP*, D, I, 1, general memorandum by German foreign ministry, 30/9/1937, 2, Bülow-Schwantz to Neurath, 2/10/1937 and 5, Hassell to foreign ministry, 8/10/1937.

20 USMM, DG, 0-A1, 'Studio circa la preparazione. Argomento I – Le forze navali', naval war plans office to Mussolini, 9/1937; Minniti, 'Il problema degli armamenti nella preparazione militare italiana', pp. 44–5.

21 Schreiber, *Revisionismus*, pp. 103–10; W. Deist, 'The Rearmament of the Wehrmacht', in W. Deist *et al.* (eds), *Germany and the Second World War. Volume I: The Build Up of German Aggression* (Clarendon Press, Oxford, 1990), pp. 472–80.

22 Schreiber, 'Political and Military Developments in the Mediterranean Area', p. 88.

23 Sullivan, 'The Italian Armed Forces', pp. 184–6; on the failure to integrate the *forze armate* into a new tri-service defence ministry, see Knox, 'Conquest Foreign and Domestic', pp. 47–8.

24 On Mussolini and Italy's élites, see Knox, *Mussolini Unleashed*, pp. 8–15 and 47. For the fears of the *Palazzo Chigi* that Hitler planned to resolve the German question either by expansion in the east or by way of 'the old *Drang nach Südosten* in the direction of Constantinople, Baghdad, and the Persian Gulf', a path which

would clash with Rome's Balkan, Mediterranean and Near Eastern interests, see Schreiber, 'Political and Military Developments on the Mediterranean Area', pp. 354–5.

25 On 30 September 1937 an internal report by the foreign ministry's directorate for European and Mediterranean affairs concluded: 'It need hardly be stated that any Italo-British rapprochement can never and will never lead to any weakening of the strong and secure friendship established between Italy and Germany.' See ASMAE, Aff. Pol. Gran Bretagna, b: 19, f: 3, 'Rapporti italo-inglesi', directorate for European and Mediterranean affairs, 30/9/1937. On the Ribbentrop visit and those of Hans Frank, Rudolf Hess and the Prince of Hessen, see Ciano, *Diario*, 21/10/1937, 22/10/1937, 24/10/1937, 27/10/1937, 30/10/1937 and 6/11/1937; *DGFP*, D, I, 10, Hassell to foreign ministry, 20/10/1937; Ciano, *Diplomatic Papers*, various conversations between Mussolini, Ciano and Ribbentrop, 22/10/1937 and 6/11/1937, pp. 139–46; on Mussolini's decision to take Italy out of the League, see *OOBM*, 29, pp. 32–3; Waddington, '*Hassgegner*', pp. 37–8. On Hassell's replacement, see Weinberg, *Starting World War Two*, pp. 285–6. On continued Italian suspicions that Germany still sought a *rapprochement* with both Paris and London, see *DGFP*, D, I, 92, Hassell to German foreign ministry, 31/12/1937.

26 Sullivan, 'The Italian Armed Forces, pp. 176–7; Ciano, *Diario*, 14/2/1938.

27 Gabriele, *Operazione C3: Malta*, pp. 16–20; USMM, CN, b: 2687, f: 4, 'Organizzazione della vigilanza del canale di Sicilia. Esaminata dopo le recenti operazioni speciali', Paladini to naval staff, 10/1937.

28 On these points, see M. Gabriele, 'Le premesse', in USMM, *La battaglia dei convogli, 1940–1943* (USMM, Rome, 1994), p. 105.

29 The lack of torpedo bombers and the reasons for it are discussed in USMM, *L'organizzazione della Marina, tomo I*, pp. 40–52. Once again, the post-war report of Eberhard Weichold offers an interesting insight into this facet of Italian defence planning. 'In June 1940, a beginning was made with the formation of torpedo bomber squadrons. By November the Italians had 13 flights of about 6 planes each, with first-class aircraft, good technical equipment and well-trained crews. These torpedo bombers came under the strategic air arm', and 'had to cover the whole expanse of the Mediterranean'. He continues, 'the main weakness of Italy's conduct of the war at sea lay in the form of her air force organisation. The navy had planned for naval air squadrons and aircraft carriers, but the Italian air force had opposed the navy's plans, and Mussolini, like Hitler in Germany, had backed the air force.' Weichold, *Axis Naval Policy and Operations*, p. 3. On Guarneri, see Ciano, *Diario*, 22/11/1937.

30 USMM, *L'organizzazione della Marina, tomo I*, pp. 180–1.

31 USMM, DG, 8-A, 'Considerazioni sulla nostra situazione militare in Mar Rosso', Bacci di Capaci to naval staff, 12/2/1937. A plans office report of mid-April on the likely strategic effects the building of a new British naval base in the Gulf of Aqaba in the northern Red Sea might have on the balance of sea power in the region concluded: 'The building of a new base at Aqaba in the event of war with Italy would not lead to any significant increase in British operational capability in the Red Sea because Britain can already deploy sufficient naval units via the Canal that would amply guarantee the defence of its interests in that sea, wherein our own naval forces could not be increased to any significant extent in time of war. Port Sudan to the north is, with regard to our own bases in the Red Sea, already in a position to interrupt all our local communications and oppose whatever operation we might launch against the Canal.' USMM, DG, 8-F, 'Appunti circa le considerazioni sul Golfo di Aqabah dal punto di vista strategico', naval war plans office, 9/4/1937. On the strategic importance of Italy's East African bases, see

USMM, *Le operazioni in Africa orientale*, p. 3.

32 USMM, DG, 8-A, 'Primo studio per la redazione del documento di guerra n.8 (D.G.8): Il problema strategico dell'A.O.', naval war plans office, 10/1937.

33 On the navy's efforts to improve bases in East Africa and on the rejection of the Chisimaio project, see USMM, *Le operazioni in Africa orientale*, pp. 4–13. The units requested for use in this theatre were three long-range cruisers, 12 ocean-going submarines, six long-range torpedo-boats, and two tankers destined to support cruiser operations in the Indian Ocean, all to be complete by 1943 and expected to operate against the Royal Navy from the new base at Chisimaio, when built. See USMM, DG, 0-C, 'Necessità di iniziare l'esecuzione del programma navale anno XVII e di accelerarlo in relazione alla importanza della nostra azione in Oceano Indiano', naval war plans office, 1/7/1939. On Italian East Africa, see USMM, *Le operazioni in Africa orientale*, pp. 12–14 and on the first strategic plans, pp. 20–1.

34 On Mussolini's final approval of the new battleship programme, see Ciano, *Diario*, 4/12/1937. For Cavagnari's views, see USMM, DG, 1-B, 'Progetti operativi', Cavagnari to Badoglio, 19/11/1937. On the views of the German military, see Schreiber, *Revisionismus*, pp. 115 and 125; and K. Jürgen-Müller, *The Army, Politics and Society in Germany, 1933–1945* (Manchester University Press, Manchester, 1987), pp. 76–80. For Hitler's views at this time, see his *Hossbach* speech delivered two week before Cavagnari's letter *DGFP*, D, I, 19, the Hossbach conference, 5/11/1937; W. Carr, *Arms, Autarky and Aggression: A Study in German Foreign Policy, 1933–39* (Edward Arnold, London, Melbourne and Auckland, 1993), Ch. 4.

35 A full record of this meeting can be found in USSME, I-4, r: 2, c: 1, 'Riunione presso l'ufficio di S.E. il Capo di Stato Maggiore generale', 2/12/1937.

36 USSME, *Verbali delle riunioni tenute dal Capo di S. M. Generale. Volume I: 26/1/1939–29/12/1940* (USSME, Rome, 1983), 'Verbale della Seduta del 26 gennaio 1939'; Ceva, 'Appunti per una storia dello Stato Maggiore generale', p. 240; Sullivan, 'The Italian Armed Forces', p. 172. On Mussolini's April order, see USMM, DG, 1-B, Cavagnari to Badoglio, 19/11/1937.

37 Weinberg, *Starting World War Two*, p. 295 and on the continuing closeness of the Rome–Berlin relationship during Hitler's May visit, p. 311. On Ribbentrop's offer of a military alliance, see Ciano, *Diario*, 5/5/1938 and DGFP, D, I, 759, Weizsäcker to foreign ministry, 9/5/1938. See also D. C. Watt, 'An Earlier Model for the Pact of Steel. The Draft Treaties Exchanged Between Germany and Italy During Hitler's Visit to Rome in May 1938', *International Affairs*, 33, 2 (1957); 'Hitler's Visit to Rome and the May Weekend Crisis: A Study in Hitler's Response to External Stimuli', *Journal of Contemporary History*, 9, 1,(1974); Schreiber, *Revisionismus*, pp. 127–9, contains a sketch of Hitler's views on Italy after the May visit. The idea that Mussolini saw the 'Nazification' of Austria taking place only after the Spanish Civil War had ended is noted in Ciano, *Diario*, 2/1/1938. On Mussolini's view of Britain, see Knox, 'The Fascist Regime, its Foreign Policy and its Wars', pp. 362–3; Weinberg, *Starting World War Two*, p. 295. Mussolini's public assertion that Italy would fight alongside Germany in the case of war over the Sudeten question is also discussed by W. Murray, 'Munich, 1938: The Military Confrontation', *Journal of Strategic Studies*, 2, 3 (1979), p. 294.

38 USMM, CN, b: 2703, naval ministry, 7/1/1938. A naval plans office memorandum on the new naval programme stressed that the building had been ordered to protect, in the words of Mussolini, 'our rights and interests' in the Mediterranean. Pointing to the naval armaments race now underway among the principal maritime powers, the report then added that the navy's chief future role as established by Mussolini,

would be that of 'maintaining communications with our immense overseas possessions and winning access to the vast ocean outside the encircled Mediterranean'. The *Littorio* class would play an integral part in the policy, constituting as they did the 'spinal cord' of the Italian fleet. See USMM, DG, Unnumbered file, 'Bilancio della Marina alla camera – esercizio 1938–1939', naval war plans office, undated. The naval estimate for the fiscal year 1938–39 totalled 2,013,000,000 lire. The breakdown of the budget and the naval ministry's official statement on new ship building can be found in *APCD*, leg. XXIX, sess. 1934–1938, doc. 2115A–27, 'Stato di previsione della spesa del ministero della Marina', 24/1/1938.

39 USMM, DG, 0-A1, 'Studio circa la preparazione. Argomento 1 – Le forze navali: aggiornamento dello studio in data settembre 1937', naval war plans office to Cavagnari, 1/1938. Santoni, 'La mancata risposta della Regia Marina alle teorie del Douhet', pp. 262–4. Santoni adds that other members of the naval staff, such as Luigi Sansonetti and Angelo Iachino, also believed that aircraft carriers were of little use to Italy, given its 'particular strategic situation', views which in turn led the political leadership to air its frequently quoted conclusion that 'Italy was an aircraft carrier'. As evidence suggests, certain elements within the naval staff, indeed within the plans office itself, remained convinced that this was not the case. Santoni's view that there were no divisions within the navy over this matter therefore appears questionable. On the conversion of the *Roma*, see pp. 264–7; Sullivan, 'Introduction', in R. Bernotti, *Fundamentals of Naval Tactics*, p. 49; Fraccaroli, *Italian Warships of World War II*, p. 23.

40 In October 1937 the Italian naval inspectorate foresaw trials for the *Vittorio Veneto* and the *Littorio* beginning in February and April 1939, respectively. By late December, the trial period for the former had been put back to June 1939. USMM, CN, b: 2688, f: 4, Falangola to Cavagnari, 6/10/1937 and 29/12/1937. On 26 January 1938 Falangola informed the naval staff that delays in allocating raw materials on the part of *Cogefag* had further put back work on the building of destroyers and torpedo-boats by up to six months, adding on 16 February that trials on the *Littorio* class would now begin in February and December 1939. USMM, CN, b:2695, Falangola to Cavagnari, 26/1/1938 and 16/2/1938. For the deficiencies facing the army and its possible effects on any rapid war in Africa, see L. Ceva, 'Un intervento di Badoglio e il mancato rinnovamento delle artiglierie italiane', *Il Risorgimento*, 28, 2 (1976), pp. 118 and 145–6.

41 Dall'Olio's letter had been in reply to a complaint from Cavagnari on 19 February that, although new supplies of materials for the 1938 programme had been approved at the same time as the programme itself, the respective shipyards were still waiting for the first batch of deliveries, scheduled for early January 1938, to arrive. See MCRR, carte Dall'Olio, b: 1122, 'Programma di costruzioni navali 1938', Cavagnari to Dall'Olio, 19/2/1938, Dall'Olio to Cavagnari, 21/2/1938, and Dall'Olio to Mussolini, 28/2/1938.

42 MCRR, carte Dall'Olio, b: 1122, 'Distribuzione di materie prime', Mussolini to all service ministries, 31/1/1938. On *Maricost*'s warning that deliveries of raw materials had not met the agreed quotas and were delaying naval building, see USMM, CN, b: 2724, f: 4, Maricost to naval ministry, 18/3/1938, and on Dall'Olio's announcement that the navy's monthly allocation would be increased, Dall'Olio to Cavagnari, 21/5/1938. For the navy's success in defeating *Cogefag* attempts to supervise shipbuilding activities, see Sullivan, 'The Italian Armed Forces', p. 173. In reality, the total amount of materials (iron, cast-iron, nickel, copper, tin and steel) allocated to the naval ministry's programmes over that summer exceeded the 10,000-ton limit imposed by Dall'Olio, as the following figures illustrate:

	original allocation	additional allocation	new total
May	7,000	3,000	10,000
June	10,000	2,000	12,000
July	10,000	1,000	11,000
August	10,000	1,000	11,000

Note: Figures in tons
Source: USMM, CN, b: 2724, f: 4, Cavagnari to Dall'Olio, 26/8/1938.

Further details of Italian raw-materials importations are to be found in Minniti, 'Le materie prime nella preparazione bellica dell'Italia', pp. 38–9.

43 MCRR, carte Dall'Olio, b:1122, 'Pro-memoria per S.E. il Capo del Governo', 8/8/1937. Interestingly, Dall'Olio noted that the navy and army had both been allocated identical quantities of iron per month. Between January and July 1938 out of 10,000 tons available monthly both received 3,000, the remaining 4,000 tons going to 'public works'. MCRR, carte Dall'Olio, b:1122, 'Materiale siderurgico per le costruzioni navali', Cavagnari to Dall'Olio, 1/9/1938; Fraccaroli, *Italian Warships of World War II*, pp. 37–40 and 121.

44 Ciano, *Diario*, 18/12/1937; Weinberg, *Starting World War Two*, pp. 284–5.

45 USMM, DG, 10, 'Rifornimento della Nazione nell'ipotesi di conflitto Italia-Germania-Giappone contro Inghilterra-Francia-Russia', naval staff, 18/1/1938. On Italian attempts to introduce import substitution, see Mack Smith, *Mussolini*, p. 220; Schreiber, 'Political and Military Developments in the Mediterranean Area', pp. 25–39.

46 The likelihood that German–Italian competition in south-eastern Europe would follow the 'vigorous Italian activity' in the Danube basin had already been raised by Hassell in March 1937. See *DGFP*, C, VI, 274, 'Political Report', Hassell to foreign ministry, 15/3/1937 and 312, 'Political Report', Hassell to foreign ministry, 12/4/1937; Schreiber, 'Political and Military Developments in the Mediterranean Area', pp. 354–5. On Italian–German competition in European markets, see Knox, *Mussolini Unleashed*, p. 31. On Spain, see P. Preston, *Franco* (HarperCollins, London, 1993), pp. 332–5, and on Japan and 'Axis' policy, see S. Hatano and S. Asada, 'The Japanese Decision to Move South, 1939–1941', in R. Boyce and E. M. Robertson (eds), *Paths to War*, pp. 383–403. For the view that Mussolini remained diametrically opposed to the *Anschluss* and attempted to use the question of safeguarding Austrian independence as the mechanism for finally concluding his long-sought-after agreement with Britain, see De Felice, *Lo stato totalitario*, pp. 466–7, see Quartararo, *Roma tra Londra e Berlin*, pp. 271–4.

47 *DGFP*, D, I, 399, 'Political Report', Plessen to foreign ministry, 25/3/1938 and on internal disquiet within Italy, see 129, Plessen to foreign ministry, 25/2/1938. On Mussolini's satisfaction at Hitler's guarantee of the Brenner on 11 March, see Ciano, *Diario*, 12/3/1938. For the view that Mussolini held private misgivings, yet 'publicly approved the long-dreaded *Anschluss* in March 1938', see Knox, 'The Fascist Regime, its Foreign Policy and its Wars', p. 354; *OOBM*, 29, pp. 67–71. On Mussolini's determination to conclude an alliance with Germany, see Ciano, *Diario*, 5/5/1938. Hitler's thinking during the so-called 'May crisis' of 1938 and his decision to annex Czechoslovakia and face the possibility of war with both Britain and France at the end of that month is discussed by Watt, 'Hitler's Visit to Rome', pp. 29–32; G. Weinberg, 'The May Crisis, 1938', *Journal of Modern History*, 29, 3 (1957); W. V. Wallace, 'The Making of the May Crisis', *The Slavonic and East European Review*, 41, 97 (1963); for Hitler's decision to 'smash Czechoslovakia by military action', see *DGFP*, D, II, 221, 'Directive for Operation

"Green"', 30/5/1938. On the Italian agreement with London, see Weinberg, *Starting World War Two*, p. 304; *DGFP*, D, I, 737, Mackensen to foreign ministry, 15/4/1938; 738, Minute by Weizsäcker, 16/4/1938; 739, Mackensen to foreign ministry, 17/4/1938 and especially 755, 'The Italo-British Agreement of April 16, 1938', unsigned memorandum, 27/4/1938. For Mussolini's notion of an Italian–German bloc, see *DGFP*, D, I, 764, 'Political Report', Mackensen to foreign ministry, 17/5/1938.

48 USMM, DG, 10, 'Il canale di Sicilia. Studio indicativo per la realizzazione e l'esercizio del dispositivo di sbarramento', naval war plans office, June 1938. See also Gabriele, 'Le premesse', p. 106.

49 USMM, DG, 1, 'Direttive generali per ogni ipotesi di guerra: classe alfa: ipotesi alfa uno', naval war plans office, 1/7/1938. The order also made provision for a supreme naval command, *Supermarina*. For details, see USMM, *La Marina italiana nella seconda guerra mondiale. XXI: L'organizzazione della Marina durante il conflitto – tomo II, evoluzione organica dal 10/6/1940 all'8/9/1943* (USMM, Rome, 1975), p. 7. Although *DG 1* made no specific mention of the navy's plans for the Red Sea, which were only considered by the Italian East African naval command in mid-1939, a report by *SIS* on 15 July did stress that western anchorage at Aden was poorly defended and thus vulnerable to attack by Italian naval units. See USMM, DG, 8-F, 'Monografia militare di Aden', SIS to naval war plans office, 15/7/1938. The idea of occupying Albania had already been discussed by Mussolini and Ciano on 10 May. See Ciano, *Diario*, 10/5/1938.

50 USSME, N: 11, c: 4030, 'Problema operativo dell'Africa settentrionale. Memoria sulla possibilità e convenienza di una offensiva aereo-terrestre in Tunisia', army war plans office, 6/1938. The army's plan anticipated the navy playing a largely logistical role in the war, namely that of transporting the expeditionary force to Libya. Offensive operations would be undertaken by the *Esercito* and the air force, whose ultimate objective was to win 'time and space' for the operations against Egypt and the Sudan. The air force should first seek to secure control of the air over Tunisia, and then land a force of between 18,000 and 20,000 troops in the region around Gabès on the Tunisian coast. A similar operation should be staged further north against the territory between Sfax and Sousse, while simultaneously a land offensive might be launched against Tunisia from Libya.

51 USMM, *I mezzi d'assalto*, pp. 20–1. Gerhard Schreiber argues that the German naval high command were not overly eager to develop too binding a relationship with their Italian counterparts during the summer of 1938. This was particularly the case after the visit of Canaris to Italy in early September, after which he spoke scathingly of the Italians, and doubted that the Italian military desired a 'parallel war' at all. See Schreiber, *Revisionismus*, pp. 138–9. The evidence from the Italian naval archive suggests that Raeder had proposed an exchange of German and Italian naval officers and technical experts while accompanying Hitler to Italy in May. Cavagnari had approved of the idea and the respective visits took place in August and September 1938. See USMM, CN, b: 2712, f: 4, Cavagnari to Raeder, 28/5/1938 and Raeder to Cavagnari, 3/6/1938. On the visits, see USMM, CN, b: 2712, f: 4, Lange to Olivia, 8/8/1938 and Pecori Giraldi to naval ministry, 9/9/1938.

52 On these points, see Ciano, *Diario*, 16/5/1938, 19/5/1938, 26/5/1938, 27/5/1938, 28/5/1938; *DGFP*, D, II, 193, 'Memorandum by the foreign minister', 23/5/1938, 211, Mackensen to foreign ministry, 26/5/1938, 220, Mackensen to foreign ministry, 29/5/1938.

53 *DGFP*, D, II, 401, 'Memorandum by the foreign minister', 27/8/1938. See also 384, 'Memorandum by the foreign minister', 23/8/1938.

54 *DGFP*, D, II, 647 Bräuer to foreign ministry, 27/9/1938 and 494, Mackensen to

foreign ministry, 15/9/1938. On Mussolini and France, see *DGFP*, D, II, 334, 'Memorandum by foreign minister', 4/8/1938; W. Murray, *The Change in the European Balance of Power, 1938–1939: The Path to Ruin* (Princeton University Press, Princeton, NJ, 1984), pp. 210–12 and 241–3.

55 *DGFP*, D, II, 414, minute by Weizsäcker for the foreign minister, 31/8/1938; Ciano, *Diario*, 2/9/1938.

56 USMM, DG, 1-A, 'DG 1 Op. AG. Studio preliminare per operazioni contro Francia-Inghilterra', naval war plans office, 2/9/1938. On further attempts by Ciano and Mussolini to discover Hitler's intentions, see Ciano, *Diario*, 3/9/1938, 5/9/1938, 6/9/1938 and 7/9/1938; and on the *Führer*'s indecision *DGFP*, D, II, 415, 'Memorandum Transmitted by Prince Philip of Hesse to the Duce', 9/1938. The order of operations was dispatched to the submarine command on 8 September. See USMM, DG, 1-A, 'Ordine generale di operazione n. 7', naval war plans office to submarine command, 8/9/1938; USMM, DG, 1-A, operational directive issued by Cavagnari, 10/9/1938.

57 On the mobilisation of the British and French navies, see *DGFP*, D, II, 444, Bräuer to foreign ministry, 9/9/1938 and 451, Kordt to German foreign ministry/naval high command, 10/9/1938. On Goering's proposal to Magistrati that Hitler meet Mussolini at the Brenner, see Ciano, *Diario*, 12/9/1938. Ciano, *Diplomatic Papers*, 'Conversation with the Yugoslav Minister', 13/9/1938, pp. 232–3. USMM, DG, 1-D, Cavagnari to all naval departments, 12/9/1938.

58 For the communication from Chamberlain to Hitler, see *DGFP*, D, II, 469, foreign ministry minute, 13/9/1938. On Munich, see Ciano, *Diario*, 29–30/9/1938, and for Mussolini's view of Britain, 14/9/1938. For discussion of Munich, see Parker, *Chamberlain and Appeasement*, Ch. 8; J. W. Wheeler-Bennett, *Munich Prologue to Tragedy* (Macmillan, London, 1966), Ch. 4; D. C. Watt, *How War Came: The Immediate Origins of the Second World War, 1938–1939* (Mandarin, London, 1990), pp. 28–9. On Mussolini's meeting with Philip of Hesse and on Pariani's confidence that Italy could win a war undertaken rapidly, see Ciano, *Diario*, 25/9/1938, and on Mussolini's strategic directives, 27/9/1938.

59 The idea that the 'Axis' was 'neither politically nor militarily prepared' to go to war over Czechoslovakia, and that Italy would in any case swiftly become a 'liability' is discussed by Murray, 'Munich 1938: The Military Confrontation', p. 295. For the views of Cavagnari and the war plans office, see Ciano, *Diario*, 26/9/1938. On Allied strategic deployments, see USMM, DG, 1-A, 'Situazione delle forze', naval staff, 22/9/1938; USMM, DG, unnumbered file, 'Riassunto delle disposizioni prese in assetto precauzionale dalle marine interessate nella crisi europea', report by *SIS*, 9-10/38. The question of Italian naval intelligence gathering is discussed by M. Knox, 'Fascist Italy Assesses its Enemies', in E. May (ed.), *Knowing One's Enemies: Intelligence Assessment Before the Two World Wars* (Princeton University Press, Princeton, NJ, 1984). On convoying and guerrilla warfare, see Gabiele, *Operazione C3: Malta*, pp. 17–21; USSM, *I mezzi d'assalto*, pp. 21–2.

4

Peace and War

The European crisis of September 1938 had illustrated all too clearly the true extent of Italian military weakness. Therefore, for Mussolini, the alliance with Berlin assumed still greater importance in the period that followed the Munich settlement. However, the *Duce*, although a firm advocate of a military agreement with the Germans for a war against the West he regarded as 'inevitable', faced continuing difficulties in making this alliance domestically popular. Solutions such as the crude anti-Semitic legislation of 1938 and his attempted 'Prussianisation' of the Italian military by ordering them to assume the German marching style (the *Passo Romano*), had largely negative effects. More successful was Mussolini's attempt, in late 1938, to conduct an anti-French campaign within Italy and to plan for an Italo-French war that, if backed by Germany, might render the 'Axis' more popular internally. Subsequently, the dictator agreed with Ribbentrop, during the German foreign minister's visit to Rome in late October 1938, that a military pact between Germany and Italy should be drawn up, the break with Britain and France now having become 'irreparable', although the idea of such an alliance should first be left to 'mature for the necessary period among the great mass of the people'. Thus, Mussolini gave the alliance a certain air of 'necessity', if not legitimacy, and even King Victor Emanuel, avowedly anti-German, cautiously agreed in early 1939 that a military agreement with Germany might prove useful in any future Italo-French war. In the meantime, Mussolini eagerly anticipated the ratification of the Anglo-Italian Easter Accords as a means of putting pressure on Paris.[1]

With Mussolini's temporary shelving of the idea of war against Britain by the end of 1938, the various service departments put aside the initial plans they had prepared for an assault on Suez. Nevertheless, the dictator's geopolitical vision had not altered. In a much-quoted speech delivered to the Fascist grand council in February 1939, he yet again emphasised the realities, as he saw them, facing Italy in the Mediterranean, where it remained 'imprisoned'. Once more he repeated his belief that 'Italian policy can only have one watchword – to march to the ocean', the Indian Ocean. Italy merely needed time to prepare. Thereafter, the naval staff in Rome approved initial plans developed by the navy's East African command for a conflict in the Red Sea against first France and later Britain, too. Moreover, the Italian occupation of Albania in April, which the naval planners had regarded as essential in securing Italian domination of the central Mediterranean in any attack on Suez, clearly constituted a further demonstration of Mussolini's 'fixity of purpose'.[2]

The dictator concluded the Pact of Steel with Germany in May, with the stipulation that Italy would not be ready for war against London and Paris before at least 1942; and on this basis, the respective military and naval staffs entered conversations with their German counterparts. Only afterwards did Mussolini realise that the *Führer* had his own agenda, and that any notion of Germany 'covering Italy's shoulders on the continent' as it fought its enemies in the Mediterranean had been rendered absurd. The consequence was that Italy found itself facing a European conflict that autumn militarily unready and effectively without a general war plan.[3]

Discussion of the continuing evolution of Mussolini's 'Axis' policy and its effect on Italian war planning forms the basis for this chapter. Naval strategic thinking in the aftermath of Munich did not foresee any outbreak of hostilities with Britain and France until at least 1942, ideas formalised by both the Pact of Steel and the Italo-German naval staff talks held at Friedrichshafen in June 1939. Subsequently, the Italian naval high command pursued a broad policy aimed at preparing the fleet and its facilities for a 'parallel' Mediterranean and Red Sea conflict alongside Germany, which they regarded as at least three years away. With the premature outbreak of hostilities a mere four months after the conclusion of the formal alliance between Rome and Berlin, the navy found itself far from ready to enter the general European war into which, despite Italian military and material debility, Mussolini appeared eager to plunge Italy. On the eve of the Second World War, the war plans office prepared a largely defensive plan of naval operations designed simply to protect the central Mediterranean, and declared itself unwilling to support any land offensive in North Africa. In the face of opposition from King Victor Emanuel and Ciano, Mussolini finally declared that Italy would remain a non-belligerent in the forthcoming conflict.

A Military Alliance with Berlin, October 1938–April 1939

Mussolini's role at the Munich conference had greatly increased his prestige. His 'mediation' over the question of the Sudeten minorities had safeguarded European peace. But, with Germany now installed both in Austria and in part of the former Czech Republic, the balance of power on the European continent had changed. Of this fact Mussolini and Ciano became swiftly aware after Ribbentrop's refusal to agree to Ciano's suggestion that a conference of the Munich powers might settle Hungarian claims against part of the former Czechoslovakia. Despite the Italian foreign minister's complaints that his German counterpart was both 'conceited' and an 'intellectual light-weight' who 'always tried to impose his own point of view', he and Mussolini could do little to prevent Berlin's siding with the Czechs. Rome, which had backed Budapest in the affair, eventually backed down.[4]

But, then, Mussolini had anticipated the rise of German power since at least the 1920s, and for him acquiescing in German hegemony on the European mainland constituted a means to an end – that of Italian expansion in the Balkans and Mediterranean. Therefore, he could overlook such 'humiliations', for Italy had the men and Germany the means to bring this war to a successful conclusion. By the end of the year, the two countries had duly taken the first tentative steps towards improving German–Italian military relations, paving the way for the full staff conversations of 1939.[5]

On 28 October, the same day that Mussolini and Ribbentrop met to discuss the need for a future military alliance between the 'Axis' powers, the naval war plans office prepared a lengthy report on how best to prepare the navy for war alongside its German ally. As regards overall naval strategy, little had changed. Beginning with the familiar geopolitical premise that Italy remained imprisoned within the Mediterranean, the report then stressed that aeronaval operations against the Mediterranean exits – Gibraltar, Suez, the Dardanelles – remained either impossible, as in the case of Gibraltar, or at least very limited in their likely effectiveness. Similarly, Italian air attacks against key enemy bases in Egypt, Syria and on Cyprus also had very limited possibilities for success. Germany and Italy intended to conduct their war in separate operational spheres – the former in the Atlantic Ocean and North Sea, the latter in the Mediterranean and Red Sea, where, in view of the above strategic facts, it would remain cut off from the oceans. This meant that the conflict had primarily to be fought out 'on the battlefield', while the navy principally concentrated on defending the central Mediterranean, attacking enemy communications, preventing the link up between enemy fleets, and, in conjunction with the army and air force, ensuring the capture of the Suez Canal.

Like operational directive *DG 1* of July 1938, the naval staff's latest strategic assessment called for the occupation of Malta and Albania at the outbreak of war, but also recommended the capture of part of the Dalmatian archipelago, Aden, and Djibouti along with the Seychelles – in order to give the Italian navy 'an advanced base' in the Indian Ocean. Finally, the planners again recommended that the battle fleet be kept at the ready to enter the conflict at the most opportune moment. Once again, they urged that guerrilla weapons be used extensively even before an actual declaration of hostilities. Repeating the conclusions reached on 1 July, the naval staff stressed once more that a highly disadvantageous strategic position faced the Italo-German alliance, and a lengthy period of preparation therefore remained an essential prerequisite for any chance of success. Only once they had fully completed this preparation, might Italy and Germany attack first in order to guarantee the element of surprise.[6]

The importance of Malta to Italy's overall grand strategy assumed even greater significance following the completion of the plans office report. On 8 December a meeting of the naval high command discussed the island's significance to the operation. Initially Campioni, Pini's replacement as deputy chief-of-staff, expressed his opposition to any capture of Malta. It would consume too many naval units, he argued, and result in 'a naval battle involving our major naval forces, forces which it remains in our interest to keep intact in order to guarantee protection for the convoys carrying the expeditionary force'. On the whole, the gathering unanimously disagreed with this view, believing the island held the key to the success of the entire Italian North African offensive. Malta, although unlikely to house the main British fleet at the outbreak of war, remained a threat. If the Italian air force failed to neutralise this threat before its own capability became reduced, then the British would inevitably redeploy there and Italy could no longer supply the operation against Egypt. The meeting concluded that both Malta and Aden should at all costs be eliminated as enemy bases of operations in order to isolate enemy naval forces in the eastern Mediterranean. Only then could supply lines with Libya be guaranteed. Once the Italian armed forces had neutralised Malta, the British, although able to make use of bases in Greece and Turkey, would not be able to attack convoys bound for North Africa with anything approaching the same level of regularity and effectiveness. Therefore, the meeting concluded that plans for the taking of the island should be developed immediately.[7]

Later that month, the naval planners finally produced their study on the supplying of the army's operations against Egypt. In the opinion of the navy's high command, any increase in enemy naval forces based on Malta and at Bizerte endangered the execution of the offensive against Suez. There were two possible solutions to this problem. The first the planners regarded as 'temporary', and involved placing both positions under constant air bombardment, blockading Malta, and reinforcing the defences in the Sicilian Channel to the maximum level possible. The second, 'definitive' solution was simply to occupy Malta – a contingency that the naval staff now believed had become 'an indispensable premise for the success of any major operations in North Africa'. The main Italian battle squadrons, as the naval leadership had already clearly established, were to engage the enemy only at the appropriate moment in the conflict. If thereby kept intact, they might continue to represent 'a real danger for the enemy' until the successful completion of the land offensive. However, only in 1942 would the navy's situation with regard to this particular dimension of the plan be satisfactory with the projected entry into service of the new *Littorio* vessels. In view of marked Italian naval inferiority and in the absence of air units able to offer protection to convoys, the navy intended to move as much material to Libya in peacetime as possible, thus limiting the chances of losing costly and irreplaceable naval units in wartime convoy defence. Finally, the planners concluded, the outcome of any Anglo-Italian war in the Middle East also depended on a swift occupation of Aden. Once more, they emphasised that the success of the strategy depended on thorough preparation and on total surprise to the enemy.[8]

However, the Italian armed forces developed no plan to capture Malta as a result of the naval staff's meticulous planning. Only in the spring of 1940 did the possibility of taking the island again become part of the navy's strategic conceptions, although, even by the eve of war, Italian planners had still not translated the idea into a concrete plan of operations. Although Mussolini did order the Italian armed forces to carry out an occupation of Albania in April 1939 in order to create a 'mighty "bulwark"' to dominate the Balkans, his attempt to capture Greece from the Italian colony in 1940 resulted in disaster and prompted German intervention in the theatre. In the aftermath of the invasion, the Italian army suffered setbacks at the hands of the Greeks, while the navy's efforts to support the Albanian offensive by attacking enemy convoys bound for Greece led to the defeat at Matapan in March 1941.[9]

Likewise, post-Munich Italian naval staff planning placed great emphasis on the importance of the German navy engaging substantial enemy forces in its theatres of operations, the Atlantic and North Sea. However, this fiercely dogmatic belief that the 'Axis' fleets should operate in independent spheres prevented closer co-operation between the two high commands, and led to a lack of agreement on joint strategic objectives, even when the two staffs finally met in June 1939. Moreover, it hardly need be repeated that the level of interservice co-operation within Italy had been negligible. The army staff, for instance, simply provided their naval counterparts with the numbers of troops and quantities of equipment that needed to be shipped, and no attempt had been made to co-ordinate the respective efforts into a coherent plan. Nor had there been any discussion on the question of providing air support for naval units making the hazardous crossing from the mainland to Tobruk in time of war. In any case, by early 1939, Mussolini, to Badoglio's great relief, shelved any idea of attacking Egypt and taking Suez. The *Duce* preferred to concentrate on improving relations with Berlin in the hope that German support for an Italian war against France might prove forthcoming.[10]

During the last months of 1938, Mussolini turned temporarily away from the idea of a Mediterranean war against Britain. Although the 'Axis' remained 'fundamental' to Italian policy, he told Ciano, he had been pleased at the British decision to ratify the April accords, and even declared himself ready to co-operate with London in Mediterranean affairs 'for as long as it remained possible to do so'. But, with France, no such arrangement could be possible, for 'against her are directed all our claims'. Yet, although the Chamberlain administration appeared eager to improve relations with Rome, seeing in the Italian dictator the means of securing a deal with Berlin – the prime minister himself even offered to meet Mussolini in Rome – the *Duce* appeared less than enthusiastic at the prospect. Only when Ciano made him aware of the 'political value' of such a visit did he grudgingly agree to it.[11]

Italian policy had already become firmly aligned with that of Berlin. France and Britain, wrote Ciano on 17 November 1938, 'represented the crystallisation and defence of political and social systems which Fascism and Nazism rejected and were ultimately determined to sweep away'. Thus, Mussolini once more stated his intent to annex Albania, and ordered Ciano to 'synchronise' Italian colonial demands with those of Berlin: Italy must win control of Tunisia and Corsica and secure a controlling interest in the Suez Canal. Subsequently, by early 1939, the Chamberlain visit aroused little more than indifference as Mussolini and Ciano moved Italy ever closer towards a military alliance with Berlin, and planned for possible future aggression against France.[12]

While Mussolini was finally approving Ribbentrop's proposal for a military alliance, a delegation from the Italian naval staff had already visited Berlin at the invitation of the German navy's high command. The discussions, which dealt initially with the German rejection of Britain's request that an upper limit of 45,000 tons be imposed on future capital-ship building, very quickly turned to the question of political relations between the 'Axis' navies. It seemed absurd, noted Admiral Otto Schniewind, the chief-of-staff, echoing an earlier pronouncement by Admiral Erich Raeder, that although the *Kriegsmarine* 'remained obliged to exchange naval information with Britain, the navies of the "Axis" powers exchanged no such information'. Therefore, would it not be a good idea to offer Italy the same information as was currently being forwarded to London, in order to 'fill the gaps' which currently existed in relations between the two naval staffs? Moreover, Schniewind believed it important to strengthen this relationship even further, and for this reason had already written to Rome requesting that exchanges of both operational and technical ideas take place between the two naval commands in future. Mussolini, having already approved the signing of a military alliance with the Reich on 2 January, readily assented to the German proposal.[13]

The naval war plans office in Rome subsequently expressed its views on the needs of the Italian navy under hypothesis *alfa uno* – the criterion governing the navy's strategic planning. The 50 per cent global formula first elaborated in July 1937 should remain the ultimate goal of the German and Italian navies, the memorandum began. Under programmes currently in progress and due for completion in 1941–42, the 'Axis' powers might expect to reach a combined fleet strength 41 per cent of that of Anglo-French naval forces. In considering how best to achieve the 50 per cent figure, future Italian naval policy needed to take account of the fact that Germany, despite having spare industrial capacity, did not intend for 'political and financial' reasons to build above the 35 per cent limit agreed with Britain in 1935. As a direct consequence, it would be left to Italy to bring 'Axis' naval power up to the global limit recommended by the naval planners. In concrete terms, this suggested that the naval ministry needed to consider building 216,000 tons of naval units in addition to those at present being built. In short, the government should immediately make available some 7,000 million lire to build two battleships, two aircraft carriers, six heavy cruisers, 20 destroyers, 20 torpedo-boats and 16 ocean-going submarines over a seven-year programme, destined for completion at the end of 1945. Once complete, Italy's 'relative strength' in the Mediterranean with regard to Britain would reach the 'acceptable' ratio of 7:10. Delaying the start date of the programme, the planners concluded, meant delaying the point at which the 'Axis' fleets reached the 50 per cent figure, and they recommended that building begin as soon as possible.

Unlike its even more ambitious predecessor, the *'flotta d'evasione'* proposal of January 1936, the *'programma settennale'* did not foresee the Italian fleet breaking out of the Mediterranean and operating in the Atlantic, where it was expected that only submarines would be deployed to attack enemy traffic alongside German U-boats. It did, however, see the need to develop an ocean-going capability in order to wage war in the Indian Ocean. If the Italian fleet could dominate the Mediterranean and Red Sea, the report continued, then Britain might only be able to supply forces defending the Suez Canal overland, after shipping supplies in via the Indian Ocean and through Iraq and Palestine. In order to place these lines of communication under attack, the navy should build the proposed base at Chisimaio, and authorise a second naval programme that included three heavy cruisers, 24 submarines and 12 destroyers, to be ready by 1942.[14]

Yet, partly as a result of Mussolini's anti-French campaign of late 1938 and early 1939, which, although apparently successful within Italy, had not unnaturally angered the French, scarce raw-materials supplies for existing armaments production were already threatened with a shortfall.

In mid-March Dall'Olio of the commissariat for war production (*Cogefag*), warned Mussolini that the risk of Italian iron imports from France and the United States ceasing as the consequence of an international 'emergency' had become very real. On 27 March Dall'Olio wrote to Mussolini again, this time complaining that his prophecy was being fulfilled. Paris had reduced the levels of both iron and steel destined for Italy, while the Americans had delayed their shipments. Worse still, coal supplies from Germany and Poland had not reached the agreed quotas; between 1 October 1938 and 1 March 1939, there had been a shortfall in total deliveries of some 550,000 tons. The Italian budget deficit for the year 1938–39, having reached a figure in excess of 8,000 million lire, placed an additional block on any substantial new naval building.[15]

Aside from yet again requesting new construction beyond the capabilities of the Italian national economy, the naval staff report contained other interesting points. First, although the plans office believed that Germany did not plan to build above the quantitative levels established with Britain in June 1935, this proved to be erroneous, particularly as Raeder and Schniewind had already informed the recent naval mission to Berlin that Germany fully intended to 'build according to its needs'. Indeed, by 27 January, Hitler ordered the German naval command to increase the pace of battleship construction, thus heralding the *Z-Plan* concept that gave naval armaments programmes priority; a fact which, if anything, illustrated the lack of communication between the staffs of the 'Axis' navies. Then, on 28 April, during the course of an elaborate speech on Nazi foreign policy, the *Führer* announced that Britain, now seemingly intent on war with Germany, had wrecked the Anglo-German Agreement; he formally stated his intention to denounce it. Also interesting is the Italian naval staff's concept of an oceanic conflict with Britain in the Indian Ocean, tentative planning for which began that summer, but which the East African naval command never completed, owing to the premature outbreak of hostilities. Finally, the fact that the navy's planners had yet again recommended aircraft-carrier building served to illustrate the difference of opinion over this question within its high command. Although Cavagnari had publicly renounced Italy's need for such vessels the year before, he quite clearly did not speak for the navy as a whole in doing so.[16]

The weakness of Italy's economic and industrial infrastructure, and the strategic debility exposed during the Mediterranean crises of 1935 and 1938, could only have confirmed Mussolini's belief that an alliance with Germany was a matter of necessity. This idea was the predominant theme at a meeting of Italy's chiefs-of-staff held in Rome on 26 January, which convened on the basis that no Italian planning would now be possible until the true extent of German military and economic support became clearer. The Italian armed forces, Badoglio informed the service chiefs, were no longer to plan for any attack on Egypt. Mussolini had ordered him to concentrate on the possibility of an Italo-French clash in the near future, and the central tenet governing overall Italian strategy could be summarised thus: 'Totally defensive on the French Alpine and Libyan fronts.' Besides, Badoglio added, the navy's recent plans illustrated all too clearly 'the precarious nature of the entire operation' against Suez. The transportation and subsequent supplying of a large expeditionary force by sea always carried a high risk of failure. Therefore, he concluded, 'we should not put our faith in such an idea'. Mussolini had already decided that transportation of troops would in future be undertaken by air, and authorised construction of the units in question. Despite protests from Pariani that the strategy under discussion 'resolved nothing', Badoglio insisted that until the German position became clearer, which it would do after Hitler made his next speech on 30 January, all Italian forces should maintain defensive positions. Italy's material and financial position remained grave, he added; a nation could not wage a 'lightning war' without gold and raw materials, and both were extremely scarce in Italy.[17]

Badoglio, who had opposed the Pariani plan to attack Egypt at least as early as December 1936, readily seized upon Mussolini's order that no offensive operations could for the moment be considered, and vetoed the entire idea. Yet, Mussolini, buoyed by the statement of support for Italy contained in Hitler's speech of 30 January, evidently did not intend simply to 'keep the doors of the house firmly secured', as Badoglio put it. On the contrary, although Mussolini had given the marshal the impression that he planned no aggression for the near future, owing to Italy's 'present military position', the *Duce* privately remarked that he did foresee a Mediterranean war against France. Indeed, later, as will be discussed, Pariani broached the idea with Wilhelm Keitel, the German chief of general staff. Meanwhile, that summer the naval command in East Africa developed plans to capture the French East African port of Djibouti in a surprise offensive. Furthermore, in the wake of Hitler's speech, Mussolini also established that, for Italy, conflict with the West as a whole, and not simply France, remained an inevitability. His famous and often-quoted political testament delivered to the Fascist grand council just four days after the *Führer*'s avowal of support, certainly left no doubt among notables such as Giuseppe Bottai as to its meaning. The 'March to the Oceans' concept, noted Bottai, was the new Mussolinian political formula 'for the future generations'. Italy remained imprisoned within a British-controlled sea whose guards were Cyprus, Malta, Tunisia and Corsica, and whose doors were Suez and Gibraltar. In order to break out of this prison, Italy needed to link her African possessions in North and East Africa and secure access to the Indian Ocean. Thus, the enemies of Roman expansion were also Greece, Turkey and Egypt, which had agreed to British 'encirclement' of Italy. In the meantime, there remained the claims against France; and if France did not concede them then Italy should be ready to go to war, a war that the Italian armed forces would fight and win not in the Alps, but in the Mediterranean, by air and by sea.[18]

Given the general Italian position, as outlined above, Mussolini could not hope to accomplish this ambitious programme of territorial expansion without German backing; and Berlin, far from being content merely to support the Italian drive towards Mediterranean dominance, had an expansionist agenda of its own, as Mussolini soon discovered. By 10 February, a deeply anxious Ciano questioned Mackensen in Rome as to the validity of rumours regarding alleged German intentions towards Albanian oil supplies. 'Albania was a purely family affair', he warned the ambassador, and Italy intended to keep it that way. Should Germany create difficulties for Mussolini there, then this would clearly undermine his considerable efforts to popularise the 'Axis' within Italy. But the dictator's efforts, if not his kudos, were to be undermined by Berlin in any case. On 15 March German troops occupied the remainder of rump Czechoslovakia created at Munich, to Mussolini's and Ciano's fury. How would it be possible, wondered the Italian foreign minister, to take the Germans at their word in future? Germany had completely humiliated the Italian people, and the latter must be compensated, perhaps in Albania. By then, however, Mussolini had already signalled his approval to the opening of staff talks with Germany. He simply swallowed his pride and congratulated the *Führer* on his prompt action.[19]

The establishment of 'Prussian hegemony in Europe', as he termed it, may temporarily have given Mussolini pause for thought, but on the whole it by no means tempered his enthusiasm for an 'Axis' alliance. Once Ciano had made it clear to Mackensen on 17 March that the dictator considered the Mediterranean as much an Italian sea as he did the Baltic a German one, and warned the German ambassador that Rome did not intend to tolerate Berlin's interference in Croatian affairs, he duly received Ribbentrop's assurances of Germany's *désintéressement* in these regions three days later. Mussolini now once more enthused over the German–Italian alliance. 'We cannot change our policy now', he told Ciano after receiving Berlin's message, 'we are after all not political whores.' Subsequently, news having reached Rome that Franco's Nationalist forces had now virtually won the bitter and prolonged Spanish Civil War, Mussolini ordered that the operation to occupy Albania proceed, but without first notifying Berlin. At the same time he demanded that the nature of the alliance with Germany be more precisely defined. Once Italian forces had taken Tirana by 8 April, London and Paris, now sure that Mussolini had definitely aligned Italy with Germany, guaranteed Greece and Romania, while Admiralty planners began to consider the possibility of a future preemptive war against Italy.[20]

Before learning of Berlin's decision to annex Bohemia–Moravia,

Mussolini and Ciano, encouraged by further Hitlerian rhetoric espousing the *Führer*'s determination to march alongside Italy, had authorised Pariani to enter into preliminary conversations with Keitel. Despite the tension in relations between Rome and Berlin that permeated the weeks that followed, Mussolini took up a German initiative at the beginning of April aimed at staging the discussions, and on 5 April they finally took place at Innsbruck, Austria. The real value of the talks was political rather than military. Keitel stressed that an Italo-French war stood little chance of remaining localised, and that it would be only a matter of time before both Britain and Germany became drawn in. Consequently, the main conclusions reached as a result of the encounter, upon which Mussolini later based his negotiations for the Pact of Steel, were that Italy and Germany required at least three years of preparation before waging their inevitable war against the west European powers. This decision for war would be taken at the political level; the present talks were merely designed to discuss the military aspects of the conflict, not its timing. Keitel, in stressing the 'inevitability' of war against Britain and France, failed to mention that he had already issued directives for the German attack on Poland, which sparked the European conflagration that autumn.[21]

Only in mid-April were there signs that the Italian naval staff had begun to strengthen its ties with the German naval command, after Raeder's and Schniewind's suggestion in January that the two navies establish closer links. The occasion to do so arose during a visit to Berlin by Admirals Silvio Salza and Raffaele De Courten in order to be present at the celebrations for Hitler's 50th birthday. During the course of the visit, which took place between 19 and 22 April, the two Italians learned from Pariani that the German navy had already begun planning for operations in the Baltic and North Sea in the event of a war with the West. But, despite Raeder's earlier enthusiasm for greater co-operation between the Axis navies, Salza noted that during his first encounter with the admiral, no specific mention was made of this fact. Neither, added Salza, did Admiral Schniewind seem prepared to raise the subject, despite having relayed the content of the Pariani–Keitel talks in some detail to the Italian. Only on 20 April, during the official reception, did Hitler affirm Germany's determination to support Italy, before emphasising his satisfaction at the recent Pariani–Keitel encounter and expressing his hope that 'these first approaches having passed successfully, similar collaboration might be extended to other areas'.

Mysteriously, however, Raeder seemed most unwilling to discuss the matter. The next day, De Courten, thanking the German commander-in-chief for his hospitality during their visit, was again left with the distinct impression that the latter 'did not wish to participate in an exchange of ideas', or at least that he expected the Italians to broach the matter first, which Cavagnari had expressly forbidden them to do. Then, on 22 April,

just as the two Italians were about to take their leave, the parting conversation with Raeder on an apparent British air-reconnaissance mission
having flown over the German battle fleet drawing to a conclusion, the
German suddenly raised the matter. 'The German navy was ready', he
stated, 'to begin discussions on future collaboration', and he would be
pleased to confer with Cavagnari on the question. Salza accordingly
expressed himself honoured to pass this message on to his chief-of-staff,
although he later informed Cavagnari privately that Pariani's dealings with
Keitel had not taken place under such an atmosphere of 'equivocation
and reticence'.[22]

Nevertheless, the stage was now set for the negotiations for an 'Axis'
military alliance to begin, and for staff talks to take place between the
respective armed forces of Germany and Italy. But, the suspicions and
resentments that had occurred at the political level – and, in particular,
after the momentous and profoundly grave events in Prague that March
– had their echoes within military circles. Keitel had, after all, misled
Pariani, while Raeder, in the words of Admiral Salza, appeared indecisive,
almost shifty, as regards the idea of closer co-operation. Equally
interesting, however, had been the fact that Pariani, rather than Pietro
Badoglio, undertook the conversations with Badoglio's German
counterpart, Keitel, head of the German supreme high command. The
available evidence suggests that Badoglio may not have been informed
about the Innsbruck talks. In any case, the marshal, always defensively
minded and anti-German, would not have approved of Pariani's visit. To
German enquiries as to whether Pariani had the same powers as Keitel,
ambassador Attolico later declined to reply.[23]

On the Brink, May–August 1939

Even before concluding the Pact of Steel with Germany on 22 May 1939,
Mussolini had been eager to stipulate that war against the British and
French would not be possible before 1942–43, at the earliest. During a
meeting in Rome with Goering in mid-April, the Italian dictator agreed
that this period would be the 'most favourable time for such a conflict'
for 'the Axis powers still needed two to three years in order to join in a
general conflict well-armed and with the prospect of victory'.[24]

In fact, the Italian military situation was worse than either Mussolini
or Ciano suspected. Reports emanating from the Italian intelligence
community informed the two men of empty magazines, antiquated
artillery and non-existent divisions. 'There has been much bluff from the
military sector', noted Ciano balefully, 'and even the *Duce* has been fooled
by it: but it is a tragic sort of bluff'. By early May, a report on the Italian
military situation by General Giacomo Carboni, soon to be appointed

head of *SIM*, confirmed how 'tragic' Italy's position with regard to armaments was. It appeared, Carboni warned, to be little short of 'disastrous'. But, much to Ciano's dismay, his father-in-law chose to overlook such facts – perhaps, as he noted in his diary, they were a little too close to the truth.[25]

Undeterred by the parlous condition of the Italian military infrastructure, Mussolini authorised Ciano to meet with his opposite number, von Ribbentrop, in Milan, and open discussions for the conclusion of a full Italo-German military alliance. Over 6 and 7 May, the two men duly met and agreed that a treaty of alliance be concluded immediately; Ribbentrop confirming to Ciano that Germany, too, remained 'convinced of the necessity for a period of peace, which should not be less than four or five years', although adding ominously that 'this does not mean to say that Germany is not ready for war before that period has elapsed'. Mussolini, who had always advocated the signing of a bilateral pact rather than the 'triangular' agreement including Japan favoured by Ribbentrop, was delighted. Even Ciano, who preferred to delay placing of the final signature on the treaty, had to admit that he had 'never seen such a pact: it was absolute dynamite'.[26]

Not everyone agreed. On his return to Rome after formalising the agreement, Ciano noted that the pact appeared more popular in Germany than Italy. 'The fact cannot be escaped', he added, 'that Italian hatred for France has not yet succeeded in generating any genuine love for Germany.' King Victor Emanuel, vehemently anti-German, warned that 'while the Germans have need of us they will be courteous even to the point of servility. But, before very long, they will show themselves to be the scoundrels that they are.' Cursing the burden imposed upon him by the Italian monarchy, Mussolini vented his anger on Percy Loraine, British ambassador to Rome since 2 January, accusing London of attempting to encircle the 'Axis', and the obstinate Poles of rejecting Hitler's 'very moderate' proposals for discussion of the Danzig question. At the end of May, Mussolini informed both Ribbentrop and Hitler that conflict with the Western powers was an 'inevitability' for which the 'Axis' would now need to prepare. Only from 1943 onwards, he repeated, would Italy and Germany be in any position to wage this war victoriously.[27]

Even as Ciano and Ribbentrop were negotiating the terms of the Pact of Steel, the naval staff took stock of the strategic situation in the Mediterranean in light of the recent turbulent events, in what proved to be a highly influential report. With the end of the civil war in Spain and the victory of Franco's Nationalist armies, the study began, the navy now assumed that Madrid would ally itself with the 'Axis' powers in the event of war against Paris and London. Therefore, the western Mediterranean basin, until recently something of a strategic backwater for the war plans office, now took on a new and greater significance. Italian control of the

Balearics offered an excellent base from which to menace French communications with North Africa, which the planners were not slow to indicate. But, they added, the enemy could easily supply French North African possessions via the Atlantic shipping lanes, and the navy's future planning ought not simply to concentrate on severing France's Mediterranean supply lines. Indeed, they noted, it remained highly likely that Anglo-French naval forces would attempt to occupy Majorca and Minorca, while keeping part of their combined fleet at Gibraltar in order to cover operations being staged from the Moroccan theatre. This, in turn, suggested that Italy's battle fleet might be compelled to seek its decisive encounter with the enemy in the western basin, and under conditions that could well prove favourable. Again, the planners stressed the value of strong central Mediterranean defences should such a strategy become considered viable; the '*sbarramento*' in the Sicilian Channel, they noted, 'must become the means whereby the enemy naval forces in the eastern basin became "compartmentalised"' from those in the west.

The naval staff report then emphasised the great improvement in Italy's strategic position that resulted from the occupation of Albania – an annexation that the high command urged from at least 1936 onwards. The navy could now easily seal off the Adriatic with few naval units, while the *Marina* had in addition gained the advantage of the port at Valona (Vlorë), whose value in the defence of the Ionian Sea was almost on a par with that of Taranto. The report also confirmed that Mussolini had ordered the 'invasion' as a means of establishing a firm strategic foothold in the Balkans. From Albania, the planners argued, Italy could easily attack and occupy Corfu and, on a wider scale, launch operations against other Balkan states.

But, the plans office report also contained more than a hint at caution. As regards North Africa, the naval staff upheld Badoglio's belief that supplying an expeditionary force in time of war remained a highly risky undertaking, if not an impossible one were the enemy to make use of Crete as a base for operations. Moreover, were London eventually to conclude an alliance with Turkey, bases could become available to the enemy that would immediately menace the Dodecanese. It was also possible that Turkish troops might be used to defend the Suez Canal. This latter eventuality rendered redundant any Italian strategy aimed at attacking British troop reinforcements passing through the Indian Ocean en route from Australia, and arriving in Egypt via Iraq and Palestine. It did, however, suggest that the navy could stage a submarine offensive against Turkish troop ships in the eastern basin, although any influx of Turkish land forces into Egypt required the strengthening of Italian land defences in eastern Libya.

Finally, the war plans office turned its attention to the enemy air threat to Italian naval units in the central Mediterranean. Air force intelligence had identified around 200 enemy bombers deployed in the air bases of French North Africa. Added to these forces were the 300 or so aircraft based on Malta, of which at least 100 would be bombers. These units posed a serious menace to Italian forces based on Sicily, and the latter should be reduced significantly.[28]

As regards Italy's other principal theatre of naval operations, the Red Sea, there is no evidence to suggest that strategic planning had made any marked progress since the deliberations of the naval staff in Rome in late 1937. Only in May 1939 did the governor and overall military commander of Italian East Africa, Duke Amadeo di Savoia, authorise the development of plans to cover the event of war in the region. On 10 May, days after the foreign ministers of Germany and Italy had determined to conclude their military pact, the navy's regional chief-of-staff, Rear-Admiral Matteucci, returned to Massawa from an East African high command meeting in Addis Ababa, and prepared a provisional study for war in the Red Sea on the orders of di Savoia. The governor had stressed that all initial planning should focus on preparing the region solely for the first days of war. Only after clear directives had been issued by the government in Rome as regards the nature of the war, the likely strength and intended strategy of the enemy as well as the additional Italian forces that would be made available for deployment in the region, could plans for the 'successive period' be drawn up. The main naval objective in the opening stages of a general conflagration, Matteucci continued, would be that of guaranteeing supplies for the East African theatre. The navy could best achieve this by seizing all enemy and neutral merchant ships operating in the southern Red Sea at the outbreak of hostilities. Using light surface units and submarines based at Massawa and the base in the Dahlak Archipelago, such an offensive, if supported by units of the air force, could secure substantial quantities of material for the Italian war effort. Concomitantly, the Italian navy's torpedo units should, operating at night, aim to attack and sink all French naval and merchant vessels passing between Djibouti and Aden. If the East African fleet carried out the two operations using all available Italian naval forces, then success could be assured, Matteucci concluded. After the initial stages of the war, greater economy needed to be exercised in the engagement of naval forces. Nevertheless, these forces needed to mount a sustained offensive against lines of communication with Djibouti in the second phase of the war, and, moreover, participate in combined operations aimed at capturing the position in question.[29]

By 15 May, both Matteucci and the other East African chiefs-of-staff had produced strategic plans which di Savoia integrated into a general operational directive, and subsequently forwarded to his superiors at the ministry for Italian East Africa in Rome. The di Savoia plan foresaw the army strengthening border defences, protecting internal lines of communication and launching a sudden offensive against French Somali-land supported by units of the air force. He hoped the latter would also participate in an aeronaval offensive aimed at attacking all enemy naval and merchant ships in the Red Sea and the Gulf of Aden, as well as launching day and night attacks against Aden and Djibouti. Finally, air units were to ensure the defence of Italy's principal regional bases (Asmara, Assab, Dire Dawa and Addis Ababa) and eventually attack the key Sudanese positions of Khartoum, Atbara, Kassala and Port Sudan. The navy, meanwhile, was to concentrate on its offensive against enemy commerce and prepare for the planned attack on French Somaliland as foreseen.[30]

The timing of the ostensibly anti-French plan is curious. In early January, as part of his campaign for territorial concessions from Paris, Mussolini had informed Ciano that France should be prepared to cede Djibouti and Corsica, before later stating that Italy would take them by force, if necessary. However, Keitel's warnings on the impossibility of localising any Italo-French war during his conversations with Pariani in early April betrayed a sense that such an offensive should have become subordinate to Germany's aims and timetable. The fact that the Italians had not done so suggests that they were not simply content to bow to German wishes and blindly follow German advice, as was to become abundantly clear at Friedrichshafen in June. How likely the governor and his regional commanders regarded the possibility of an 'isolated' war against France, whose objective was to be the 'sudden' annexation of Djibouti and French Somaliland, is perhaps best revealed by the fact that the East African high command had also begun preparing additional plans aimed at capturing British Somaliland, Kenya and Aden – after an expeditionary force had landed in the Yemen. Assessments of the likely success of the naval plan should take into consideration the absence of combined strategic planning, the limited number of naval forces deployed in the region – which Cavagnari undoubtedly did not wish to increase in the event of war, owing to the vulnerability of this theatre – the fleet's lack of night-fighting capability, and its poor base defences. Finally, the likelihood that Britain planned to remain neutral after attacks on French forces deployed at Aden remained, to say the least, a remote possibility.[31]

Initially, the naval leadership in Rome approved the Matteucci plan for naval war in the Red Sea. Admiral Odoardo Somigli, the new deputy chief-of-staff, informed Massawa that the idea of launching an aggressive offensive with 'all available forces' before entering a secondary phase in the war that would require greater tactical caution to be shown, remained a sound concept. Only later, in early July, did Cavagnari order changes to the plan. Matteucci should on no account seize neutral ships and he should make sure that any operations against enemy shipping followed closely the guidelines clearly set out by the existing 'Regulations for War at Sea' (the *Norme di Diritto Marittimo di Guerra*). Moreover, he concluded, only submarines should undertake any future offensive against enemy units operating in the southern Red Sea, and in particular between Aden and Djibouti; clearly, the chief-of-staff did not wish to risk surface-vessel losses in this theatre that could affect the navy's position in the Mediterranean.[32]

Cavagnari had already outlined the inferiority of this position in mid-May, while the commanders in East Africa were planning their respective campaigns. Highlighting one of the main themes of the war plans office's strategic appreciation of 18 May – the question of enemy air power in the central Mediterranean – the navy's chief-of-staff warned that Italy faced a naval coalition with a combined fleet strength at least double that of the Italian navy. In a letter addressed to Pietro Badoglio and Giuseppe Valle, still under-secretary at the air ministry, Cavagnari stressed that in any 'Axis' war against Britain and France the enemy regarded deployment to the Mediterranean as a priority, although, as events the previous autumn had shown, no major naval units would be based at Bizerte or on Malta, given the threat posed by Italian air bases on Sardinia and Sicily. The enemy intended to deploy their battle fleets to both Mediterranean basins, and also planned to conduct operations against Italy in the central region of the sea. It was at this point that the navy's battle squadrons had the greatest possibility for success against one, if not both, of the enemy formations in question.

Italian naval strategy, Cavagnari emphasised, intended to secure the Italian fleet's domination of the central Mediterranean theatre in time of war. Light cruiser divisions and other smaller surface units dispersed between the bases at Cagliari, Trapani, Palermo, Messina and Augusta assured Italian naval predominance in this region, and permitted operations aimed at defending the '*sbarramento*' in the Sicilian Channel to pass off successfully. However, given enemy air strength in this theatre, it remained inevitable that if the Anglo-French coalition achieved air superiority, then this might compel the Italian navy to abandon each of these bases. Should the enemy in fact force them to do so, then this rendered extremely unlikely the 'timely intervention' of Italian naval forces in the war. In turn, this abandonment had clear repercussions on the navy's capability to ship troops and military equipment to North Africa – whether destined for the defence of Libya's Tunisian front or a 'land offensive to the east'. In short, he concluded, for the navy to achieve domination of the central Mediterranean, total Italian air superiority in the region also became a vital prerequisite. The air force should therefore ensure that at the outbreak of hostilities, it was ready to attack all enemy air bases in the region, and able to place Malta and Bizerte under such pressure as to invalidate their use as naval facilities.[33]

In reply to Cavagnari's request that he explain how the air force expected to co-operate with the navy in wartime, Valle argued that Italy's general mobilisation plan – *PR 12* – had already established that air offensives were to be launched against key enemy positions in time of war, while concurrent operations should be staged whose scope included the defence of metropolitan territory. Guided by these two criteria, air staff strategy also encompassed attacks aimed at destroying, or at least damaging as severely as possible, all enemy shipping. From their bases in Sicily, Sardinia and Libya, ten Italian squadrons – comprising seven bomber formations, two-and-a-half fighter and one *'stormo d'assalto'* (assault squadron) – could attack Malta and French bases in Tunisia. Therefore, the air force could indeed render inoperative enemy naval facilities on Malta and at Bizerte in any war, and thereby prevent the deployment of large naval units there. These same Italian air units could also attack any enemy fleet attempting to break through Italian defences in the Sicilian Channel. Further squadrons currently based in Puglia and Tuscany could readily redeploy to Sicilian and Sardinian air fields, should reinforcements be necessary. But, he added, the air force could not guarantee absolute Italian air superiority over the entire central Mediterranean. Even if Italian air units assured superiority on a 'partial' basis, this did not prevent the enemy from launching air attacks against important Italian air and naval facilities in Sardinia and Sicily. However, Valle concluded, Italian air power, although inferior to that of the British and French, could 'easily guarantee control of a specific theatre of operations for a limited period of time', although very little beyond this.[34]

The Cavagnari–Valle exchange of May and June 1939 constituted a fitting finale to the question of air cover for Italian fleet operations. Not only had the navy's chief-of-staff blocked the construction of carrier units, despite the pleas of his planning department, but navy–air force bickering also prevented the creation of torpedo bombers; Valle informed Mussolini in June that the air staff 'did not believe in the effectiveness of this type of weapon'. Only after the Italian declaration of war was any progress made on the development of this type of aircraft. Nor did the navy's planners significantly raise the issue of fleet air cover again before Italy's entry into the war in June 1940. Thereafter, once under combat conditions, the range of Italian land-based aircraft proved inadequate and, in turn, placed severe limitations on the range of naval forces reluctant to operate without air support. Moreover, air and naval staff co-operation continued to prove as dysfunctional in wartime as it had done in peacetime. A member of the Italian naval staff provided a telling epitaph to the entire question in late June 1939. Italy's foreign policy, the officer noted, had led the country into a situation where it now faced the real threat of a naval war in the Mediterranean – at a time when the level of air and navy co-operation in preparing for this conflict had been frankly dreadful. In short, he concluded, 'there is now an almost total absence of any clear and rational doctrine' for aeronaval warfare in the Mediterranean.[35]

In their report of 18 May, the naval staff also placed substantial emphasis on the navy's need to consider anew the strategic position *vis-à-vis* the western Mediterranean basin. Although the naval archives in Rome offer no evidence that this resulted in any specific new plans for operations being drawn up, the war plans office did continue to stress the importance of this theatre, which Cavagnari later underlined during his conversations with Admiral Erich Raeder in late June 1939. The French, the planners argued in reports in May and June, were highly likely to attempt to occupy the Balearics in the event of a European war; this had been 'an objective of French naval policy for centuries'. Added to this possibility was the fact that Britain now actively sought a Turkish alliance, which, in the event of war, effectively closed Italy's only remaining means of supplying itself by sea in wartime, the Dardenelles. Echoing the report produced by the naval staff in January 1938, and discussed in the previous chapter, the planners noted that Spain was now the only transit point open for Italian commerce arriving from outside the Mediterranean by sea. Naturally, the Balearics were crucial if Spain did agree to ship goods arriving at Atlantic ports overland to the Mediterranean coast, from where they could be transported to Italy. If Majorca and Minorca fell into enemy hands, Italy could no longer regard this economic strategy as possible, and therefore Franco should be requested to strengthen defences on the islands as soon as possible. Once the Spanish had significantly improved the network of fortresses already in existence on the two islands, then any attempted French annexation would require the concentration of large numbers of forces in the region 'for several days'. In sum, were an enemy to become bogged down in trying to break through the formidable Balearic defences, the Italian navy might find an ideal opportunity to engage them in what might prove a decisive aeronaval confrontation. This matter should be discussed with the Spanish as soon as possible.[36]

The opportunity for Cavagnari and the naval staff finally to delineate and define the nature of their relationship with the German navy, theoretically their ally under the aegis of the Pact of Steel and officially the Italian navy's cohort since July 1937, came shortly after that treaty's conclusion. Despite being aware of Raeder's 'reticence' during the visit of De Courten and Salza to Berlin in mid-April, Cavagnari expressed his pleasure at the idea of developing closer links with the German naval command, and assented to the opening of staff conversations 'at any time and in any location which you might deem appropriate'. Raeder should also inform the Italian naval staff of the intended topics for discussion, in order that the Italian delegation might come to the meetings well prepared. On 17 May the German commander-in-chief duly expressed his 'great joy' at the possibility of closer German–Italian naval collaboration, and looked forward to the prospect of a personal exchange of views with his Italian opposite number. If the admiral had no objections, Friedrichshafen on Lake Constance – a 'mid-way point' between Rome and Berlin – should be the location, and the talks could take place there between 19 and 23 June.[37]

The precise scope and likely depth of any exchange of ideas between the armed forces of the 'Axis' powers had already been established some time before the conversations that were to follow took place. On 22 March Hitler stressed that in any talks with the Italians, 'the military-political bases and the strategical and operational questions arising therefrom are to be *deferred* for the present'. General Walter von Brauchitsch, commander-in-chief of the German army, re-affirmed this directive during the course of a visit to Italy in early May. There was to be no operational co-operation between the 'Axis' armed forces; as Pariani had conveniently requested, joint operations were not to be envisaged for the time being. This explains the largely innocuous list of proposed discussion points submitted by the German naval attaché to Rome, Werner Löwish, on 27 May, and accepted by the Italian naval high command on 1 June. The three-point agenda established for Friedrichshafen was as follows: (1) discussion of the 'aims and principles' for further German–Italian naval co-operation; (2) establishing spheres for further collaboration; (3) agreements on the methodology to be followed in any further discussions.[38]

Having made the journey to Lake Constance on the German–Swiss border, the Italians found Raeder eager to discuss operational rather than purely technical matters. Expecting opposition from the German naval leadership to the Italian concept of German units' 'drawing off' enemy battleships in the Atlantic, Cavagnari later expressed his surprise at Raeder's readiness to consider the value of such a strategy. Believing that the *Kriegsmarine* would opt to deploy in the Baltic and North Sea, as De Courten and Salza had been informed in April, the Italian delegation appeared pleased at German willingness to attack the enemy in the Atlantic shipping lanes.

By 19 September 1938, Raeder had already begun to examine the possibility of a German war against Britain and France in the Atlantic. A special planning committee set up by the grand admiral eventually con-cluded that Germany could not hope to outbuild Britain in capital ships, and that the *Kriegsmarine* should, rather, concentrate on creating a special cruiser fleet supported by supply ships in order to wage an oceanic conflict against the Royal Navy. Resonant of the 'escape fleet' proposed by Italian naval planners in January 1936, the proposed German programme was, to say the least, ambitious; by 1948 the Germany navy would have built ten battleships, 12 new pocket battleships, five heavy cruisers, 24 light cruisers, 36 small cruisers, eight aircraft carriers, 249 U-boats, 70 destroyers and 78 torpedo boats. Fearing that even such a vast programme would still not provide Germany with a fleet powerful enough to defeat Britain, Raeder also urged Hitler to consider an alternative building policy focused on the rapid expansion of the Germany navy's submarine arm, an objective which German shipyards could accomplish far more quickly. Hitler rejected the latter scheme in favour of the former – the *Z plan* concept – on 27 January 1939. The *Führer* believed that a war with Britain was not imminent, and as late as 22 August ruled out such a possibility and continued to give priority to battleship construction.[39]

At Friedrichshafen, marked differences of opinion between the Italian and German naval delegations occurred over the conduct of the naval war in the Mediterranean. Raeder secretly believed that Italy's role in any sea war should be a 'diversionary' one. He strongly pressed Cavagnari to abandon the idea of defending the central Mediterranean – the fundamental basis of Italian naval strategy – and focus instead on defeating the French in the western Mediterranean, thereby achieving dominion in that sea and forcing France to supply North Africa via the Atlantic route. The British, he added, would not constitute a problem; units of the Royal Navy sent to fight in the eastern Mediterranean would make 'excellent targets for Italian submarines'. There even remained the chance, added Admiral Schniewind, of the British deploying the five battleships of the Mediterranean Fleet to the Far East.

Cavagnari strongly disagreed with these views. Britain showed no evidence of abandoning the Mediterranean. The French would not attempt to move large numbers of troops to North Africa in time of war. Were they to attempt to occupy the Balearics, then Italy could launch an air and sea offensive against them in the western basin, but not at the expense of defending the central Mediterranean and the lines of communication between Italy and Libya. Later, in September 1940, Raeder stressed to Hitler the importance to Germany of ousting Britain from the Mediterranean and winning control of Gibraltar and Suez. Were Germany and Italy to win control of the sea, Raeder noted, new sources of raw materials might be secured as well as new bases for 'further operations against the British Empire'. But Hitler, increasingly obsessed with the impending German campaign against Russia – operation *Barbarossa* – effectively rejected Raeder's proposed Mediterranean strategy. German intervention in the Mediterranean theatre, following Mussolini's disastrously ill-conceived assault on Greece in October 1940, was only intended by the *Führer* as a means of preventing an Italian collapse, and of safeguarding Germany's southern flank in anticipation of the Russian campaign the following summer.

After Friedrichshafen, it became clear that the success of the naval talks had been limited. The Italo-German conversations had established respective operational spheres – Italy in the Mediterranean and Red Sea, Germany in the oceans, the most 'sensitive spot' of the British – and seen agreement reached on the need to operate jointly in the Indian Ocean from the projected new Italian base at Chisimaio, once the Italian navy had completed work on it. However, Friedrichshafen constituted only a preliminary round of talks that neither side offered to resume prior to the Italian declaration of hostilities the following year. Clear differences of opinion emerged, which would only become more pronounced in later conversations. In June 1939 the German naval command regarded Suez and Egypt as 'prestige objectives', whose capture would be difficult to achieve and even harder to consolidate. 'We must see to it', noted Captain Kurt Fricke, head of the German naval operations division, that 'Italy does not go running after all sorts of prestige targets', but that in the common interest 'she displays the most vigorous activity in the western Mediterranean.' But, this was not to be the case. Cavagnari, in his report on the Friedrichshafen meetings, placed great emphasis on the 'separate' nature of the operational spheres, and expressed his great relief that no time had been devoted towards discussing a unitary command structure. He would conduct his Mediterranean war in the way he thought most fit, and this meant concentrating primarily on defence of the central Mediterranean. Interestingly, neither delegation raised the thorny question of air force–navy co-operation; the issue being as sensitive in Germany as it proved to be in Italy.[40]

Duplicity also prevailed at Friedrichshafen. Raeder assured the Italians that his *Führer* did not foresee war as being imminent, despite having been present at a secret conference chaired by Hitler on 23 May, during which the German dictator stated his intent to wage war against Poland, even should it entail conflict with the British and French. Similarly, the Italian naval staff did not mention the fact that it was considering a possible annexation of French Somaliland and Djibouti at this time, despite the fact that Keitel had expressly advised against any Italian colonial war with France. No further talks were held after the premature outbreak of European hostilities just two months later. Had there been a greater effort at establishing a truly common 'Axis' strategy for war, with common goals, then the realities facing Italy in the Mediterranean in June 1940 might have proved altogether different. As it transpired, both naval commands, although heralding Friedrichshafen as a success, undertook no written agreements. No coalition had been formed.[41]

In a memorandum to Italy's service chiefs dated 27 May 1939, Mussolini elaborated in some detail his ideas on how best to wage the 'inevitable' 'Axis' war against the 'plutocratic and therefore selfishly conservative' Western powers. Only after the international exhibition to commemorate the 20th anniversary of the march on Rome in 1922 would Italy be in any shape to undertake such a conflict. Thus, not before 1943 should the Italian armed forces plan to wage it. Meanwhile, Libya, Ethiopia and Albania should be strengthened militarily, the six new and rebuilt battleships be completed, new artillery replace antiquated equipment currently still in service, and the alliance with Germany itself be promoted more positively among the Italian people. No 'dynamic' offensives were anticipated on the Alpine, Rhine and Libyan fronts, Mussolini noted; only from Italian East Africa could the *forze armate* successfully mount operations against enemy possessions. The 'Axis' powers might also aim to occupy the Danube basin and the Balkans to forestall any enemy offensive there, while Poland should be 'paralysed' before the Soviet Union could intervene.[42]

But, in believing that Hitler conveniently concurred with this strategic vision, or indeed this timetable, the *Duce* miscalculated badly. By mid-June, Ciano and Mussolini became aware that the international temperature had risen as a consequence of Berlin's claims against Danzig, established as a free city under the terms of Versailles. On 26 June, Attolico, Italy's ambassador to the Reich, warned Ciano that alarming rumours were circulating in Berlin of German intentions to settle claims against Poland by force as early as mid-August. The Italian foreign minister, although rather complacently convinced that such claims were exaggerated and alarmist, nevertheless expressed quiet concern; the Germans had informed him of nothing, which remained difficult to reconcile with the terms of the Pact of Steel. Mussolini's solution to the problem – a plebiscite – Ciano dismissed as 'Utopian', before convincing himself that Berlin's silence suggested nothing sinister was afoot.[43]

Then, on 4 July, a note from the British ambassador Loraine spoke of the 'ominous preparations' being taken by Germans in Polish-controlled Danzig, and of the serious threat 'of a European war' that was now looming. Mussolini, undeterred by such threats of war, informed Loraine three days later that, should London choose conflict to resolve Germany's legitimate claims against Danzig, 'then there must not be the slightest doubt that Italy would equally be on Germany's side'.[44]

However, now seemingly aware that the British and French governments would not this time stand aside and allow Hitler the pleasure of yet another coup, Mussolini, still avowing his support for Berlin, suggested a conference be held 'to disrupt the unity of the front opposing us'. A prior meeting between himself and the *Führer* 'would cause such a sensation that it would be impossible for such a conference not to produce positive results'. Yet, despite having reminded Berlin of the fact that Italy could not enter a war at present, Mussolini's appeal fell on deaf ears. Ribbentrop, although not able to speak for Hitler, agreed that a more favourable time for war would be 'four or five years hence', but rejected the conference proposal out of hand. What advantages lay in such an idea for the 'Axis'? Would not the enemy powers regard any peace initiative by the 'Axis' as a 'sign of weakness'?[45]

By the first days of August, a worried Mussolini had agreed to Ciano's proposal that he visit Germany and confer with Hitler. If Italy were to 'shadow German policy' too closely, Ciano argued, it would find itself in a war for which it remained wholly unprepared. It was imperative that Rome found a 'way out' of its military commitments to Berlin. In mid-August, at Salzburg, Ciano laid out with some frankness the Italian economic and strategic position. The Italian fleet had only two battleships; Italian artillery was still in the process of modernisation; both metro-politan and colonial defences remained weak; raw materials and money were extremely scarce. Italy could not fight; but Britain and France almost certainly would. Hitler disagreed, maintaining that the West would not and could not support Poland. Furthermore, he hinted, Paris and London could do nothing to prevent Italy from taking Yugoslavia while Germany dealt with Warsaw. Ciano, 'disgusted with Germany, and her leaders', returned to Rome determined to keep Italy out of the war.[46]

For the Italian navy, the reasons for avoiding war in 1939 were glaringly obvious; neither the fleet nor its facilities were ready for it. Before the dramatic European events of late July and early August 1939 unfolded, the naval staff, following the return of the Italian delegation from Friedrichshafen, continued further to consider the long-term strategic ideas laid out in the study of mid-May in a series of reports in which the level of unreadiness became all too apparent. Naval war plans office attention now turned from the western Mediterranean basin to the east, where the high command believed that an enemy attack against the Dodecanese remained practically inevitable in any war – as, in fact, Cavagnari had informed Raeder and Schniewind in late June. In any 'Axis' confrontation with Britain and France, a study of 5 July noted, the likelihood of Soviet and Turkish support for the West, whether active or indirect, remained certain. The consequence for Italy in either case would be the closure of maritime communications with the Black Sea, while Greek hostility might also lead to the severing of all lines of communi-cations with Italy's Aegean possessions. Counter-measures against this enemy offensive remained the only operational possibility at present open to the navy under the existing hypothesis for war, *alfa uno*. However, any operations foreseen in this theatre would find the fleet confronted with greatly superior forces, and the planners recommended that no additional naval units be deployed in this region, given the vulnerability of all Italian surface vessels to attack from enemy forces based at Iraklion on Crete and at Morea.

Perhaps the only way open to Italy of countering the operational and logistical advantages enjoyed by the enemy in the eastern basin was to capture the north-eastern Greek port of Thessaloniki. '*Salonicco*', the study argued, 'enjoyed an optimum strategic position in the northern Aegean', making it a valuable point from which to launch Italian offensives in the waters of the Dardanelles. Although roughly the same distance from the Bosphorus as the Italian island of Leros, Thessaloniki would be less vulnerable to air attack, while the former more easily formed part of the

Tobruk–Taranto system of naval bases. Thus, the port constituted an 'excellent departure point for operations whose aim was the severing of enemy communications between Greece and the Dardanelles'. On the other hand, Italian shipping passing between Thessaloniki and Leros in wartime remained exposed to enemy attack for the entire extent of the 300-mile journey. Therefore, keeping the Dodecanese supplied via this route did not appear noticeably easier than along lines of communication passing entirely by sea from Italy to southern Greece. Furthermore, the study concluded, any 'direct' advantage resulting from an Italian capture of Thessaloniki would be limited to using the base simply as an auxiliary position for naval forces based on Leros; Italy's overall geostrategic position in the theatre seemed unlikely to improve markedly. 'Indirectly', a successful Italian annexation of the port prevented the enemy from using it either as a naval base or as a point from which to supply the Greek army in time of war.[47]

The naval staff report made pessimistic reading for Mussolini, who by May 1939 increasingly began to consider the possibility of 'jumping upon Greece at the first opportunity'. In any general war, he had somewhat optimistically maintained, an Italian occupation of Greece would force the British to abandon the eastern Mediterranean basin, rendering it as much an 'Italian lake' as the Adriatic had become after the annexation of Albania. Duly, he ordered the building of a new highway towards Greece in the southern region of Albania, from where Italian air and land units might eventually launch their attack.[48]

Evidently, the naval staff did not concur with the dictator's aims. They argued that the navy should station no additional naval forces in the Aegean other than those already destined for deployment there. To do so would merely risk their immediate loss at the hands of the enemy. Even if the army and air force could launch offensives from southern Albania that might lead to the capture of Thessaloniki, this by no means significantly improved Italy's strategic position in the eastern basin. Nor could supply lines to the Dodecanese possessions as a whole be guaranteed in time of war, given the preponderance of enemy power in the region. The naval staff believed that Italy quite clearly could not dominate the eastern Mediterranean at all, let alone transform it into a theatre controlled totally by its armed forces.

In addition, the Spanish had proved anything but willing to offer support for Italy, with clear implications for the navy's western Mediterranean theatre. Spain, emphasised Serrano Suñer, Franco's foreign minister, during a visit to Italy in June, needed at least two or three years before it would be ready to participate in an 'Axis' war. For the time being, he added, there was no need to conclude any written agreements between Madrid and Rome. In the face of the Spaniard's bitter criticism of Nazi religious policy, Ciano and Mussolini clearly felt it expedient not to press him further. The question of asking Franco to strengthen fortifications on the Balearics, as recommended by the naval staff, could not be broached.[49]

Equally pessimistic was the navy's view of its logistical position as regards metropolitan bases. Four days before the naval staff had pronounced their verdict on the strategic situation in the eastern Mediterranean, the war plans office produced a study on the availability of well-defended ports able to house the six new and remodernised battleships scheduled to enter service by the autumn of 1940. In effect, the planners concluded, there were none – or at least none anywhere in the vicinity of the navy's principal theatre of operations, the Sicilian Channel. Thus, even if the enemy's own position regarding the availability of bases in the eastern basin able to house capital-ship units remained serious, Italy's situation was no better. Of the two facilities able to harbour ships of the *Littorio* class, Genoa was too exposed to enemy attack, being highly vulnerable to air and sea offensives, while Venice remained too far from the main theatre of operations and could only be considered as a 'makeshift' port. Even more seriously, the latter did not have sufficient repair facilities. The work destined to create the new base at Taranto – the *Mar Grande* project – would not be complete before 1942, and the current facilities there could not hold the entire Italian battle fleet in case of emergency. In short, the Italian fleet at present had no point from which to conduct its strategic operations in time of war, should it erupt prior to that date. The only solution would be rapidly to accelerate the construction work currently being undertaken on the harbour at Naples.[50]

Similar levels of deficiency and all-round unpreparedness hampered the navy's planning for war in Italian East Africa, where in late August Mussolini ordered Badoglio to consider afresh plans to capture Djibouti and British Somaliland, after various Italian planning departments had strongly cautioned against the *Duce*'s desired Balkan offensive. The problem was that Italian East Africa remained almost entirely unprepared for any type of war. On 1 July the navy's planners again urged the Fascist administration to delay no longer in releasing the funds necessary to render Italian East Africa effective as a naval theatre of operations. Requesting that money for the naval programme announced earlier that year be made available in order to build three long-range cruisers, 12 ocean-going submarines and six torpedo-boats for use in the Red Sea by 1943, the plans office also placed great stress on the need finally to begin work on the new naval facility at Chisimaio in Italian Somaliland. Operations from this position, they argued, greatly relieved the pressure on Italy's naval forces in the Mediterranean and could influence the outcome of the entire war. Therefore, the German navy, which had requested the use of the port for its own naval units, should be reminded of its promise, made at Friedrichshafen, that it would supply 2,000 tons of steel and 20,000 tons of sheet iron for the construction work there.[51]

By early August, Matteucci, commander-in-chief of the East African naval command, stressed the undoubtedly high value of the Italian possession in attacking all shipping passing through the Indian Ocean and heading for the Sudan and Suez, as well as all enemy naval units operating between Aden and Djibouti. Similarly, Italy could make use of its positions at Assab, within the Dahlak Archipelago and the Farasan Islands, to cover future operations against Egypt and the Sudan, as well as in protecting traffic with the Italian colonies. The principal problem, however, was that only Massawa had to date reached anything approaching the level of readiness for use as a naval base in war. Furthermore, it would be four years before Chisimaio would be able to house the ocean-going fleets of the 'Axis' navies, and, in Italy's case, before those forces would actually be ready. In the summer of 1939, any offensive war in East Africa in which the Italian navy played an integral role, clearly could not be contemplated.[52]

On 16 August, Mussolini summoned Marshal Pietro Badoglio to his office in the *Palazzo Venezia* and informed him that Italy would remain 'strictly defensive' in the fast-approaching European conflagration. Berlin, he informed Badoglio, would go to war over Danzig on 21 August, firm in the belief that the conflict would remain localised. Mussolini fundamentally disagreed with Hitler's decision and the basis upon which he had made it, remaining convinced that London and Paris intended to fight. Thus, because the Germans adamantly intended to resolve the question themselves, they could not expect Italy to offer men or equipment for their war effort. If Italy became the victim of a pre-emptive offensive by the Western powers, then the Italian armed forces should seize this moment in order to attack Greece and capture Thessaloniki. An annexation of Croatia might also be considered, provided the conditions were right. The strategic situation in Libya was serious, both men agreed, and Mussolini ominously promised to 'discuss' the matter with Pariani at the most appropriate moment. In the meantime, the respective military staffs should consider the operations he had requested.[53]

The next day, Mussolini changed his mind. Believing that Italy should remain loyal to its German ally, he informed Ciano and Attolico, in Rome to confer on the crisis, that he wanted Italy to march alongside Germany if the Allies declared war. By 20 August, with Ciano absent on an official visit to Albania, Mussolini appeared more determined then ever to enter the war and secure the territorial concessions in the Balkans Hitler had recommended to Ciano two weeks earlier.[54]

That same day, the navy's war plans office issued its operational directives in the event of Italy's declaring war. Recent periods of international tension had clearly shown that, in any conflict, the Anglo-French coalition would deploy their principal naval forces to the Mediterranean basins, leaving only light surface units and submarines to operate in the

centre. The navy foresaw no 'decisive operations' in the extremes of the
sea and faced the overwhelming superiority of enemy sea power there
alone. The German fleet, although able to draw off a certain number of
enemy forces through its planned offensives in the Atlantic Ocean and in
the Baltic and North Seas, ultimately could not create diversions
significant enough to prevent Britain and France from reinforcing their
Mediterranean position. The enemy could also count on support from
their regional allies, Turkey and Greece, and possibly the Soviet Union
and Yugoslavia too, all of whom had significant numbers of modern naval
units, not to mention bases, to commit to the conflict. While the enemy,
who controlled the three points of entry into the Mediterranean, might
simply block off these positions and attempt to win the war by isolating
Italy within that sea (concentrating primarily on prosecuting a land
offensive), it remained unlikely that the naval war would continue on such
a limited basis. Italy's control of the Straits of Sicily constituted a serious
threat to Allied communications with India and the Black Sea, and it was
inevitable that they would more than likely attempt to resolve the conflict
by conducting offensives in the central Mediterranean. Were they indeed
to do so, then the main Italian battle fleet should at all costs be maintained
intact and committed to fight only when victory seemed certain.

All the available evidence suggested that the Anglo-French fleets
planned to focus primarily on engaging the Italian navy in the central
Mediterranean. Enemy bases there had recently been strengthened, and
the distribution of forces suggested that they had been deployed with this
type of strategy in mind. Thus, with any idea of the Italian fleet conducting
its war against the Mediterranean exits precluded, its planned operations
also concentrated on this theatre. Aside from seeking a decisive fleet
action, the navy's Sicilian Channel defences should aim to prevent enemy
transit through the sea and any link-up between their respective fleets.
Protecting Italian troop convoys destined for North Africa in wartime was
risky and involved the use of almost the entire Italian battle fleet, and the
naval leadership was most unwilling to undertake this task. The British
and French could very easily attack Italian communications with Libya
from their air and sea bases in Tunisia, Egypt and Greece, and, as the naval
staff had noted in July, the navy could commit no additional units to the
Dodecanese to counter these attacks. Eventually, the opportunity for a
naval offensive in the western basin might present itself, but only if the
Western powers chose to attack the Balearics. Otherwise, strategy there,
as well as in the eastern basin, should remain strictly defensive. In the
Indian Ocean, Italian submarines should operate with German units
against enemy traffic, while similar actions should be undertaken in the
Red Sea 'with the forces available there'. The first and second squadrons
should now assume a war footing at Taranto and a squadron of light
cruisers should make ready at Naples. By 31 August, 87 Italian submarines

were also to be made ready for war. All harbour defences were now to be placed on full alert and the minefields in the Sicilian Channel laid. On 26 August the naval high command gave the order to place all central Mediterranean naval departments on a full war footing.[55]

Despite the evident limitations of the navy's overall plan – the absence of any co-ordinated aeronaval strategy, quantitative and qualitative inferiority, a poorly defended main base – Mussolini's bellicose frame of mind had not altered, notwithstanding the protestations of Ciano, who bitterly condemned Germany's 'betrayal' of its 'Axis' partner after the Salzburg '*Diktat*'. Influenced by Pariani, who continued to argue that the army was ready for war, Mussolini seemed prepared to attack Croatia and Dalmatia in order to secure Italy's 'share of the booty', and especially so after the German–Russian Non-Aggression Pact of 24 August appeared to remove the possibility of Western aid reaching Poland, and the likelihood of Soviet naval intervention in the Mediterranean. But, following King Victor Emanuel's firm protestations that the army was entirely unready for war, Italian frontier defences far from secure and the alliance with Germany widely unpopular domestically, Ciano convinced the still belligerent Mussolini that Italy should not enter the war. To the foreign minister's relief, the *Duce* authorised the dispatch, on 25 August, of a letter to Berlin containing Rome's reasons for not marching alongside Germany, followed the next day by a comprehensive list of raw materials Italy would need immediately if it were to initiate hostilities. On 31 August, after Mussolini again proposed a conference of the 'Munich' powers to resolve the conflict, London cut its telephone links with Italy in response to Italian measures taken in Europe and the Mediterranean. Ciano swiftly informed Mussolini, who, clearly taken aback, ordered his son-in-law immediately to contact Loraine, pointing out that Italy did not intend to declare war against Britain and France. At 5.25 a.m. central European time on 1 September, Germany attacked Poland. That afternoon, Mussolini informed the Fascist grand council, the forum for much bombast from the dictator in the past, that Italy would remain a non-participant in the German war against Britain and France.[56]

So ended the first phase of Mussolini's relationship with Hitler's Reich. The 'Axis', the 'vehicle of Mussolini's imperial ambitions', had not worked in Italy's favour to date. Berlin had followed its own agenda, occupying the Rhineland, Austria, part of Czechoslovakia and, finally, Prague, before entering into war contrary to specific agreements reached in Munich in September 1938 and Milan in May 1939. Mussolini felt betrayed. For him, Italy's neutrality amounted to little more than a humiliation. As the evidence suggests, non-participation in the war was not a choice for Mussolini but a necessity. After the drama of the autumn of 1938, any notion of waging an offensive against Egypt and Suez appeared evidently impracticable. The naval high command had warned that logistical support for Pariani's intended campaign carried a high risk of failure. In the period that followed the shelving of the plans in January 1939, the navy requested further costly, long-term building of ships and bases that in its opinion would improve the Italian strategic position in both the Mediterranean and the Red Sea.[57]

Mussolini clearly agreed with the need to prepare both the navy and the nation for war by 1943. Quite simply, in aligning his country to a Hitlerian Germany already redrawing the territorial map of Europe according to its own agenda, he surrendered his right to decide the timing of the 'inevitable' 'Axis' clash with the Western powers. On the eve of the Second World War, the Italian navy, its existing programmes incomplete, could do little more than attempt to defend the Straits of Sicily from the overwhelming might of Allied sea power it believed faced no serious challenge from Rome's German ally.

NOTES

1 On Mussolini's efforts to popularise Italy's relationship with Germany, see Mack Smith, *Mussolini*, pp. 253–8. On the anti-French campaign, see Knox, 'L'ultima guerra dell'Italia fascista', p. 22; and on the infamous anti-French outburst by Fascist deputies during a speech by Ciano, see Ciano, *Diario*, 30/11/1938. The idea that Rome planned an 'isolated' war against France with German help is discussed in M. Toscano, 'Le conversazioni militari italo-tedesche alla vigilia della seconda guerra mondiale', *Rivista Storica Italiana*, 69,1 (1957), pp. 349–50. Accounts of the Ribbentrop visit can be found in Ciano, *Diplomatic Papers*, 'Conversation between the Duce and the Foreign Minister of the Reich, von Ribbentrop', 28/10/1938, pp. 242–6; *DGFP*, D, IV, 400, 'Memorandum by an Official of the Foreign Minister's secretariat', 28/10/1938. For the views of King Victor Emanuel, see Ciano, *Diario*, 5/1/1939. On the Easter Accords, see Knox, *Mussolini Unleashed*, p. 38.
2 Sullivan, 'The Italian Armed Forces', pp. 179–80; Bottai, *Diario*, 4/2/1939. On the naval plans for war in East Africa, see USMM, *Le operazioni in Africa orientale*, p. 20; on Albania, Knox, *Mussolini Unleashed*, p. 41.
3 Ceva, *Le forze armate*, pp. 250–1; USMM, *L'organizzazione della Marina durante il conflitto, tomo I*, appendix 5, Mussolini to Cavagnari, 27/5/1939, pp. 348–50.
4 Sullivan, 'The Italian Armed Forces', p. 185; Ciano, *Diario*, 22–24/10/1938 and 28/10/1938; Ciano, *Diplomatic Papers*, conversations between Ciano and Ribbentrop, 22/10/1938, 23/10/1938 and 28/10/1938, pp. 238–41.
5 *DGFP*, D, IV, 402, Mackensen to foreign ministry, 5/11/1938, 403, 'Memorandum by the Director of the Political Department', 7/11/1938, 406, 'Memorandum by the Ambassador in Italy', 8/11/1938 and 411, Keitel to Ribbentrop, 30/11/1938; Toscano, 'Le conversazioni militari italo-tedesche', pp. 336–44. For the argument that Hitler, although having authorised greater military co-operation with Italy, remained opposed to a unitary high command and foresaw separate theatres of war, see Schreiber, *Revisionismus*, pp. 147–8.
6 USMM, DG, 0-A1, 'Documento zero: studio sulla preparazione', naval war plans office, 28/10/1938. In the period which followed the Czech crisis the Italian naval staff continued to show limited interest in guerrilla warfare. Although the navy

authorised work on man-guided torpedoes and '*barchini*' to begin afresh, and made provision for a special team of officers based at La Spezia secretly to develop new weapons, at the moment of Italy's entry into the European conflict few of the weapons had passed even the developmental stage. See USMM, *I mezzi d'assalto*, pp. 22–33.

7 A report by Riccardo Paladini, by now commander-in-chief of the lower Ionian naval division, had already emphasised the value of Malta to the enemy as a possible landing point for carrier-borne air units, which had attacked the Italian base at Taranto. See USMM, DG, 10, 'Impiego delle forze di superficie del settore Jonio e basso Adriatico nelle prime 24 ore di conflitto', Paladini to naval war plans office, 6/10/1938. The increasing strategic importance of Malta to the plan to supply the army's offensive in North Africa is discussed by Gabriele, *Operazione C3: Malta*, pp. 17–20; USMM, DG, 10, 'Riunione dello Stato Maggiore', 8/12/1938.

8 USMM, DG, 10, 'DG 10/A2. Studio generale per il trasporto di un corpo di spedizione in Africa settentrionale', naval war plans office, 12/1938; cited in part in Gabriele, *Operazione C3: Malta*, appendix 1; USMM, *La Marina Italiana nella seconda guerra mondiale. VI: La difesa del traffico con l'Africa settentrionale dal 10 giugno 1940 al 30 settembre 1941* (USMM, Rome, 1958), p. 4.

9 Gabriele, *Operazione C3: Malta*, pp. 34–43; USSME, *Verbali delle riunioni*, meeting of 5/6/1940; D. Brown, 'Malta 1940–1942: The Influential Island', draft paper, London, 1990, pp. 2–3. On the Balkan offensive and Matapan, see I. S. O. Playfair, *The Mediterranean and the Middle East. Volume I – The Early Successes Against Italy* (Her Majesty's Stationery Office, London, 1954), pp. 333–8; Admiral of the Fleet Viscount Cunningham, *A Sailor's Odyssey* (Hutchinson, London, 1951), pp. 326–37 and 341.

10 Schreiber, *Revisionismus*, pp. 170–1; Ceva, 'Altre notizie sulle conversazioni militari italo-tedesche alla vigilia della seconda guerra mondiale', pp. 156–9.

11 Ciano, *Diario*, 16/11/1938; DGFP, D, IV, 409, 'Political Report', Mackensen to foreign ministry, 28/11/1938 and 410, Mackensen to foreign ministry, 28/11/1938; Watt, *How War Came*, p. 51; Parker, *Chamberlain and Appeasement*, pp. 192–6. For the argument that Chamberlain viewed the visit as a means of encouraging Mussolini to put pressure on Hitler in order to secure 'a lasting European settlement', see P. Stafford, 'The Chamberlain–Halifax Visit to Rome: A Reappraisal', *English Historical Review*, 98, 386 (1983). Stafford's judgement that Mussolini did not agree to Ribbentrop's October alliance proposal for fear that Britain and France might 'close ranks behind him', and, moreover, that he valued British 'friendship' as a means of pressurising Paris, appears somewhat erroneous in the face of abundant evidence regarding the dictator's anti-British orientation. See P. Stafford, 'Italy and Anglo-French Strategy and Diplomacy, October 1938–September 1939' (DPhil, Oxon, 1985), pp. 5–6 and 56, for Stafford's support of the De Felice '*peso determinante*' thesis. For the Italian record of the Chamberlain–Halifax visit to Rome in mid-January 1939, see ASMAE, carte Grandi, b: 55, f: 145, 'Colloquio del Duce col signor Chamberlain', meetings of 11/1/1939 and 12/1/1939; Ciano, *Diario*, 12/1/1939.

12 Ciano, *Diario*, 17/11/1938, 30/11/1938, 2/12/1938, 6/12/1938, 1–3/1/1939, 5/1/1939, 7–9/1/1939; Ciano, *Diplomatic Papers*, 'Letter to Reich Minister von Ribbentrop', 2/1/1939, pp. 258–9; DGFP, D, IV, 421, Ciano to Ribbentrop, 2/1/1939 and 422, memorandum by Mackensen, 3/1/1939; Knox, 'The Fascist Regime, its Foreign Policy and its Wars', p. 363.

13 USMM, DG, Studi politici, 'Conversazioni navali italo–tedesche', Olivia to naval staff, 12/1/1939. The German naval programme revealed to the Italian delegation amounted to one 40,000-ton battleship, 13 destroyers, six torpedo-boats, and 35

submarines. On Mussolini's assent, see USSME, I: 4, r: 3, c: 5, 'Pro-memoria per S.E. il Capo di Stato Maggiore generale', report for Badoglio by the office of the supreme high command, 13/1/1939.

14 USMM, DG, 0-A1, 'Pro-memoria sul programma anno XVII e seguenti', naval war plans office, 1/1939.

15 On the effects of the anti-French campaign within Italy, see Ciano, *Diario*, 8/12/1938 and 5/1/1939. On raw materials, see MCRR, carte Dall'Olio, b: 1122, 'Disponibilità di materie prime in caso di emergenza', Dall'Olio to Mussolini, 13/3/1939 and 'Materie prime', Dall'Olio to Mussolini, 27/3/1939. On the transportation difficulties affecting Italo-German coal trade, see *DGFP*, D, IV, 432, Clodius to transport ministry, 15/1/1939, and on complaints by the Italian government about the shortfall, 457, memorandum by Weizsäcker, 8/3/1939. Figures on the Italian budget deficit can be found in PRO, FO 371/23810, 'Report of Budget Commission of the Chamber of Fascist Deputies on the Naval Estimates', 10/6/1939.

16 For discussion of Hitler's *Z-Plan* for massive German naval expansion of January 1939 and its part in the dictator's overall expansionist thinking, see Hillgruber, 'England's Place in Hitler's Plans for World Domination', p. 15; W. Rahn, 'German Naval Power in the First and Second World War', draft conference paper, Exeter, 1994, pp. 11–13. On Hitler's views on sea power in a war against Britain, see Hildebrand, *The Foreign Policy of the Third Reich*, pp. 75–6. Hitler's speech of 28 April 1939 is cited in A. Bullock, *Hitler: A Study in Tyranny* (Penguin Books, London, 1981), pp. 500–4.

17 USSME, *Verbali delle riunioni*, meeting of 26/1/1939.

18 For official Italian reaction to Hitler's speech, see Ciano, *Diario*, 31/1/1939 and 2/2/1939. For comment on Mussolini's speech, see Bottai, *Diario*, 4/2/1939; the full text of the speech can be found in ACS, Joint Allied Intelligence Agency (JAIA), Personal Papers of Benito Mussolini, Job 2, Roll 229, 'Relazione per il Gran Consiglio', 2/1939.

19 *DGFP*, D, IV, 449, Mackensen to foreign ministry, 10/2/1939; Ciano, *Diario*, 10/2/1939 and 15/3/1939. On Mussolini's agreement to the opening of full staff conversations, see *DGFP*, D, IV, 461, 'Memorandum by an Official of the Foreign Minister's Personal Staff', 11/3/1939. On his message of approval for the German occupation of Prague, see 463, Mackensen to foreign ministry, 15/3/1939 and D, VI, 15, Mackensen to foreign ministry, 17/3/1939.

20 Ciano, *Diario*, 16/3/1939, 17/3/1939 and 20/3/1939; *DGFP*, D, VI, 15, Mackensen to foreign ministry, 17/3/1939 and 45, Mackensen to foreign ministry, 20/3/1939. On Spain, Bargoni, *L'impegno navale italiano nella guerra civile spagnola*, pp. 411–12; Ciano, *Diario*, 11/3/1939 and 26/3/1939. On the decision to take Albania and proceed with the German alliance 22–3/3/1939; Bottai, *Diario*, 10/4/1939 and 13/4/1939. On British guarantees to Greece and Romania, see Parker, *Chamberlain and Appeasement*, p. 219–22; on British strategic planning, see PRO, ADM 1/9900, 'Operations against Italy in the Event of War', February–April 1939; Playfair, *The Mediterranean and Middle East, Vol. I*, pp. 25–9.

21 For Mussolini's approval of the talks, see Ciano, *Diario*, 10/3/1939. On the political background to this decision, see Toscano, 'Le conversazioni militari italo–tedesche', pp. 337–47 and on the Keitel–Pariani talks, pp. 349–65. DDI, 8, XIII, appendix III, 'Le conversazioni militari italo–tedesche di Innsbruck', 5/4/1939. Hitler's instructions regarding the extent of the conversations can be found in *DGFP*, D, VI, appendix I, no. I, 'Directive by the Chief of the High Command of the Wehrmacht. Wehrmacht Conversations with Italy', 22/3/1939. On Hitler's authorisation of the Polish offensive, see *DGFP*, D, VI, 149, 'Directive by the Chief

of the High Command of the Wehrmacht', 3/4/1939; and on the levels of mistrust that dominated German–Italian military conversations between April and June 1939, see Schreiber, 'Political and Military Developments in the Mediterranean Area', p. 9; H. Umbreit, 'Italy's Entry into the War', in W. Deist *et al.* (eds), *Germany and the Second World War. Volume II: Germany's Initial Conquests in Europe* (Clarendon Press, Oxford, 1991), pp. 304–5.

22 USMM, CN, b: 2741, f: 1, 'Rapporto di missione a Berlino', Salza to Cavagnari, 24/4/1939; Schreiber, *Revisionismus*, p. 163.

23 Ceva, 'Altre notizie sulle conversazioni militari italo–tedesche', pp. 166–9; *DDI*, 8, XII, 47, Attolico to Ciano, 27/5/1939.

24 *DGFP*, D, VI, 211, 'Record of the Conversation between Field Marshal Goering and the Duce', 18/4/1939.

25 Ciano, *Diario*, 29/4/1939, 30/4/1939 and 2/5/1939. On Carboni and *SIM*, see Knox, 'Fascist Italy Assesses its Enemies', pp. 349–51.

26 *DGFP*, D, VI, 341, 'The Discussions between the Reich Foreign Minister and the Italian Foreign Minister', 18/5/1939; Ciano, *Diplomatic Papers*, 'Conversation with the Reich Foreign Minister, von Ribbentrop', 6–7/5/1939, pp. 283–6; Ciano, *Diario*, 6–7/5/1939, 13/5/1939 and 14/5/1939. For various interpretations of the Pact of Steel, see M. Toscano, *The Origins of the Pact of Steel* (Johns Hopkins University Press, Baltimore, MD, 1967), pp. 307–402; Schreiber, 'Political and Military Developments in the Mediterranean Area', pp. 39–41; Watt, *How War Came*, pp. 408–11; Weinberg, *Starting World War Two*, pp. 566–7 and 596–7.

27 Ciano, *Diario*, 24/5/1939, 25/5/1939 and 27–28/5/1939; *DGFP*, D, VI, 456, Mackensen to foreign ministry, 31/5/1939; G. Waterfield, *Professional Diplomat: Sir Percy Loraine of Kirkharle, 1880–1961* (John Murray, London, 1973), pp. 229–33; USMM, *L'organizzazione della Marina durante il conflitto, tomo I*, appendix 5, pp. 348–50; *DDI*, 8, XII, 59, Mussolini to Hitler, 30/5/1939.

28 USMM, DG, 0-A1, 'Nuovi aspetti della situazione mediterranea rispetto alla situazione del settembre 1938', naval war plans office, 18/5/1939. On British and French planning for the Mediterranean theatre in May and June 1939, see Playfair, *The Mediterranean and Middle East. Vol. I*, pp. 25–9, on Malta, pp. 29–31 and 69–70, and on the position in May 1940, p. 95. The figure of around 200 air units in French North Africa provided by Italian air intelligence, *SIA*, clashes with the figures for this period presented by Martin Thomas, who notes that French air strength for the Mediterranean and Middle East as a whole totalled 166 aircraft, of which 103 were bombers. See M. Thomas, 'Plans and Problems of the *Armée de l' Air* in the Defence of French North Africa before the Fall of France', *French History*, 7, 4 (1993), pp. 484–5. On the effectiveness of Italian air intelligence, see Schreiber, 'Political and Military Developments in the Mediterranean Area', p. 84.

29 USMM, DG, 8-A, 'Possibilità di azione in caso di conflitto', Matteucci to naval staff, 10/5/1939.

30 USSME, N: 8, r: 1513, 'Direttive per l'azione delle forze armate dell'Impero in caso di improvviso conflitto', di Savoia to ministry for Italian East Africa, 15/5/1939. On the general Italian military situation in East Africa, see Playfair, *The Mediterranean and Middle East. Vol. I*, pp. 165–6.

31 Ciano, *Diario*, 8/1/1939. During his conversation with Keitel, Pariani had spoken of his belief that Italian demands against France 'would be settled through a "colonial war", and not through a European war. The war would remain localized [*sic*] to France–Italy'. Keitel was left with the impression that 'Pariani made these apparently spontaneous statements on the basis of strict instructions which he had brought with him from Rome'. *DGFP*, D, VI, appendix I, no. III, record of the

Pariani–Keitel conversations, 4/4/1939. On plans against British East African positions, see USSME, N: 8, r: 1513, di Savoia to ministry for Italian East Africa, 15/5/1939.

32 USMM, DG, 8-A, 'Studio sulle azioni offensive e sulla dislocazione iniziale', Somigli to naval command, Massawa, undated (1939). The naval staff's approval of the Matteucci plan is most likely that referred to in USMM, *Le operazioni in Africa orientale*, p. 20. USMM, DG, 8-A, 'Piani operativi', Cavagnari to ministry for Italian Africa, 5/7/1939. The order from Cavagnari came at a time when Badoglio, in his capacity as chief of the general staff, assumed control of Italy's colonial armed forces. And, as MacGregor Knox notes, 'the monarch's role and Badoglio's defensive mentality prevented most of the offensive planning necessary to translate Mussolini's vision into a reality', Knox, 'Fascist Italy Assesses its Enemies', p. 366.

33 USMM, DG, 0-M, 'Operazioni aeree iniziali interessanti la guerra marittima', Cavagnari to Badoglio/Valle, 16/5/1939.

34 USMM, DG, 0-M, 'Operazioni aeree iniziali interessanti la guerra marittima', Valle to Cavagnari/Badoglio, 6/6/1939.

35 On torpedo bombers, see USMM, *L'organizzazione della Marina durante il conflitto, tomo I*, p. 51; USMM, DG, 0-M, 'Pro-memoria sul problema della cooperazione aereo-navale', report by Vittorio Bacigalupi, 23/6/1939.

36 USMM, DG 10, 'Difesa delle Baleari', naval war plans office, 24/5/1939 and 12/6/1939. On Raeder's view that the Italian navy should seek to secure control of the western Mediterranean, see Schreiber, *Revisionismus*, pp. 170–1. *SIS* reports on Anglo-Turkish relations in this period claimed that London had been attempting to secure Ankara's co-operation in eventual operations against the Dodecanese, and expected to make use of the southern Turkish port of Marmaris as an operational base. See USMM, CN, b: 3276, f: 6, 'Bolletino verde, n.1070. Turchia (fonte SIM)', 10/3/1939. For a naval staff report on the Anglo-Turkish declaration of 12 May 1939 and its possible implications for Italy in the eastern Mediterranean, see USMM, CN, b: 3276, f: 8, 'Gli accordi anglo-turchi', naval staff, 13/5/1939; on this point, see also Playfair, *The Mediterranean and the Middle East. Vol. I*, p. 25.

37 USMM, CN, b: 2741, b: 1, Cavagnari to Raeder, 3/5/193, and Raeder to Cavagnari, 17/5/1939.

38 *DGFP*, D, VI, appendix I, I, 'Directive by the Chief of the High Command of the Wehrmacht', 22/3/1939 (italics in original), and VI, 'Visit of the Commander-in-Chief of the Army to Italy', Löwisch to the high command of the navy, 13/5/1939; USMM, CN, b: 2741, f: 1, Löwisch to Cavagnari, 27/5/1939 and 'Schema di risposta alla lettera dell'addetto navale germanico', unsigned, 1/6/1939; *DGFP*, D, VI, appendix I, VIII, 'Meeting of the Commander-in-Chief of the Navy with the Italian Admiral Cavagnari', Schniewind to naval attaché group, 17/5/1939.

39 B. Stegemann, 'Germany's Second Attempt to Become a Naval Power', in Deist *et al.* (eds), *Germany and the Second World War. Volume II*, pp. 60–6.

40 *DDI*, 8, XIII, appendix IV, Cavagnari to Ciano, 20–1/6/1939; *DGFP*, D, VI, appendix I, XII, 'Record of the Conversations at Friedrichshafen', and XIII, 'Conversation between the Italian Admirals Sansonetti and De Courten and Rear-Admiral Schniewind and Captain Fricke', Fricke to head of operations division, naval war staff, 21/6/1939; conversations cited in part in Toscano, 'Le conversazioni militari italo–tedesche', pp. 365–77; Schreiber, *Revisionismus*, pp. 172–5 and on Raeder's thoughts prior to the conversations pp. 168–72. On Raeder and the Mediterranean see *Fuehrer Conferences on Naval Affairs, 1940*, unpublished Admiralty Report, September 1947, 'Report of the Commander-in-Chief, Navy

to the Fuehrer', 6 September 1940 and 26 September 1940; B. Stegemann, 'Politics and Warfare in the First Phase of the German Offensive', in Deist *et al.* (eds), *Germany and the Second World War. Volume II*, pp. 25–6. At the time of the naval talks the German Vice-Admiral Zeiger had visited Italy and requested a tour of inspection of the new *Littorio*-class ships. While the Italian naval ministry proved outwardly forthcoming, there could be no disguising the sense of discomfiture generated by the visit, as revealed by the 'hurried' and limited nature of the visits in question. See USMM, b: 2741, f: 1, reports on the visit of Vice-Admiral Zeiger to the Ansaldo shipyard and the battleship *Littorio*, 22/6/1939 and 23/6/1939.

41 Toscano, 'Le conversazioni militari italo–tedesche', p. 379; Ceva, 'Altre notizie sulle conversazioni militari italo–tedesche', pp. 158 and 168. Ceva argues that even by 1940 greater attempts at co-ordinating the German–Italian war effort could have seen successes in exploiting the aeronaval potential of Italian East Africa, Chisimaio (provided its land defences were rendered adequate) and the *sbarramento* in the Sicilian Channel, and could also have led to a successful attempt to take Malta, all of which were within the operational capabilities of the 'Axis' and particularly so after the fall of France. For views on Friedrichshafen, see USMM, *L'organizzazione della Marina durante il conflitto, tomo I*, pp. 313–15; Schreiber, *Revisionismus*, pp. 175–7.

42 USMM, *L'organizzazione della Marina durante il conflitto, tomo I*, appendix 5, Mussolini to Cavagnari, 27/5/1939, pp. 348–50. On 14 June 1939 Mussolini expressed his opinion on the role of Spain in future Italian strategy in a conversation with Ciano. Morocco should become totally Spanish, while Algeria and Tunisia should become Italian possessions. Through alliance with Spain Italy could thereby secure access to the oceans. See Ciano, *Diario*, 14/6/1939. On Mussolini's belief that the 'Axis' should dominate the Balkans in order to secure raw materials supplies there, see Bottai, *Diario*, 9/6/1939.

43 Ciano, *Diario*, 13/6/1939 and 3–4/7/1939; *DDI*, 8, XII, 255, Arone to Ciano, 16/6/1939, 367, Attolico to Ciano, 26/6/1939 and 432, Ciano to Attolico, 2/7/1939.

44 *DDI*, 8, XII, 463, Loraine to Ciano, 4/7/1939; Waterfield, *Professional Diplomat*, p. 234. On Mussolini's statement to Loraine, see *DDI*, 8, XII, 505, Mussolini to Ciano, 7/7/1939; Ciano, *Diario*, 7/7/1939.

45 Knox, *Mussolini Unleashed*, p. 42; *DGFP*, D, VI, 718, 'Record of the Conversation between Foreign Minister Ribbentrop and Ambassador Attolico', 25/7/1939; *DDI*, 8, XII, 687, Attolico to Ciano, 26/7/1939. For Hitler's view of Mussolini's conference idea, see 717, Attolico to Ciano, 28/7/1939 and 732, Attolico to Ciano, 31/7/1939.

46 Ciano, *Diario*, 6/8/1939, 7/8/1939 and 9/8/1939. On the Salzburg meetings, see *DDI*, 8, XIII, 1, 'Verbale del colloquio tra il ministro degli Esteri Ciano e il ministro degli Esteri tedesco, von Ribbentrop', 12/8/1939 and 4 and 21, 'Verbale del colloquio tra il ministro degli Esteri, Ciano, e il Cancelliere del Reich, Hitler', 12–13/8/1939; *DGFP*, D, VII, 43 and 47, meeting between Ciano and Hitler, 12–13/8/1939; Ciano, *Diario*, 11/8/1939, 12/8/1939 and 13/8/1939.

47 USMM, DG, 9-C, 'Valore del possesso di Salonicco da parte nostra nei riguardi della guerra marittima nell'Egeo', naval war plans office, 5/7/1939.

48 Knox, *Mussolini Unleashed*, p. 41; Ciano, *Diario*, 12/5/1939; Schreiber, 'Political and Military Developments in the Mediterranean and Middle East', pp. 53–4.

49 Ciano, *Diario*, 5–7/6/1939 and 14/6/1939.

50 USMM, DG, 0-C1, 'Necessità di accelerare l'approntamento dei bacini adatti per le nuove corazzate da 35,000 tonn. in corso di costruzione', naval war plans office, 1/7/1939.

51 USSME, I: 4, r: 6, c: 13, 'Direttive di carattere operativo per le terre italiane d'oltremare in dipendenza dell'attuale situazione internazionale', Badoglio to all service departments, 29/8/1939; Schreiber, 'Military and Political Developments in the Mediterranean and Middle East', p. 54; USMM, DG, 0-C, 'Necessità di iniziare l'esecuzione del programma navale anno XVII', 1/7/1939.

52 USMM, CN, b: 2765, f: 18, Matteucci to naval staff, 2/8/1939.

53 USSME, I: 4, r: 6, c: 13, 'Direttive di carattere operativo in dipendenza della situazione internazionale', Badoglio to all chiefs-of-staff, 17/8/1939; Schreiber, 'Political and Military Developments in the Mediterranean and Middle East', p. 53; see also Ciano, *Diario*, 16/8/1939, for Mussolini's views of Germany at this point.

54 Ciano, *Diario*, 17/8/1939 and 20/8/1939.

55 USMM, DG, 0-A1, 'Esame del programma strategico in caso di conflitto nella attuale situazione politica', naval war plans office, 20/8/1939; USMM, DG, 10, 'Ordine generale di operazione n. 1', Barone to all naval departments, 26/8/1939.

56 Ciano, *Diario*, 21–6/8/1939, 31/8/1939 and 1/9/1939; Schreiber, 'Political and Military Developments in the Mediterranean and Middle East', p. 54. On Mussolini's views of the situation of the Italian fleet, see also *DGFP*, D, VII, 280, Mackensen to foreign ministry, 25/8/1939; Ceva, 'Appunti per una storia dello Stato Maggiore generale', p. 246; *DDI*, 8, XIII, 250, Mussolini to Hitler, 25/8/1939 and 293, Mussolini to Hitler, 26/8/1939. On British peace initiatives, see Waterfield, *Professional Diplomat*, pp. 242–7. On Italian measures taken, see *DGFP*, D, VII, 349, Mackensen to foreign ministry, 27/8/1939, 350, Mussolini to Hitler, 27/8/1939 and 423, Mackensen to foreign ministry, 29/8/1939.

57 Knox, *Mussolini Unleashed*, p. 50.

War

Italian '*non-belligeranza*' was greeted with as much relief in Paris and London as it had been throughout Italy. Yet, for Mussolini, the sense of failure had been profound, and in the period that followed the outbreak of European war on 3 September 1939 he attempted both to seek a negotiated peace in order to end Italy's 'shame' and to preserve his tarnished relationship with Berlin. Concomitantly, he also readied the Italian armed forces for the possibility of an eventual entry into the general conflict now in progress. Ignoring the warnings of drastic raw-material shortages voiced by Dall'Olio and *Cogefag* in late August, the dictator ordered an increase in the production of all armaments that autumn.[1]

Then, clearly determined to ready the Italian armed forces for war and at the same time to rid himself of incompetent military leaders, he dismissed both Pariani and Valle from their respective posts at the war and air ministries, replacing the former with Rodolfo Graziani, who became chief-of-staff, and Ubaldo Soddu, who assumed the role of undersecretary. Giuseppe Valle, who had assured the dictator that Italy could boast of some 2,300 first-line aircraft when, in fact, only 640 were combat ready, lost his own position to Francesco Pricolo. Only Cavagnari, who in 1935 had warned Mussolini of the dangers of war against Britain and now urged that Rome distance itself from Berlin's requests for naval assistance, remained at his desk after the widespread administrative changes of the autumn of 1939. Ciano advised Mussolini against replacing the admiral given his 'excellent performance' in the recent period of tension. Only after the Taranto disaster a year later did the *Duce* finally replace him with Arturo Riccardi.[2]

By the spring of 1940, as Mussolini turned once more towards the idea of war against the west European powers, Cavagnari again expressed doubts as to the wisdom of Italian participation in the conflict against the British, given the weakness of Italy's position. But, Mussolini, although aware of the true extent of continued Italian material and military debility, none the less believed that Italy could successfully undertake a war of short duration, thereby earning it the right to participate in the peace talks. It was merely a question of entering the conflict at the most opportune moment, he informed the chiefs-of-staff on 31 March. Following the German military successes that spring and early summer, that moment appeared to have arrived.[3]

To the navy, Mussolini assigned the specific task of attacking the enemy 'in the Mediterranean and outside', provoking its commander-in-chief once more to reject any idea of an offensive war against the Royal Navy. The Italian navy could not achieve precise strategic objectives, Cavagnari insisted, nor could it defeat the markedly superior enemy forces, or replace lost ships as easily as they could. Thus, a purely defensive strategy in the Mediterranean did not justify entry into the conflict. Cavagnari's appeal failed. On 10 June, with France all but defeated following the devastating German offensive of that year, Mussolini declared war against the West in order irrevocably to resolve the question of Italy's imprisonment in the Mediterranean, his stated aim for the past two decades.[4]

This chapter examines the part played by Cavagnari and the naval staff in Mussolini's well-documented decision to take Italy into a general war at a time of widespread national and military unreadiness. The continuing developments in the dictator's relationship with Berlin will be addressed, and the reasons underpinning the naval high command's determination to avoid conflict will be examined in the light of this relationship. The fleet's readiness for war will be assessed, as will naval strategic planning throughout the period of non-belligerence and up to Italy's entry into the conflict in June 1940.[5]

Non-belligerence: Phase One, September 1939–February 1940

Although Italy remained a non-participant in the European war which erupted in early September 1939, there could be no question of Mussolini changing sides. The Allies had extended the economic blockade of Germany imposed by them at the initiation of hostilities to the Mediterranean, a fact that served still further to underline the disparity between Italian demands for free access to the world's oceans and British and French control of that sea. It might be added that were Rome to conclude a second treaty of London similar to the one signed in 1915, no one would take Italy or its leader seriously ever again. Prestige built up over 'so many years of struggle', as the Fascist zealot Roberto Farinacci noted, would evaporate overnight. Even if those Italians in favour of the alliance with Germany remained a small minority indeed, Mussolini, despite predicting a German defeat following Ciano's 1 October meeting with Hitler and Ribbentrop, soon rediscovered his faith in the 'Axis'. By the middle of the month he was speaking of Italy as Berlin's 'economic and moral reserve', adding that it might yet find a military role for itself.[6]

As far as the naval leadership was concerned, no such 'role' could exist for the foreseeable future: war in the Mediterranean theatre against the overwhelming might of the Allied air and sea forces based there remained out of the question. Moreover, although in late September the naval staff finally approved the May 1939 Matteucci plan for offensive operations in the Red Sea, the evolving political and strategic situation radically, indeed swiftly, altered its nature.

The original plan foresaw aggressive and undeclared attacks being launched from Italian bases in East Africa, whose aim was the capture of merchant shipping, the destruction of enemy naval forces, and ultimately the armed occupation of Djibouti and French Somaliland. Some four weeks after the outbreak of hostilities, Cavagnari informed Matteucci's replacement at Massawa, Rear Admiral Balsamo, that he had now approved the original idea as developed in May, and issued the admiral with directive *Di. Na. 4* authorising its prosecution. Interestingly, the chief-of-staff now rescinded his instruction of July that only submarine forces were to take part in the operations in question, and authorised all Italian naval units in the region to engage the enemy in the event of war. Furthermore, he also agreed to Matteucci's original idea of capturing both enemy and neutral cargo vessels at the outbreak of hostilities.

In the event of war, the naval high command in Rome expected torpedo units to menace enemy communications between Aden and Djibouti at night, a task to which the navy assigned contingents of human torpedoes. Both were to attack the naval units of the adversary in their bases at Aden, Perim, Djibouti and Port Said, while other *'mezzi insidiosi'* would destroy as many enemy stores and military facilities as possible. Cavagnari also ordered the main Italian surface forces based in the region – the 3rd and 5th destroyer squadrons – to operate against allied sea communications, while concurrently protecting those between Italian territories and 'the Arab coastline'. The air force should be requested to launch attacks against all enemy positions, and in particular aim at 'neutralising' Aden. The high command in Rome foresaw Italian submarines attacking enemy units in the Gulfs of Aden and Oman, without a prior declaration of hostilities if necessary, while the navy assisted in the occupation of French Somaliland.

However, once it became clear that Rome's non-belligerence did not preclude allied reinforcement of the Red Sea theatre, the East African naval command 'recognise[d] … the need to revise this directive'. By March 1940, Balsamo noted that if the Allies were to increase their naval presence in the theatre – which, not surprisingly, he considered likely after the outbreak of war – he was not prepared to risk Italian surface units in any offensive. To do so risked incurring losses that the navy could not replace. Aggressive operations by submarines and torpedo-boats might be possible, he added, provided that naval intelligence and air reconnaissance could provide accurate and up-to-the-minute information on the deployment of enemy forces. In the meantime, in the event of hostilities, the regional naval command had already decided that the best option open to the navy would be laying a *'sbarramento'* of mines from a point ten miles south-east of the Bab-el-Mandeb Straits, in order to threaten communications between Aden and Perim. The naval staff in Rome ultimately agreed with Balsamo's prognosis, adding that the East African command should only undertake the planned operations if 'concrete results' could be assured.[7]

Such caution was by no means exclusive to Italy's East African territories. Overall strategic directives issued by Badoglio at the end of August 1939 focused on the defence of Italian overseas territories, rather than Pariani-style campaigns of territorial conquest for which the Italian armed forces were generally unprepared and seriously ill equipped. Any offensive or counter-offensive operations, such as those proposed by Matteucci and Italo Balbo – one of the original Fascist *squadristi* and now governor of Libya, who aimed to revive the Pariani plan to conquer Suez from Libya, probably as a means of furthering his own political ambitions – could not be considered. Mussolini and Badoglio duly rejected Balbo's idea, which was indefinitely shelved after the dismissal of Pariani in October. Meanwhile, the naval high command tactfully replaced the aggressively minded Matteucci with the rather more cautious Balsamo.[8]

Clearly, the new commander-in-chief at Massawa had been unprepared to risk precious surface units in any war against the Allies, unless the odds for success were significantly stacked in the navy's favour. Balsamo believed that the East African fleet could not replace losses incurred in the Red Sea while hostilities remained in progress. Rome now no longer mentioned the possibility of co-operation with the German navy in the Indian Ocean, and neither had the naval ministry approved the projected new base at Chisimaio or the ocean-going cruiser units destined for this theatre, facts which influenced Balsamo's views. His 'perplexity' at any idea of committing the limited naval assets at his disposal to 'risky night time operations' is therefore understandable. Similarly, although *Di. Na. 4* cited the importance of guerrilla-warfare tactics to the success of the planned offensives, only the previous July, with the threat of war growing, the war plans office in Rome had authorised work to begin on preparing and testing new weapons and specialised training to commence. At the outbreak of hostilities, the entire *'mezzi d'assalto'* programme was still far from complete. Only in 1941 did the naval staff finally appreciate the true value of this inexpensive, yet effective, form of warfare.[9]

Other, even more serious, problems faced the naval high command in the Mediterranean theatre. The premature outbreak of hostilities found work on the *Mar Grande* harbour-construction project at Taranto, initiated in 1937, still far from complete, leaving the Italian battle squadrons – by July 1940 containing six capital ships – without an adequately defended logistical base, should they find themselves suddenly at war. Even the existing system of defences at the port were considered seriously deficient. In late October Admiral Giulio Valli, a former deputy chief-of-staff and now a senator, warned Cavagnari that in the event of an air or underwater torpedo attack against naval units based at Taranto, the navy risked grave losses if it did not significantly improve harbour defences there. Although the naval staff had considered the likelihood of enemy attack by torpedo bombers since at least 1913, history had shown that this form of offensive had limited success to date. However, attack by torpedo bombers was still a threat, as was the possibility of Italian naval forces being attacked in their bases by enemy guerrilla weapons such as midget submarines. During recent tours of inspection undertaken at Taranto, Augusta and La Spezia, Valli had noted with some alarm the vulnerability of the fleet's large surface units at times of international tension. Subsequently, he urged the chief-of-staff to consider a project he personally had developed for the placing of anti-torpedo netting around individual vessels in order to protect them from this form of warfare. Only by making use of 'vertical' nets of this type could the surface vessels of the Italian fleet be defended against all forms of torpedo attack, both in port and at sea. The resulting reduction in speed, he concluded, would be more than compensated for by a substantial increase in protection.[10]

Cavagnari flatly rejected the idea as financially and materially far too costly. Some 12–15,000 metres of materials would be required if the idea were to be adopted, and the naval ministry could not afford such a capital outlay at this time. Considerable industrial problems arose in producing such large quantities of netting, while widespread use of this type of anti-torpedo defence would incur a substantial increase in the number of tugs required within naval ports. Finally, he added, the navy needed to overcome significant 'nautical and logistical' difficulties, and address the question of ship manoeuvrability if this system were accepted. For these reasons, he had decided to continue with the current anti-torpedo protection policy of the navy, and simply improve the 'compartmentalised' system of nets within the outer harbour at Taranto. This seemed to him the most 'practical and economical' solution to the entire problem.[11]

In July 1940 Valli examined the problem once again, still warning that the current 'compartmentalised' anti-torpedo defences of the outer harbour were unlikely to offer much protection from aerial offensives. Improving the defences would invariably be costly, but worth the endeavour, he stressed, otherwise Cavagnari might as well order the fleet to 'sail for Alexandria'. Once more, Cavagnari overlooked Valli's recommendations and the existing defensive system at *Mar Grande* was left in place, as the chief-of-staff had ordered. That November, squadrons of British *Swordfish* torpedo bombers settled the dispute. In spite of the 'strength of the defences' at *Mar Grande* Andrew Cunningham, commander-in-chief of the British Mediterranean Fleet, ordered the successful attack on the Italian base – operation 'Judgement' – which left the battleship *Cavour* beached and the *Duilio* and *Littorio* damaged and out of action for some six months.[12]

A naval war plans office report of mid-November highlighted not only the weakness of the navy's port defences, but other major problems as well. Even if the Italian fleet found its battleship nucleus increased by four new and remodernised vessels by the summer of 1940, the memorandum began, the navy needed to offset the change this brought to the balance of Mediterranean naval power against its own shortages in other ship types. In particular, the Italian naval squadrons, once ready for war, remained bereft of an appropriate level of modern destroyer escorts. Once the remodernised *Doria* class and the new *Littorio* ships entered service, the only way of providing them with destroyer protection would be to 'pilfer' ships destined for deployment in North Africa and the Dodecanese; theatres where the navy already faced shortages in all types of vessel. Worse still, the planners argued, once at war, the navy might incur destroyer losses – which, in any conflict, were normally likely to be fairly heavy – which it could not replace. In short, the Italian fleet would find itself permanently deprived of this type of vessel, leaving the battleship formations accordingly exposed to attack.

Shortages in key raw materials such as oil, iron and steel affected the navy's ability to undertake training exercises at sea and gunnery practice, the report continued. So bad was the situation, that the naval staff had suspended all forms of training for the remainder of November. By January, the plans office hoped to resume training at a greatly increased level. The overall capability of the navy would be seriously undermined, however, if raw-material deficiencies further prevented fleet exercises from taking place at the beginning of 1940. The only possible solution was that the government allocate greater material resources to the fleet in order to replenish its stocks, and thereby not delay its preparations for war any further. In particular, the navy should seek to secure greater fuel stocks in order to ensure adequate levels of training, and that enough oil entered the navy's bunkers for use in wartime. At present, the fleet had sufficient supplies of oil for five-and-a-half months of combat. Once the new storage facilities were complete and filled to capacity in the early months of the following year, there would be fuel enough for seven months of war.

In turn, the planners addressed two other serious, if not familiar, problems confronting the navy's high command: the questions of air support and base defences. The Italian navy, the planners emphasised, remained without any adequate means of air cover for its fleet operations.

171

Forcing it to sea against an enemy well versed and properly equipped in the requirements of aeronaval warfare amounted to little more than suicide. Indeed, so behind was Italy in air and sea co-operation that it constituted the 'gravest preoccupation' for the naval leadership in any war. The current situation regarding harbour defences was scarcely better. Great expense and effort had in recent years been expended on increasing Italy's surface and underwater forces, without a similar effort being undertaken to provide them with secure facilities. In particular, the report concluded, ammunition was in short supply, with the consequence that anti-aircraft defences as a whole were appallingly weak, being 'wholly inadequate for the defence either of ships or installations'. Mussolini, aware of the navy's current state of readiness, having read and absorbed this report, needed to act swiftly in order to rectify the serious problems affecting naval combat effectiveness. He should make greater resources available immediately if the situation was in any way to improve.[13]

Clearly, the navy's overall situation was far from adequate. Short of effective air cover, destroyer escorts for its precious capital ships, and a well-defended principal base, its vulnerability in time of war was self-evident. Furthermore, the shortages in raw materials reduced fleet efficiency, prevented gunnery practice and sea exercises, and left overall fuel stocks sufficient only for five months of combat. Even including the additional storage facilities still under completion in the autumn of 1939, the navy's bunkers could not, notably, hold more than seven months worth of stocks at any one time. Moreover, there remained other, equally serious, deficiencies. Although other naval powers had not yet completed their developments in radar technology when war broke out, neither had the Italians proved wholly successful in developing a working prototype by the time Mussolini chose to declare war the following year. Despite experiments by the navy's technical specialist, Professor Ugo Tiberio, which began in 1936 at the Livorno Naval Institute of Electronics, the fleet entered the war without Italian industry being able to mass produce radar equipment, or even to secure the necessary parts from the United States. If, Tiberio noted after the war, he had managed to build an effective prototype sooner, and not wasted time and scarce money on developing other models, Italy would have been at least two years ahead of the race. As it was, not until 1941 were 60 instruments finally ordered by the naval ministry.[14]

Added to this, the navy's mines, the mainstay of the central Mediterranean strategy advocated by Cavagnari and the navy's planners, were woefully outdated and in short supply; at the outbreak of war there were some 25,000 mines in the navy's arsenals, a quantity well below that required for a lengthy conflict. Existing anti-submarine technology remained limited and backward. Destroyers, the principal vessels assigned to this task, were not only in short supply – as a consequence of the decision taken by Mussolini and Badoglio to reduce naval construction costs by using armed merchant men in such operations – but were also unable to operate at night. Torpedo-boats, the other type of vessel the navy deployed to counter enemy submarine attacks, were often of dubious seaworthiness and had a limited operational range.[15]

Finally, equally as serious were the tactical weaknesses of the Italian navy. The naval high command had been slow to follow a general post-Great War trend in less rigid naval tactics. German officers present at Italian naval exercises noted the rigid insistence on controlling naval units from land, an adherence to 'compact formations at sea', and concurrently little use being made of detached units or independent operations. Admirals and commanding officers on the whole seemed to lack initiative, while training in night actions and scouting duties proved largely insufficient. A further grave oversight was the navy's failure to assign a commander-in-chief afloat. The naval ministry's policy was merely to place the senior flag officer in command of the fleet, a procedure that proved 'extremely detrimental to uniformity of training in peacetime, and prevented smooth co-operation between detached squadrons during the war'. The temperamental performance of Italian naval radio transmitters and receivers aboard ship could hardly improve the deficiencies imposed by such structural inflexibility. So poor was the quality of on-board radio equipment, that inter-ship and ship-to-shore communication often proved difficult. The navy abandoned attempts at sea-to-air communication two months into the conflict.[16]

The material condition of the other armed forces proved equally as bad, if not even worse. At a meeting of the supreme high command held two days after the navy's war planners had reported on the overall position of the Italian fleet, a pessimistic picture emerged of the national military capability. Italy's overseas possessions were desperately short of materials. Food, ammunition and fuel were in short supply; so short, that in neither East Africa, nor the Aegean, nor Libya did there exist more than six months' worth of stocks; and Badoglio stressed that the Italian colonies needed at least a full year's worth before contemplating any war. Anti-aircraft defences were generally in poor shape. Odoardo Somigli, deputy chief-of-staff for the navy, argued that Italian naval bases needed a further 5–6,000 anti-aircraft guns, together with ammunition, before even training of the gunners could take place. In short, concluded Badoglio, any idea of Italy's taking the Suez Canal had become wholly unrealistic, and the planning staffs should waste no further time considering unrealistic operations. Not before 1942 would the Italian position be likely to improve. The respective chiefs-of-staff should in the meantime concentrate all their efforts solely on securing national defences. Only when the *forze armate* had completed this task, could the possibility of any offensives be considered.[17]

But Mussolini was growing restless. After reports appeared in the British press claiming that the dictator intended to 'assume leadership of a neutral bloc and veer away from the Axis', he responded angrily by emphasising that he detested the very word 'neutrality'. Italy's status, Ciano informed Mackensen in mid-October, 'remained that of maximum preparedness', although, 'owing to gaps in preparedness', Italy must for the moment remain in the background.[18]

Clearly, Mussolini did not intend to remain away from the limelight for long. On 15 November he informed a demonstration of university students in Rome that Fascist Italy's peace was not the peace of a weakling, but 'an armed peace'. He went on to demand of the supreme autarky commission that the tempo of Italy's march towards a full war economy 'be accelerated beyond the limits of the possible', whatever sacrifices might be required, eliminating all 'sceptics', all 'laggards' while doing so. By early December, a despondent Ciano, who had seemingly lost none of his anti-German feelings, noted that Mussolini felt himself 'excluded from great events'. The *Duce* now proposed writing to Hitler in order to assure him that Italy supported any German diplomatic initiative aimed at ending the war, or, alternatively, of entering the conflict in 1942, as originally agreed in Milan the previous May. On the evening of 7 December, during the foreign minister's speech to the Fascist grand council on the theme of Italo-German relations since 1935, Mussolini, while tacitly approving the anti-German tenor of Ciano's argument, nevertheless seemed determined that the 'Axis' alliance should survive the recent traumas. Far from speaking of peace, the *Duce* called for the 'greater numbers of cannons, aircraft and tanks' that Italy needed in order to be ready to intervene at the end of 1941.[19]

In view of such pronouncements, Mussolini's eventual, exhaustively discussed, letter to Hitler of 5 January 1940 cannot, as has often been argued, easily be interpreted as a sign of crisis in 'Axis' relations. Mussolini assured the *Führer* that he was 'accelerating the tempo of military preparations', and that Italian intervention would come only 'at the most profitable and decisive moment'. Italy remained fully committed to its alliance; only by so doing could Mussolini realise his dreams of a Mediterranean and Balkan empire.[20]

The cardinal problem for Mussolini was that the most 'profitable' moment for Italian entry into the war seemed far off, and Hitler simply might not choose to wait very long before initiating hostilities in earnest. In mid-December Carlo Favagrossa, the new head of *Cogefag*, acting on data provided by the respective service departments on material deficiencies, produced for Mussolini a generally pessimistic report on the approximate date of Italian military readiness. The air force would have 3,000 new aircraft only by 1941. The army could not expect completion of its programme of artillery modernisation until 1945 and, moreover, remained critically short of tanks. Only after the declaration of war did Mussolini approve production to begin of around 3,500 new tanks of all types. Italian armaments factories had not completed the programme before Italy concluded its armistice with the Allied powers in 1943. The navy, too, could not expect completion of its artillery programme until 1944–45, while current building, aimed at increasing the battleship nucleus of the fleet to eight vessels, was not destined to be ready until at least 1943. Accordingly, Mussolini reconsidered his position and ruled out any possibility of intervention in the New Year. Italy could not enter the war before late 1941, at the earliest.[21]

Certainly, the naval high command were not, by late January 1940, seriously contemplating any immediate Mediterranean or Red Sea conflict against the Allies. The war plans office had given vague consideration, in early December 1939, to an early occupation of Corfu in wartime, thereby preventing its use as a naval base by the British, who would, in making use of Cephalonia 90 miles further south as an alternative, find a position 'far less hydrographically favourable' for use as a base. Apart from this, by the beginning of 1940, the navy's planners had produced no new strategic plans to follow the operational directives issued in late August – directives that dealt exclusively with defending the central Mediterranean from the overwhelming superiority of enemy air and sea power. There seemed little point in doing so. 'The control exercised by Britain and France over the two main Mediterranean exits and on the stretches of coastline in proximity to these exits, amounts to no less that a total *strategic encirclement* of Italy', noted a gloomy naval staff report of 26 January 1940. The only theatre where the navy could avoid this encirclement, in effect mirrored by the Italian position in the Red Sea, and consider aggressive operations, was in the Indian Ocean. There, however, the naval high command had already noted the strategic limitations imposed by the absence of a secure base in Italian Somaliland, and by the limited number of naval forces available, which the navy could not replace in time of war. This left the plans office again concentrating purely on the defence of the central Mediterranean, where, despite Italy's advantageous position in the Sicilian Channel, the navy's six battleships, once in service, still faced an enemy naval coalition whose superiority the planners regarded as crushing.

The Italian fleet could do little against the eight battleships (including the new French *Dunquerque* class), nine heavy cruisers, aircraft carriers and other substantial naval units confronting it, while Italy's naval bases remained unable to defend themselves from enemy air offensives from Malta and Bizerte. The entry into the conflict of Greece and Turkey, while not markedly improving the overall force strengths of the British and French fleets, improved substantially their strategic position with regard to bases and, in turn, threatened greatly Italy's position in the Aegean.

This overall situation might only change, the naval staff concluded cautiously, if and when the enemy deployed additional naval units to cover losses in other theatres of war. In line with the general strategic conclusions reached at the supreme high command meeting the previous November, the naval staff suggested little more than a strengthening of the defences in the Sicilian Channel. The 'calibre and the total of guns required' for the protection of Pantelleria, in particular, should be 'studied at length' in order to ensure that in any naval war, the island might be in a strong position to play a key role in the defence of the central Mediterranean.[22]

Despite the grave strategic situation in which Italy found itself, Mussolini turned increasingly towards ideas of intervention. By mid-January, influenced by interventionists like Graziani, who, in the words of Ciano, 'had more ambition than brains', Mussolini spoke of his belief that Italy could enter the war alongside Germany in the second half of 1941. Undeterred by a near-disastrous national economic and industrial situation, exacerbated further after he broke off trade talks with London in February under pressure from Berlin – a move which stripped Italy of British coal supplies and potential hard currency amounting to £20 million – Mussolini demonstrated a clear determination to declare war. At the final meeting of the supreme defence commission, held between 8 and 14 February, Mussolini warned that he would empty the reserves of the Bank of Italy in order to ready Italy for conflict. 'No-one should believe', he declared 'that our deficiencies could ever constitute an alibi for Italy. We cannot possibly remain absent from this drama, which will re-write the history of entire continents.' The Allies would lose the war, he told Ciano afterwards, once again reaffirming his familiar thesis that Italy 'needed free access to the oceans, without which it could never become an imperial power'. The Duce was determined to have his 'parallel war'. He did not have long to wait for it.[23]

Non-belligerence: Phase Two, March–June 1940

Given the precarious position of the Italian armed forces and the Italian economy, it is hardly surprising that Italy's various planning departments had largely not considered the offensive operations needed to secure territorial conquest in the first period of Mussolini's non-intervention. The risk of failure remained far too great. In early March the completion of *PR 12*, the overall strategic blueprint for any possible Italian war effort, showed that war ministry planning had followed to the letter Mussolini's and Badoglio's instructions of August and November 1939, which established that the chief military priority facing the armed forces was the defence of metropolitan and colonial territories from attack. On all fronts, the army's operations department prepared contingencies for a strategy designed principally to counter possible enemy aggression. Mainland Italy, its various islands and the Aegean possessions should be defended against the likelihood of amphibious landings and air attack; Libya should be secured from the threat of invasion from either Egypt or Tunisia, and in particular the port of Tobruk should be prevented from falling into Allied hands; Italian East African territories should be defended from enemy offensives launched from the Sudan and British and French Somaliland; and, somewhat cryptically, the Italian Alpine fronts should also be strong enough to counter a possible land invasion of Italy. By no means precluding the likelihood of eventual offensives by the Italian armed forces, *PR 12* focused on eastern Libya, Italian East Africa and the eastern Alpine frontier as the theatres where counter-offensive strategies might in time be considered, once 'circumstances became favourable'.[24]

Undoubtedly, *PR 12* was the product of Pietro Badoglio's defensively-minded strategic philosophy, and therefore differed from the war plan eventually revealed by Mussolini at the end of the month. Although the *Duce* also foresaw the army remaining largely on the defensive, the navy was to act offensively against the enemy, while air force strategy was to be 'integrated' with that of ground troops and naval forces.[25]

Throughout March, Italy moved ever closer towards a 'parallel' war of the kind envisaged by Mussolini. Bitterly angered by the British decision to prevent German ship-borne supplies of coal reaching Italy after Anglo-Italian conversations had broken down in February, and under increased pressure from Berlin to sever links with the British, Mussolini appeared increasingly bellicose. On 6 March, during the course of a particularly vociferous anti-British tirade, the *Duce* warned Ciano that he, of all people, did not intend to become the 'laughing stock of all Europe' by remaining out of the war, soon to begin in earnest. On the contrary, he did not wish to suffer any further humiliation at the hands of London in Italy's 'own sea'. Rather, he would make the British regret their recent actions, and Italy's entry into the war 'would lead to their defeat'. Britain would be 'resoundingly beaten', and Ciano should get used to the idea very quickly indeed.[26]

Once Ribbentrop had descended on Rome on 10 March, promising an imminent German offensive on the western front and monthly German deliveries of coal amounting to 1 million tons – Italy's total national requirement – which promised to relieve Rome of its dependence on Britain, the stage was firmly set for Italian intervention. Italy, a prisoner in the Mediterranean, simply needed to be patient, Mussolini informed the Reich's foreign minister. It would remain so until ready, 'just as the boxer in the ring must at certain moments be able to take a great many punches'.[27]

If Mussolini, having now committed Italy, continued to doubt the successful outcome of the coming German onslaught, then Hitler's letter, delivered by Ribbentrop, made him clearly aware of the consequences for Italy if Germany failed:

> I believe, Duce, that there can be no doubt that the outcome of this war will also decide the future of Italy. If that future is viewed in your country merely as the continued survival of a modest European state, then I am wrong. But if that future is conceived as a guarantee of the existence of the Italian people from the historical, geopolitical, and general moral viewpoints, that is, according to the criteria of your people's right to existence, Duce, then you will some day be confronted by the same opponents who are fighting Germany today.

At their meeting on the Brenner a week later, the *Führer* spoke even more graphically. The fates of Germany and Italy were 'indissolubly connected'. A German victory would also be an Italian one. The 'defeat of Germany also implied the end of the Italian empire'. Mussolini, doubtlessly vulnerable to Hitler's promises of uncontested Italian mastery in the Mediterranean after France 'was disposed of', left unanswered Hitler's proposal for a joint German–Italian land offensive against the Rhone Valley. But, fatefully, he did confirm that Italy would soon declare war, despite the seriousness of its financial and material position. It was now merely a question of timing.[28]

By 23 March, Mussolini had privately informed Ciano of the strategy Italy would pursue in its coming war against the West, informing the king and the service chiefs in his detailed and frequently cited memorandum of seven days later. The *Duce's* plan contained few, if any, surprises. Aside from the familiar, even clichéd statements regarding Italy's geostrategic and geopolitical 'imprisonment' – the justification for Mussolini's decision to fight – the overall grand strategy envisaged a land offensive only in East Africa. The army should remain on a defensive footing on all fronts – the French and Yugoslavian Alpine fronts, those of Libya, Albania and the Aegean. The Italian armed forces might attempt an annexation of Corsica, but no attack on France should proceed, unless German victories proved overwhelming. Similarly, Italy might only attempt an attack on Yugoslavia in the event of internal collapse. Otherwise, he considered offensive operations viable only in East Africa, where he ordered the armed forces to proceed with their planned occupation of Djibouti and Kassala. The navy, however, should consider itself on an offensive footing both 'in the Mediterranean and outside it'.[29]

Clearly, given the universal pessimism that permeated the naval staff, and in particular the reports of the war plans office in November 1939 and January 1940, the prospect of war against Britain and France would have been viewed with some alarm by the high command. By mid-March, the naval staff had already warned Cavagnari that Italy could not even adequately defend the Adriatic in time of war. The army staff were unable to increase the number of divisions currently based in Albania (five) and, as a result, could not now successfully counter any attempted enemy occupation of Corfu. The British and French would subsequently force the navy to abandon its base at Port Edda, in southern Albania, with the overall consequence that Allied forces, once in full possession of the Greek island, could easily menace Italian traffic in the Straits of Otranto. This could only have the gravest consequences for Italy's lines of communication.[30]

Even worse, however, was the fact that on the eve of Italy's entry into the conflict the navy's planners had not yet given full consideration as to how they intended to deploy the main battle squadrons in the Mediterranean. During his March meetings with Hitler and Ribbentrop, Mussolini had placed great emphasis on the value of his surface fleet, boasting of the imminent entry into service of the navy's new and remodernised capital ships. The Italian fleet, he stressed, would be ready for war in three to four months. Italy would have the advantage in battleship strength, given that she had 'at her disposal four vessels of 35,000 tons as compared with only two on the British side' – a patent untruth. Furthermore, he followed these statements, fuelled more by his characteristic *braggadocio* than reality, by issuing a directive to the naval command to wage a sea offensive against the enemy fleets. This order in no way corresponded with the strategic realities confronting the naval staff. A report by the plans office in April stressed that there would be difficulty enough concentrating the battle fleet for the decisive encounter in the central Mediterranean, long foreseen by the navy's strategists, let alone contemplating war in other Mediterranean theatres or even outside that sea.

The first naval squadron, an internal memorandum for Cavagnari noted, would be composed of all six operational battleships, which, once finding themselves *en route* to a combat situation had, in the first instance, to be protected from enemy air and undersea attack. Moreover, the navy's sea reconnaissance forces had to co-operate fully with the respective air units in order to offer 'guidance' to the fleet at sea as it approached any enemy formation. The principal problem lay with the vessels themselves as much as with other material or tactical questions. 'The fundamental differences in armaments, protection and speed' between the ships implied that the composition of the battle fleet would need to be 'elastic'. The navy should avoid creating too 'rigid' a formation at all costs. By this the planners meant that the older and slower *Doria* and *Cavour* classes, when operating 'under normal conditions of visibility', should steam four or five miles ahead of their newer *Littorio*-type counterparts in order to ensure that, once deployed to battle stations, the former were not left lagging behind in the event of a decisive engagement. Therefore, the navy should not group the six units in question together but, rather, allocate them to separate formations, which, in the event of a naval encounter calling for the deployment of the entire fleet, should be distributed in such a way as to permit a timely intervention.[31]

The implications of both naval staff memoranda were grave. The Adriatic, claimed by Mussolini to be an 'Italian lake' after the occupation of Albania in April 1939, was nothing of the sort. The armed forces based in the Italian-occupied territory could not prevent enemy possession of Corfu by staging a pre-emptive annexation of the island. Subsequently, the Allies were free to use the position as a base from which to menace Italian traffic in the Straits of Otranto in the southern Adriatic. Meanwhile, the April report on the battle fleet highlighted still more serious problems. It appeared that the naval high command had given no consideration to battleship deployment in poor weather conditions or at night, when visibility would invariably be 'abnormal'; it remained unlikely that the enemy would obligingly seek a confrontation merely when the Mediterranean climate best suited the leadership of the *Marina*. Moreover, the emphasis placed on guaranteeing protection from enemy air attack and on sound aerial reconnaissance underlined the fact that the vessels could only operate within the range of land-based air units, and not beyond, as Mussolini's vague yet ambitious directive of 31 March demanded. The lack of anti-submarine technology and the deficiencies of Italian naval 'scouting' have already been illustrated. The differences in speed – which ranged from a trial speed of 27 knots for the older ships to 31.5 for the newer ones – suggest that concentration of the fleet would have been problematical. Having said this, the performance of the Italian vessels nevertheless compared favourably with those of the British. In fact, the trial speeds achieved by the remodernised *Doria* and *Cavour* classes were faster than those reached by the *Warspite*, the *Barham* and the *Valiant*, whose speeds averaged at 23 knots. Although greater velocity might prove advantageous in terms of disengagement, the vulnerability of the Italian ships to modern ordnance and air attack would prove to be decidedly disadvantageous. At the outbreak of hostilities in June, the naval high command chose to deploy its capital-ship assets to Taranto and, in conformity with the recommendations of the planners, grouped the *Littorio* class separately from the two older ships in service at that point (see appendix 1). Clearly, the lack of adequately protected bases in the main theatre of operations made such a distribution of forces necessary. It did not, however, make them any less vulnerable to enemy air attack, as the naval leadership soon discovered.[32]

Cavagnari's marked reluctance to consider a naval war against the British, expressed in his well-documented statements to the supreme high command on 9 April, and in his letter to Mussolini five days later, is therefore both understandable and identical to the doubts he had raised during the spring of 1935. In line with the main strategic precept contained within the naval staff report of January 1940, the chief-of-staff could only confirm that what the navy's planners had predicted had now become a reality – the enemy could deploy fleets at Gibraltar and Suez, leaving Italy to 'asphyxiate within the Mediterranean'. The Italian fleet, strategically confined to the defence of the Sicilian Channel, could do little to counter adversaries who were most likely to reduce their own communications passing through the Mediterranean and conduct a war of attrition against Italy. Furthermore, Italy could not replace losses as easily as the enemy. Under such circumstances, the purely defensive strategy planned for the Italian fleet would not lead to the defeat of the Allied navies. Hence, in the absence of clear and achievable objectives, Italy's entry into the war simply 'could not be justified'. The navy lacked adequate air reconnaissance, air support, well-defended bases as well as a sufficient number of units with torpedo-carrying capability. Mussolini could find himself at the peace conference without a navy or an air force.[33]

Yet, the undeniable tendency to overestimate the strength of the enemy, a characteristic of each of the Italian armed services, cannot be overlooked. The naval staff's gloomy prognoses of an awesome preponderance of Allied air and sea power confronting Italy in the Mediterranean failed to consider the possible weaknesses that also existed, possibly as a consequence of a faulty naval intelligence-gathering mechanism. In the words of the wartime chief of the *Servizio Informazioni Segreti*, Commander Max Ponzo:

> Before the war our offensive service was built up on foundations which it had been proved did not correspond to the necessities of war and were without any precise organic scheme. Expenditure was cut down, there was no confidence in the service, and it was considered absolutely undesirable to employ active service officers on these delicate and important duties. Indeed in every country the work depended almost exclusively on the naval attachés, each of whom, according to his own judgement and with the limited means at his disposal, organised for [*sic*] his own satisfaction an intelligence service in the country or countries to which he was accredited; these organisations in nearly every case regarded the naval attaché as their head who examined the information and transmitted it to the centre.[34]

Italian naval intelligence analysed the nation's enemies within a somewhat restricted paradigmatic framework, simply assessing the composition of enemy forces, their activities and location, and their likely future operational activities. Indeed, as already noted, the naval war plans office largely based its assessments of the British and French fleets simply on quantitative analyses of battleship strength. Had the naval leadership placed greater emphasis on broadening the methodological basis of assessment, then the naval staff might have been more aware of the vulnerable points of their future adversary. For example, the naval high command might have discovered that Andrew Cunningham could not 'take his whole battle fleet to sea at the same time without stopping all other activities', owing to the equally limited number of destroyers available to him. They might also have learned that although the British capital ships possessed 15" guns, compared with the 12.5" weapons of their remodernised Italian counterparts, the latter could in fact out-range the guns of the Royal Navy. The navy's planners might also have become aware of the scant resources available to the Royal Navy to provide escorts for Red Sea shipping, the attacking of which had been an integral component of naval strategy in the East African theatre.[35]

On a wider basis, faulty intelligence also accounts for the excessively pessimistic Italian assessment of British defences on Malta, whose occupation the navy's planners considered afresh in April 1940, after which Cavagnari vetoed the idea as too risky during the high command meeting of 5 June. Believing the British to have some 105 aircraft on the island, together with a formidable system of defences, the naval staff erred. Prior to the outbreak of hostilities in the Mediterranean, the only air units based there were seaplanes. Britain had deployed no fighter units to the island and only completed work on a new Maltese airfield in May 1940. Nor had Malta received appropriate quantities of anti-aircraft guns. Indeed, so grave had been the situation, that the Allied military committee in London concluded that 'in the case of Malta, no direct relief can be afforded in the initial stages of the war, and we should hope that the garrison would be able to hold out until relieved'.[36]

More generally, intelligence gathering within Italy as a whole proved equally ineffective. At the meeting of the Italian chiefs-of-staff held on 6 May, which discussed the necessity of strengthening manpower levels in Libya – in itself a useless and time-consuming strategy without the necessary means being available – Badoglio produced figures for enemy-force strengths in the theatre that hardly corresponded with reality. Maxim Weygand's Syrian army totalled not the 200,000 men cited by Badoglio, but three poorly equipped and inadequately trained divisions – around 40,000 men. The figure of 100,000 British and Egyptian troops based in Egypt in reality translated into the 36,000 men of Archibald Wavell's army, again insufficiently equipped, and the native army whose support would be doubtful – Egypt not being at war with Germany. Political motives may be attributed to such serious miscalculations of allied strength; after all, Giacomo Carboni, head of SIM, reportedly held 'anti-German convictions', and accordingly the figures may have been distorted to influence Mussolini. But, more likely, the failures of Italian intelligence work can be attributed, as suggested by Max Ponzo, to lack of confidence, limited resources and, certainly in the case of SIS, far too narrow a set of criteria for assessment.[37]

In any case, Mussolini soon swept away Cavagnari's reservations, and, on 12 April, ordered the fleet to mobilise. Then, as the German offensive of that spring and summer got underway, swallowing first Norway and Denmark before consuming Holland, Belgium and, ultimately, France, the *Duce*, in the words of Ciano, growing more 'warlike and Germanophile' by the day, finally decided to launch his parallel war of conquest in the Mediterranean. Despite having approved the idea of opening new staff conversations with Germany, Mussolini rejected Hitler's Brenner proposal of a common Upper Rhine front, and, by implication, any notion of a 'coalition war', and finally announced, on 13 May, that he would launch Italy's own Mediterranean war within a month. The British and French had lost the conflict, he told Ciano, and he would wage it against them by air and sea. At the end of the month, Mussolini finally succeeded in wresting control of the armed forces 'in combat' from King Victor Emanuel, at the same time informing the service chiefs, gathered at the *Palazzo Venezia*, that they should be ready for war by 5 June. Hitler then requested that Mussolini postpone the date of Italian entry into the war for a further five days, in order not to jeopardise forthcoming German operations against French air fields. The *Duce* concurred. Italy would initiate hostilities on the morning of 11 June.[38]

The operational directives duly issued by the naval high command, renamed *Supermarina*, on 29 May promised very little, mirroring almost exactly those issued in August 1939. In the eastern and western basins, the fleet should maintain a defensive footing, leaving the Sicilian Channel as the principal theatre for fleet operations. There, the navy should prevent the enemy fleets from uniting, and protect communications with North Africa. Lines of communication with Albania and the Aegean were also to be safeguarded, while the Italian metropolitan coastline should be defended from the expected Allied aeronaval onslaught. Only at the most propitious moment would the Italian battle fleet seek any decisive naval encounter, and then only when the engagement seemed likely to take place nearer to Italian naval bases than those of the enemy.[39]

The next day, the supreme high command 'concentrated on achieving the most effective possible defence capacity on all fronts', the idea of an offensive in East Africa having already evaporated. Quickly, it became apparent that Cavagnari envisaged no major fleet action. Strategy for the navy, summarised as 'defensive to the right and left; control of the Straits of Messina', had, in the words of Francesco Pricolo, 'no precise objectives'. It became clear that only Italy's submarines would carry out an offensive in the Mediterranean. On 2 June *Supermarina* accordingly dispatched orders to all Italian submarine commands to attack enemy naval units, with the exception of 'torpedo-boats and light surface vessels'. Merchant ships should not be spared.[40]

Mussolini wanted a brief but genuine Italian war against the West. As the German victories of that year mounted, so he grew increasingly determined on real intervention, firm in the belief that Italy could not remain neutral, and sure that the Italian people 'wanted war'. He would strike no deal with an almost vanquished France. Even if the dictator eventually bowed to Badoglio's pleas for a total ban on all offensive action against the French – after they themselves had promised not to attack Italy first – this proved more a 'temporary expedient to pacify Badoglio' than any genuine belief in a post-war *rapprochement* with Paris. Nor, as Giorgio Rochat has argued, did Mussolini wish to see German European hegemony checked by an only partially defeated Britain. The *Duce* despised the Western powers; they were fundamentally opposed to Italian expansion: 'We hate them', he had told Hitler at the Brenner in March. 'Co-operation with these countries was out of the question ... Therefore, Italy's entry into the war was inevitable'; her honour and her interests demanded that it be so.[41]

Certainly, when the high command met on 5 June, Badoglio ordered the chiefs-of-staff to focus on attacking the British in the Mediterranean and abstain from any offensives against French territory. But, Cavagnari's orders for the fleet dispatched three days later, betrayed a sense that the navy could hardly avoid combat with the French. All enemy aircraft in flight over the La Maddalena naval base were to be shot down. French naval units encountered by day should be engaged, if hostile. At night, they were to be attacked in any case. Even Badoglio was not averse to French shipping being attacked by 'anonymous' Italian submarines, provided they could get away with it. Shortly after war broke out, the fallacy of any deal between Rome and Paris was truly exposed as the French fleet bombarded Genoa and sank an Italian submarine. In response, Cavagnari did nothing. As the British official history notes, 'the enemy's inaction at sea suggested no great desire to seek battle', a situation that did not alter even after the total capitulation of France. Rather than strike boldly at Malta, as the enemy expected and, as had been planned in September 1938, launch guerrilla operations against the British fleet and its bases, the chief-of-staff simply chose to keep his priceless fleet in being. Whether through strategic narrow-mindedness or fear, or even awe, of his enemy, Cavagnari's principal preoccupation was simply to defend communications with Libya. Determined to avoid ship losses, and apparently resistant to the authority of the supreme high command, the *Comando Supremo*, Cavagnari refused to contemplate action against a British navy that for him had not lost its 'fighting spirit' or for that matter its 'hardness and aggression'. At the moment when his much-vaunted battleships first exchanged fire with the enemy while on convoy duty off Calabria in July, they failed to secure even one hit. Meanwhile, the first encounter with the enemy amply illustrated the appalling ineffectiveness of air and navy co-operation. The Italians had not damaged even one

British ship, while the *Aeronautica*'s bombers even attacked their own fleet by mistake. The Italian navy's submarine arm, of which Mussolini had also boasted during his spring meeting with Ribbentrop, proved hugely disappointing. Just three weeks after Mussolini declared war, Cavagnari could only declare his alarm at the rate of losses.[42]

Mussolini's chagrin with his German allies in the autumn of 1939 by no means tempered his appetite for territorial conquest through armed aggression. Ignoring the desperate condition of the Italian economy, the shortage of strategic raw materials, and in spite of the wholesale unpreparedness of the armed forces, he plunged Italy into war in June 1940, a war he clearly believed already won by Germany. Although the chiefs-of-staff, including Cavagnari, believed that 'they were doing no more than taking a seat at the negotiating table after the Wehrmacht had crushed the West', Mussolini remained convinced that the armed forces, and particularly the navy, would, once thrust into war, drive Britain from the Mediterranean. Aside from highlighting the nature of Fascist politico-military relations, this decision also underlines the tenuous grasp Mussolini had on strategic matters. He was fully aware that the battleship nucleus remained far from complete in June 1940. He was aware, too, of Cavagnari's opposition to Italian entry into a war already in progress, and of the limitations naval unpreparedness would place on strategy (the naval staff after all had anticipated war no sooner than 1943). Yet, he still ordered a naval offensive both within the Mediterranean and outside. This time, unlike during the spring and summer of 1935, Cavagnari could not hope for a political solution to prevent Italy's being hurled into an abyss. The Italian fleet faced Britain alone, no operational alliance with Germany having been concluded, with no concrete strategic objectives, and clinging to the hope that the war would be over quickly. Paralysis of will prevented its leadership from even attempting to strike directly at its adversary.[43]

NOTES

1 Playfair, *The Mediterranean and Middle East. Vol. I*, pp. 39–45; D. Dilks (ed.), *The Diaries of Sir Alexander Cadogan, 1938–1945* (Cassell, London, 1971), p. 171. On Italy see Ciano, *Diario*, 2/9/1939; Bottai, *Diario*, 2/9/1939; Schreiber, 'Political and Military Developments in the Mediterranean Area', pp. 54–5. On Mussolini's continuing enthusiasm for the 'Axis' see Ciano, *Diario: 1937–1943*, 3/9/1939 and 4/9/1939.

2 Ciano, *Diario*, 27/10/1939; L. Ceva, 'Vertici politici e militari nel 1940–1943: Interrogativi e temi d'indagine', *Il Politico*, 46, 4 (1981), pp. 691–2; R. Bernotti, *Cinquant'anni nella Marina Militare* (Mursia, Milan, 1971), pp. 255–6.

3 Schreiber, 'Political and Military Developments in the Mediterranean Area', p. 55–6; Knox, *Mussolini Unleashed*, p. 89.

4 *DDI*, nona serie (vols. I–IV) (Istituto Poligrafico dello Stato, Rome, 1954–60), III, 669, Mussolini to all service chiefs, 31/3/1940. The original document can be found in ACS, JAIA, Mussolini Papers, Job 1, Roll 228; USMM, *L'organizzazione*

della Marina durante il conflitto, tomo I, appendix 6, Cavagnari to Mussolini, 14/4/1940, pp. 351–2. Cavagnari's opposition to Italian entry into the war is also discussed in Ciano, *Diario*, 3/5/1940; Gabriele, 'Le Premesse', p. 112; Playfair, *The Mediterranean and the Middle East. Vol. I*, pp. 145–6; G. Rochat, 'Mussolini, Chef de Guerre, 1940–1943', *Revue d'Histoire de la Deuxième Guerre Mondiale*, 100 (1975), pp. 50–2.

5 A widespread literature exists on the reasoning behind Mussolini's decision to declare war in June 1940, despite the opposition of various key figures in Italy. See, for example, the first-hand account of Ciano's *chef de cabinet* Filippo Anfuso, *Da Palazzo Venezia al lago di Garda* (Cappelli, Bologna, 1957), pp. 117–32, which argues that Mussolini entered the war on the basis that failure to do so would leave Italy without territorial spoils. For the argument that Mussolini wanted Italy actively to fight in the war in order to give legitimacy to Italy's claims at the peace conference see Knox, 'L'ultima guerra dell'Italia fascista', p. 26, and Schreiber, 'Military and Political Developments in the Mediterranean Area', pp. 55 and 59–60. For the contrary view that Mussolini planned to 'declare war but not make war' see Mack Smith, *Mussolini*, p. 291. For a thorough discussion of the historiography of Italian intervention, and in particular the theme of Italo-German relations during 1939–40 see E. Di Nolfo, 'Mussolini e la decisione Italiana di entrare nella seconda guerra mondiale', in E. Di Nolfo, R. H. Rainero and B. Vigezzi (eds), *L' Italia e la politica di potenza in Europa, 1938–1940* (Marzorati, Milan, 1988), pp. 19–38. The view that Italy faced a genuine threat of German invasion at this point and also met with the 'intimidation' of Paris and London in the face of this threat is maintained in V. Gayda, *Italia e Inghilterra: l'inevitabile conflitto* (Edizioni del Giornale d'Italia, Rome, 1941). That Mussolini's decision was based on a mixture of fear of German aggression against Italy as well as a determination to share in the 'glory' of a German victory is argued by D. Alfieri, *Due dittatori di fronte* (Rizzoli, Milan, 1948), pp. 40–1. The 'threat of German intervention' against Italy is also discussed in H. Cliadakis, 'Neutrality and War in Italian Policy, 1939–1940', *Journal of Contemporary History*, 9, 3 (1974). For the view that Mussolini continued to seek consensus with the West during this period while attempting to restrain Hitler, only opting for war when German victories 'compelled' him to do so, see De Felice, *Lo stato totalitario*, pp. 832–3. For a similar argument with the proviso that Mussolini declared war only 'reluctantly' in the very last hours of peace – the De Felice argument taken to its extreme – see Quartararo, *Roma tra Londra e Berlino*, pp. 606–25.

6 G. Bastianini, *Uomini, cose, fatti: memorie di un ambasciatore* (Edizioni Vitagliano, Milan, 1959), pp. 71–3. The Allied blockade of the Mediterranean is discussed in the official British accounts of the Mediterranean war, see Playfair, *The Mediterranean and Middle East. Vol. I*, pp. 44–8 and W. N. Medlicott, *The Economic Blockade: Volume I* (Her Majesty's Stationery Office, London, 1952), Ch. 8. British policy towards Italy, the ultimate effects of contraband control and London's failed attempts to reach an economic agreement with Mussolini over the period 1939–40 are discussed in R. Mallett, 'The Anglo-Italian War Trade Negotiations, Contraband Control and the Failure to Appease Mussolini, 1939–1940', *Diplomacy and Statecraft*, 8, 1 (1997). On Italo-German relations see Ciano, *Diario*, 13/9/1939 and 1–2/10/1939; and on Mussolini's temporary belief in an Allied victory, 3/10/1939. For his reaffirmation of the 'Axis' see entry for 25/10/1939. On Ciano's meetings with Hitler and Ribbentrop see Ciano, *Diplomatic Papers*, 'Conversation with the Fuehrer', 1/10/1939, pp. 309–16. Ciano's attempts to use these discussions as a means of securing Italy's long-range interests in the Balkans, and Hitler's rejection of the 'Balkan neutral bloc' plan is

discussed in F. Marzari, 'Projects for an Italian-led Balkan Bloc of Neutrals, September–December 1939', *The Historical Journal*, 13, 4 (1970), pp. 770–4.

7 For British air and naval forces deployed to the Mediterranean see Playfair, *The Mediterranean and Middle East. Vol. I*, pp. 41–2; on Italian East Africa see USMM, *Le operazioni in Africa orientale*, pp. 20–7; on the final authorisation of the plan USMM, DG, 8-A, 'Direttive di azione per le forze navali in AOI', Somigli to Massawa naval command, 29/9/1939. The overall strategy for the East Africa theatre, revised at the request of Mussolini in late August, foresaw Italian forces in the first instance annexing both French and British Somaliland before attempting a sudden occupation of the Sudan. See USSME, N: 8, r: 1513, 'Direttive per le operazioni nel teatro d'operazioni dell'AOI', war ministry to di Savoia, 18/9/1939.

8 USSME, I: 4, r: 6, c: 13, 'Direttive di carattere operativo per le terre italiane d'oltremare in dipendenza dell'attuale situazione internazionale', Badoglio to all service departments, 29/8/1939; Schreiber, 'Political and Military Developments in the Mediterranean Area', p. 55.

9 USMM, *Le operazioni in Africa orientale*, p. 26; USMM, *I mezzi d'assalto*, pp. 26–33; G. Rochat, 'Lo sforzo bellico 1940–1943: analisi di una sconfitta', *Italia Contemporanea*, 160 (1985), pp. 13–14.

10 USMM, *L'organizzazione della Marina durante il conflitto, tomo I*, pp. 180–1; USMM, DG, 0-G, 'Protezione delle navi nelle radi e nei porti – progetto riservato', Valli to Cavagnari, 22/10/1939.

11 USMM, DG, 0-G, Cavagnari to Valli, 15/11/1939.

12 USMM, DG, 0-G, Valli to Cavagnari, 7/1940; Playfair, *The Mediterranean and Middle East. Vol. I*, pp. 235–8 and, on the defences at Taranto, see map 4; Cunningham, *A Sailor's Odyssey*, pp. 282–7.

13 USMM, DG, 1-A, 'Rapporto', naval war plans office, 16/11/1939. The navy's fuel stocks on 15 February 1940 totalled 1,479,272 tons, enough, the naval staff estimated, for 5.8 months of war. By September 1940 it was anticipated that the total would rise only to 1,566.000 tons, enough for six months. See USMM, DG, 1-A, 'Esame scorte di nafta', naval staff, 18/2/1940. The deficiencies facing the navy at the outbreak of war are discussed in Schreiber, 'Political and Military Developments in the Mediterranean Area', pp. 86–90; C. Favagrossa, *Perchè perdemmo la guerra: Mussolini e la produzione bellica* (Rizzoli, Milan, 1946), pp. 20–1; Bragadin, *Che ha fatto la Marina?*, pp. 2–5; Bocca, *Storia d'Italia nella guerra fascista*, pp. 130–3.

14 USMM, *L'organizzazione della Marina durante il conflitto, tomo I*, pp. 163–4 and 168–9.

15 Weichold, *Axis Naval Policy and Operations in the Mediterranean*, p. 3; USMM, *La guerra di mine*, p. 14; USMM, *La lotta antisommergibile*, p. 6. The official history charts the various studies in anti-submarine warfare undertaken by the naval staff between 1936 and 1939, concluding that Mussolini and Badoglio rejected the navy's requests for ships destined to carry out this task substituting them with armed merchant vessels. Ultimately, on the eve of war the limited number of vessels available, 20 per cent of which were over 20 years old, were forced to cover 'vast' theatres of operations in the Mediterranean, Red Sea and Indian Ocean.

16 USMM, *L'organizzazione della Marina durante il conflitto, tomo I*, pp. 169–74; Weichold, *Axis Naval Policy and Operations in the Mediterranean*, pp. 3–4; PRO, HW 11/33, 'GC and CS Naval History, Volume XX. The Mediterranean 1940–43', p. 13.

17 USSME, *Verbali delle riunioni*, meeting of 18/11/1939. On 2 November the operations department at the war ministry confirmed that Italian grand strategy

as outlined by Mussolini for Badoglio in mid-August remained focused on plan *PR 12*. In the first instance the overall objective was to ensure the territorial integrity of both the metropolitan and colonial spheres, before any possible offensives against Greece and Yugoslavia (once the internal 'political' situation there permitted) might be considered. Offensives might be possible against Egypt from Libya and against the Sudan and French Somaliland from East Africa. Again, these too were subordinate to the defensive security of the Italian territories in question. The Aegean theatre should remain strictly on the defensive. Other grand plans, *PR 10* – war against France and Yugoslavia only, and *PR 16* – war against Germany, were at present ready but were unlikely to be issued, owing to the 'political' situation. See USSME, H: 5, r: 46, 'Sintesi operativa', operations department, war ministry, 2/11/1939.

18 *DGFP*, D, VIII, 266, Mackensen to foreign ministry, 17/10/1939; B. Vigezzi, 'Mussolini, Ciano, la diplomazia italiana e la percezione della "politica della potenza" all'inizio della seconda guerra mondiale', in Di Nolfo *et al*. (eds), *L'Italia e la politica di potenza in Europa*, pp. 9–11.

19 Knox, *Mussolini Unleashed*, pp. 58–9; Ciano, *Diario*, 3/12/1939; Bottai, *Diario*, 8/12/1939; In a second speech delivered to the Fascist chamber of deputies on 16 December, Ciano had included, on Mussolini's orders, a reaffirmation of the German–Italian alliance. See Ciano, *Diario*, 13/12/1939 and for the speech itself see 'Discorso pronunciato da Ciano alla camera il 16 dicembre 1939, Ciano, *Diario*, pp. 701–24.

20 For this line of argument see, in particular, Wiskeman, *The Rome–Berlin Axis*, pp. 187–8 and Bullock, *Hitler: A Study in Tyranny*, pp. 570–2. Mussolini's letter to Hitler can be found in *DDI*, 9, III, 33, Mussolini to Hitler 5/1/1940. MacGregor Knox sees the letter as Mussolini's means of preventing Hitler 'from taking the offensive before Italy could participate', and of safeguarding Rome's position as Germany's ally undermined by the Ribbentrop–Molotov Pact of August 1939, Knox, *Mussolini Unleashed*, pp. 67–9. For further analysis of the letter and the resulting historical debate see also di Nolfo, 'Mussolini e la decisione Italiana di entrare nella seconda guerra mondiale', pp. 25–31.

21 F. Minniti, 'La politica industriale del Ministero dell'Aeronautica: mercato, pianificazione, sviluppo, 1935–1943: parte prima', *Storia Contemporanea*, 12, 1 (1981), pp. 39–41; Favagrossa, *Perché perdemmo la guerra*, pp. 48–50; F. Minniti, 'Il problema degli armamenti', pp. 11–22; idem, 'Due anni di attività del "Fabbri-guerra" per la produzione bellica, 1939–1941', *Storia Contemporanea*, 6, 4 (1975), pp. 858–9; Ciano, *Diario*, 31/12/1939; Knox, *Mussolini Unleashed*, p. 75; on the qualitative aspects of the navy's artillery see L. Ceva, 'L'evoluzione dei materiali bellici in Italia', in Di Nolfo *et al*. (eds), *L'Italia e la politica di potenza in Europa*, pp. 388–90; A. Santoni, 'Perché le navi italiane in guerra non colpivano il bersaglio', *Rivista Storica* (March 1994). For a considerably more positive view of the navy's gunnery see E. Cernuschi, 'Colpito e occultato', *Rivista Storica* (July 1994), pp. 22–33. As regards the projected date of Italian intervention, Gerhard Schreiber maintains that in late 1939/early 1940 Badoglio had no reason to suppose that this would occur before 1943, as agreed in Milan in May 1939. See Schreiber, 'Political and Military Developments in the Mediterranean Area', pp. 55–6.

22 USMM, DG, 0-B1, 'Pro-memoria – problema offensivo–difensivo del tratto di costa prospiciente Corfù-Butrinto', naval war plans office, 7/12/1939; USMM, DG, 0-A1, naval staff, 26/1/1940. The naval staff, as in May 1939, clearly overestimated the extent of the Allied air threat within the central Mediterranean theatre. The figure of 300 bombers based at Bizerte and Malta given by the January report does not correspond with reality. Even after Britain had increased its air

strength after January 1939 the Royal Air Force command in the Mediterranean could boast of only 96 bombers (*Blenheim Mark I* and *Bombay*) and 75 *Gladiator* fighters to cover the entire central and eastern Mediterranean and Middle East. The French air force had some 85 bombers and 65 fighters in North Africa as a whole, with a further 13 bombers and 26 fighters based in Syria. See Playfair, *The Mediterranean and Middle East*. Vol. I, pp. 94–5. On Pantelleria see USMM, DG, 10, 'Rafforzamento della difesi di Pantelleria', naval staff, 1/1940. On the possibilities of Italian–German joint submarine offensives from Spanish bases see USMM, *La Marina italiana nella seconda guerra mondiale. XII: I sommergibili negli oceani* (USMM, Rome, 1963), pp. 24–5.

23 Ciano, *Diario*, 10/1/1940, 12/1/1940, 23/1/1940 and 25/2/1940. Mussolini's decision to end all negotiations of the Anglo-Italian standing committee on possible sales of Italian war materials in return for British coal in early February 1940 marked a turning point on Italy's road to war. See Schreiber, 'Political and Military Developments in the Mediterranean Area', pp. 38–9; Mallett, 'The Anglo-Italian War Trade Negotiations', pp. 155–8. Accounts of the supreme defence commission meetings can be found in Bottai, Diario, 14/2/1940; MCRR, carte Dall'Olio, b: 1121, 'XVIIa sessione della Commissione suprema di difesa', 8–14/2/1940.

24 USSME, H: 6, r: 14, 'Piano PR 12 – II', 3/3/1940.

25 Pieri and Rochat, *Badoglio*, pp. 744–5; Schreiber, 'Political and Military Developments in the Mediterranean Area', pp. 56–7.

26 Ciano, *Diario*, 3/3/1940, 4/3/1940 and 6–7/3/1940; Bottai, *Diario*, 1/3/1940.

27 *DGFP*, D, VIII, 665 and 669, 'Conversation between the Reich Foreign Minister and the Duce', 10–11/3/1940; Ciano, *Diplomatic Papers*, 'Conversation between the Reich Foreign Minister and the Duce', 10–11/3/1940, pp. 339–60;

28 On Mussolini's doubts see Ciano, *Diario*, 10/3/1940 and 12/3/1940; for Hitler's letter see *DGFP*, D, VIII, 663, Hitler to Mussolini, 8/3/1940; DDI, 9, III, 492, Hitler to Mussolini, 8/3/1940. A record of the Brenner encounter can be found in Ciano, *Diplomatic Papers*, 'Conversation between the Duce and the Fuehrer', 18/3/1940, pp. 361–5; Bottai, *Diario*, 29/3/1940.

29 Ciano, *Diario*, 23/3/1940; DDI, 9, III, 669, Mussolini to all service chiefs, 31/3/1940.

30 USMM DG, 0-B1, 'Organizzazione difensiva della costiera albanese', naval staff, 18/3/1940.

31 USMM, DG, 0-B1, 'Pro-memoria sulla costituzione e sui criteri generali di impiego della 1a squadra navale', naval war plans office, 4/1940.

32 A. Raven and J. Roberts, *British Battleships of World War Two: The Development and Technical History of the Royal Navy's Battleships and Battlecruisers, 1911–1946* (Arms and Armour Press, London, 1976), pp. 206 and 234–47; USMM, *L'organizzazione della Marina durante il conflitto, tomo I*, pp. 338–47; Schreiber, 'Political and Military Developments in the Mediterranean Area', pp. 86–7.

33 USSME, *Verbali delle riunioni*, meeting of 9/4/1940; USMM, *L'organizzazione della Marina durante il conflitto, tomo I*, appendix 6, Cavagnari to Mussolini, 14/4/1940, pp. 351–2.

34 PRO, ADM 1/16229, 'Report on the Organisation of the Intelligence Division of the Italian Navy and the Activities of the I.S. Service during the War, 1940–1943', report by commander M. Ponzo, undated.

35 F. Maugeri, *From the Ashes of Disgrace* (Reynal and Hitchcock, New York, 1948), p. 31; Playfair, *The Mediterranean and Middle East. Vol. I*, pp. 90–2.

36 USSME, *Verbali delle riunioni*, 5/6/1940. For the plan of operations eventually produced in mid-June see USMM, *L'organizzazione della Marina durante il conflitto, tomo I*, appendix 8, 'Investimento di Malta', naval staff, 18/6/1940,

pp. 356–60; PRO, FO 371/24944, 'Allied Military Action in the Event of War with Italy', allied military committee, May 1940; Playfair, *The Mediterranean and the Middle East. Vol. I*, pp. 70, 98 and 121; Brown, 'Malta the Influential Island', p. 5; Gabriele, *Operazione C3: Malta*, pp. 39–42.

37 USSME, *Verbali delle riunioni*, meeting of 6/5/1940; comparative figures in Playfair, *The Mediterranean and the Middle East. Vol. I*, pp. 92–3; G. Rochat, 'I servizi di informazione e l'alto commando italiano nella guerra parallela del 1940', *Studi Piacentini*, 4, 1 (1989), pp. 75–8.

38 *DGFP*, D, IX, 92, Mussolini to Hitler, 11/4/1940 and 357, Hitler to Mussolini, 31/5/1940; Ciano, *Diario*, 20/4/1940 and 13/5/1940; *DDI*, 9, IV, 642, 'Verbale della riunione tenuta nella stanza del Duce', 29/5/1940; on Mussolini's assumption of command and on his institution of a high command, the *Comando Supremo* see also USMM, Comando Supremo, busta: A, fascicolo: 1, sottofascicolo: 2, 'Costituzione e funzionamento del Comando Supremo delle FF.AA. in caso di guerra', Badoglio to all service ministries, 4/6/1940; Q. Armellini, *Diario di guerra: nove mesi al Comando Supremo* (Garzanti, Milan, 1946), entries for 11/5/1940, 29/5/1940 and 30/5/1940; Ceva, *La condotta della guerra*, pp. 24–5.

39 USMM, *L'organizzazione della Marina durante il conflitto. tomo I*, appendix 7, 'Di. N.A. n.0. (zero). Concetti generali di azione nel Mediterraneo', operational directive issued by Cavagnari, 29/5/1940, pp. 353–5.

40 Schreiber, 'Political and Military Developments in the Mediterranean Area', p. 58; Armellini, *Diario di guerra*, 11/5/1940; USSME, *Verbali delle riunioni*, meeting of 30/5/1940; USMM. *L'organizzazione della Marina durante il conflitto, tomo I*, appendix 9, 'Ordine generale di operazioni n. 1', Falangola to all submarine commands, 2/6/1940, pp. 361–5. The original order for the submarine command had been issued by *Supermarina* on 25 May. See USMM, DG, 10, 'Ordine generale di operazione n. 8 per l'impiego iniziale dei sommergibili', naval high command, 25/5/1940.

41 Ciano, *Diario*, 11/4/1940, 8/5/1940 and 10/5/1940; Anfuso, *Da Palazzo Venezia al Lago di Garda*, pp. 125–30; Knox, *Mussolini Unleashed*, p. 122; for Badoglio's comments on this see Armellini, *Diario di guerra*, 4/6/1940. On the argument that Mussolini genuinely sought an Italo-French *rapprochement* as late as 5 June, but that this possibility was blocked by London, see Quartararo, *Roma tra Londra e Berlino*, p. 623. The idea that 'Mussolini wanted to declare war on France, while at the same time forbidding any shooting' is expressed by Schreiber, 'Political and Military Developments in the Mediterranean Area', p. 62; Rochat, 'Mussolini, Chef de guerre', pp. 53–4; *DGFP*, D, IX, 1, 'Conversation between the Führer and the Duce', 17/3/1940.

42 USSME, *Verbali delle riunioni*, meeting of 5/6/1940; USMM, CS, b:B, f:1, Cavagnari to La Maddalena naval command, 8/6/1940 and 'Nostro contegno contro la Francia all'apertura delle ostilità', Badolglio to all chiefs-of-staff, 7/6/1940; Playfair, *The Mediterranean and the Middle East. Vol. I*, p. 110; Armellini, *Diario di guerra*, 27/6/1940, 21/7/1940 and 3/9/1940; Ciano, Diario, 4/7/1940; Playfair, *The Mediterranean and the Middle East. Vol. I*, pp. 151–4. In mid-August retired admiral Alfredo Baistrocchi, adviser to Mussolini on naval strategic matters, noted that had less been spent on preparing a battle fleet for a Jutland-style encounter, and more resources gone into preparing for a truly aeronaval war then the initial Italian encounters with the enemy would have proved far more successful. See ACS, Segretaria particolare del Duce, carteggio riservato 1922–1943, busta: 2, fascicolo: 3, Baistrocchi to Mussolini, 21/8/1940.

43 J. Gooch, 'Italian Military Incompetence', *Journal of Strategic Studies*, 5, 2 (1982), p. 259.

Conclusion

Mussolini believed that Italy should become a great power, and concurrently an imperial one. Throughout the early years of Fascist rule he repeatedly spoke of his country's need to secure free access to the world's oceans. Aggressive war in conjunction with Hitler's revived German Reich constituted the means of driving Britain and France from the Mediterranean and Red Sea – in the same way that Ancient Rome had defeated Carthage and won its empire. If the Mediterranean was not to 'remain a jail that stifles our life force', the *Duce* declared in late 1934, 'we must become powerful on that sea'.[1] This study, in focusing on the period that followed this pronouncement, has discussed Italian efforts to prepare for its naval confrontation with the predominant powers in Mediterranean politics in the context of Fascist foreign policy during those years.

Examination of the relationship between the foreign policy pursued by Mussolini from 1935–1940 and the course duly taken by naval policy, shows that the formation of the 'Axis' alliance drove Fascist planning for war in the Mediterranean and Red Sea. After the Italo-Ethiopian crisis had beyond any doubt demonstrated the level of resistance to Italian imperialism the *Duce* might expect from London, the need for alignment with other, ideologically sympathetic revisionist powers became all too clear. When the breach between Rome and the West, long predicted by Mussolini, finally came over the question of Italian ambitions in East Africa, the path to this alliance lay open. The weak material and financial position of the Italian state, and the effects this was to have on the national rearmament effort, only served to generate further impetus towards improving Italo-German relations.

Thus, by late 1936, Mussolini had ruthlessly removed those, such as Fulvio Suvich, who opposed any strengthening of bilateral ties, had conceded German predominance in Austrian affairs, and promised Hitler that Italy would never engage in staff talks with the Locarno nations whose scope was anti-German. In the subsequent two years, he further strengthened ties by visiting Berlin, taking Italy out of the League of Nations,

191

adhering to the Anti-Comintern Pact and conducting a joint German–Italian war effort in support of General Franco in Spain, before welcoming the *Führer* to Rome in the summer of 1938 amid the growing international furore over German territorial claims in central Europe.

The effect of Mussolini's pro-German policy upon Italian strategic policy and planning as a whole was immediate. Over the period 1934–35 the naval high command moved away from its anti-French and anti-Yugoslav planning policy and, in the spring of 1935, albeit reluctantly, contemplated war against Britain's Royal Navy on the specific orders of Mussolini. Then, as relations between Rome and the western European powers deteriorated over the Italo-Abyssinian question, so did the navy's policy gradually encompass the idea of a war against those nations. Subsequently, in the wake of the Mediterranean crisis of 1935–36, the idea that this war would be conducted alongside the German navy – a direct product of improved political relations between the two countries – became a central tenet of naval staff thinking.

By December 1936, the Pariani plan to capture Egypt and the Sudan – a plan contingent upon a parallel German drive towards Paris, and whose origins are to be found during the period of Italo-British tension a year earlier – was being discussed by the various service chiefs. Despite the resistance of the highly conservative Badoglio, who consistently argued against foreign adventures of this kind and who preferred to strengthen metropolitan and colonial defences, the design took root. In the two years that followed, preparations proceeded in earnest. While the army planned to create its African expeditionary force, the navy's war plans office examined the possibilities of a naval coalition with Germany and Imperial Japan that would form the political basis for the conflict. In turn, the naval staff under Cavagnari considered how best to strengthen Italy's naval position in the Mediterranean – opting for a battleship-heavy fleet – and how the navy might operate in the event of war.

Basing all planning on the concept that the army would primarily undertake, and win, the conflict, the naval staff focused on defence of the central Mediterranean and the protection of communications between the mainland and North Africa. Any encounter involving the Italian battle squadrons should only take place at the moment when success seemed assured. Otherwise, the planners foresaw submarines, light surface units, and the fixed defences of the Sicilian Channel being used to sever enemy communications between the eastern and western basins, and also to prevent combined enemy fleets from staging operations in the central theatre. In the Red Sea, units of the East African naval command were to attack enemy traffic between Djibouti and Aden. The naval leadership gave primary consideration to the neutralisation of these two positions in order that, while the army captured the Suez Canal, a corresponding operation by the *forze armate* further to the south would seize control of the Bab-el-Mandeb Strait, thereby securing Mussolini's much-trumpeted 'free access to the ocean'.

By the summer of 1938, naval planning for these contingencies was already underway, although the fleet would not be ready to stage them, as Pariani hoped, by the spring of 1939. In fact, the navy's building programmes and its efforts to strengthen base facilities would not be complete before 1943, at the earliest, which clearly highlighted the deficiencies of an Italian military planning infrastructure wherein individual staffs planned in isolation, and on orders transmitted individually by Mussolini to the respective chiefs-of-staff. The *Duce*'s failure to address this issue, and foster greater co-operation between the various staffs, and his refusal to consider the possibility of establishing a unitary command, created widespread confusion. At the time of the 1935 Anglo-Italian crisis, air and navy collaboration was virtually non-existent. In the final days before the declaration of war in 1940, the situation was scarcely better, and co-operation between the two planning departments proved tortuous once the conflict began.

By the end of 1938, Berlin's expansionist agenda, and Mussolini's vocal support for it, brought the navy to the very brink of a Mediterranean war with the West which, even if initiated without a prior declaration of hostilities, as the navy's planners recommended, would have found it outgunned and outnumbered. Accordingly, Mussolini himself shelved the idea of taking Suez in the immediate wake of the Munich settlement. Ordering Badoglio to concentrate the efforts of the armed forces on strengthening national and overseas defences, Mussolini finally agreed to conclude a formal political and military alliance with Germany, which foresaw an 'Axis' war with Britain and France. However, such an effort required at least three years preparation, and on this basis Rome and Berlin concluded the Pact of Steel in May 1939.

In reality, duplicity prevailed on both sides. German designs against Poland, and Italian plans to wage a limited colonial war in East Africa against France, after Wilhelm Keitel expressly advised Pariani against it in April, most certainly did not form part of the agenda for the Italo-German naval conversations at Friedrichshafen the following June. Furthermore, despite the formation of an alliance at the political level, none of the respective armed forces achieved a working partnership with their German counterparts before war broke out the following September. Even at the moment when Mussolini, adamant that Hitler had won the war, plunged Italy into a conflict for which it was so glaringly unprepared in the summer of 1940, the two countries had still not formed a working and effective military partnership. Thus, joint operations which the 'Axis' could have undertaken successfully, such as the capture of Malta and the launching of an aeronaval offensive in East Africa, had not been considered in any detail. The navy entered the war in trepidation, its programmes incomplete, with no clear objectives, and with a defensive war plan wholly inconsistent with the expectations laid down by Mussolini in late March.

As regards the policy pursued by the naval high command between 1934, the point at which the navy initiated major new building programmes, and Italy's entry into war in June 1940, this study has argued that, in spite of the clear financial and material limitations facing it, the navy's leadership could have better prepared the Italian fleet for the anti-British war envisaged by Mussolini. Cavagnari's rejection of carrier-borne air support for the fleet in August 1936, and his opting for an expensive second capital-ship programme in early 1937, left the navy operationally confined to the central Mediterranean and lacking other types of vessel – such as destroyers – without which the battle squadrons, once at sea, would remain seriously exposed to enemy attack.

The stifling of internal debate within the navy clearly did not help matters. Ignoring the views of intelligent and experienced naval theorists such as Romeo Bernotti, Alfredo Baistrocchi, Giulio Valli and even the navy's war planners themselves, who warned variously of the dangers of concentrating so many resources on further *Littorio* building at the expense of other units, primarily aircraft carriers, of Italy's lack of anti-submarine technology and, equally tellingly, of the vulnerability of Taranto's harbour defences on the eve of war, Cavagnari doggedly maintained that only battleships could decide the naval struggle in the Mediterranean. Insisting that the experience of the Great War had demonstrated beyond doubt that 'only this type of ship had the absolute capacity to resist attack from the air' while their 'high calibre guns kept all types of vessel at a distance', the conservative Cavagnari failed to realise that times had changed. Once at war, the fallacy of his views was rapidly exposed, and after Taranto, Mussolini promptly dismissed him.[2]

Had Cavagnari considered other, less expensive options, such as the innovations offered by the guerrilla warfare arm, virtually ignored until the post-Munich period, and the possibilities of extensive mining, instead of focusing on creating a 'fleet in being' suitable only for defence of the Straits of Sicily and a 'decisive' naval encounter with the enemy under conditions favourable to Italy, the navy could have taken the offensive to the enemy, and with good possibilities for success. On the eve of war in 1940, Malta, whose defences were significantly weaker than the estimates of the Italian naval staff suggested, could have been attacked; an operation which, following the fall of France and the withdrawal of the French fleet from the conflict, might well have met with some success. The inevitable strengthening of Italy's central Mediterranean position that would have resulted, would only have made Britain's task harder, while the early loss of the island would have come as a serious psychological blow at a critical juncture in the war against Germany.

Moreover, had naval tactics concentrated less on controlling naval units from the land, and more on fostering a sense of initiative among officers at sea, then the naval high command might have eliminated the rigidity which paralysed initiative. By so doing, training would have been rendered more effective in peacetime, while co-operation between detached squadrons would have been smoother, once the navy found itself at war. Similarly, had Cavagnari given greater thought to developing sub-marine tactics, moving away from the 'static' conceptions that governed undersea warfare to a position in which Italian submarines were used as more mobile and manoeuvrable weapons, then the possibilities for success might have been greater and losses of these units in the early days of war might have been significantly reduced.[3]

Finally, a tendency to overestimate enemy strengths remained a collective deficiency of the Italian military intelligence services as a whole. Greater efforts and resources spent on developing the naval intelligence department might have improved all-round confidence in this vitally important service, and strengthened its intelligence-gathering capability. An awareness of British weaknesses, such as the poor level of defences on Malta and the difficulties facing the Royal Navy in both the Mediterranean and Red Sea, might then have resulted. As it was, the criteria governing SIS's assessments of the enemy were far too narrow, while fatally 'the weakest spot of all was the poor liaison which existed between operations and Intelligence, between *Supermarina* and *SIS*'.[4]

However, nothing could compensate for Italy's dependence on imported strategic raw materials. Despite the self-sufficiency programmes initiated by the Mussolini regime, little could be done to alter the fact that, to cite but two examples, national annual coal requirements, totalling 12 million tons, and petroleum consumption, amounting to 2 million, had to be met almost entirely through costly importation. This drove up armament-production costs, created insuperable delays – such as those which perennially dogged the *Littorio* programmes – reduced quality, and ultimately lowered the quantity of arms that the Italian armaments industries could manufacture. The navy's domination of the armed services in gaining access to the industrial and technological base, such as it was, concomitantly reduced the quality of army and air force weaponry.[5]

These facts alone should have demonstrated to Mussolini that he should not have contemplated war against the powerful and comparatively wealthier Western democracies alongside a German Reich that could barely spare resources it required for its own armed struggle in continental Europe. Yet, far from doing so, the *Duce*'s 'unscrupulous personal ambi-tion', his vision of the Italian people as omnipotent masters of a new Roman Empire, drove both to a national disaster that ultimately swept Mussolini and his Fascist regime away in its wake.[6]

NOTES

1 *OOBM*, XXVI, pp. 322–4.
2 ACS, SpD, b: 2, f: 3, Cavagnari to Mussolini, 3/9/1940; Sullivan, 'Intoduction', in Bernotti, *Fundamentals of Naval Tactics*, p. 27. The question of internal debate within the navy is also discussed by James Sadkovich, whose conclusions once more appear ill judged. His attempt to separate the autocratic style of Cavagnari's leadership from Mussolini and the Fascist regime misses the fundamental, indeed, rather obvious point that Fascism as a political concept did not tolerate diversity of opinion. Cavagnari, a convinced Fascist, acted according to his political instincts and did not permit 'dissent'. Likewise, Sadkovich's assertion that both the navy and the institute for maritime warfare were 'apolitical' institutions is patently absurd. A report by the institute on Fascist Italy's need to win supremacy of the Mediterranean and Red Sea by prosecuting a war against Britain and France, illustrates all too clearly its political compliance with the overall strategic goals of the regime. See Sadkovich, *The Italian Navy in World War II*, pp. 4–5 and 9; USMM, b: 2715, f: 6, 'Il nostro problema militare marittimo del Mediterraneo', Istituto di guerra marittima, undated, but most probably 1937–38.
3 Weichold, *Axis Naval Policy and Operations*, p. 3; USMM, *I sommergibili in Mediterraneo*, p. 17.
4 Maugeri, *From the Ashes of Disgrace*, pp. 31–3.
5 Sullivan, 'The Italian Armed Forces', pp. 173–4.
6 Knox, *Mussolini Unleashed*, p. 286.

Appendix 1

Italian Fleet Disposition Plan, 10 June 1940

Surface Fleet

1st Naval Squadron (Taranto)*
(Admiral Campioni)

5th battleship division	9th battleship division	1st heavy cruiser division
Conte di Cavour	*Littorio*	*Gorizia*
Giulio Cesare	*Vittorio Veneto*	*Fiume*
	(actually in service	
	2 August)	

4th light cruiser squadron	8th light cruiser squadron	Aircraft transporters
Da Barbiano	*Duca degli Abruzzi*	*Miraglia*
Cadorna	*Garibaldi*	
Di Giussano		
Diaz		

7th destroyer squadron	8th destroyer squadron	9th destroyer squadron
Freccia	*Folgore*	*Alfieri*
Dardo	*Fulmine*	*Oriani*
Saetta	*Baleno*	*Carducci*
Strale	*Lampo*	*Gioberti*

14th destroyer squadron	15th destroyer squadron	16th destroyer squadron
Vivaldi	*Pigafetta*	*Da Recco*
Da Noli	*Zeno*	*Usodimare*
Pancaldo	*Da Mosto*	*Tarigo*
	Da Verazzano	*Pessagno*
	Malocello	

* Remodernisation work on the battleships *Caio Duilio* and *Andrea Doria* was not completed until 15 July and 26 October 1940, respectively. Therefore, neither vessel is included in the naval staff fleet deployment plan.

Water tankers
Isonzo
Po
Garda

2nd Naval Squadron (La Spezia)
(Admiral Paladini)

Heavy cruiser	3rd heavy cruiser division	7th heavy cruiser division
Pola	*Trento*	*Eugenio di Savoia*
	Bolzano	*Duca d'Aosta*
	Trieste	*Attendola*
		Montecuccoli

2nd light cruiser division	10th destroyer squadron	11th destroyer squadron
Bande Nere	*Maestrale*	*Artigliere*
Colleoni	*Libeccio*	*Camicia Nera*
	Grecale	*Aviere*
	Scirocco	*Geniere*

12th destroyer squadron	13th destroyer squadron	Repair ship
Lanciere	*Granatiere*	*Quarnaro*
Carabiniere	*Fuciliere*	
Corazziere	*Bersagliere*	
Ascari	*Alpino*	

Water tankers	Petrol tankers
Volturno	*Cocito*
Istria	
Flegetone	
Mincio	

Submarine Arm
(Admiral Falangola)

1st submarine group (La Spezia)

11th squadron	13th squadron	16th squadron
Calvi	*Berillo*	*Micca*
Finzi	*Onice*	*Foca*
Tazzoli	*Gemma*	
Fieramosca		

12th squadron	14th squadron	17th squadron
Cappelini	*Iride*	*H1*
Faà di Bruno	*Argo*	*H2*
Mocenigo	*Velella*	*H4*
Veniero		*H6*
Glauco	15th squadron	*H8*
Otaria	*Gondar*	
	Neghelli	
	Ascianghi	

2nd submarine group (Naples)

21st squadron	22nd squadron
Marcello	*Barbarigo*
Nani	*Emo*
Dandolo	*Morosini*
Provana	*Marconi*
	Leonardo da Vinci

3rd submarine group (Messina)

31st squadron	34th squadron	37th squadron
Pisani	*Mameli*	*Bragadino*
Colonna	*Capponi*	*X2*
Bausan	*Speri*	*X3*
Des Geneys	*Da Procida*	

33rd squadron	35th squadron
Bandiera	*Durbo*
Manara	*Tembien*
Menotti	*Beilul*
Santarosa	

4th submarine group (Taranto)

40th squadron	43rd squadron	47th squadron
Balilla	*Ruggiero Settimo*	*Malachite*
Sciesa	*Settembrini*	*Rubino*
Toti		*Ambra*
Millelie	44th squadron	
	Anfirite	48th squadron
41st squadron		*Ondina*
Liuzzi	45th squadron	
Bagnolini	*Salpa*	49th squadron
Giuliani	*Serpente*	*Atropo*
Tarantini		*Zoea*
	46th squadron	*Corridoni*
42nd squadron	*Dessié*	
Brin	*Dagabur*	
	Uarsciek	
	Uebi-Scebeli	

7th submarine group (Cagliari)

71st squadron	72nd squadron
Alagi	*Diasporo*
Adua	*Corallo*
Axum	*Turchese*
Aradam	*Medusa*

Other Naval Departments

Upper Tyrrhenian Sector (La Spezia)
(Admiral Savoia-Aosta)

10th motor torpedo-boat squadron	16th motor torpedo-boat squadron	Mine-layers
Vega	*Monzambano*	*Orlando*
Curatone	*Sagittario*	*Gasperi*
Perseo	*Castelfidardo*	*Crotone*
Sirio	*Calatafimi*	
	Carini	Water tankers
1st flotilla special motor torpedo-boats	*La Masa*	*Dalmazia*
(*MAS*)		
20 vessels		
(1st, 5th, 12th, 13th and 14th squadrons)		

Lower Tyrrhenian Sector (Naples)
(Admiral Pini)

NAPLES

3rd motor torpedo-boat squadron	4th motor torpedo-boat squadron	Mine-layers
Prestinari	*Procione*	*Partenope*
Cantore	*Orione*	*Buffoluto*
	Orsa	Water tankers
	Pegaso	*Arno*
		Metauro

SARDINIA (La Maddalena)
(Admiral Sportiello)

2nd motor torpedo-boat squadron	9th motor torpedo-boat squadron	4th *MAS* squadron
Papa	*Cassiopea*	4 vessels
Montanari	*Canopo*	
Cascino	*Cairoli*	Mine-layers
Chinotto	*Mosto*	*Durazzo*
		Pelagosa
		Caralis
		A. Deffenu
		Mazara

SICILY (Messina)
(Admiral Barone)

1st torpedo-boat
flotilla

13th squadron	14th squadron
Circe	*Partenope*
Clio	*Polluce*
Calliope	*Pleiadi*
Calipso	*Pallade*

2nd torpedo-boat
flotilla

1st squadron	12th squadron	1st *MAS* flotilla
Airone	*Altair*	16 vessels
Ariel	*Antares*	(2nd, 9th, 10th and 15th
Aretusa	*Aldebran*	squadrons)
Alcione	*Andromeda*	

5th motor torpedo-boat squadron	Mine-layers	Support ships
		Pacinotti
Schialfino	*Buccari*	*Volta*
Dezza	*Scilla*	
La Farina	*Brioni*	Water tankers
Abba	*Adriatico*	*Verde*
Albatros		*Prometeo*
		Bormida
		Brenta

Ionian and Lower Adriatic Sector (Taranto)
(Admiral Pasetti)

TARANTO

Light cruisers	2nd motor torpedo-boat squadron	6th motor torpedo-boat squadron
Bari		
Taranto	*Espero*	*Pilo*
	Borea	*Stocco*
	Zeffiro	*Missori*
	Ostro	*Sirtori*

Mine-layers	Transport ships	Water tankers
Barletta	*Cherso*	*Sesia*
Vieste	*Lussino*	*Garigliano*
Otranto		*Tirso*
Gallipoli		

BRINDISI
(Vice-Admiral Spalice)

Destroyers	7th motor torpedo-	3rd *MAS* squadron
Riboty	boat squadron	Two vessels
Mirabello	*Bassini*	
	Cosenz	
	Fabrizi	
	Medici	

Gun boats	Water tankers
Cirene	*Adige*

Upper Adriatic Sector (Venice)
(Admiral Savoia Genova)

VENICE

15th motor torpedo-	Training ships	Mine-layers
boat squadron	*Colombo*	*Albona*
Confienza	*Vespucci*	*Laurana*
Solferino		*Rovigno*
San Martino		
Palestro		

POLA
(Rear-Admiral Bobbiese)

Motor torpedo-boats	6th *MAS* squadron
Giovannini	4 vessels

Mine-layers	Oil tankers	Water tankers
Azio	*Lete*	*Scrivia*
San Giorgio		*Verbano*
San Giusto		

Albanian Sector (Durazzo)
(Admiral Tur)

Water tankers	Motor patrol vessels
Pagano	*Vivilante*
	Vedetta

Aegean Sector (Rhodes)
(Rear-Admiral Biancheri)

4th destroyer squadron	8th motor torpedo-	5th submarine group
Crispi	boat squadron	51st squadron
Sella	*Lupo*	*Narvalo*
	Lince	*Squalo*
	Lira	*Tricheco*
	Libra	*Delfino*

52nd squadron
Ialea
Iantina
Ametista
Zaffiro

3rd *MAS* flotilla
5 vessels   Mine-layers   Gun boats
(7th, 1th, 16th and 22nd   *Lero*   *Sonzini*
squadrons)   *Legnano*   *Caboto*

Libyan Sector (Benghazi)
(Admiral Brivonesi)

TRIPOLI

11th motor torpedo-   Mine-layers   Gun boats
boat squadron   *Monte Gargano*   *Alula*
Cigno
Castore
Climente
Centauro

TOBRUK

Heavy cruisers   1st destroyer squadron
San Giorgio   *Turbine*
                             Aquilone
                             Euro
                             Nembo

6th submarine group
61st squadron   62nd squadron   Gun boats
Sirena   *Diamante*   *Palmaiola*
Argonauta   *Topazio*   *De Lutti*
Fisalia   *Nereide*   *Grazioli Lante*
Smeraldo   *Galatea*   *G. Berta*
Naiade   *Lafolè*   *Valoroso*

Water tankers
Lina Campanella
Ticino
Polifemo

East African Naval Command (Massawa)
(Rear-Admiral Balsamo)

Colonial sloops   5th destroyer squadron 2nd submarine
Eritrea   *Nullo*   squadron
                             Sauro   *Macallè*
                             Manin   *Archimede*
                             Battisti   *Torricelli*
                                                     Perla

81st submarine squadron	Motor torpedo-boats	21st *MAS* squadron
Guglielmotti	*Acerbi*	Five vessels
Ferraris	*Orsini*	
Galvani		
Galileo		

Gun boats	Mine-layers	Water tankers
Porto Corsini	*Ostia*	*Sile*
Biglieri		*Sebeto*

Far Eastern Naval Command
(Captain Galletti)

Mine-layers	Gun boats
Lepanto	*Carlotto*

Sources: USMM, *L'organizzazione della Marina durante il conflitto. Tomo I* (USSM, Rome, 1972), pp. 338-45; A. Fraccaroli, *Italian Warships of World War II* (Ian Allan, London, 1968), pp. 16-19; G. Schreiber, 'Political and Military Developments in the Mediterranean Area 1939–1940', in W. Deist *et al.* (eds), *Germany and the Second World War, Volume III* (Clarendon Press, Oxford, 1995), pp. 86-7.

Appendix 2

Meeting of the Supreme High Command held at the *Palazzo Viminale*, Rome, 13 August 1935

Present:
Marshall Pietro Badoglio – chief of the supreme high command
General Federico Baistrocchi – under-secretary of state for war
Admiral Domenico Cavagnari – under-secretary of state for the navy
General Giuseppe Valle – under-secretary of state for the air force
General Alberto Pariani – deputy chief-of-staff for the army
Rear-Admiral Vladimiro Pini – deputy chief-of-staff for the navy
General Pietro Pinna – deputy chief-of-staff for the air force

The meeting began at 10 am. The first to speak was His Excellency the Marshal of Italy, Pietro Badoglio.
Badoglio: 'Today's meeting has two aims: the first executive, the other informative.
The executive aim is the consequence of the following letter which I have received from His Excellency the Head of Government:

> In the event that we may face a period of extreme tension with Britain I ask Your Excellency to examine our strategic situation immediately, and to ensure that the three General Staffs have taken the necessary precautions.
> Rome, 9 August 1935–year XIII
>
> Mussolini.

My intention is to be in a position to advise the Head of Government:

1) What orders have been issued, and to present him with an assessment of our military position in the event that we are ordered to initiate hostilities;
2) What situation confronts us.

The Navy has already completed detailed studies: therefore I beg His Excellency Admiral Cavagnari briefly to outline the measures he has taken.'

Cavagnari: 'I will simply give a general overview and leave Admiral Pini to give a more detailed outline.'

Badoglio: 'If I might just make a further point: in the event that we are faced with the extreme tension referred to in His Excellency the Head of Government's letter it remains vital that the Libyan formations, which we had planned to deploy to East Africa, remain where they are, not only in order to reduce troop movements, but also so that this sector should be able to defend itself.'

Baistrocchi: 'The Libyan division will begin assembling on 1 September, although no transportation has been organised for it as yet; only the formation of the units and the arrangements for the creation of the division are underway at present.'

Badoglio: 'It is vital that the Head of Government inform the high commissioner for East Africa that if the tension with Britain should worsen no troops will be transferred from Libya; this is all the more important given that the high commissioner insists that he should have Libyan forces deployed in East Africa. Now, over to His Excellency Cavagnari.'

Cavagnari: 'All existing naval units are armed and ready for deployment. Two complete battle squadrons can, after 30 August, be in position as foreseen by the current operational plan.

All fully operational submarines – totalling around 50 in number – have already been deployed to the positions set out in the war plan.

All ships are fully equipped (although reserve supplies of torpedoes are still in production).

Ships still have to reach their war time complements, which they will do as soon as the order to mobilise is issued.

A naval division, composed of units able to operate in that theatre, has already been deployed to the Red Sea, and its task has been limited to defending the most vulnerable parts of the coastline from seaborne attack, while also offering support to land defences (Assab, etc.).

Other naval units for use in the Red Sea have been deployed at Leros and Tobruk.

Modern naval units (that is faster and better armed ones) will not be deployed to the Red Sea, because, in the event of hostilities with Britain, the latter could concentrate naval forces from India and the Cape in the region, which could only be neutralised by a large force of our own vessels that had been redeployed from the Mediterranean theatre, which would then be concomitantly weakened.

In East Africa we have already stockpiled the supplies of ammunition, torpedoes, provisions and materials required to keep the ships and shore facilities of the Navy supplied for many months.

The coastal defences, communications systems and harbour facilities of the two colonies are efficient and nearing war readiness.

Metropolitan coastal defences are as ready as the current availability of materials will permit.

Artillery pieces are being installed at Naples, Genoa and Palermo; at La Spezia, La Maddalena, Cagliari, Trapani, Augusta, Taranto, Brindisi, Venice, Leros and Tobruk the existing port defences are fully operational.

THE FIXED ANTI-AIRCRAFT DEFENCES ALONG THE ENTIRE METROPOLITAN COASTLINE ARE WEAK, with the exception of those at La Spezia, which could fire a barrage of short duration.

Fixed underwater defences at key strategic points are in place.

Current fuel stocks now total one-third of those required to wage war for one year.

During September three new 6–7,000 ton cruisers will enter service.

We are at present either remodernising or building: four battleships, a further three cruisers, four large destroyers, 16 torpedo-boats, four destroyer escorts, 16 submarines and other small ships.

The raw materials needed to complete this construction are for the most part already in Italy.

Instructions to request shelter for merchant vessels in neutral ports in the event of hostilities have been sent to all Consular offices.

The various departments of the naval high command, communications systems, etc. are ready.

The decree instituting the central naval command is ready for issue.

The high commands of the eastern and western naval sectors have been established.'

Badoglio: 'Before we begin any in-depth examination of the situation we might face in the event of war, I would like us to turn to the executive question that I mentioned earlier. Therefore, I beg Admiral Pini to fill us in on the details.'

Pini: 'In April of this year it was decided to keep the class of 1913, which had been due to be replaced by the class of 1915, in service. In certain categories we have recalled all available specialists, some of whom have been transferred for service with the Air Force (wireless operators); 500 officers and 850 non-commissioned officers have also been recalled.

Instead of the normal total of 52,000 men in service, the Navy now has 57,500. The wartime complements recalled will report to their respective ships immediately. With the recalled personnel we have been able to man reserve naval vessels, along with the two old battleships *Doria* and *Duilio*, which cannot be discounted given their level of armaments, but all the same cause us great concern given their poor level of buoyancy in the event of undersea attack. Various coastal defence and anti-aircraft batteries of maritime importance have now been readied, as have most of the signal stations in Sardinia, Sicily and the Aegean. Personnel has been found for many of the ten medium-calibre armoured trains. In the case of many of the coastal batteries we have had to build barracks and shelters, fit aiming equipment, provide provisions and secure supplies of munitions. The gun batteries at present available have been positioned around La Spezia, Maddalena, Cagliari, all of Sicily, Taranto, Leros, Tobruk and Eritrea. Genoa has been assigned a pontoon with two 381-mm main guns and six 76-mm anti-aircraft weapons as well as two 152-mm guns. Among the Navy's guns destined for use by colonial troops, are the 190-mm weapons that have been installed at Tripoli.

Various armoured trains have also been manned. One, armed with a 120-mm main gun is already in place at Cogoleto. Another, with 120- and 152-mm weapons will operate from La Spezia along the Gulf of Genoa in order to protect the Ligurian coastline. A third train armed with 76-mm anti-aircraft guns is currently being prepared and will be deployed to the Polcevera valley in order to defend the industrial zone there. Another train fitted with 102-mm anti-aircraft weapons has already been sent to Augusta. La Spezia has three more medium-calibre trains and five more are based at Taranto; these will operate either on the Ionian coastline or along that of southern Sicily. Among the other armoured trains at present in service we have three or four fitted with 380-mm guns, although their characteristics render them inappropriate for operations against naval targets. We are at this moment preparing rail and housing facilities for the super gun (210 mm) which will be deployed in southern Sicily, from where it can be used against Malta (range 100 km).

We plan to lay a minefield in a stretch of the Sicilian Channel in order to interrupt enemy commerce, at the same time we will have to respect the waters near the French coast and notify all neutral states of the dangers that might be incurred by entering them; meanwhile the waters off the coast of Messina will remain open and free.

The base at Augusta would no longer be suitable if the British were to deploy their naval forces around the Balearics. In the event that this happened the base at Maddalena would appear to be a more appropriate choice. On the other hand, should the British fleet deploy to the eastern Mediterranean, it would be advisable for us to operate out of Augusta, although we should bear in mind that Augusta cannot easily be defended against sea offensives. The rocky sea bed does not permit the laying of mines, and the heavy guns positioned there total only two 203-mm weapons (not yet in place), two 190-mm and two 305-mm guns, all of which are on pontoons. The outer defences at Augusta must therefore rely on the use of submarines and air units on Sicily.

We also intend to deploy various batteries at Leros and Tobruk.

We have recalled Admiral Bertonelli to service so that he can organise the military preparations on the Italian Aegean islands. It should be noted that the defences at Leros and Tobruk are modest to say the least, and particularly so when compared to the naval and air forces at Britain's disposal and the resources that it could stockpile in the region by occupying one of the islands, probably Stampalia. If these positions were to fall to the enemy our ability to protect key lines of communication with the Black Sea would be compromised. The defensive capability of our Red Sea base at Massawa is good. We have sent four 120-mm and two 152-mm guns, two 76-mm anti-aircraft batteries and a number of 13.2-mm machine-guns to Assab. We are sending 400 torpedoes to the region on the 'Lussin'; we will place a barrage of torpedoes at the entrance to Assab.

In Somaliland we have four 120-mm guns in position at Chisimaio, and a further four at Mogadishu, where, however, the difficulty of unloading ships is considerable at this time of year.

We have already established High Commands in two naval sectors with the aim of co-ordinating and directing preparations along the extensive coastlines of the mainland and the Italian islands. Our naval forces, as His Excellency Cavagnari has already pointed out, are at the maximum level of efficiency, and by 30 August will be able to move to their battle stations within 48 hours of the order being given. The first naval squadron and a division from the second will deploy to Augusta; the other division of the second naval squadron will deploy either at Taranto or Brindisi, and the fifth division will operate in the Adriatic while a division of scout ships will operate from Cagliari. We also have small nuclei of light naval vessels composed of *MAS* for departmental use, and the forces deployed in the Red Sea, limited to the cruiser *Bari* and a small number of light naval vessels suited to the tasks that will be undertaken by the navy in that theatre, which are inevitably inferior to the British forces that will be based there.

Our submarines have been deployed at La Spezia, Naples, Messina and Taranto, while single squadrons have been sent to Cagliari, Trapani and Augusta. Two submarines are stationed at Leros and can be moved to the Red Sea if circumstances require it. We would send the support ship *Volta* to operate with them.

From their predetermined bases submarines will fan out in order to carry out their tasks in various regions of the Mediterranean and, if it becomes advisable, in the Atlantic. Our naval operations will be under-taken principally by submarines and units of the air arm, given that our surface units will not be in a position to operate against objectives at great distance from their bases. But, while we have an advantage over our enemy in numbers of submarines, we should also note that only with great difficulty can we keep more than 20 or so submarines at sea at any one time, while their operational zones cover extremely vast areas. Even for submarine operations in waters close to the mainland it would be very useful to have air support: at present, however, the navy's coastal air squadrons are not in the best of condition, and this is also true of our ship-borne aircraft. This state of affairs only increases the net inferiority of our naval forces should they find themselves confronted with those of the enemy, especially as we will have a limited air reconnaissance capability guiding our naval forces at sea.'

Badoglio: 'So, to sum up: as regards the calling up of personnel and the mobilising of resources the navy is ready to assume battle stations as of 30 August.

The navy does not consider it worthwhile or appropriate to reinforce its position in the Red Sea in order not to weaken the efficiency of our naval forces in the Mediterranean.

The navy highlights the weakness of our position in the Aegean, where it is possible that superior enemy forces might well occupy Leros. It also highlights the weakness of Tobruk given the close proximity of enemy bases.

Hostilities with Britain might break out before or after the commencement of our operations against Ethiopia, in other words war might follow or precede the beginning of our offensive in East Africa; if it should be the latter then we need to examine the enormous difficulties that we will encounter in keeping our colonies supplied. These supplies might arrive sporadically in Libya, and might not even arrive at all in East Africa. This factor significantly affects our entire plan of operations in East Africa. We will be forced to undertake a strictly defensive strategy, and the colony will have to survive with the supplies it already has. Furthermore, we will not be able to send any more air units to East Africa.

I beg His Excellency General Valle to give us his appreciation.'

Valle: 'The possibility of hostilities between Italy and Britain comes at a time of crisis for the Air Force.

Our aircraft are already dated (ten years old); they have served and continue to serve as trainers for the pilots of the Air Force.

In any case, we have issued orders for the building of new airfields in Sicily, for the building of new storage facilities, new bases, etc.

Work on these has begun, and as regards the bases, these will be complete before the end of August.

In order to carry out Operation B we have at our disposal 12 squadrons of BRs (84 aircraft), 12 squadrons of S55s (72 aircraft), totalling 156 bombers.[1] In all, the air force has 346 aircraft in service. Our initial position will be quite strong, given that the British have at present 92 aircraft stationed on Malta, and a total of 250 units in the Mediterranean, including those carried aboard ships and aircraft carriers. Our situation will improve from 1 October. In June 1936 we will have 1,500 aircraft in service. After 15 September of this year our 346 first-line aircraft will be strengthened by the addition of units destined for East Africa: between 15 September and 15 December around 200 new aircraft will come into service. Squadrons can be at battle stations in 70 hours.'

Badoglio: 'His Excellency Valle has clearly outlined the position: at this moment in time our Air Force is in crisis, because it has inherited aircraft which are out of date and which are being used to train its 2,000 pilots. The mechanisms are in place which will allow 346 aircraft to be deployed within 70 hours by the end of August.

However, they are aircraft with very limited capabilities. The new production currently in progress will replace existing aircraft that will be lost during the course of operations.'

Valle: 'I might add that our 346 aircraft will have to undertake defensive operations over a range of around 1,000 km, while the British will be able to concentrate their 200 aircraft at points of their own choosing. In any case, we have the capability to bombard Malta daily with 100 tons of bombs.'

Badoglio: 'His Excellency General Valle rightly draws our attention to the great expanses of territory which he will have to defend compared to the tasks facing the British Air Force, which operates roughly the same number of aircraft as we do.

I beg His Excellency General Baistrocchi to inform us of the measures taken by the Army.'

Baistrocchi: 'Orders have already been issued for the readying of military bases and islands as well as coastal defences and artillery. It should be taken into account that coastal defence will be undertaken by the MVSN,[2] but that at present the Army has not yet withdrawn its units from these positions. As regards coastal-defence guns, we have no reason to be concerned.

In the Aegean we are taking steps to ensure that defences are as strong as possible. In Sicily and Sardinia we are in a position to mobilise and assume defensive positions at a moment's notice.

At present we have two CCNN[3] divisions mobilised and fully operational and two army divisions (the '*Sila*' and '*Gran Sasso*'). A further two CCNN divisions will be ready in two months' time and a third in three months'.

The '*Cosseria*' and '*Assietta*' divisions will begin mobilisation in a few days.

Various other units (tanks, engineers, etc.) of considerable strength are now ready to leave for East Africa.

These units, for the reasons set out by His Excellency Marshal Badoglio, could be used for national defence and to undertake operations which might become necessary in the event that this new situation became a reality.

Concerning the difficulties of supplying East Africa and Libya mentioned by His Excellency Admiral Cavagnari, I might point out that we have recently increased our supplies of provisions and ammunition in East Africa. According to the officer in charge of this operation, who is in Rome at this moment, we have more supplies down there than we had planned to have. Should the units destined for deployment in East Africa be kept at home and not sent to the colony, the materials projected to run out in November, would last until January. Therefore, we would not need to worry for quite some time.'

Badoglio: 'The position of the army does not warrant concern. There is no possibility of a British amphibious landing on national territory.'

Pariani: 'As regards supplies for East Africa it should be noted that we have two months' worth already there and a month of reserve stocks – 500,000 head of livestock – 4,000,000 tins of food. By the beginning of September we will have ten days' supply of munitions for the artillery and 50 days' worth of ammunition for the infantry, which has been allocated, however, only to units we had already planned to deploy to East Africa.'

Badoglio: 'Given that it is impossible for the British to stage landings on our national territory, the security of our territory is not under any threat and this also applies to our land forces.

His Excellency General Baistrocchi has indicated that he will prepare Leros to resist attack.

I have been warned by His Excellency Admiral Cavagnari that in the event of hostilities with Britain all our lines of communication with East Africa, with the exception of wireless communications, will be severed. The odd merchant vessel might be able to reach Libya. In conclusion, as regards the executive part of the order issued by His Excellency the Head of Government, we can assure him that all the necessary steps have been taken in case of worsening tension with Britain.

By 30 August the fleet, our air forces and our land forces, will be in a position to assume battle stations within four days.'

Valle: 'It's worth bearing in mind that we will shortly have at our disposal squadrons able to mount an attack on London.'

Badoglio: 'OK. But this can only be authorised by the Head of Government, and moreover it also remains to be seen whether we will be permitted to fly over neutral territory.

To summarise: I can assure His Excellency the Head of Government that in terms of the executive part of his order, all the necessary steps will be taken. But our work does not end here. We must also inform His Excellency the Head of Government what the position of the enemy forces might be and what situation we might find ourselves in.'

Cavagnari: 'I will begin by noting that the first squadron will be at La Spezia for careening until 30 August and the second squadron will be ready towards the 25th. Both have been ordered to be ready for the 30th. We have learned that British naval forces in the Mediterranean will undertake their summer cruise which includes a visit to Yugoslav ports on the 29th of this month. I will now compare British naval force strength with our own.

Britain possesses:

- Fifteen battleships, with an average of eight 381/406 mm guns each. In total there are 120 high-calibre weapons. (We do not possess even one).
- Around 60 ships of 8/10,000 tons displacement (we have seven 10,000 tonners and six 6,000 ton ships, which could soon become eight or nine).
- Numerous ships of 3/4,000 tons displacement, and around 100 modern destroyers (we have around 50 modern, not so modern and very old destroyers).
- Around 50–60 submarines (in this category of vessel we practically match them; in fact, we have a slight superiority).

The British at the moment have two organically structured naval squadrons, and also naval forces based in India, the Cape, the Far East, etc.

Each squadron is composed of seven ships of the line (five battleships and two battle cruisers), ten *Washington*[4] type cruisers, two destroyer flotillas and a submarine flotilla.

Currently, Britain's fastest battleships (the *Queen Elisabeth* class) are deployed in the Mediterranean, along with two battle cruisers (the *Hood* and the *Renown*) and a flotilla of modern submarines.

Britain also has six aircraft carriers (each of which can carry 40 fighter, bomber and reconnaissance aircraft) for deployment in European waters.

To sum up: Italy's total lack of battleship capability and the limited operational value of its air force render the possibility of war against Britain an extremely onerous undertaking.

If we already had our new capital-ship nucleus, we might then be able to reach somewhat different conclusions, even if only from the point of view that Britain might not then wish to take the risk of engaging us in any war.

The two old battleships *Duilio* and *Doria* cannot be deployed to any theatre of strategic operations. They will therefore be assigned to the defence of Augusta, Naples or La Maddalena.

WHAT MIGHT THE BRITISH ORDER OF OPERATIONS BE?

With the great preponderance of naval power they have at their disposal, the British could easily blockade Gibraltar and Suez, even by using comparatively few naval units.

With the rest they could sweep the Mediterranean.

They could also form numerous groups of ships, always superior to our own. Anyhow, because of the presence of British battleships, our squadrons and divisions will always find themselves ballistically inferior.

Any naval forces at Malta will almost certainly be quickly moved from there. Any operation by us against the island would have to overcome its considerable static defences. Even if we were lucky enough to achieve an early success, after a surprise operation that took place prior to Malta's total evacuation, only with great difficulty could we consolidate it. Time would always be on the side of the enemy, given that they could concentrate ever more powerful air and naval forces in the Mediterranean.

The enemy will probably make use of Gibraltar, Haifa and Aqaba as operational bases, and quite possibly Argostoli, Candia, the Balearics or Leros.

The Dodecanese might well have been offered to Greece as a reward for the use of a port in the central Mediterranean.

Our ports at Leros and Tobruk undoubtedly have a very precarious capacity to resist attack.

Neither can we exclude the possibility that Maddalena might be captured in order to establish an operational base in the region.

Air and naval operations against our coastline are always a possibility, and especially in the stretch of water between the frontier[5] and Elba, where we would not be in any position to retaliate.'

Badoglio: 'I don't believe the British will try and capture La Maddalena.'

Cavagnari: 'Above all else we will have to rely on the element of surprise in order to secure the odd success in the opening phase.

Our submarine operations and the eventual blockading of the Maltese channel could well paralyse British merchant traffic in the Maltese channel and disrupt oceanic traffic as well.'

Badoglio: 'We can certainly disrupt British traffic in the Mediterranean. On the other hand, we should be under no illusions as to how sympathetic the other Mediterranean nations are likely to be.'

Cavagnari: 'Our successes in the first days of the war would not, in time, be worth very much, since the disproportionate balance of power will only act against us during the course of the conflict.

From every point of view, and simply limiting ourselves to the idea of a war between Italy and Britain alone, the passing of time can only act against us, given our lack of reserves, and given that Britain, once it has mobilised its awesome war machine, can rely on inexhaustible resources.

Merchant traffic destined for Italy will increasingly be confined to the few ships that are able to slip through the enemy blockade. It is also doubtful whether we will be able to rely on supplies reaching us from the Black Sea for very long.

Basically, the conflict will be a very hard one for Italy and especially so for the Navy.'

Badoglio: 'Evidently once the war has started East Africa will be forced to make do with the means available to it at that time.

In the Mediterranean any initial advantages we might enjoy will subsequently evaporate as the British reinforce the theatre with additional air and naval forces, and neither will it be possible for us to counter this on land.'

Cavagnari: 'I might point out that if were we to give the impression that we intend to throw all our available resources into this war, this might cause Britain to hesitate in the face of the possible global and imperial complications that might be a consequence of the conflict.

What we have ascertained as regards the geostrategic situation and the availability of means has led us to prepare a plan of operations in which is reflected our lack of battleships and, even more seriously, the weakness of our air forces.

As a matter of fact, were we able to count on a truly effective air arm, composed of no fewer than a thousand modern, effective aircraft, it would be possible to initiate hostilities by launching an intensive surprise aeronaval attack on Malta (either prior to Britain's evacuation of its fleet or during the evacuation), or against any blockade of the Suez Canal.

Subsequently, vigorous pressure could be put on British bases and forces from Gibraltar to Haifa, or even on their naval forces at sea.

But, in order to guarantee the success of such operations they must be supported for days or even weeks by substantial reserves of material, and especially reserves of aircraft.

In the absence of all this, Plan B represents only an emergency measure undertaken by the currently available means.'

Badoglio: 'In conclusion, His Excellency the Head of Government can count on the bravery and spirit of dedication and self-sacrifice that characterises the Italian people. But, it is our duty to outline for his benefit the situation in which we may well find ourselves, a situation which seems grave. It is only right and proper that His Excellency the Head of Government be aware of the facts, so that he can make his decisions.

Today's meeting has not covered the question of East Africa because this loses its significance when compared to the problem that we have discussed, that is, Italy's situation in the Mediterranean in the event of conflict with Britain.

Our East African colonies would need to be entirely self-reliant should this become a reality.

I was already aware of the position of the navy and air force before today's discussion. I had not yet spoken with His Excellency General Baistrocchi, because the contribution of land forces to the conflict in question would not be particularly significant.'

Baistrocchi: 'I would like to examine what contribution land forces operating out of our colonies against neighbouring British territories might make to the conflict.'

Badoglio: 'Fair enough, but there is no need to undertake in-depth studies, given that such operations are of little significance compared to the central question.'

Pini: 'I wish to point out that the naval ministry has issued the necessary instructions to national merchant ships in the event of a war. We have issued circulars which ships' captains will receive from Consular and port authorities. We are not yet able to say whether all vessels will have received their instructions by 30 August.'

Cavagnari: 'It is anticipated that by the end of the current month all merchant vessels, except one or two, will have returned to home waters.'

Baistrocchi: 'Given what has been said today and considering the situation in which we may soon find ourselves, it seems to me that we need to examine the wider politico-military picture. We might examine, therefore, whether we need accept this struggle at all, for various reasons and not just because of our inferiority.

What I'm saying is, in order to provide as much information as possible for the Head of Government, we should examine whether it would be possible for us find some alternative strategy, while carrying out our obligations as a great power.'

Badoglio: 'What I have said today has simply been in response to the orders of the Head of Government. In reference to these I can confirm:

1) that from 30 August and within the space of four days, the navy, the air force and the army will have taken all the necessary precautions in the event of extreme tension with Britain;
2) that the military situation is precisely as outlined today.

The political implications of this can only be assessed by His Excellency the Head of Government. In military terms the Head knows that we are all prepared to make whatever sacrifice might be necessary.'

Baistrocchi: 'But anyway, we will need directions.'

Badoglio: 'Yes. We will have these directions after the Head of Government has issued his orders.'

Pariani: 'But if we have to go into action which plan should we adopt?'

Badoglio: 'Plan B.'

Pariani: 'Can't we cross the Maltese channel in order to prevent the British from becoming absolute masters of the Mediterranean?'

Badoglio: 'We have taken the precautions necessary for us to adopt 'wait and see' positions. For now, we cannot predict what might happen in operational terms. Our future actions will be the consequence of events.'

Baistrocchi: 'So, we are to remain on the defensive on all fronts.'

Badoglio: 'No. Our planned operations against Malta, and the operations planned for the Red Sea are fundamentally offensive. On the other hand, we don't yet know what the enemy might do. Only then can we decide. For the moment we cannot think of preparing any plan for a land war. We must limit ourselves to preparing all our available means and comparing these with those of the enemy.'

Baistrocchi: 'We must hint that we intend to assume a non-passive defensive position.'

Badoglio: 'That, in fact, is what the navy and air force have done, at least as far as they can.'

Valle: 'The air force plan is totally offensive.'

Cavagnari: 'Naval operations, foreseen by Plan B, are also offensive.'

Baistrocchi: 'My remarks have been made in ignorance of Plan B, because no one told me anything about it. Consequently, given what His Excellency Marshal Badoglio and Their Excellencies Valle and Cavagnari have said, I have nothing to add.'

The meeting ended at 12 pm.
Rome, 13 August 1935–XIII.

NOTES

1   Valle seems to refer here to the Fiat BR.20, which did not enter service until 1936. The S55 he mentions is the SIAI Marchetti S55.
2   *Milizia Volontaria per la Sicurezza Nazionale* (the Fascist militia).
3   Fascist blackshirt divisions.
4   As stipulated by the Washington Naval Treaty.
5   The French–Italian frontier.

Archival and Documentary Sources

Britain

Public Record Office, London

ADM 1   Admiralty Secretariat Papers
ADM 116 Admiralty General Correspondence

AIR 2   Air Ministry Papers
AIR 8/9 Air Ministry Directorate of Plans

CAB 2/6 Committee of Imperial Defence Papers
CAB 21   Cabinet Minutes
CAB 53   Chiefs-of-Staff Papers

FO 371   Foreign Office General Correspondence
FO 837   Papers of the Ministry of Economic Warfare
FO 954   Papers of Lord Avon

HW 11   Government Code and Cipher School: World War Two
         Official Histories, 1938–45

Italy

Archivio Centrale dello Stato, Rome
Ministero della Marina
• Gabinetto

Joint Allied Intelligence Agency
• Personal Papers of Benito Mussolini

Presidenza del Consiglio dei ministri

Segretaria particolare del Duce
- Carte Alfredo Baistrocchi
- Carte Italo Balbo
- Carte Antonio Sorice
- Guerra civile in Spagna

Ministero dell'Interno
- Direzione affari generali e riservati della pubblica sicurezza

Ufficio Storico della Marina Militare, Rome

- Cartelle Numerate
- Comando Supremo
- Direzioni Generali
- Promemoria di Supermarina
- Pubblicazioni

Archivio Storico del Ministero degli Affari Esteri, Rome

Affari Politici
- Albania
- Francia
- Germania
- Gran Bretagna
- Italia
- Italia (colonie)

Rappresentanze diplomatiche
- Ambasciata di Berlino
- Ambasciata di Londra

Archivio De Felice
- Carte Dino Grandi

Archivio di Gabinetto

Archivio del Museo Centrale del Risorgimento, Rome
- Carte Dall'Olio

Ufficio Storico dello Stato Maggiore dell'Esercito, Rome

I-4	Carteggio Stato Maggiore generale, 1924–48
H-1	Ministero della Guerra – Gabinetto
H-3	SIM: Notiziari stati esteri – bollettini
H-5	Stato Maggiore dell'Regio Esercito
H-6	Piani operativi
H-9	Carteggio del Capo del Governo

H-10   Verbali riunioni, 1924–1943
L-10   Stato Maggiore dell'Regio Esercito: vari uffici

Published Documents

Germany

Documents on German Foreign Policy, Series C, 1933–37, Vols III–VI (Her Majesty's Stationery Office, London, Washington and Paris, 1957–83).
Documents on German Foreign Policy, Series D, 1936–41, Vols I–IX (Her Majesty's Stationery Office, London, Washington and Paris, 1949–56).

Britain

Documents on British Foreign Policy, Second Series, 1929–38, Vols XIII–XVIII (Her Majesty's Stationery Office, London, 1946–85).
Documents on British Foreign Policy, Third Series, 1938–39, Vols I–IX (Her Majesty's Stationery Office, London, 1949–55).
British Documents on Foreign Affairs: Reports and Papers from the Foreign Office and Confidential Print, Series F: Europe 1919–39, Vols XI–XV (University Publications of America, Washington, DC, 1992).

Italy

I documenti diplomatici italiani, settima serie, 1922–35, Vol. XIV (Istituto Poligrafico dello Stato, Rome, 1990).
I documenti diplomatici italiani, ottava serie, 1935–39, Vols I–IV and XII–XIII (Istituto Poligrafico dello Stato, Rome, 1952–92).
I documenti diplomatici italiani, nona serie, 1939–43, Vols I–IV (Istituto Poligrafico dello Stato, Rome, 1952–53).
Atti Parlamentari. Camera dei deputati, legislatura XXIX, sessione 1934–38 (various volumes).

Bibliography

Books

Adams, H. *Italy at War: World War II* (Time Life Books, Chicago, 1982).

Alexander, M. S. *The Republic in Danger: General Maurice Gamelin and the Politics of French Defence, 1933–1940* (Cambridge University Press, Cambridge, 1992).

Alfieri, D. *Due dittatori di fronte* (Rizzoli, Milan, 1948).

Anfuso, P. *Da Palazzo Venezia al Lago di Garda* (Cappelli, Bologna, 1957).

Armellini, Q. *Diario di guerra: nove mesi al Comando Supremo* (Garzanti, Milan, 1946).

Avon, Earl of. *The Eden Memoirs. Volume I: Facing the Dictators* (Cassell, London, 1962).

Baer, G. W. *The Coming of the Italian–Ethiopian War* (Harvard University Press, Cambridge, MA, 1967).

Bargoni, F. *L'impegno navale italiano durante la guerra civile spagnola* (Ufficio Storico della Marina Militare [USMM], Rome, 1992).

Barros, J. *The Corfu Incident of 1923* (Princeton University Press, Princeton, NJ, 1965).

Bastianini, G. *Uomini, cose, fatti: memorie di un ambasciatore* (Edizioni Vitagliano, Milan, 1959).

Bell, P. M. H. *The Origins of the Second World War in Europe* (Longman, London and New York, 1996).

Bernardi, G. *Il disarmo navale fra le due guerre mondiali, 1919–1939* (USMM, Rome, 1975).

Bernotti, R. *La guerra sui mari nel conflitto mondiale, 1939–41* (Società Editrice Tirrena, Livorno, 1948).

Bernotti, R. *Cinquant'anni nella Marina militare* (Mursia, Milan, 1971).

Birkenhead, Earl of. *Halifax: The Life of Lord Halifax* (Hamish Hamilton, London, 1965).

Blinkhorn, M. *Fascists and Conservatives: The Radical Right and the Establishment in Twentieth-century Europe* (Unwin Hyman, London, 1990).

Bocca, G. *Storia d'Italia nella guerra fascista, 1940–1943* (Laterza, Bari, 1969).

Bosworth, R. J. B. *Italy: The Least of the Great Powers* (Cambridge University Press, Cambridge, 1979).

Bottai, G. Diario, *1935–1944*, ed. G. B. Guerri (Rizzoli, Milan, 1994).

Botti, F. and Ilari, V. *Il pensiero militare italiano dal primo al secondo doppoguerra* (Stato Maggiore dell'Esercito, Ufficio Storico [USSME], Rome, 1995).

Boyce, R. and Robertson, E. (eds), *Paths to War: New Essays on the Origins of the Second World War* (Macmillan, London, 1989).

Bragadin, M. *Che ha fatto la Marina, 1940–45?* (Garzanti, Rome, 1950).

Buccianti, G. *Verso gli accordi Mussolini–Laval. Il riavvicinamento italo-francese fra il 1931 e il 1934* (Giuffrè, Milan, 1984).

Bullock, A. *Hitler: A Study in Tyranny* (Penguin Books, London, 1981).

Butler, J. R. M. (gen. ed.) *History of the Second World War.*
    Playfair, I. S. O. *The Mediterranean and Middle East. Volume I: The Early Successes Against Italy (to May 1941)* (Her Majesty's Stationery Office [HMSO], London, 1954).
    Gibbs, N. H. *Grand Strategy. Volume I: Rearmament Policy* (HMSO, London, 1976).

Butler, J. R. M. *Grand Strategy. Volume II: September 1939–June 1941* (HMSO, London, 1957).

Calvocoressi, P., Wint, G. and Pritchard, J. *Total War: The Causes and Courses of the Second World War. Volume I: The Western Hemisphere* (Penguin Books, London, 1989).

Carr, W. *Arms, Autarky and Aggression: A Study in German Foreign Policy, 1933–39* (Edward Arnold, London, Melbourne and Auckland, 1972).

Cassels, A. *Mussolini's Early Diplomacy* (Princeton University Press, Princeton, NJ, 1970).

Catalano, F. *L'economia italiana di guerra: la politica economia-finanziaria del fascismo dalla guerra d'Etiopia alla caduta del regime, 1935–1943* (Istituto Nazionale per la Storia, Milan, 1969).

Centre National de la Recherche Scientifique. *Les Relations Franco-Britanniques, 1935–1939* (Paris, 1975).

Ceva, L. *La condotta italiana della guerra: Cavallero e il Comando Supremo, 1941–1942* (Feltrinelli, Milan, 1975).

Ceva, L. *Le forze armate* (Unione Tipografico Editrice Torinese [UTET], Turin, 1981).

Ceva, L. and Curami, A. *Industria bellica anni trenta* (Franco Angeli, Milan, 1992).

Chatfield, Lord. *It Might Happen Again* (Heinemann, London, 1947).

Churchill, W. S. *The Second World War. Volume I: The Gathering Storm* (Cassell, London, 1948).

Ciano, G. *Diplomatic Papers*, ed. M. Muggeridge (Odhams Press, London, 1948).

Ciano, G. *Diario: 1937–1943*, ed. R. De Felice (Rizzoli, Milan, 1994).

Connell, J. *Wavell: Scholar and Soldier, Volume I* (Collins, London, 1964).

Cooper, Duff. *Old Men Forget* (Rupert Hart-Davis, London, 1953).

Coverdale, J. F. *Italian Intervention in the Spanish Civil War* (Princeton University Press, Princeton, NJ, 1975).

Craig, G. A. and Gilbert, F. (eds) *The Diplomats, 1919–1939* (Princeton University Press, Princeton, NJ, 1953).

Cunningham, Admiral of the Fleet, Viscount. *A Sailor's Odyssey* (Hutchinson, London, 1951).

Dann, U. (ed.) *The Great Powers and the Middle East, 1919–1939* (Holmes & Meier, New York, 1988).

De Felice, R. *Mussolini il Duce. I: Gli anni del consenso, 1929–1936* (Giulio Einaudi, Turin, 1974).

De Felice, R. *Mussolini il Duce. II: Lo stato totalitario, 1936–1940* (Giulio Einaudi, Turin, 1981).

De Felice, R. *Mussolini il alleato, 1940–1945. L'Italia in guerra, 1940–1943. I: Dalla guerra 'breve' alla guerra lunga* (Giulio Einaudi, Turin, 1990).

De Grand, A. *Italian Fascism* (University of Nebraska Press, London, 1982).

Deist, W. *et al.* (eds) *Germany and the Second World War.*
Volume I: The Build-up of German Aggression (Clarendon Press, Oxford, 1990).
Volume II: Germany's Initial Conquests in Europe (Clarendon Press, Oxford, 1991).
Volume III: The Mediterranean, South-East Europe and North Africa, 1939–1941 (Clarendon Press, Oxford, 1995).

Dilks, D. (ed.) *The Diaries of Sir Alexander Cadogan, 1938–1945* (Cassell, London, 1971).

Dilks, D. (ed.) *Retreat from Power* (Macmillan, London, 1981).

Di Nolfo, E. *Mussolini e la politica estera italiana, 1919–1933* (Ledam, Padua, 1960).

Di Nolfo, E. Rainero, R. H. and Vigezzi, B. (eds) *L'Italia e la politica di potenza in Europa, 1938–1940* (Marzorati, Milan, 1988).

Duroselle, J. B. *La Décadence, 1932–1939* (Imprimerie Nationale, Paris, 1979).

Duroselle, J. B. *L'Abîme, 1939–1944* (Imprimerie Nationale, Paris, 1986).

Favagrossa, C. *Perchè perdemmo la guerra: Mussolini e la produzione bellica* (Rizzoli, Milan, 1946).

Fraccaroli, A. *Italian Warships of World War II* (Ian Allan, London, 1968).

Fraccaroli, A. *Italian Warships of World War I* (Ian Allan, London, 1970).

Gabriele, M. *Operazione C3: Malta* (USMM, Rome, 1965).

Gabriele, M. *Le convenzioni navali della Triplice* (USMM, Rome, 1969).

Gabriele, M. and Friz, G. *La politica navale italiana dal 1885 al 1915* (USMM, Rome, 1982).

Garzke, W. H. and Dullin, R. O. *Battleships: Axis and Neutral Battleships in World War II* (Naval Institute Press, Annapolis, MD, 1985).

Gayda, V. *Italia e Inghilterra: l'inevitabile conflitto* (Edizioni del Giornale d'Italia, Rome, 1941).

Gooch, J. *Armies in Europe* (Routledge, Kegan & Paul, London, 1980).

Gooch, J. *Esercito, stato e società in Italia, 1870–1915* (Franco Angeli, Milan, 1994).

Gordon, G. A. H. *British Seapower and Procurement between the Wars* (Macmillan, London, 1988).

Grandi, D. *Il mio paese: ricordi autobiografici* (Il Mulino, Bologna, 1985).

Guerri, G. B. *Galeazzo Ciano: una vita, 1903–1944* (Bompiani, Milan, 1979).

Hardie, F. *The Abyssinian Crisis* (Batsford, London, 1974).

Hibbert, C. *Benito Mussolini* (Reprint Society, London, 1962).

Hildebrand, K. *The Foreign Policy of the Third Reich* (Batsford, London, 1973).

James, Admiral Sir W. *Admiral Sir W. Fisher* (Macmillan, London, 1943).

Joll, J. *Europe since 1870: An International History* (Penguin Books, London, 1981).

Jürgen-Müller, K. *The Army, Politics and Society in Germany, 1933–1945* (Manchester University Press, Manchester, 1987).

Katz, R. *The Fall of the House of Savoy* (Macmillan, London and New York, 1971).

Kennedy, P. *The Realities behind Diplomacy: Background Influences on British External Policy 1865–1980* (Fontana Press, London, 1981).

Kennedy, P. *Strategy and Diplomacy* (Fontana Press, London, 1989).

Kershaw, I. *The Nazi Dictatorship: Problems and Perspectives of Interpretation* (Edward Arnold, London, 1996).

Knox, M. *Mussolini Unleashed, 1939–1941: Politics and Strategy in Fascist Italy's Last War* (Cambridge University Press, Cambridge, 1982).

Lenton, H. T. and Colledge, J. J. *Warships of World War Two* (Ian Allan, London, 1964).

Liddell Hart, B. H. *History of the Second World War* (Book Club Associates, London, 1970).

Lowe, C. J. and Marzari, F. *Italian Foreign Policy, 1870–1940* (Routledge, Kegan & Paul, London, 1975).

Mack Smith, D. *Mussolini's Roman Empire* (Longman, London, 1976).

Mack Smith, D. *Mussolini* (Paladin, London, 1983).

Magistrati, M. *L'Italia a Berlino, 1937–1939* (Arnoldo Mondadori, Verona, 1956).

Marder, A. *From the Dardanelles to Oran* (Oxford University Press, London, 1951).

Marder, A. *From the Dreadnought to Scapa Flow. Volume V: Victory and Aftermath, January 1918–June 1919* (Oxford University Press, London, 1974).

Marks, S. *The Illusion of Peace* (Macmillan, London, 1976).

Maugeri, F. *From the Ashes of Disgrace* (Reynal & Hitchcock, New York, 1948).

May, E. R. (ed.) *Knowing One's Enemies: Intelligence Assessments before the Two World Wars* (Princeton University Press, Princeton, NJ, 1984).

Medlicott, W. N. *British Foreign Policy since Versailles* (Methuen, London, 1940).

Medlicott, W. N. *The Economic Blockade: Volume I* (HMSO, London, 1952).

Millett, A. R. and Murray, W. (eds) *Military Effectiveness. Volume II: The Interwar Period* (Allen & Unwin, Boston, MA, 1988).

Millett, A. R. and Murray, W. (eds) *Military Effectiveness. Volume III: The Second World War* (Allen & Unwin, Boston, MA, 1988).

Millett, A. R. and Murray, W. (eds) *Calculations: Net Assessments and the Coming of World War II* (The Free Press, New York, 1992).

Mommsen, W. J. and Kettenacker, L. *The Fascist Challenge and the Policy of Appeasement* (Allen & Unwin, London, 1983).

Morgan, P. *Italian Fascism 1919–1945* (Macmillan, London, 1995).

Mori, R. *Mussolini e la conquista dell'Etiopia* (Felice le Monnier, Florence, 1978).

Müller, K. J. *The Army, Politics and Society in Germany: 1933–1945* (Manchester University Press, Manchester, 1987).

Murray, W. *The Change in the European Balance of Power, 1938–1939: The Path to Ruin* (Princeton University Press, Princeton, NJ, 1984).

Mussolini, B. *Opera Omnia di Benito Mussolini* (various volumes) (La Fenice, Florence and Rome, 1951–1980).

Parker, R. A. C. *Europe, 1919–1945* (Weidenfeld & Nicolson, London, 1969).

Parker, R. A. C. *Chamberlain and Appeasement: British Policy and the Coming of the Second World War* (Macmillan, London, 1993).

Pastorelli, P. (ed.) *Sidney Sonnino: carteggio 1914–1916* (Laterza, Bari, 1974).

Pedrocini, G. (ed.) *Histoire Militaire de la France. Volume 3: De 1871 à 1940* (Presses Universitaires de France, Paris, 1992).

Petersen, J. *Hitler e Mussolini: la difficile alleanza* (Laterza, Milan, 1975).

Pieri, P. and Rochat, G. *Badoglio* (UTET, Turin, 1974).

Post, G. Jr. *Dilemmas of Appeasement. British Deterrence and Defense, 1934–1937* (Cornell University Press, London, 1993).

Pratt, L. *East of Malta, West of Suez: Britain's Mediterranean Crisis, 1936–1939* (Cambridge University Press, Cambridge, 1975).

Preston, P. *Franco* (HarperCollins, London, 1993).

Quartararo, R. *Roma tra Londra e Berlino: la politica estera fascista dal 1930 al 1940* (Bonacci, Rome, 1980).

Raven, A. and Roberts, J. *British Battleships of World War Two: The Development and Technological History of the Royal Navy's Battleships and Battlecruisers, 1911–1946* (Arms and Armour Press, London, 1976).

Robertson, E. M. *Mussolini as Empire Builder* (Macmillan, London, 1977).

Rochat, G. *Militari e politici nella preparazione della campagna d'Etiopia: studio e documenti, 1932–1936* (Franco Angeli, Milan, 1971).

Rochat, G. *Italo Balbo: aviatore e ministro dell'Aeronautica, 1926–1933* (Italo Bovolenta, Ferrara, 1979).

Roskill, S. *Hankey Man of Secrets. Volume III: 1931–1963* (Collins, London, 1974).

Roskill, S. *Naval Policy Between the Wars. Volume II: The Period of Reluctant Rearmament, 1930–1939* (Collins, London, 1976).

Rostow, N. *Anglo-French Relations, 1934–1936* (Macmillan, London, 1984).

Rusinow, D. I. *Italy's Austria Heritage, 1919–1946* (Oxford University Press, London, 1969).

Sadkovich, J. J. *The Italian Navy in World War II* (Greenwood Press, Westport, CT, 1994).

Salvatorelli, L. *Il fascismo nella politica internazionale* (Giulio Einaudi, Rome-Modena, 1956).

Salvatorelli, L. and Mira, G. *Storia d'Italia nel periodo fascista* (Giulio Einaudi, Rome, 1959).

Salvemini, G. *Mussolini diplomatico* (Laterza, Bari, 1952).

Santoni, A. *Il vero traditore* (Mursia, Milan, 1981).

Sbacchi, A. *Il colonialismo italiano in Etiopia, 1936–1940* (Mursia, Milan, 1980).

Schmidt, G. *The Politics of Appeasement* (Berg, Leamington Spa, 1986).

Schreiber, G. *Revisionismus und Weltmachtstreben: Marineführung und deutsch-italienische Beziehungen, 1919–1944* (Deutsch Verlags-Anstalt, Stuttgart, 1978).

Segrè, C. *Italo Balbo: A Fascist Life* (University of California Press, London, 1987).

Seton-Watson, R. W. *Britain and the Dictators* (Cambridge University Press, London, 1939).

Shorrock, W. I. *From Ally to Enemy: The Enigma of Fascist Italy in French Diplomacy, 1920–1940* (Kent State University Press, London, 1988).

Suvich, F. *Memorie, 1932–1936*, ed. G. Bianchi (Rizzoli, Milan, 1984).

Tasso, A. *Italia e Croazia* (Tipografia S. Giuseppe, Macerata, 1967).

Taylor, A. J. P. *The Origins of the Second World War* (Penguin, London, 1987).

Toscano, M. *The Origins of the Pact of Steel* (Johns Hopkins University Press, Baltimore, MD, 1967).

Uberti, U. *La Marina da guerra* (Adriano Salani, Florence, 1940).

Ufficio Storico dello Stato Maggiore del Esercito (USSME). *Verbali delle riunoni tenute dal Capo di S.M. generale. Volume I: 26/1/1939– 29/12/1940* (USSME, Rome, 1983).

Ufficio Storico della Marina Militare (USMM). *La Marina italiana nella seconda guerra mondiale.*
II: La guerra nel Mediterraneo: le azioni navali, tomo I, dal 10 giugno 1940 al 31 marzo 1941 (USMM, Rome, 1949).
VI: La difesa del traffico con l'Africa settentrionale dal 10/6/1940 al 30/9/1941 (USMM, Rome, 1958).
X: Le operazioni in Africa orientale (USMM, Rome, 1961).
XII: I sommergibili negli oceani (USMM, Rome, 1963).
XIII: I sommergibili in Mediterraneo (USMM, Rome 1967).
XIV: I mezzi d'assalto (USMM, Rome 1964).
XVIII: La guerra di mine (USMM, Rome, 1966).
XXI: L'organizzazione della Marina durante il conflitto: Tomo I: Efficienza all'apertura delle ostilità (USMM, Rome, 1972). *Tomo II: Evoluzione organica dal 10/6/1940 al 8/9/1943* (USMM, Rome, 1975).
XXII: La lotta antisommergibile (USMM, Rome, 1978).

Ufficio Storico della Marina Militare. *La battaglia dei convogli, 1940–1943* (USMM, Rome, 1994).

Vergani, O. *Ciano: Una lunga confessione* (Longanesi, Milan, 1974).

Waterfield, G. *Professional Diplomat: Sir Percy Loraine, 1880–1961* (John Murray, London, 1973).

Watt, D. C. *Personalities and Policies* (Longmans, London, 1965).

Watt, D. C. *How War Came: The Immediate Origins of the Second World War, 1938–1939* (Mandarin, London, 1990).

Weinberg, G. *The Foreign Policy of Hitler's Germany.*
Volume I: Diplomatic Revolution in Europe, 1933–36 (University of Chicago Press, Chicago, IL, 1970).
Volume II: Starting World War Two, 1937–39 (University of Chicago Press, Chicago, 1980).

Wheeler-Bennett, J. W. *Munich: Prologue to Tragedy* (Macmillan, London, 1966).

Wiskemann, E. *The Rome–Berlin Axis: A History of Relations Between Hitler and Mussolini* (Oxford University Press, Oxford, 1949).

Young, R. J. *In Command of France: French Foreign Policy and Military Planning, 1933–1940* (Harvard University Press, Cambridge, MA, 1988).

Articles and Essays

Ando, E. 'Capitani Romani', in *Warship: Volume II* (Conway Maritime Press, London, 1980), pp. 247–57.

Blatt, J. 'The Parity that Meant Superiority: French Naval Policy towards Italy at the Washington Naval Conference, 1921–22, and Interwar French Foreign Policy', *French Historical Studies*, 12, 2 (1981), pp. 223–48.

Botti, F. 'La strategia marittima negli anni venti', *Bolletino d'Archivio dell'Ufficio Storico della Marina Militare*, 2, 3 (1988), pp. 241–58.

Botti, F. 'Da flotta secondaria a grande Marina: la strategia marittima italiana negli anni trenta', *Bolletino d'Archivio dell'Ufficio Storico della Marina Militare*, 2, 4 (1988), pp. 135–57.

Cassels, A. 'Mussolini and German Nationalism, 1922–25', *Journal of Modern History*, 35, 2 (1963), pp. 137–57.

Cassels, A. 'Was There a Fascist Foreign Policy? Tradition and Novelty', *International History Review*, 5, 2 (1983), pp. 255–68.

Cavagnari, D. 'La Marina italiana nella vigilia e nel primo periodo della guerra', *Nuova Antologia*, 357 (1947), pp. 370–86.

Cernuschi, E. 'Colpito e occultato', *Rivista Storica* (July 1994), pp. 22–35.

Ceva, L. 'Un intervento di Badoglio e il mancato rinnovamento delle artiglierie italiane', *Il Risorgimento*, 28, 2 (1976), pp. 117–72.

Ceva, L. 'Altre notizie sulle conversazioni militari italo-tedesche alla vigilia della seconda guerra mondiale (aprile–giugno 1939)', *Il Risorgimento*, 30, 3 (1978), pp. 151–82.

Ceva, L. 'Appunti per una storia dello Stato Maggiore generale fino all vigilia della "non-belligeranza", giugno 1925–luglio 1939', *Storia Contemporanea*, 10, 2 (1979), pp. 207–52.

Ceva, L. 'Vertici politici e militari nel 1940–1943: interrogativi e temi d'indagine', *Il Politico*, 46, 4 (1981), pp. 691–700.

Ceva, L. '1927: una riunione fra Mussolini e I vertici militari', *Il Politico*, 50, 2 (1985), pp. 329–37.

Cliadakis, H. 'Neutrality and War in Italian Policy, 1939–1940', *Journal of Contemporary History*, 9, 3 (1974), pp. 171–90.

Davis, R. 'Mésentente Cordiale: The Failure of the Anglo-French Alliance: Anglo-French Relations during the Ethiopian and Rhineland Crises, 1935–1936', *European History Quarterly*, 23, 4 (1993), pp. 513–25.

Douglas, R. 'Chamberlain and Eden, 1937–1938', *Journal of Contemporary History*, 13, 1 (1978), pp. 97–116.

Edwards, P. G. 'The Foreign Office and Fascism, 1924–1929', *Journal of Contemporary History*, 5, 2 (1970), pp. 153–61.

Edwards, P. G. 'Britain, Mussolini and the Locarno–Geneva System', *European Studies Review*, 10, 1 (1986), pp. 1–16.

Ferrante, E, 'Il pensiero strategic navale in Italia', *Rivista Marittima*, special issue (1988), pp. 3–151.

Ferretti, V. 'La politica estera italiana e il Giappone imperiale (gennaio 1934–giugno 1937)', *Storia Contemporanea*, 10, 4/5 (1979), pp. 873–923.

Fioravanzo, G. 'Studi e progetti per la presa di Malta: una verità da ristabilire', *Rivista Marittima* (July 1954), pp. 2–6.

French, D. *'Perfidious Albion* Faces the Powers', *Canadian Journal of History*, 28, special issue (1993), pp. 177–87.

Funke, M. 'Le relazioni italo-tedesche al momento del conflitto etiopico e delle sanzioni della Società delle Nazioni', *Storia Contemporanea*, 2, 3 (1975), pp. 475–93.

Gabriele, M. '1939. Vigilia di guerra nel Mediterraneo', *Rivista Marittima* (July 1984), pp. 17–40.

Gabriele, M. 'L'Italia nel Mediterraneo tra tedeschi e alleati, 1938–1940', *Rivista Marittima* (December 1984), pp. 17–36.

Gabriele, M. 'Mediterraneo 1935–1936: la situazione militare marittima nella visione britannica', *Rivista Marittima* (May 1986), pp. 21–36.

Gabriele, M. 'Una voce degli anni venti nel dibattito sulle portaerei', *Rivista Marittima* (May 1988), pp. 11–18.

Gabriele, M. 'I piani della Marina francese contro l'Italia', *Bollettino d'Archivio dell'Ufficio Storico della Marina Militare*, 2, 3 (1988), pp. 175–206.

Goldman, A. L. 'Sir Robert Vansittart's Search for Italian Co-operation against Hitler, 1933–1936', *Journal of Contemporary History*, 9, 3 (1988), pp. 93–130.

Gooch, J. 'Italian Military Incompetence', *Journal of Strategic Studies*, 5, 2 (1982), pp. 258–65.

Gretton, P. 'The Nyon Conference: The Naval Aspect', *English Historical Review*, 90, 1 (1975), pp. 103–12.

Hillgruber, A. 'England's Place in Hitler's Plans for World Dominion', *Journal of Contemporary History*, 9, 1 (1974), pp. 5–22.

Knox, M. 'Conquest, Foreign and Domestic, in Fascist Italy and Nazi Germany', *Journal of Modern History*, 56, 1 (1984), pp. 1–57.

Knox, M. 'L'ultima guerra dell'Italia fascista', in B. Micheletti and P. Poggio (eds), *L'Italia in guerra, 1940–1943* (Annali della Fondazione 'Luigi Marchetti', Brescia, 1990–91), pp. 17–32.

Knox, M. 'Il fascismo e la politica estera italiana', in R. J. Bosworth and S. Romano (eds), *La politica estera italiana, 1860–1985* (Il Mulino, Bologna, 1991), pp. 287–330.

Knox, M. 'The Fascist Regime, its Foreign Policy and its Wars: "An Anti–Fascist" Orthodoxy?', *Contemporary European History*, 4, 3 (1995), pp. 347–65.

Leitz, C. 'Nazi Germany's Intervention in the Spanish Civil War and the Foundation of HISMA/ROWAK', in P. Preston and A. L. Mackenzie (eds), *The Republic Besieged: Civil War in Spain, 1936–1939* (Edinburgh University Press, Edinburgh, 1996), pp. 53–85.

Little, D. 'Red Scare, 1936: Anti-Bolshevism and the Origins of British Non-Intervention in the Spanish Civil War', *Journal of Contemporary History*, 23, 2 (1988), pp. 291–311.

MacDonald, C. A. 'Britain, France and the April Crisis of 1939', *European Studies Review*, 2, 2 (1972), pp. 151–69.

MacDonald, C. A. 'Radio Bari: Italian Wireless Propaganda in the Middle East and British Countermeasures, 1934–38', *Middle Eastern Studies*, 13, 1 (1977), pp. 195–207.

Mallett, R. 'The Anglo-Italian War Trade Negotiations, Contraband Control and the Failure to Appease Mussolini, 1939–1940', *Diplomacy and Statecraft*, 8, 1 (1997), pp. 137–67.

Marder, A. 'The Royal Navy and the Ethiopian Crisis of 1935–1936', *American Historical Review*, 75, 5 (1969), pp. 1327–56.

Marzari, F. 'Projects for an Italian-led Balkan Bloc of Neutrals, September–December 1939', *The Historical Journal*, 13, 4 (1970), pp. 767–88.

Michaelis, M. 'Italy's Strategy in the Mediterranean, 1935–1939', in M. J. Cohen and M. Kolinsky (eds), *Britain and the Middle East in the 1930s* (Macmillan, London, 1992), pp. 41–60.

Mills, W. C. 'The Nyon Conference: Neville Chamberlain, Anthony Eden, and the Appeasement of Italy in 1937', *International History Review*, 15, 1 (1993), pp. 1–22.

Minniti, F. 'Due anni di attività del "Fabbiguerra" per la produzione bellica, 1939–1941', *Storia Contemporanea*, 6, 4 (1975), pp. 849–79.

Minniti, F. 'Il problema degli armamenti nella preparazione militare italiana dal 1935 al 1943', *Storia Contemporanea*, 9, 1 (1978), pp. 5–61.

Minniti, F. 'La politica industriale del Ministero dell'Aeronautica: mercato, pianificazione, sviluppo, 1935–1943: parte prima', *Storia Contemporanea*, 12, 1 (1981), pp. 5–55; 'parte seconda', 12, 2 (1981), pp. 271–312.

Minniti, F. 'Le materie prime nella preparazione bellica dell'Italia, 1935–1943 (parte prima)', *Storia Contemporanea*, 17, 1 (1986), pp. 5–40.

Minniti, F. 'Piano e ordinamento nella preparazione italiana alla guerra negli anni trenta', *Dimensioni e problemi della ricerca storico*, 1 (1990), pp. 1–41.

Minniti, F. '"Il nemico vero": gli obiettivi dei piani di operazione contro la Gran Bretagna nel contesto etiopico (maggio 1935–maggio 1936)', *Storia Contemporanea*, 26, 4 (1995), pp. 575–602.

Morewood, S. 'Protecting the Jugular Vein of Empire: The Suez Canal in British Defence Strategy, 1919–1941', *War and Society*, 10, 1 (1992), pp. 81–107.

Morewood, S. 'The Chiefs-of-Staff, the "Men on the Spot", and the Italo-

Abyssinian Emergency, 1935–36', in D. Richardson and G. Stone (eds), *Decisions and Diplomacy – Essays in Twentieth Century International History* (LSE/Routledge, London, 1995), pp. 83–107.

Murfett, M. H. 'Living in the Past: A Critical Re-examination of the Singapore Naval Strategy, 1918–1941', *War and Society*, 11, 1 (1993), pp. 73–103.

Murray, W. 'Munich, 1938: The Military Confrontation', *Journal of Strategic Studies*, 2, 3 (1979), pp. 282–302.

Ortona, E. 'La caduta di Eden nel 1938', *Storia Contemporanea*, 15, 3 (1984), pp. 47–61.

Painter, B. W. Jr. 'Renzo De Felice and the Historiography of Italian Fascism', *American Historical Review*, 95, 2 (1990), pp. 391–405.

Parker, R. A. C. 'Great Britain, France and the Ethiopian Crisis, 1935–1936', *English Historical Review*, 89, 351 (1974), pp. 293–332.

Petersen, J. 'La politica estera fascista come problema storiografico', *Storia Contemporanea*, 3, 4 (1972), pp. 5–61.

Pizzigalo, M. 'La Regia Marina e il petrolio: un lungimirante progetto del 1919', *Rivista Marittima* 109, 10 (1976), pp. 56–62.

Polastro, W. 'La Marina Militare italiana nel primo dopoguerra, 1918–1925', *Il Risorgimento*, 3 (1977), pp. 127–70.

Post, G. Jr. 'The Machinery of British Policy in the Ethiopian Crisis', *International History Review*, 1, 4 (1979), pp. 522–41.

Preston, P. 'Mussolini's Spanish Adventure: From Limited Risk to War', in P. Preston and A. L. Mackenzie (eds), *The Republic Besieged: Civil War in Spain, 1936–1939* (Edinburgh University Press, Edinburgh, 1996), pp. 21–51.

Quartararo, R. 'La crisi mediterranea nel 1935–1936', *Storia Contemporanea*, 6, 4 (1975), pp. 801–46.

Quartararo, R. 'Imperial Defence in the Mediterranean on the Eve of the Ethiopian Crisis (July–October 1935)', *The Historical Journal*, 20, 1 (1977), pp. 185–220.

Robertson, J. C. 'The Hoare–Laval Plan', *Journal of Contemporary History*, 10, 3 (1975), pp. 433–59.

Rochat, G. 'Il controllo politico delle forze armate dall'unità d'Italia alla seconda guerra mondiale', in E. Forcella (ed.), *Il potere militare in Italia* (Laterza, Bari, 1971).

Rochat, G. 'Mussolini, Chef de Guerre, 1940–1943', *Revue d'Histoire de la Deuxième Guerre Mondiale*, 100 (1975), pp. 43–66.

Rochat, G, 'Lo sforzo bellico 1940–1943: analasi di una sconfitta', *Italia Contemporanea*, 160 (1985), pp. 7–24.

Rochat, G. 'I servizi di informazione e l'alto commando italiano nella guerra parallela del 1940', *Studi Piacentini*, 4, 1 (1989), pp. 69–84.

Rose, N. 'The Resignation of Anthony Eden', *The Historical Journal*, 25, 4 (1982), pp. 911–31.

Sadkovich, J.J. 'Re-evaluating Who Won the Italo-British Naval Conflict, 1940–1942', *European History Quarterly*, 18, 4 (1988), pp. 455–71.

Sadkovich, J. J. 'Understanding Defeat: Reappraising Italy's Role in World War II', *Journal of Contemporary History*, 24, 1 (1989), pp. 27–61.

Sadkovich, J. J. 'German Military Incompetence through Italian Eyes', *War in History*, 1, 1 (1994), pp. 39–62.

Salerno, R. N. 'Multilateral Strategy and Diplomacy: The Anglo-German Naval Agreement and the Mediterranean Crisis of 1935–1936', *Journal of Strategic Studies*, 17, 2 (1994), pp. 39–78.

Santoni, A. 'La mancata risposta della Regia Marina alle teorie del Douhet', in *La figura e l'opera di Giulio Douhet* (Società di Storia Patria, Caserta, 1988), pp. 257–69.

Santoni, A. 'Perchè le navi italiane in guerra non colpivano il bersaglio', *Rivista Storica* (March 1994), pp. 26–38.

Shorrock, W. I. 'France, Italy, and the Eastern Mediterranean in the late 1920s', *International History Review*, 8, 1 (1986), pp. 70–82.

Stafford, P. 'The Chamberlain–Halifax Visit to Rome: A Reappraisal', *English Historical Review*, 98, 386 (1983), pp. 61–100.

Sullivan, B. R. 'Roosevelt, Mussolini e la guerra d'Etiopia: una lezione sulla diplomazia americana', *Storia Contemporanea*, 19, 1 (1988), pp. 85–105.

Sullivan, B. R. 'A Fleet in Being: The Rise and Fall of Italian Sea Power, 1861–1943', *International History Review*, 10, 1 (1988), pp. 106–24.

Sullivan, B. R. 'Italian Naval Power and the Washington Disarmament Conference of 1921–1922', *Diplomacy and Statecraft*, 4, 3 (1993), pp. 220–48.

Sullivan, B. R. 'Introduction', in R. Bernotti, *Fundamentals of Naval Tactics and Fundamentals of Naval Strategy* (Naval Institute Press, Annapolis, MD, 1998), pp. 1–65.

Thomas, M. 'Plans and Problems of the *Armée de l'Air* in the Defence of French North Africa before the Fall of France', *French History*, 7, 4 (1993), pp. 472–95.

Toscano, M. 'Le conversazioni militari italo-tedesche alla vigilia della seconda guerra mondiale', *Rivista Storica Italiana*, 69, 1 (1957), pp. 336–82.

Waddington, G. '*Hassgegner*: German Views of Great Britain in the Later 1930s', *History*, 81, 261 (1996), pp. 22–39.

Waddington, G. 'An Idyllic and Unruffled Atmosphere of Complete Anglo-German Misunderstanding: Aspects of the Operations of the Dientstelle Ribbentrop in Great Britain, 1934–1938', *History*, 82, 265 (1997), pp. 44–72.

Wallace, W. V. 'The Making of the May Crisis', *The Slavonic and East European Review*, 41, 97 (1963), pp. 368–90.

Watt, D. C. 'An Earlier Model for the Pact of Steel: The Draft Treaties

Exchanged Between Germany and Italy during Hitler's Visit to Rome in May 1938', *International Affairs*, 33, 2 (1957), pp. 185–97.

Watt, D. C. 'Hitler's Visit to Rome and the May Weekend Crisis: A Study in Hitler's Response to External Stimuli', *Journal of Contemporary History*, 9, 1 (1974), pp. 23–32.

Weinberg, G. 'The May Crisis, 1938', *Journal of Modern History*, 29, 3 (1957), pp. 213–25.

Whealey, R. H. 'Mussolini's Ideological Diplomacy: An Unpublished Document', *Journal of Modern History*, 39, 4 (1967), pp. 432–37.

Young, R. J. 'Soldiers and Diplomats: The French Embassy and Franco-Italian Relations, 1935–6', *Journal of Strategic Studies*, 7, 1 (1984), pp. 74–91.

Young, R. J. 'French Military Intelligence and the Franco-Italian Alliance, 1933–1939', *The Historical Journal*, 28, 1 (1985), pp. 143–68.

Unpublished Sources

Brown, D. 'Malta 1940–1942: The Influential Island', Anglo-Italian Conference, Imperial War Museum, 1990.

Dingli, A. 'Diaries, 1938–1940', ASMAE, carte Grandi, b:66, f:2.

Fuehrer Conferences on Naval Affairs, 1940, Admiralty Report, September 1947, Brotherton Library, University of Leeds.

Patterson. T. 'Chatfield', Courtesy of Dr Eric Grove, Department of Politics, University of Hull.

Rahn, W. 'German Naval Power in the First and Second World War', 'Parameters of Naval Power' conference paper, University of Exeter, 1994.

Sadkovich, J. J. 'The Indispensable Navy: Italy as a Great Power, 1911–1943', 'Parameters of Naval Power' conference paper, University of Exeter, 1994.

Stone, G. 'Britain, France and the Spanish Problem, 1936–1939', courtesy of Dr Glynn Stone, University of the West of England, Bristol.

Weichold, E. *Axis Naval Policy and Operations in the Mediterranean, 1939 to May 1943*, Naval Historical Branch, Ministry of Defence Library, London.

Doctoral Theses

Morewood, S. 'The British Defence of Egypt, 1935–September 1937', PhD thesis, University of Bristol, 1985.

Stafford, P. 'Italy and Anglo-French Strategy and Diplomacy, October 1938–September 1939', DPhil, Oxon, 1985.

Index